Data Science: Foundations
and Hands-on Experience

Fatwa Ramdani

Data Science: Foundations and Hands-on Experience

Handling Economic, Spatial, and Multidimensional Data with R

Springer

Fatwa Ramdani
International Public Policy, Graduate
School of Humanities and Social Studies
University of Tsukuba
Tsukuba, Ibaraki, Japan

ISBN 978-981-96-4682-1 ISBN 978-981-96-4683-8 (eBook)
https://doi.org/10.1007/978-981-96-4683-8

This Springer imprint is published by the registered company Springer Nature Singapore Pte Ltd.
The registered company address is: 152 Beach Road, #21-01/04 Gateway East, Singapore 189721, Singapore

For Putri Setiani, Alidrisi Sorai Ramdani, Albiruni Keiji Ramdani, and Alina Hikari Ramdani

Preface

Every spring semester at the University of Tsukuba, Japan, I teach a course titled **"Data Science for Social Sciences."** Only a handful of students enrolled when it was first introduced a few years ago. However, the course gained popularity over time, and the number of students steadily increased each year. Today, the classroom is bustling with local and international students from diverse backgrounds, making it a truly global learning experience.

Initially, my focus was on introducing the basics—questions like "What is data science?" and "How can it help in research?" were at the core of the course. However, as I got to know my students better, I realized they belong to a digitally native generation, eager to dive into the world of data and technology. This insight inspired me to enhance the course materials, incorporating real-world case studies and practical applications using the R programming language.

We live in an era of overwhelming data—vast, abundant, and often unmanageable. Students need a strong foundation to navigate this complexity: the ability to search and collect data effectively, filter relevant information, and critically assess its validity and reliability. Equipping them with these skills, alongside hands-on experience with real-world datasets, is crucial to addressing modern societal challenges. This realization became the driving force behind the creation of this book.

While many data science tools and programming languages are available, R stands out for its ease of learning, intuitive scripting, and the support of a vibrant, adaptive community. Its user-friendly interface, especially through RStudio, makes it an excellent choice for beginners and experienced users alike. Furthermore, although numerous books exist on data science, few highlight the unique power of spatial data—a critical and underexplored area in the field. This book seeks to fill that gap, offering in-depth explanations and step-by-step guidance on leveraging spatial data in research.

The book is structured to cover the entire data science process, presented in ten comprehensive chapters. Each chapter is divided into two parts:

1. **Theoretical Foundations**—laying the groundwork for key concepts.
2. **Practical Applications**—featuring exercises in RStudio using real-world datasets.

By the end of this book, readers will not only gain foundational knowledge and technical expertise but also develop a keen sense of ethical awareness. They will be empowered to conduct rigorous, reliable, and socially conscious research. No prior experience in programming and data science is required—just curiosity and a willingness to explore the transformative power of data in understanding and shaping society. This book is designed for both undergraduate and graduate students, helping them build a strong theoretical base while acquiring practical skills in RStudio.

This book is a heartfelt dedication to my parents, teachers, and professors, whose guidance shaped my journey; to my students, who inspire me to continue learning and growing; and most importantly, to my family, whose unwavering love and support have been my greatest source of strength. Through this book, I hope to channel that love and passion into every page, sharing it with all who read it.

Tsukuba, Ibaraki, Japan Fatwa Ramdani
2025

Competing Interests The author has no competing interests to declare that are relevant to the content of this manuscript.

Contents

Chapter 1
Introduction to Data Science and Basics of R

Abstract The first part of this chapter introduces the difference between data and information, along with definitions, roles, importance, and real-world applications of data science. The first part of this chapter provides a strong foundation for understanding data science principles. Additionally, it walks through key steps in data science projects: defining objectives, planning, collecting and analyzing data, interpreting results, and effectively communicating complex findings to non-technical audiences. The second part covers the basics of R: what R is, why it's useful, how to download and install it, an introduction to the R interface, and fundamental operations, including working with variables, data types, operators, and functions.

Relation to Other Chapters: Sets the foundational concepts and skills required for the chapters that follow, especially for data types (Chap. 2) and data exploration (Chap. 3).

1.1 Introduction

Data science is a multidisciplinary field that combines scientific methods, statistical analysis, and computer programming to extract valuable insights, patterns, and knowledge from large and complex datasets. It integrates techniques from mathematics, statistics, computer science, and domain-specific knowledge to solve real-world problems. This chapter introduces the fundamental concepts of data science, explaining its significance in today's data-driven world. By leveraging data science, organizations can make better decisions, optimize processes, and uncover hidden trends that can drive innovation and growth. This chapter sets the foundation for understanding the key principles and applications of data science.

F. Ramdani, *Data Science: Foundations and Hands-on Experience*,
https://doi.org/10.1007/978-981-96-4683-8_1

Table 1.1 Difference between data and information

Category	Data	Information
Definition	Raw facts, figures, or statistics without context or meaning	Processed, organized, and contextualized data that conveys meaning
Characteristics	Unstructured, unordered, and lacks interpretation	Structured, ordered, and has interpretation
Form	Typically represented as numbers, text, or symbols	Presented in a meaningful format, such as charts, graphs, or reports
Purposes	Serves as the foundation for generating information	Provides insights, knowledge, and understanding for decision-making
Context	Lack of context and relevance on its own	Provides context and relevance through analysis, interpretation, and contextualization
Importance	Crucial for information generation	Transforms data into valuable insights for decision-making
Example	Raw sales data, temperature readings, survey responses	Sales report, weather forecast, market analysis
Value	Holds potential value when processed and analyzed	Provides actionable insights and knowledge for informed decision-making
Example of use	Data is used to collect, store, and process information	Information is used for planning, strategizing, and decision-making

1.2 Data Versus Information

Before we go into details of what data science is, it is better to understand what data and information first. Data and information are closely related but the two are distinct concepts. Data refers to raw facts, figures, or statistics without context or meaning, while information is processed, organized, and contextualized data that conveys meaning.

Understanding the difference between data and information is crucial for effective data analysis and decision-making. Table 1.1 summarizes the difference between data and information

1.3 Science, Data Science, and Statistics

According to the English dictionary, science has multiple definitions. As a noun, science can be defined as a branch of knowledge or study dealing with a body of facts or truths systematically arranged and showing the operation of general laws such as the mathematical sciences. Another definition of science is a systematic knowledge of the physical or material world gained through observation and experimentation. Science is also knowledge, as of facts or principles. Science can also be defined as knowledge gained by systematic study.

From the many definitions above, we have some keywords for science. It must be systematic, gained through observation and experimentation, and must produce a piece of knowledge. So, if we combine the word "science" with "data" to get a new word for "data science," it means we are dealing with raw facts, processing the raw facts with systematic observation or experiments to produce a piece of knowledge that was hidden before.

In more complex words, data science is a multidisciplinary field that combines scientific methods, statistical analysis, and computer programming to extract insights, patterns, and knowledge from large and complex datasets (Fig. 1.1). It involves using various tools, techniques, and algorithms to process, analyze, and interpret data, and derive actionable insights to solve real-world problems and make informed decisions.

How about statistics? While both are dealing with raw data, there are several basic differences. Table 1.2 summarizes the difference between data science and statistics.

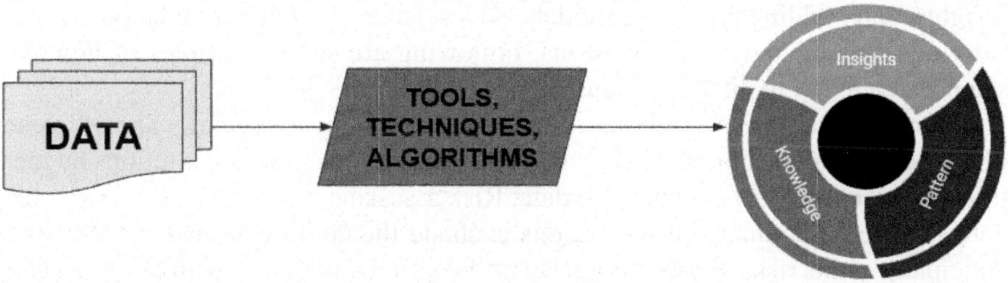

Fig. 1.1 Data science is a multidisciplinary field that combines scientific methods, statistical analysis, and computer programming to extract insights, patterns, and knowledge

Table 1.2 Difference between data science and statistics

Aspect	Data science	Statistics
Focus	Extracting insights, patterns, and knowledge from various data types	Analyzing quantitative data to make inferences or conclusions about a population
Methodology	Utilizes a combination of statistics, machine learning, and computer science techniques/multi- or transdisciplinary approach	Emphasizes probability theory and mathematical modeling/sole approach
Objective	To uncover actionable insights, predictive models, and solutions to complex problems for business	To understand and describe data distributions, relationships, and variability/causal effect for research
Data handling	Handles diverse data types including structured, unstructured, and big datasets	Typically deals with structured data and smaller sample sizes
Scope	It encompasses a broader range of techniques including machine learning, deep learning, and data visualization	Traditionally focused on hypothesis testing, regression analysis, and experimental design

1.4 Role, Importance, and Applications of Data Science

Data science is crucial in transforming businesses, industries, and societies. It has become a driving force behind many technological advancements and innovations and is being increasingly used across various domains for data-driven decision-making, predictive modeling, and process optimization.

The importance of data science lies in its ability to extract valuable insights from the vast amounts of data that are generated and collected in today's digital world.

With the explosion of data from various sources such as social media, sensors, devices, and transactions, organizations can leverage data science to gain a competitive advantage, optimize operations, improve customer experiences, and drive innovation (Fig. 1.2).

The applications of data science are incredibly diverse and impactful, cutting across many industries. By analyzing large amounts of data, extracting valuable insights, and building predictive models, data science has transformed the way organizations operate and make decisions. Following are some examples of how data science is applied in different industries.

In **finance**, data science plays a crucial role in ensuring the security and efficiency of financial systems. For instance, it is used to detect fraudulent transactions by identifying unusual patterns in financial data. Risk assessment is another key area where data science helps financial institutions evaluate the creditworthiness of clients or anticipate market risks. Furthermore, portfolio optimization, which involves selecting the best combination of financial assets to maximize returns while minimizing risk, is also driven by data science models.

In **healthcare,** data science has paved the way for groundbreaking innovations. Predictive modeling helps doctors and researchers forecast disease outbreaks or individual patient outcomes based on historical data. Personalized medicine, which tailors treatment plans to individual patients, leverages data science to analyze genetic information and patient records. Health monitoring systems, such as wearable devices, use data science to track vital signs and detect health issues early.

In the **marketing** sector, data science is a powerful tool for understanding consumer behavior. Companies use it for customer segmentation, dividing their audience into smaller groups based on shared characteristics to offer targeted products or services. Recommendation systems, like those used by streaming platforms or

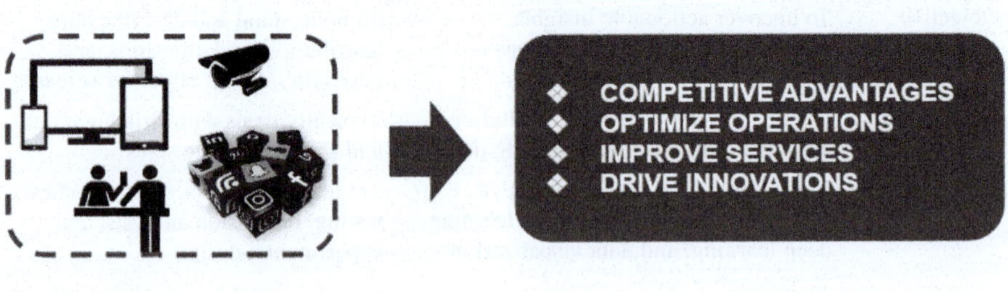

Fig. 1.2 Importance of data science

online retailers, suggest items to users based on their preferences and past behaviors. Additionally, sentiment analysis helps businesses gauge customer opinions by analyzing text from social media, reviews, and surveys.

The **transportation** industry also benefits significantly from Data Science. Route optimization, for example, uses algorithms to identify the most efficient paths for deliveries or public transportation, reducing costs and travel times. Demand forecasting helps predict the need for transportation services, enabling better resource allocation. Predictive maintenance, another application, analyzes data from vehicles or equipment to anticipate failures before they occur, improving safety and reducing downtime.

Data science is revolutionizing **education** by harnessing the power of data to improve learning experiences, enhance educational outcomes, and inform decision-making at various levels. One significant application is personalized learning, where machine learning algorithms analyze students' learning patterns, preferences, and progress to deliver tailored content. Predictive analytics also plays a crucial role in education, particularly in identifying at-risk students. By analyzing data such as attendance records, test scores, and participation metrics, schools can implement early interventions to support these students and reduce dropout rates. Higher education institutions, for example, use predictive models to flag students who may need academic or emotional support, helping them stay on track to complete their studies. Another vital area is curriculum design and policymaking, where data-driven insights inform decisions about resource allocation and curriculum improvements. By analyzing standardized test results and demographic data, policymakers can identify underserved regions and prioritize building schools or training teachers in those areas. Additionally, learning analytics provides real-time feedback to educators, enabling them to fine-tune their teaching methods.

In the fight against **climate change**, data science has become an indispensable tool for understanding and addressing environmental challenges. Climate modeling and prediction are among its most critical applications. Using machine learning and statistical models, researchers can analyze vast datasets from satellites and weather stations to predict future climate patterns. This includes forecasting temperature changes, rainfall variations, and the likelihood of extreme weather events, which are essential for crafting effective climate policies and adaptation strategies. Monitoring carbon emissions is another area where data science excels. Remote sensing and Geographic Information Systems (GIS) allow for the tracking of greenhouse gas emissions from deforestation, industrial activities, and urban development. Satellites such as Sentinel-5P provide high-resolution data on air pollutants, enabling governments to enforce emissions regulations and measure the impact of mitigation efforts.

Additionally, data science aids in assessing the **environmental impact** of human activities. For example, analyzing vegetation indices like NDVI helps monitor deforestation rates and ecosystem health, providing crucial information for conservation efforts. Renewable energy optimization is another critical application, where data science helps determine the best locations for solar panels and wind turbines by analyzing geospatial and meteorological data. Machine learning algorithms are also used to forecast energy production, ensuring efficient grid management and reducing reliance on fossil fuels. Furthermore, in the field of **disaster management**, predictive analytics helps anticipate natural disasters such as floods, hurricanes, and wildfires. Combining real-time data with machine learning models, early warning systems enable proactive responses, reducing the loss of life and property.

Beyond these industries, data science has applications in retail, manufacturing, sports, energy, agriculture, and government. Retailers use it to manage inventory and improve the customer experience. Manufacturers rely on data science for quality control and optimizing production processes. In sports, it enhances performance analysis and injury prevention. Energy companies use it to forecast demand and manage renewable energy sources. Agriculture benefits from data science in precision farming, which helps monitor crops and improve yields. Governments utilize data science for urban planning, public safety, and policy development.

By integrating data science into their operations, organizations across various fields can make better decisions, increase efficiency, and drive innovation. Its ability to provide actionable insights from data makes it a cornerstone of modern industries.

1.5 The Data Science Process

The data science process is a systematic approach that involves several key steps to ensure meaningful insights are derived from data. These steps include defining the problem or objective, planning the methodology, collecting relevant data, analyzing the data using appropriate tools and techniques, interpreting the results to draw meaningful conclusions, and finally, communicating these findings effectively to stakeholders. Each of these steps is crucial and builds on the previous one, as illustrated in Fig. 1.3.

One unique feature of the data science process is its iterative nature. After completing the final step, which is communication, we have the opportunity to reflect on the entire process. If the results do not fully meet the expectations of stakeholders or fail to achieve the desired outcomes, we can revisit earlier stages. For instance, the data might be reinterpreted for deeper insights, re-analyzed using different methods, or even recollected to fill any gaps or address new questions that arise. This iterative approach allows for continuous improvement, ensuring that the process is flexible and adaptable to changing needs. By repeating this cycle as necessary, we can work toward achieving an optimal result that satisfies all stakeholders and meets the defined objectives.

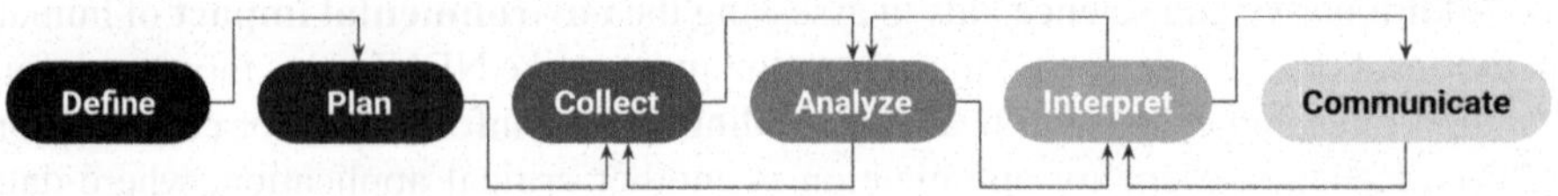

Fig. 1.3 Key steps of the data science process

A. Define

What is “define?” In define step, we try to understand the problem statement or objective of the data science project. This involves understanding the business context, identifying the data science goals, and setting expectations. This step is crucial as it lays the foundation for the entire data science project. It helps set clear objectives and expectations, aligning the project with the business needs. It involves understanding the problem statement, identifying the objectives and goals of the project, and formulating research questions or hypotheses. Let’s take a closer look at each of these steps:

- **Understanding the problem statement**
  The first step is to thoroughly understand the problem statement or the business problem that needs to be addressed. This involves gathering information from stakeholders, domain experts, and other relevant sources to define the problem and its context clearly. It is important to understand the scope and constraints of the problem, as well as any specific requirements or expectations from the project.
- **Identifying the objectives and goals**
  Once the problem statement is understood, the next step is to identify the data science project’s objectives and goals. Objectives are the specific outcomes that the project aims to achieve, while goals are the broader, strategic outcomes that align with the overall business or organizational goals. To ensure clarity and achievableness, objectives and goals should be specific, measurable, achievable, relevant, and time-bound (SMART).

An example of SMART objectives/goals for a data science project studying the impact of social media usage on mental health among adolescents.

Specific: The objective is clear and well-defined.
Example: Identify the relationship between social media usage patterns (measured by daily usage time and types of activities) and mental health outcomes (measured by self-reported depression and anxiety scores) among adolescents aged 13–18 years old.

Measurable: The objective can be quantified or measured.
Example: Collect and analyze data from at least 500 adolescents using validated surveys to measure social media usage patterns and mental health outcomes.

Achievable: The objective is realistic and attainable within the available resources and constraints.
Example: Conduct the study within a 6-month timeframe, with adequate resources including access to relevant data, appropriate statistical analysis tools, and a research team with expertise in data science and social science research.

Relevant: The objective is aligned with the research question and the overall goals of the social science study.
Example: The objective directly addresses the research question of the impact of social media usage on mental health among adolescents, which is relevant to the field of social science and has practical implications for understanding and improving adolescent mental health outcomes.

Time-bound: The objective has a specific timeline or deadline for completion.
Example: Complete data collection and analysis within 6 months, and present the findings at a national social science conference within 1 year from the start of the project.

A SMART objective for a data science project on the impact of social media usage on mental health among adolescents in social science research could be:
"Identify the relationship between social media usage patterns and mental health outcomes among 500 adolescents aged 13–18 years old using validated surveys, within a 6-month timeframe, and present findings at a national conference within 1 year from the start of the project."

Formulating research questions or hypotheses

Research questions or hypotheses are the guiding principles that help in defining the direction of the data science project. Research questions are typically used in exploratory studies where the aim is to explore and describe a phenomenon, while hypotheses are used in hypothesis-driven studies where the aim is to test a specific relationship or effect. Research questions or hypotheses should be formulated based on the problem statement and objectives of the project, and they should be well-defined, specific, and testable.

It is important to note that the problem statement, objectives, and research questions/hypotheses may evolve and be refined as the project progresses and more information is gathered. However, a clear and well-defined problem statement, objectives, and research questions/hypotheses at the outset of the project provide a solid foundation for the data science project and ensure that it is focused and aligned with the desired outcomes.

B. Plan

The next step is to "Plan." We need to plan the approach and methodology for the data science project. This involves designing the project framework, identifying required data and resources, and creating a timeline and budget. Planning is essential as it ensures that the project is executed in a systematic and organized manner, and helps in making informed decisions about the data and techniques to be used.

- **Designing the project framework**

  i. **Define the Project Objective**
  Clearly define the objective of your data science project. What problem are you trying to solve or what goal are you trying to achieve? This will be the foundation f your project and will guide all your subsequent decisions.

  ii. **Identify the Scope**
  Determine the scope of your project by specifying what will be included and what will be excluded. Define the boundaries of your project and set realistic expectations for what can be achieved within the given timeline and

  iii. **Define Deliverables**
  Clearly outline the deliverables of your project. What are the tangible outcomes or results that you expect to produce? This could include reports, dashboards, models, or any other outputs that will be generated as part of the project.

  iv. **Define Stakeholders**
  Identify all the stakeholders involved in the project, including team members, sponsors, clients, and any other relevant parties. Clearly define their roles and responsibilities, and establish communication channels to ensure effective collaboration throughout the project.

- **Identifying Required Data and Resources**

  i. **Data Requirements**
  Identify the data that is required for your project. This could include internal data from your organization, external data from third-party sources, or a combination of both. Define the data variables, formats, and quality requirements that are necessary for your project.

  ii. **Data Collection**
  Plan how you will collect the required data. This could involve data scraping, data acquisition from APIs, data cleaning and preprocessing, or any other relevant data collection methods. Consider the data privacy and security requirements and ensure that you comply with all relevant regulations.

  iii. **Resource Requirements**
  Identify the resources that are needed for your project. This could include hardware, software, tools, and any other resources required for data analysis, modeling, and visualization. Allocate resources based on the project timeline and budget.

- **Developing a Timeline and Budget**

  i. **Timeline**
  Create a detailed timeline for your project, including all the major milestones, tasks, and deadlines. Consider dependencies between tasks and allocate sufficient time for each task, taking into account any potential delays

or unforeseen circumstances. Regularly review and update the timeline throughout the project to ensure that it stays on track.

ii. **Budget**

Develop a budget for your project, including all the estimated costs for data collection, data processing, modeling, visualization, and any other relevant expenses. Consider the cost of resources, tools, software licenses, and any other expenses that may arise during the project. Regularly monitor and control the budget to ensure that it remains within the allocated limits.

iii. **Contingency Plan**

Develop a contingency plan to address any potential risks or issues that may arise during the project. This could include risks related to data quality, resource availability, or any other potential roadblocks. Have a plan in place to mitigate risks and minimize their impact on the project timeline and budget.

iv. **Project Management**

Choose a project management approach and tools to help you effectively manage the project. This could include using project management software, setting up regular progress meetings, and assigning responsibilities to team members. Regularly review the project status, update the timeline and budget as needed, and communicate any changes to stakeholders.

C. Collect

Collecting the data required for the data science project. This involves gathering, storing, and preparing the data for analysis. Data collection is critical as the quality and quantity of data directly impact the accuracy and reliability of the results. Proper data collection ensures that the data used for analysis is relevant, accurate, and complete. Several factors to consider include which sources of data that will be used, types of data organization that is required, data collection methods and measuring data quality and validation.

- **Sources of data**

i. **Internal Data**

Internal data refers to the data generated or collected within an organization, such as sales data, customer data, employee data, and financial data. Internal data is typically structured and can be easily accessed from the organization's databases, data management systems, or other internal sources.

ii. **External Data**

External data refers to the data that is obtained from sources outside the organization, such as publicly available data, third-party data providers, social media data, market research reports, and government data. External data can be structured or unstructured, and it may require data integration and cleaning before it can be used for analysis.

- **Types of data organization**

  i. **Structured Data**
  Structured data is organized and formatted in a specific way, making it easy to store, retrieve, and analyze. Structured data can be obtained from various sources, such as databases, spreadsheets, and other structured formats, and is typically in a tabular form with rows and columns.

  ii. **Unstructured Data**
  Unstructured data refers to data that does not have a specific format or structure, making it more challenging to store, retrieve, and analyze. Unstructured data can include text data from social media posts, customer reviews, emails, images, videos, audio files, etc. Unstructured data may require data preprocessing techniques such as natural language processing (NLP) or image recognition to extract meaningful insights.

- **Data collection methods**

  i. **Surveys**
  Surveys involve collecting data through questionnaires or interviews to gather information from individuals or groups. They can be conducted in person, over the phone, through mail, or online. Depending on the type of questions asked and the response format, surveys can provide quantitative or qualitative data.

  ii. **Interviews**
  Interviews involve collecting data through direct conversations with individuals or groups. Interviews can be structured, semi-structured, or unstructured, depending on the level of formality and flexibility in the questions and responses. Interviews can provide rich qualitative data, allowing for in-depth understanding of individuals' perspectives, experiences, and opinions.

  iii. **Observations**
  Observations involve collecting data by observing and recording behaviors, events, or processes in their natural settings. Observations can be structured, where specific variables are measured, or unstructured, where the observer records qualitative descriptions. Observations can provide valuable insights into real-world behaviors and interactions.

  iv. **Web Scraping**
  Web scraping involves collecting data from websites or web pages using automated tools or scripts. Web scraping can be used to collect structured data, such as product prices, customer reviews, or stock prices, or unstructured data, such as text from news articles or social media posts. Web scraping requires technical skills and knowledge of web technologies and may have legal and ethical considerations. You will learn more detail about web scraping in Chap. 8 of this book.

- **Data quality and validation considerations**

  i. **Accuracy**
  Data should be accurate, free from errors, and reflect the true state of the phenomenon being measured. Data quality checks should be performed to identify and correct errors or inconsistencies in the data, such as missing values, data entry mistakes, or data outliers.

  ii. **Reliability**
  Data should be reliable and consistent, meaning that similar results should be obtained when the data is collected or measured repeatedly. Data collection methods should be standardized and followed consistently to ensure reliability. Validation techniques, such as comparing data with known benchmarks or using multiple data sources, can help ensure data reliability.

  iii. **Completeness**
  Data should be complete, meaning that all relevant data points are captured and included in the analysis. Missing data can introduce biases and errors in the analysis, and efforts should be made to minimize missing data through careful data collection and data validation.

  iv. **Validity**
  Data should be valid, meaning that it measures what it is intended to measure. Data collection methods should be designed to capture the relevant information accurately and appropriately.

D. Data Analysis

The next step is to analyze the data using appropriate data science techniques and algorithms. This involves exploring the data, and then performing appropriate analysis techniques such as statistical analysis, natural language processing (NLP), machine learning (ML), or other advanced techniques. Analysis is the heart of the data science process as it involves extracting insights, patterns, and trends from the data to derive meaningful conclusions.

Exploratory data analysis or EDA is a critical step in the data analysis process that involves examining and analyzing datasets to gain insights, identify patterns, and summarize the main characteristics of the data. Here are some common techniques used in EDA:

v. **Data Cleaning:** This involves identifying and handling missing values, outliers, and inconsistencies in the data to ensure that the data is accurate and reliable for analysis.

vi. **Univariate Analysis:** This focuses on analyzing individual variables in the dataset. Descriptive statistics such as measures of central tendency (mean, median, mode) and measures of dispersion (range, variance, standard deviation) are commonly used to summarize the main characteristics of a variable.

vii. **Bivariate Analysis:** This involves analyzing the relationship between two variables in the dataset. Scatter plots, correlation coefficients, and contingency tables are commonly used techniques for bivariate analysis. These techniques can help identify patterns, trends, and associations between variables.

viii. **Multivariate Analysis:** This involves analyzing the relationship between three or more variables in the dataset. Techniques such as heat maps, parallel coordinates plots, and scatterplot matrices can be used to visualize and understand complex relationships between multiple variables.

ix. **Data Visualization:** Data visualization is a powerful tool in EDA that helps to present data in a visual format for better understanding. Bar charts, line charts, and scatter plots are commonly used visualization techniques for exploring and summarizing data. Bar charts are used to display categorical data, line charts are used to display trends over time, and scatter plots are used to display the relationship between two continuous variables.

E. Data Interpretation

After we finish the analysis, then we need to interpret the results obtained from the data analysis to understand the implications of the findings, drawing conclusions, and validating the results against the research question or problem statement. Interpretation is crucial as it helps in making informed decisions based on the insights gained from the data analysis. Following are some key steps and considerations for effective data interpretation:

- **Drawing insights from the data analysis**

i **Review and understand the data**

Before interpreting the data, it is important to have a thorough understanding of the data that has been collected or analyzed. This includes reviewing the data collection methods, data quality, and any limitations or biases in the data.

- **Identifying patterns, trends, and relationships**

i. Identify patterns and trends

Look for patterns and trends in the data by examining the data from different angles and perspectives. This can involve analyzing data visually through graphs, charts, or other visualizations, as well as conducting statistical analysis to identify significant findings.

ii. Look for relationships

Explore relationships between different variables or factors in the data. This can involve conducting correlation analysis or regression analysis to determine if there are any statistically significant associations between variables.

- **Interpreting the results**

i. **Contextualize the results**

Interpret the results in the context of the research question or hypothesis. Consider how the findings align with the research question or hypothesis, and whether they support or contradict the original research question or hypothesis. It is important to avoid making unsupported assumptions or overgeneralizing the results.

ii. **Consider alternative explanations**

Be mindful of alternative explanations for the findings. Consider possible confounding variables, limitations of the data or analysis, and other factors that could impact the interpretation of the results.

iii. **Draw meaningful insights**

Based on the patterns, trends, relationships, and contextual understanding of the results, draw meaningful insights that address the research question or hypothesis. These insights should be supported by evidence from the data and should be relevant and applicable to the research context.

F. Communicate

The last step is to communicate the findings and results to stakeholders. This involves creating visualizations, reports, and presentations to convey the results and insights clearly. Communication is essential as it helps in conveying the outcomes of the data science project to stakeholders and guiding them toward taking action based on the results. Some key points in communicating the findings are as follows:

- **Presenting findings to stakeholders**

i. **Know your audience**

Understanding your stakeholders' level of technical expertise, familiarity with the subject matter, and their specific interests will help you tailor your presentation accordingly. Use language and concepts that are familiar and accessible to your audience.

ii. **Use a clear and concise format**

Organize your findings in a logical and structured manner. Use bullet points, headings, and subheadings to make it easy for stakeholders to follow along. Avoid jargon and technical terms unless necessary, and define them when used.

iii. **Highlight key findings**

Clearly identify and emphasize the most important findings that are relevant to your stakeholders. Use visuals such as charts, graphs, and infographics to make your findings visually appealing and easy to understand.

iv. **Provide context**

Help stakeholders understand the significance and implications of your findings by providing relevant context. Explain the methodology used, the limitations of the data, and any assumptions made during the analysis. This will help stakeholders interpret the results accurately.

- **Data visualization techniques**
  1. **Choose the right type of visualization**
     Select the appropriate type of visualization that best represents your data and conveys your message effectively. Common types of visualizations include bar charts, line charts, pie charts, scatter plots, and maps. Consider factors such as data type, relationships between variables, and the story you want to tell.
  2. **Keep it simple**
     Avoid cluttering your visualizations with unnecessary details or overwhelming amounts of data. Use clean and simple designs that are easy to read and understand. Use labels, legends, and annotations to provide context and guide interpretation.
  3. **Use color and visual cues strategically**
     Choose colors that are visually appealing and convey meaning. Use visual cues such as size, shape, and position to highlight important data points or trends. Be mindful of accessibility considerations, such as using color-blind-friendly palettes.
  4. **Tell a story with your visuals**
     Use visualizations to tell a compelling story that supports your findings. Use annotations, captions, and titles to guide the reader through the visualization and explain the key insights. Use narratives and storytelling techniques to make your findings more engaging and memorable.

- **Interpreting and explaining complex results**
  1. **Use simple and accessible language**
     Avoid technical jargon and use plain language to explain complex concepts. Use analogies, metaphors, and real-life examples to make your explanations relatable and understandable to non-technical audiences.
  2. **Provide context**
     Help non-technical audiences understand the relevance and implications of the results by providing relevant context. Explain the background, methodology, and significance of the findings in simple terms.
  3. **Use visual aids**
     Visual aids such as charts, graphs, and infographics can help simplify complex results and make them more accessible. Use visual aids to illustrate key points and provide visual representations of data or trends.
  4. **Focus on key messages**
     Identify the most important findings and key messages that are relevant to your non-technical audience. Highlight these key messages in your explanations and use them as the main focus of your communication. Avoid overwhelming your audience with too much information.

v. **Be responsive to questions**

Be prepared to answer questions and provide further explanations as needed. Listen to your audience's concerns and feedback, and adapt your explanations accordingly. Encourage questions and provide clarifications to ensure that your non-technical audience fully understands the results.

Effective communication of results to stakeholders and non-technical audiences requires clear, concise, and accessible language, visual aids, and context that focuses on the most relevant findings and key messages. By using these techniques, you can effectively communicate complex results and ensure that your audience understands the implications and significance of the findings.

Each step in the data science process is important and contributes to the overall success of the project. Properly defining the problem, planning the approach, collecting relevant data, analyzing the data using appropriate techniques, interpreting the results, and effectively communicating the findings are all crucial for obtaining meaningful insights and making data-driven decisions. Neglecting any of these steps can lead to inaccurate or incomplete results and can adversely impact the outcomes of the data science project.

Simple Project: Social Media Usage and Mental Health

This project investigates the impact of social media usage on mental health among adolescents. The project would involve defining the research question, planning the approach, collecting data through surveys, analyzing the data to identify patterns, interpreting the results, and communicating the findings.

- **Define**: The first step in the project would be to define the research question and objectives. For example, the research question could be "How does social media usage affect the mental health of adolescents aged 13–18?" The objectives could be to investigate the relationship between social media usage and mental health outcomes such as depression and anxiety among adolescents.
- **Plan**: This would involve deciding on the appropriate data sources, sample size, and data collection methods. For example, the data could be collected through surveys administered to adolescents in schools, along with their social media usage patterns and mental health outcomes measured using standardized questionnaires.
- **Collect**: This administering surveys to a sample of adolescents, collecting data on their social media usage patterns, and collecting data on their mental health outcomes.
- **Analyze**: The data could be analyzed to determine if there is a significant association between the amount of time adolescents spend on social media and their levels of depression and anxiety.
- **Interpret**: The results are interpreted to determine if there is evidence of a significant relationship between social media usage and mental health

outcomes among adolescents and to identify any patterns or trends in the data.
- **Communicate**: The final step is about presenting the results clearly through reports, presentations, or data visualizations. The implications of the findings for social science research and policy could be discussed, and recommendations for future research or interventions could be provided

1.6 The Future of Data Scientist

As highlighted in the World Economic Forum's *Future of Jobs Report 2025*, the future of data scientists is promising. Data science roles are becoming increasingly pivotal across industries due to the rapid adoption of technologies like cloud computing, big data analytics, and artificial intelligence. These tools rely heavily on data, making the expertise of data scientists indispensable. Businesses today require professionals who can analyze complex datasets and transform them into actionable insights that drive strategic decisions.

The demand for data scientists is not confined to the tech sector. Industries such as finance, healthcare, retail, manufacturing, and transportation are integrating data science into their operations. For instance, in the financial sector, data scientists are optimizing risk management and fraud detection through predictive analytics. Healthcare providers are using AI-driven data solutions for personalized medicine and early disease detection, while retailers rely on consumer data to refine supply chains and forecast market trends. This widespread adoption of data-driven strategies underscores the growing importance of data science expertise.

As the role of data scientists evolves, so do the skills required to thrive in this field. Technical proficiency in machine learning frameworks such as TensorFlow and PyTorch, expertise in big data platforms like Hadoop and Spark, and programming languages like R, Python, and SQL remain critical. However, the job increasingly demands more than technical know-how. Data scientists must also possess strong critical thinking and problem-solving abilities to interpret data patterns and communicate findings effectively to non-technical stakeholders. Creativity is equally vital, as businesses look for innovative ways to leverage data for competitive advantage.

Moreover, the future of data science will demand a multidisciplinary approach. Combining technical skills with domain knowledge in fields such as finance, environmental science, or healthcare will enhance a data scientist's relevance and value. At the same time, an understanding of ethical considerations and data governance will become crucial as regulations around data privacy and responsible AI use become stricter. Ethical data handling and compliance with frameworks like GDPR and CCPA are essential to building trust and ensuring the sustainability of data-driven practices. We will learn more detail about it in Chap. 10.

Looking ahead, some key areas are poised for significant growth in the field of data science. Integration with AI and automation will see data scientists designing, validating, and improving systems for tasks like autonomous vehicles and robotics. Similarly, sustainability and environmental data analysis are becoming vital as organizations use geospatial and climate data to address pressing global challenges like deforestation and carbon emissions. Healthcare will also remain a fertile ground for data science innovation, with applications ranging from epidemic tracking to telemedicine and vaccine research. Additionally, the retail sector's push toward hyperpersonalized marketing and consumer insights will further fuel the need for skilled data professionals.

Despite its promising future, the field of data science is not without challenges. A notable concern is the skills gap, as the rapid evolution of AI and data science tools outpaces the supply of qualified professionals. This creates a need for lifelong learning and upskilling to stay relevant. Ethical and legal risks, such as data misuse and breaches, pose another challenge, emphasizing the importance of governance and accountability. Furthermore, while automation simplifies repetitive tasks, it may reduce the demand for entry-level data roles, shifting the focus toward higher-level strategic positions.

For aspiring data scientists, continuous skill development and adaptability will be essential. Pursuing advanced certifications, gaining practical experience through real-world projects, and staying informed about industry trends are key strategies to remain competitive. Developing strong communication skills and an ethical mindset will further enhance their ability to succeed in this evolving landscape.

Data scientists will play a central role in shaping the future of industries. As businesses become increasingly data-driven, the need for skilled professionals who can analyze, interpret, and apply data creatively will only grow. By embracing innovation, upskilling, and ethical practices, data scientists can position themselves as the architects of a data-powered future.

Easy to Digest Box

Data Science is a way of understanding and using information to solve problems and make better decisions. Imagine you have a huge pile of toys in a toy box. If you want to find out how many blue toys there are, or which toy is the most expensive, you would need to sort through them and count. That's kind of like what data scientists do, but instead of toys, they work with numbers, pictures, words, and other types of information called "data."

Data scientists have exciting jobs because they can work in many areas. For example, they can help doctors predict diseases, help farmers grow better crops, or even help game designers create fun video games. In the future, as we have more technology and more data, data scientists will be needed even more. They will help solve big problems, like finding ways to protect the earth or make cities safer and smarter. Give human more time to thinks, talks, discuss, collaborate, and acts rather than wasting time on data processing.

1.7 Summary of Key Points

- Data serves as the raw material, while information is the processed data and meaningful output that facilitates decision-making and understanding.
- Data science has become a critical discipline in modern society, enabling organizations to harness the power of data to drive innovation, improve decision-making, and achieve meaningful outcomes in diverse domains.
- The problem statement, objectives, and research questions/hypotheses may evolve and be refined as the project progresses and more information is gathered.
- A clear and well-defined problem statement, objectives, and research questions/hypotheses at the outset of the project provide a solid foundation for the data science project.
- EDA techniques, including descriptive statistics and data visualization, are essential tools for exploring and understanding data, identifying patterns, and gaining insights that can inform further data analysis and decision-making.
- Data interpretation is a critical step in the research process as it helps researchers make sense of the data and derive meaningful insights.
- Effective communication of results to stakeholders and non-technical audiences requires clear, concise, and accessible language, visual aids, and context that focuses on the most relevant findings and key messages
- Consider the data privacy and security requirements and ensure that you comply with all relevant regulations. Be careful with laws that could be different in many countries.

1.8 Hands-on Experience

What is R?

R is a powerful programming language and an open-source environment specifically designed for statistical computing and creating graphics. It allows users to analyze and manipulate data efficiently, making it a vital tool in the field of data science and research. R has gained global recognition for its versatility, offering a wide range of built-in functions and packages to handle complex statistical tasks and produce high-quality visualizations.

The development of R began in the mid-1990s by Ross Ihaka and Robert Gentleman at the University of Auckland in New Zealand. Their goal was to create a tool that would allow statisticians and researchers to perform advanced data analysis with ease. Inspired by the S programming language, R built upon its predecessor's strengths while introducing new features and an open-source framework, which enabled a community of users to contribute to its development and improvement.

Today, R is widely used by statisticians, data scientists, and researchers across various disciplines. Its popularity stems from its ability to support a wide array of applications, such as data analysis, statistical modeling, and data visualization.

Researchers use R to explore data patterns, test hypotheses, and communicate results effectively through clear and attractive charts and graphs. Its extensive library of user-created packages further enhances its functionality, making it suitable for specialized fields, including machine learning, bioinformatics, and geospatial analysis.

The open-source nature of R also fosters a collaborative environment, where users worldwide can share their expertise and resources. This community-driven approach has contributed to R's continuous growth and adoption in academia, industry, and government organizations. As a result, R remains an essential tool for anyone working with data.

Why R?

R is a powerful programming language and software environment widely used for data analysis and statistical computing. It offers several key features that make it a preferred choice for researchers, data scientists, and analysts across diverse disciplines. Several strong points of R includes:

Versatility

R is highly versatile, offering a comprehensive suite of statistical and graphical techniques. It supports tasks ranging from basic exploratory data analysis to complex statistical modeling, making it suitable for a wide range of applications. For instance, researchers can use R to summarize datasets using descriptive statistics, visualize data through plots and graphs, and perform advanced statistical tests like regression analysis or time series modeling. This versatility makes R an essential tool in fields like healthcare, finance, social sciences, and environmental studies.

Open-source environment

One of the most attractive features of R is that it is open-source, meaning it is free to use, modify, and distribute. This accessibility has contributed to the rapid growth of its user base and an active global community of developers and contributors. The collaborative nature of the R community ensures continuous updates, bug fixes, and the availability of extensive learning resources. New users can easily access tutorials, forums, and discussions to solve problems and share ideas.

Extensibility

R's extensibility is another key advantage. It has a rich ecosystem of packages contributed by the community that enhances its core functionalities. Whether for data visualization with packages like ggplot2, machine learning with caret, or data manipulation with dplyr, R users can find specialized tools for nearly any task. Furthermore, users can create custom functions or packages tailored to their unique needs, making R a flexible tool for solving specific problems.

Reproducibility

R is built with reproducibility in mind. It offers tools for documenting and sharing code, which is crucial for transparent and verifiable data analysis. By using tools like R Markdown, users can create dynamic reports that combine code, analysis, and visualizations in a single document. This ensures that others can easily reproduce and validate results, which is especially important in research and collaborative projects.

These features empower users to tackle complex data challenges efficiently while fostering a collaborative and transparent approach to solving real-world problems.

Where to download R?

To begin using R for data analysis, the first step is to download and install R. It can be obtained from the Comprehensive R Archive Network (CRAN) website at https://cran.r-project.org/. The CRAN website provides the latest version of R and supports all major operating systems, including Windows, macOS, and Linux. Clear instructions are available for downloading and installing R for your operating system.

R provides a command-line interface where users can enter commands to interact directly with the R environment. This allows for precise control and customization, but it may feel less intuitive for beginners. To make R more accessible, several graphical user interfaces (GUIs) have been developed. One of the most popular GUIs is RStudio, which offers a user-friendly and interactive platform for working with R. Once R is installed, the next step is to download RStudio Desktop, a popular integrated development environment (IDE) for R. RStudio Desktop can be downloaded from the official Posit website at https://posit.co/download/rstudio-desktop/. The free version of RStudio is suitable for students, researchers, and professionals working on data analysis projects.

RStudio provides tools for code editing, debugging, and visualization, offering a seamless workflow for R users. Detailed guidance on RStudio's features, setup, and compatibility can be found on the official Posit website.

By combining R and RStudio, users can efficiently explore data, create graphs, and perform advanced statistical analysis. Proper setup of these tools ensures a smooth and productive experience in data science and analytics projects.

Introduction to R interface

Toolbar

The toolbar in RStudio contains buttons for performing common actions such as saving scripts, running code, and debugging. These shortcuts provide quick access to frequently used features, helping users save time and focus on their work. For example, instead of typing out commands, users can click a button to execute scripts or access debugging tools, making the interface more efficient and beginner-friendly.

Source Editor

The source editor is where users write their R code. It includes several advanced features such as syntax highlighting, which visually distinguishes different elements of the code; autocompletion, which suggests commands and functions as you type; and code folding, which allows users to hide or collapse sections of code for better organization. These features make coding less error-prone and more efficient, especially when working on complex projects. **Throughout this book, you will use the source editor to input your code.**

Console

The console in RStudio is the interactive component where users can directly input R commands and see the immediate output. It displays the results of executed commands, along with any error messages or warnings, which are critical for debugging. Additionally, the console maintains a history of previously entered commands, allowing users to review and reuse past work without retyping.

Environment and History Panes

The Environment pane provides an overview of the current R session, including loaded packages, data objects, and functions. Users can view, modify, and manage these objects easily. The History pane complements this by displaying a record of all commands executed during the session. This combination of tools simplifies project management and enhances workflow by keeping all session-related information readily accessible.

Plots and Viewer Panes

RStudio is well-equipped for data visualization. The Plots pane displays any visualizations generated using R's plotting functions, such as graphs or charts, in an organized way. Meanwhile, the Viewer pane is designed for interacting with web-based content, such as HTML files or Shiny apps, directly within RStudio. These features make RStudio versatile for both exploratory data analysis and presenting results.

Help and Files Panes

To assist users, RStudio includes a Help pane that provides access to R's extensive documentation. This includes detailed help files for functions, packages, and commands, ensuring users can find support when needed. Additionally, the Files pane shows the files and folders in the current working directory, making it easy to navigate and organize project files without leaving the RStudio environment.

Tabs

RStudio supports multitasking by allowing users to open multiple documents (such as scripts or files) simultaneously. Each document appears in its tab, enabling users to switch between different scripts or projects effortlessly. This feature is particularly useful for working on large projects that involve multiple code files. Figure 1.4 shows the locations of each feature and tool of RStudio.

If your RStudio interface is different from Fig. 1.4, you can adjust it. Go to View > Panes > Pane Layout… (Fig. 1.5)

R basics

Variables

In R, **variables** are essential components used to store data for further analysis and computations. Variables act like containers that hold different types of data, such as numbers, text, or logical values. To create a variable, you use an **assignment**

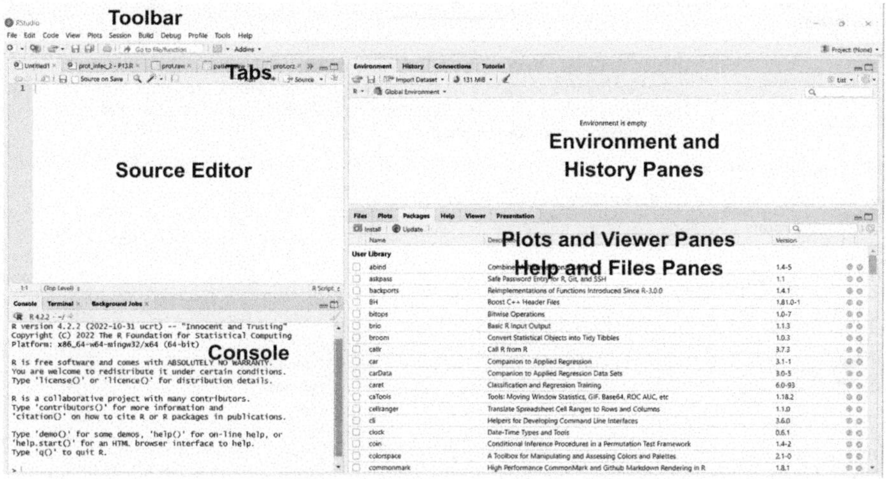

Fig. 1.4 Locations of each feature and tool of RStudio

operator (<- or). For instance, if you want to store the number 10 in a variable called x, you can write in the source editor:

```
x <- 10
# or
x = 10
```

Both assignment operators are commonly used, but <- is more conventional in R programming. Once a variable is created, you can use it in calculations, pass it as input to functions, or modify its value.

In R code, the # symbol is used to indicate a comment. Everything after the # on that line is ignored by R when the code is executed. Comments are useful for explaining what the code does, adding notes for clarity, or temporarily disabling a line of code without deleting it.

Data Types

R supports multiple **data types** to handle various kinds of data. These include:

- **Numeric:** Represents decimal numbers, such as `3.14`.
- **Integer:** Represents whole numbers, such as `42`.
- **Character:** Represents text data, such as `"hello"`.
- **Logical:** Represents Boolean values, such as `TRUE or FALSE`.

Fig. 1.5 Adjusting the layout of RStudio interface

For example, creating variables of different types looks like this:

```
num_var <- 3.14 #                        Numeric
int_var <- as.integer(5)                   # Integer
char_var <- "hello"                          #
Character
log_var <- TRUE                             # Logical
```

Understanding data types is crucial because certain operations or functions work only with specific types of data.

Operators

R provides a wide range of **operators** for performing tasks such as arithmetic calculations, logical comparisons, and more. These include:

- **Arithmetic operators** (e.g., +, −, *, /, ^ for power): Used for mathematical operations.
- **Logical operators** (e.g., &, |, !): Used for combining or negating logical conditions.
- **Comparison operators** (e.g., <, >, = =, ! =): Used for comparing values.

For example,

```
sum <- 5 + 3                                    #
Arithmetic: sum is 8
is_equal <- 10 == 10                    # Comparison:
is_equal is TRUE
logical_and <- TRUE & FALSE # Logical: logical_and
is FALSE
```

Operators are the backbone of performing calculations and logical evaluations in R.

In R, %>% is the pipe operator from the dplyr package (part of the tidyverse). It is used to pass the result of one operation to the next operation in a sequence, making the code more readable and efficient.

Here's how it works:

- ***The left-hand side of %>% is passed as the first argument to the function on the right-hand side.***
- ***It allows you to chain multiple operations together in a clear, step-by-step manner.***

It's commonly used in data wrangling and analysis tasks in R. You will practice using the pipe operator in Chapter 3.

Functions

R is known for its **rich set of built-in functions** that allow users to perform tasks ranging from simple arithmetic to complex statistical analysis. Functions are reusable pieces of code that perform specific tasks. For example, the function `sum()` calculates the total of a series of numbers, while `mean()` calculates their average.

You can also create custom functions to tailor computations to your specific needs. Here's an example of using both built-in and custom functions:

```
# Built-in function
total <- sum(1, 2, 3) # total is 6

# Custom function
add_two_numbers <- function(a, b) {
 return(a + b)
}
Result <- add_two_numbers(5, 7) # result is 12
```

Functions are a powerful tool in R programming, making it easier to organize and reuse code.

PRACTICE 1

Learning objectives

Understand the Importance of Setting the Working Directory:

- Define what a working directory is and explain its significance in R programming.
- Demonstrate how to set the working directory using the `setwd()` function to avoid file path errors.

Familiarize with Built-in Datasets in R:

- Access and explore the structure of the built-in `mtcars` dataset.
- Use the `head()` function to preview the dataset's first few rows.
- Utilize the `attach()` function to simplify referencing dataset variables.

Create Basic Scatterplots in R:

- Use the `plot()` function to visualize relationships between two variables in a dataset.
- Add a regression line to the scatterplot using the `abline()` function.
- Interpret the trend shown by the scatterplot and regression line.

Explore Advanced Visualizations Using ggplot2:

- Install and load the `ggplot2` package in R for advanced plotting.
- Create customized scatterplots using the `ggplot()` function and associated functions like `geom_point()`, `labs()`, and `theme()`.
- Apply themes and design elements to make visualizations professional and aesthetically appealing.

Enhance Reproducibility and Workflow Efficiency in R:

- Understand how to write and run R scripts in RStudio using keyboard shortcuts and the source code window.
- Recognize the importance of clear and reproducible code practices in data analysis.

Apply R Functions to Data Analysis Tasks:

- Combine visualization techniques with regression modeling (e.g., using `lm()`) to explore and summarize data trends.
- Identify the key components of effective data visualization, including clear labels, titles, and clean designs.

When working in R, it is important to always set your working directory at the start of your session. The working directory is the folder on your computer where R reads and saves files. You can set it using the `setwd()` function. For example, if your files are in a folder called "Week_1," you can set your working directory by typing `setwd(""your_path/Week_1")`. This ensures that R knows exactly where to find or save your files, which avoids errors related to file paths.

Next, let's work with the built-in `mtcars` dataset in R. To access the dataset, use the `attach()` function. This makes the variables in the dataset accessible without needing to use the $ operator every time. For example, after running `attach(mtcars)`, you can directly refer to variables like wt (weight) and mpg (miles per gallon). To view the first few rows of the dataset, use the `head(mtcars)` function. This provides a quick preview of the data, allowing you to understand its structure and content.

One common task is creating a simple scatterplot to explore the relationship between two variables. For example, you can use the `plot()` function to visualize the relationship between the weight of a car (`wt`) and its fuel efficiency (`mpg`). The following code creates a scatterplot of `wt` versus mpg and adds a regression line to the plot using the `abline()` function. Copy and paste the code into your source code window of RStudio, then click **ctrl + Enter for Windows** or **command + Enter for macOS** or click on the **"Run" icon** on the top-left of the source code window.

```
plot(wt, mpg)
abline(lm(mpg ~ wt))
title("Regression of MPG on Weight")
```

The **plot will be shown in the Plot and View Panes**; it is located on the right side of the source code window. This plot (Fig. 1.6) shows how miles per gallon

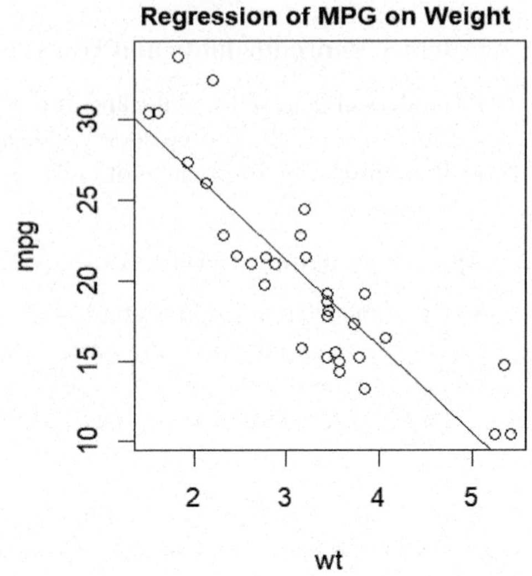

Fig. 1.6 Simple scatterplot to explore the relationship between car weight and fuel efficiency

changes as car weight increases. The regression line, calculated by the `lm()` function, summarizes the trend in the data.

For more advanced visualizations, the `ggplot2` package is a powerful and flexible tool. If you don't have it installed, you can add it to your R environment using `install.packages("ggplot2")`. Once installed, load the package with `library(ggplot2). Using ggplot2`, you can create a customized scatterplot with the following code:

```
scatter_plot <- ggplot(mtcars, aes(x = wt, y =
mpg, color = "#f7aa58")) +
 geom_point() + Add points to the plot
 labs(x = "Weight", y = "MPG", title = "Scatterplot
of MPG vs Weight") + # Add axis labels and plot
title
 theme(plot.title = element_text(face = "bold")) +
 theme(legend.position = 'none')
print(scatter_plot)
```

This code generates a polished scatterplot (Fig. 1.7) where each point represents a car, showing its weight (`wt`) on the x-axis and fuel efficiency (`mpg`) on the y-axis. The plot includes clear axis labels, a bold title, and a consistent color for the points. The `theme()` function is used to remove the legend and enhance the title's appearance, making the visualization clean and professional.

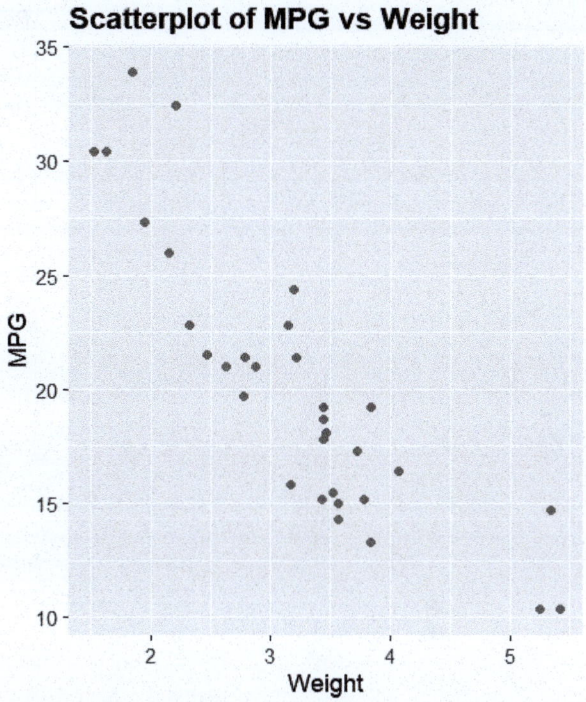

Fig. 1.7 A polished scatterplot showing its weight (`wt`) on the x-axis and fuel efficiency (`mpg`) on the y-axis

Chapter 2
Data Types and Measurement Scale

Abstract The first part of this chapter will cover key aspects of data structure, including types such as structured, unstructured, semi-structured, and metadata. This chapter will also discuss data types, such as categorical, ordinal, numerical, and binary data, and explain the differences between numeric, integer, Boolean, and string data. Additionally, measurement and rating scales, including the Likert Scale, Semantic Differential Scale, Numerical Rating Scale, and Visual Analog Scale, will be introduced. Finally, this chapter explores the characteristics and challenges of big data, providing a comprehensive overview for all readers. The second part will explain how to start a new project, introduce the types of data that R can handle, show where to find reliable datasets, guide us in creating or importing our owned data, and review how to assess data quality.

Relation to Other Chapters: Links to data preprocessing and quality control (Chap. 3), as it sets the groundwork for understanding data forms and accuracy needs.

2.1 Introduction

The discipline of data science has increasingly become vital to social sciences, facilitating in-depth analysis of diverse datasets and revealing patterns that drive informed decisions. A solid grasp of data structures, types, and measurement scales lays the groundwork for selecting the proper analytical tools and approaches. In this chapter, we delve into these core concepts, examining the role each plays in enhancing data management, accuracy, and analytical rigor in social science research.

F. Ramdani, *Data Science: Foundations and Hands-on Experience*,
https://doi.org/10.1007/978-981-96-4683-8_2

2.2 Understanding Data Structure

Data structure is a way of organizing and storing data so that it can be accessed and modified efficiently. The structure of data has significant implications for how it can be stored, analyzed, and used in various applications.

1. Structured Data
   Structured data follows a set format, making it easy to analyze. It is organized in tables with rows and columns that are related to each other (Fig. 2.1). Examples of structured data include Excel files or SQL databases, where the rows and columns can be sorted.

   Structured data relies on a data model, which shows how the data is stored, processed, and accessed. Because of this model, each piece of data is separate and can be accessed on its own or together with other data. This makes structured data very useful, as it allows for quick gathering of data from different parts of the database. Structured data is seen as the most "traditional" way of storing data, as the first database systems were designed to handle this type of data.
2. Unstructured Data
   Unstructured data refers to information that does not follow a specific format or organization, meaning it lacks a clear, predefined structure. This type of data is often made up of large amounts of text but can also include numbers, dates, facts, and other types of information as shown in Fig. 2.2. Since it doesn't follow a consistent or organized format, unstructured data can be hard to analyze and interpret using traditional software tools, unlike structured data that is neatly organized in databases. Examples of unstructured data include images, audio, video files, and data stored in No-SQL databases, all of which can vary greatly in format and content, adding to their complexity.

   The capacity to store and process unstructured data has advanced significantly in recent years. This progress is largely due to the emergence of various new technologies and tools designed to handle specific types of unstructured data.

   The ability to analyze unstructured data has become particularly important in the era of big data. In many organizations, a significant portion of the data they deal with is unstructured, including formats like images, dates, audios and videos, numbers, facts, and PDF files. The ability to extract meaningful insights and value from this unstructured data is one of the key factors driving the rapid

Fig. 2.1 Illustration of simple structured data

	Category	Example
1	ID	1
2	Name	Alice
3	Age	30
4	Salary	50000

	text
1	Yamamoto's birthday is on 1994-12-12. He turned 30 years old.
2	The project deadline is January 15, 2025, with a budget of $2,000,000.
3	On 2022/11/30, a record high temperature of 45.6°C was reported in the city.
4	No specific date was mentioned, but sales increased by 15% last month.

Fig. 2.2 Illustration of simple unstructured data containing data such as dates, numbers, and facts

growth of data science, as it allows companies to unlock information that would otherwise remain hidden or underutilized.

3. Semi-structured Data
   Semi-structured data is a type of data that falls somewhere between fully structured and unstructured data. Unlike structured data, which fits neatly into tables with rows and columns like in relational databases, semi-structured data doesn't follow a strict schema or predefined format. However, it still has some organization, usually in the form of tags or markers that help separate and label different parts of the data, creating a hierarchy of records and fields. Because of this self-describing nature, it's often referred to as having a flexible structure. Common examples of semi-structured data include formats like JSON and XML. Illustration and difference between these two types of data are shown in Fig. 2.3.

   The reason for this middle category is that semi-structured data is easier to work with than completely unstructured data. While unstructured data, like text documents or images, can be difficult to analyze because they lack organization, semi-structured data contains enough structure for data analysis tools to process and interpret it. Many data science tools and platforms can easily read and work with formats like JSON or XML, making it simpler to analyze compared to fully

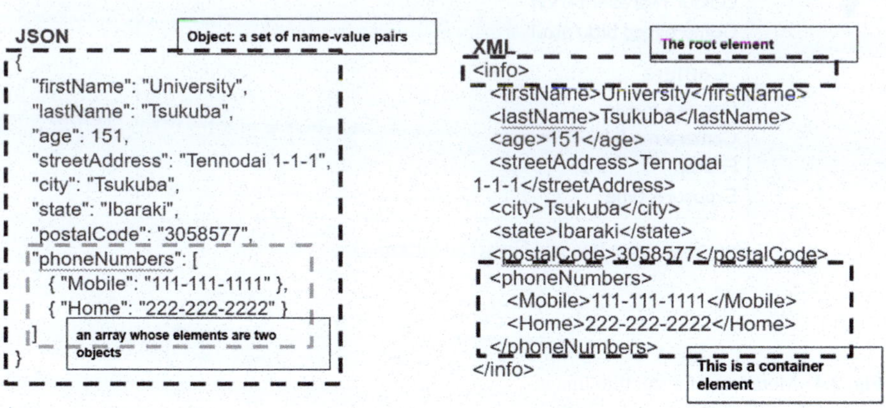

Fig. 2.3 Difference between JSON and XML

unstructured data. This makes semi-structured data an ideal option for situations where flexibility and ease of processing are important.

4. Metadata

   Metadata means data about data. From a technical standpoint, metadata is not a separate type of data, but rather an essential component for data science analysis and problem-solving. It gives extra details about a specific dataset. For instance, in a collection of photos, the metadata might include information about when and where the photos were taken. This extra information, like dates and locations, can be seen as structured data on its own. Because of its importance, metadata is often used in data science to help with initial analysis. For example, Fig. 2.4 shows metadata from a satellite image, demonstrating how this additional information supports the understanding of the image itself. Data like image dimensions, width, height, horizontal and vertical resolution, bit depth, compression type, and many more are available in the metadata.

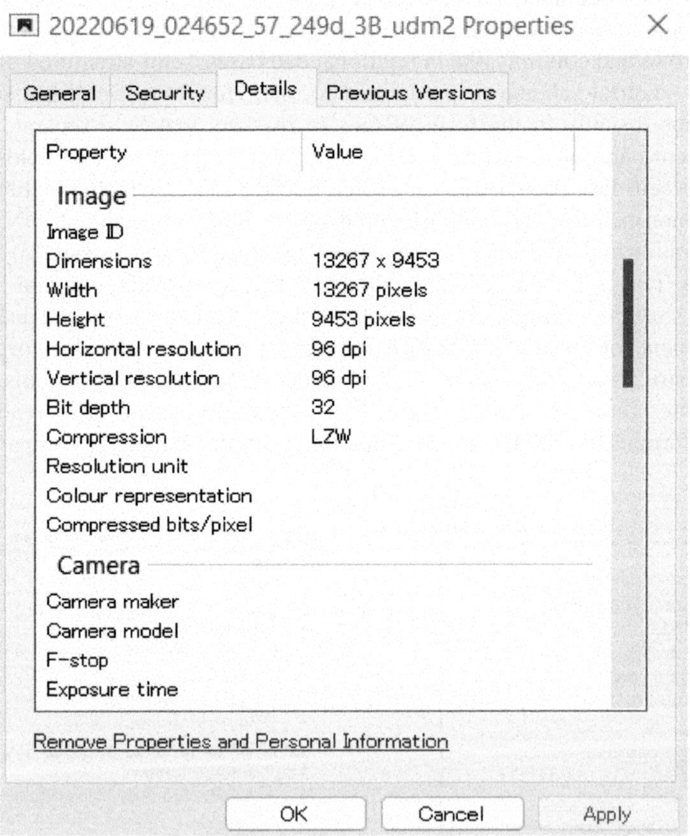

Fig. 2.4 Metadata of a satellite image

2.3 Types of Data

In data science, a data type is a classification that helps determine the kind of value a variable holds and what types of operations can be performed on it without causing errors. These operations can be mathematical, relational, or logical. For instance, a string is a data type used to classify text, while an integer is a data type used for whole numbers. However, it is important to remember that strings and integers cannot be used together in certain operations, as this will result in an error. Understanding data types is essential because it allows us to know how data can be manipulated and analyzed.

Data types also serve as the foundation for statistical analysis. By knowing the type of data we are working with, we can choose the appropriate methods and tools for analysis and visualization. For example, numerical data might be analyzed using different techniques compared to categorical data. Each data type requires specific approaches to make sure the analysis is accurate and meaningful.

Categorical Data

Categorical data is a type of data that can be divided into groups or categories. There are two main types of categorical data: nominal and ordinal.

Nominal Data refers to categories that do not have any specific order or ranking. Examples of nominal data include gender, nationality, or eye color. These categories simply represent different groups, and there is no inherent hierarchy among them. Nominal data is often used in frequency-based analysis, where the goal is to see how often each category appears in the dataset.

Ordinal Data, on the other hand, has a natural order, but the intervals between the categories are not necessarily consistent. For example, educational levels such as "high school," "bachelor's degree," and "master's degree" are ordinal because they represent a progression, but the difference in years of education between each level may vary. Ordinal data allows researchers to identify rankings or hierarchies, such as customer satisfaction ratings or income levels.

Numerical Data

Numerical data involves values that are expressed as numbers. There are two types of numerical data: continuous and discrete.

Continuous Data is data that can take any value within a given range. Examples include measurements like temperature, weight, or income. Continuous data is important in statistical techniques such as regression analysis and correlation studies, where precise numerical input is required. These data types allow for more detailed and refined analysis, especially when we are trying to predict trends or relationships.

Discrete Data consists of fixed values, usually counted data. For example, the number of children in a family or the number of cars in a parking lot are discrete data. Discrete data is often visualized using bar graphs or histograms, where the data points are represented as distinct bars or categories. Discrete data is commonly used in surveys or studies where we are counting occurrences of certain events.

One important distinction between discrete and continuous data is the types of statistical analysis that can be used.

- Discrete data can be analyzed using methods such as frequency distributions, measures of central tendency, and measures of dispersion.
- Continuous data, on the other hand, requires more advanced statistical techniques such as regression analysis and correlation analysis.

Binary Data

Binary data is a special type of data that can take on only two possible values. These values are typically represented as true/false, yes/no, or 1/0. Binary data is often used in social science research to predict outcomes with two possible results, such as whether someone will vote in an election or whether they will be employed. Logistic regression models and decision trees are common tools for analyzing binary data, as they help predict the likelihood of one of the two outcomes occurring.

Figure 2.5 shows examples of each data type presented in plot.

Data Types in R

Categorization of data types for statistical analysis in R is a little different. In the statistical software R, data types are essential for handling different formats of data. R supports various data types, including *numeric, integer, character, logical, and factor*. These data types are crucial for cleaning, transforming, and analyzing data in social science research. *Numeric* data is used for continuous numbers, while *integer*

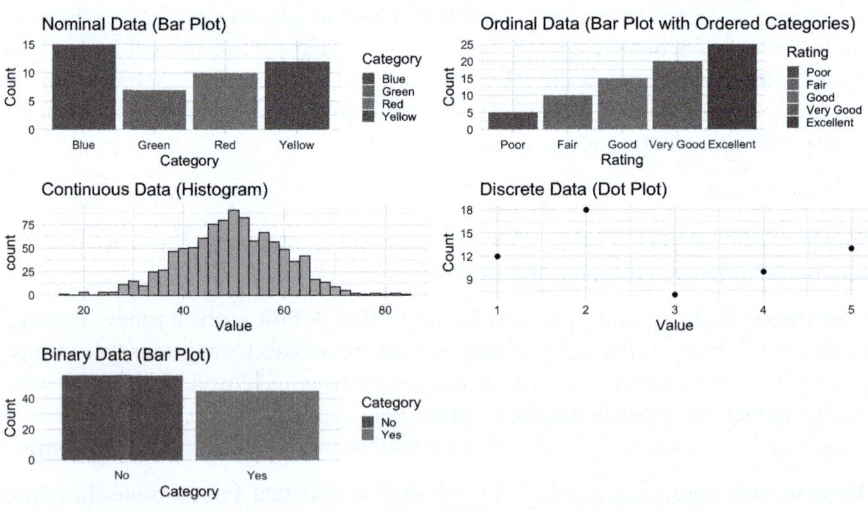

Fig. 2.5 Illustration of nominal, ordinal, continuous, discrete, and binary data plot in bar plot, histogram, and scatterplot

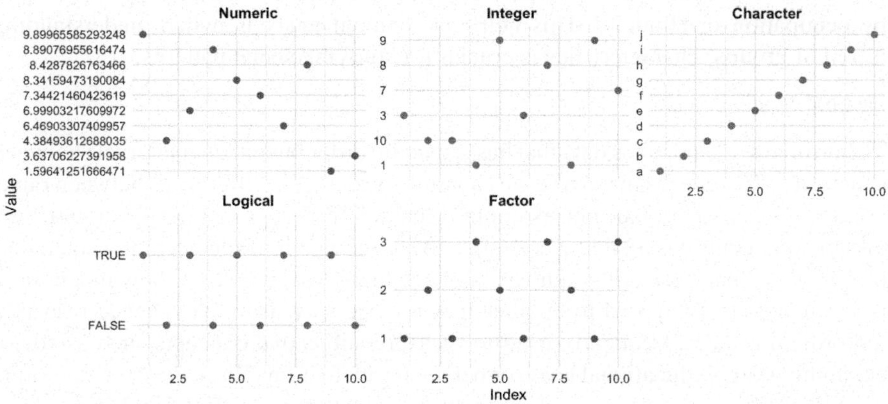

Fig. 2.6 Illustration of different data types plot in R

data stores whole numbers. *Character* data holds text, *logical* data stores Boolean values (true or false), and *factor* data is used for categorical variables, especially when they have a fixed number of levels (Fig. 2.6). Understanding how to use these data types in R is key for managing and analyzing complex datasets.

By understanding the different data types, researchers can make informed decisions about how to analyze their data, choose the right techniques for their studies, and visualize it most suitably. Whether working with text, numbers, or categories, selecting the appropriate data type ensures accurate and efficient data analysis.

2.4 Measurement Scales

Measurement scales are an important concept in data analysis because they determine which mathematical operations can be applied to data. These scales also influence how data is visualized and analyzed in statistical studies. Understanding the different types of measurement scales is essential for choosing the right methods to analyze data effectively.

Nominal Scale

The nominal scale is the simplest level of measurement. It categorizes data without any specific order or ranking. For example, variables like types of employment (e.g., teacher, doctor, engineer) or language groups (e.g., English, Spanish, French) are classified using the nominal scale. The main operation that can be applied to nominal data is counting the frequency of categories, which helps describe the data. Descriptive statistics like the mode (the most common category) and frequency distributions are commonly used with nominal data. In the social sciences, this scale is often used for classification purposes. For instance, researchers might categorize participants by occupation or ethnicity. This helps in segment analysis, where understanding different groups' characteristics is crucial for studying social patterns.

Ordinal Scale

The ordinal scale involves data that has a specific order but unequal intervals between categories. This means that while we can rank the data, the differences between ranks are not necessarily equal. For example, satisfaction ratings (e.g., very dissatisfied, dissatisfied, neutral, satisfied, very satisfied) or income brackets (e.g., low, medium, high) are ordinal data. Although we can rank them, we cannot say how much more one category is compared to another in a precise way. In social science research, the ordinal scale is frequently used to measure subjective concepts such as socio-economic status, educational level, or personal satisfaction. These measures are often used in studies that explore social inequality, as they help classify and rank individuals based on their social standing.

Interval Scale

Interval data is characterized by equal intervals between values, but it lacks an absolute zero point. This means that while you can measure the difference between values, you cannot make meaningful statements about ratios. For example, temperature measurements in Celsius or Fahrenheit are interval data because the difference between 10 and 20 °C is the same as between 20 and 30 °C, but there is no true zero point that represents the absence of temperature. In social science, interval data is useful for analyzing standardized measures, such as IQ scores or test results. These measures allow for statistical operations like calculating means, standard deviations, and correlations, but you cannot make direct ratio comparisons.

Ratio Scale

The ratio scale is the highest level of measurement. It shares the properties of the interval scale but with the added benefit of having an absolute zero. This allows for a wide range of mathematical operations, including the calculation of means, standard deviations, and meaningful ratio comparisons. For example, data such as income, age, and weight are measured on a ratio scale. In social science, ratio scales are crucial for economic analysis, such as studying income disparities or population growth rates. The ability to compare proportions (e.g., a person earning twice as much as another) makes the ratio scale powerful for understanding trends and making accurate statistical comparisons.

Figure 2.7 summarizes common categorization of data types in relation to the applicable measurement scale in data science.

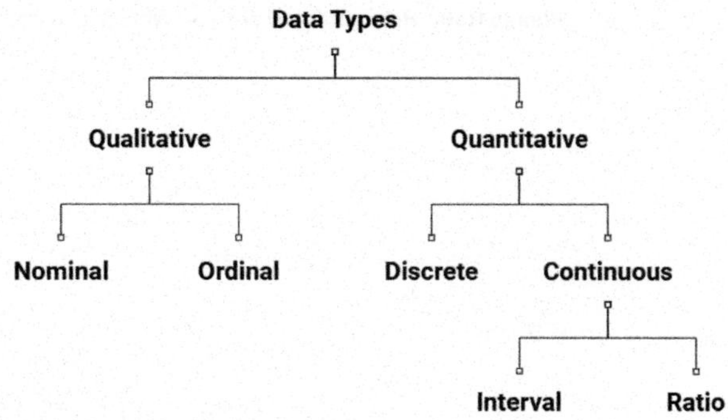

Fig. 2.7 Data types and the measurement scale

2.5 Rating Scale

Rating scale techniques are a type of research tool used to measure and quantify subjective opinions, attitudes, perceptions, or behaviors of individuals or groups.

They are commonly used in fields such as psychology, marketing, social sciences, and market research to gather data on people's opinions or preferences.

Rating scales typically consist of a series of items or statements that are presented to respondents, who then rate or rank their level of agreement or disagreement, satisfaction, preference, or other subjective evaluations.

The responses are usually collected using numerical or descriptive scales, where respondents assign a value or choose a response option that best represents their opinion or perception.

Following are examples of rating scales:

- **Likert Scale**: This is a commonly used rating scale that asks respondents to indicate their level of agreement or disagreement with a series of statements. The scale typically ranges from “strongly agree” to “strongly disagree,” with options in between such as “agree,” “neutral,” and “disagree.“ Respondents select the option that best reflects their opinion or attitude toward each statement. Figure 2.8 illustrates the question with the Likert Scale
- **Semantic Differential Scale**: This type of rating scale measures the meaning or connotation of a concept or object using bipolar adjectives or opposite pairs, such as “good” versus “bad” or “happy” versus “sad.“ Respondents rate the concept or object on each adjective along a continuum, indicating their perception or evaluation of the item. Figure 2.9 illustrates the question with the Semantic Differential Scale.
- **Numerical Rating Scale**: This type of rating scale involves assigning a numerical value to a particular item or statement, typically on a scale of 1 to 10 or 1 to 5, where higher numbers indicate a more favorable evaluation and lower numbers indicate a less positive or less favorable evaluation. Figure 2.10 illustrates the question with the Numerical Rating Scale.
- **Visual Analog Scale:** This rating scale uses a line or bar where respondents mark their responses along a continuum to indicate their opinion or perception. The

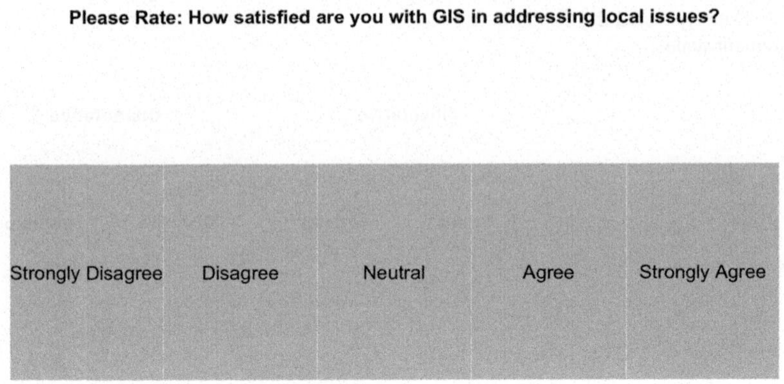

Fig. 2.8 Illustration of Likert Scale application

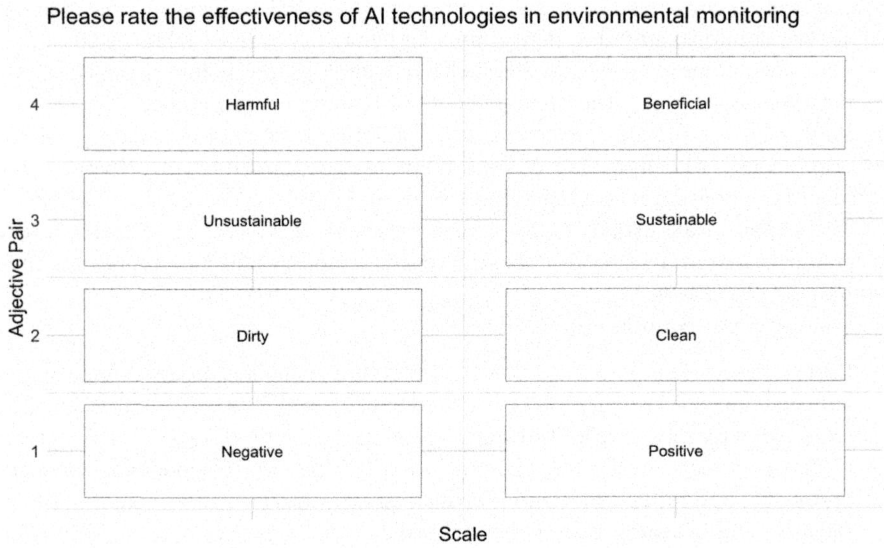

Fig. 2.9 Illustration of Semantic Differential Scale application

length of the line or bar represents the range of possible responses, and respondents mark their response at the appropriate point along the line. Figure 2.11 illustrates the question with the Visual Analog Scale.

Advantages and Limitations

Rating scale techniques are widely used in research and surveys due to several advantages. One key benefit is their ease of administration, which allows researchers to gather responses from a large number of participants efficiently. This simplicity is

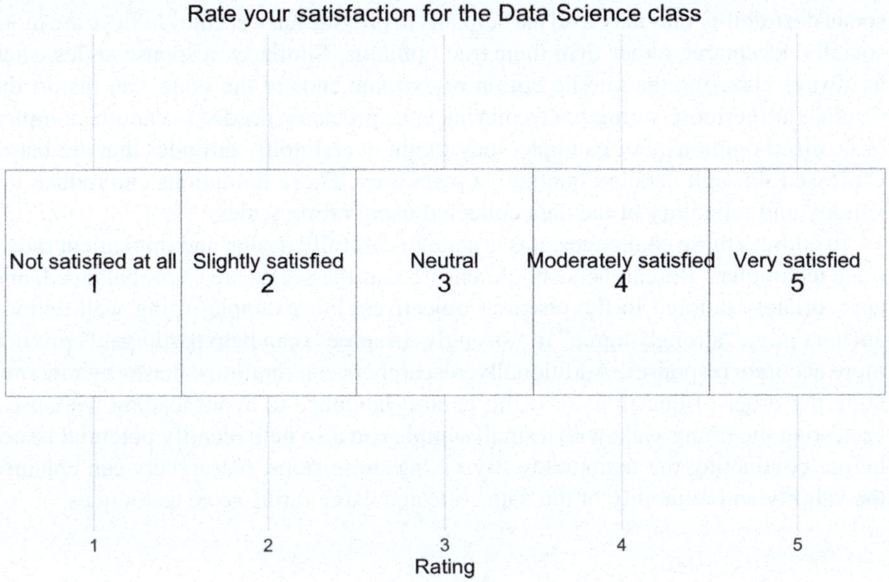

Fig. 2.10 Illustration of Numerical Rating Scale application

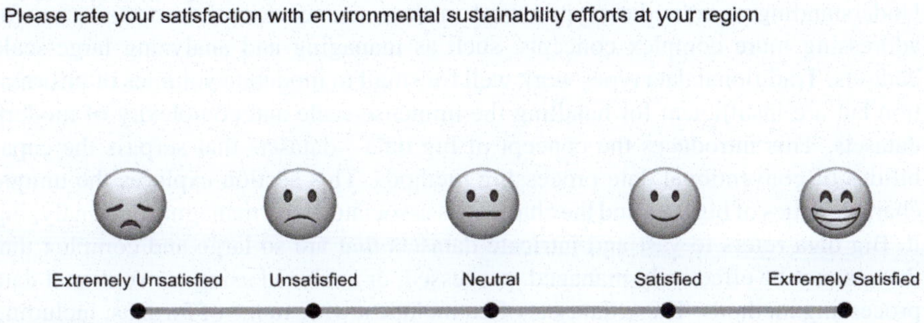

Fig. 2.11 Illustration of Visual Analog Scale application

beneficial in studies with limited time or resources, as rating scales are straightforward for participants to understand and complete. Additionally, these techniques facilitate efficient data collection by standardizing responses, making it easier to organize and analyze the data. Since the responses are often numerical, rating scales lend themselves to quantitative data analysis, enabling researchers to apply statistical techniques to identify patterns, relationships, and trends in the data. These characteristics make rating scale techniques a valuable tool in social science, market research, and educational assessments.

Despite their advantages, rating scale techniques also have certain limitations. One common challenge is the potential for biases in participant responses. For instance, social desirability bias may lead participants to provide answers they believe are more socially acceptable rather than their true opinions. Similarly, response styles, such as always choosing the middle option or extreme ends of the scale, can distort the results. Furthermore, rating scales may lack the precision needed to capture complex or nuanced opinions. For example, they might oversimplify attitudes that are better expressed through detailed qualitative responses. These limitations can reduce the validity and reliability of the data collected using rating scales.

To address these challenges, it is crucial to carefully design and implement rating scale techniques. Researchers should ensure that the scales are clear, balanced, and appropriately tailored to the research objectives. For example, using well-defined anchors (e.g., "strongly agree" to "strongly disagree") can help participants provide more accurate responses. Additionally, researchers can minimize biases by randomizing the order of questions or using neutral language to avoid leading responses. Pretesting the rating scale with a small sample can also help identify potential issues before conducting the main study. By taking these steps, researchers can enhance the validity and reliability of the data collected using rating scale techniques.

2.6 Data Types and Big Data

Understanding various data types used in data science forms the foundation for addressing more complex concepts, such as managing and analyzing large-scale datasets. Traditional data types work well for small to moderate volumes of information but are insufficient for handling the immense scale and complexity of modern datasets. This introduces the concept of big data—datasets that surpass the capabilities of conventional data processing methods. This section explores the unique characteristics of big data and the challenges associated with managing and analyzing it. Big data refers to vast and intricate datasets that are so large and complex that they cannot be effectively managed, processed, or analyzed using conventional data processing methods. These datasets often include a wide range of formats, including structured, semi-structured, and unstructured data, which complicate traditional analysis techniques. The challenge lies not only in storing and managing such data but also in extracting meaningful insights from it.

To better understand the unique nature of big data and the difficulties in handling it, experts often refer to the "Five Vs" of big data. These characteristics—*Volume, Velocity, Variety, Veracity*, and *Value*—are essential in defining the scope and complexity of big data (Fig. 2.12).

Volume refers to the size or massive amount of data generated and collected from various sources such as social media, sensors, devices, websites, and more. This data can be in structured or unstructured formats, and its sheer size can overwhelm traditional data processing systems. Managing and analyzing large volumes of data requires specialized tools and technologies that can handle the scale and complexity of big data. Social scientists often deal with massive datasets generated from diverse sources, such as social media, government records, and surveys.

Fig. 2.12 "Five Vs" of big data and its relationship

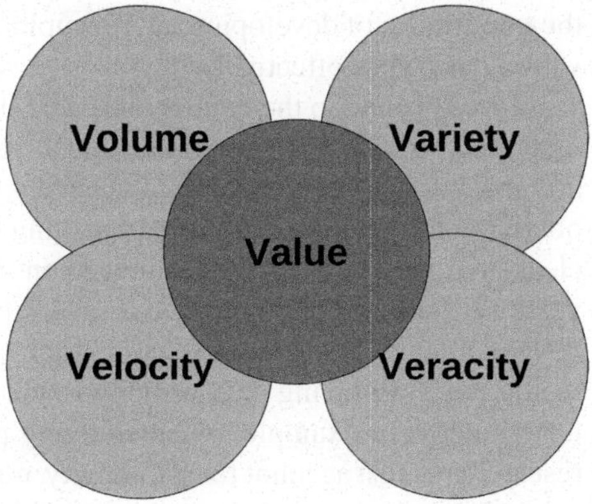

For instance, analyzing millions of Twitter posts to gauge public sentiment during elections involves handling vast quantities of data. Such datasets require advanced tools for storage, processing, and analysis. Boyd and Crawford (2012) emphasize that while big data allows unprecedented access to social behaviors, managing these massive datasets poses ethical and logistical challenges, especially in terms of privacy and accessibility.

Velocity refers to the speed at which data is generated, processed, and analyzed. With the increasing use of real-time data and the Internet of Things (IoT), data is being generated and transmitted at an unprecedented rate. The ability to process and analyze data in real-time or near real-time is crucial to gain actionable insights and make informed decisions. In social science research, real-time data streams, such as live traffic feeds or social media updates, can provide immediate insights into societal trends. For example, during natural disasters, real-time analysis of social media platforms can help track public reactions and coordinate relief efforts. The speed at which such data arrives necessitates advanced algorithms and computing capabilities to analyze it in real-time. Chen et al. (2014) highlight the role of big data technologies in facilitating rapid analytics, particularly in decision-making processes for social and economic challenges.

Variety refers to the diversity and heterogeneity of data. Big data can come in different formats such as structured data (e.g., relational databases), unstructured data (e.g., text, images, videos), semi-structured data (e.g., XML, JSON), and more. Big data can also come from various sources, including social media, mobile devices, sensors, and more. Analyzing and integrating data from different sources and formats poses significant challenges in terms of data integration, data quality, and data consistency. Social scientists frequently work with structured data, such as census records; semi-structured data, like social media posts; and unstructured data, such as videos and images. For example, researchers studying urban poverty might integrate geospatial data, policy documents, and qualitative interviews to understand the phenomenon comprehensively. The ability to analyze such heterogeneous datasets is critical for addressing multifaceted issues. Kitchin (2014), in *The Data Revolution*, emphasizes the importance of developing interdisciplinary approaches and tools to manage these varied data types effectively.

Veracity refers to the quality and reliability of data. Big data can be noisy, incomplete, inconsistent, and unreliable due to various reasons such as data errors, biases, and inaccuracies. Ensuring data accuracy, consistency, and reliability is crucial to obtaining trustworthy insights and making informed decisions. Data validation, data cleansing, and data quality management are important steps in dealing with the veracity challenge of big data. Social science research often involves data that may be incomplete, biased, or inaccurate, such as self-reported survey responses or social media posts. Ensuring data veracity requires rigorous validation and preprocessing techniques. For example, when studying public opinions using social media data, researchers must account for bot activity, misinformation, and sampling biases. Lazer et al. (2009) underscore the importance of addressing these issues in computational social science, advocating for methodological rigor to enhance data reliability.

Value refers to the potential insights, knowledge, and business value that can be extracted from big data. The ultimate goal of analyzing big data is to derive meaningful and actionable insights that can drive business decisions, improve processes, and gain a competitive advantage. Extracting value from big data requires advanced analytics techniques such as machine learning, data mining, and predictive analytics to uncover patterns, trends, and correlations in the data. In social science, extracting value from big data often involves identifying relationships between variables that inform policy decisions. For instance, understanding the correlation between socio-economic factors and health outcomes can guide resource allocation in public health initiatives. Janssen et al. (2017) explore how big data generates value in governance contexts, highlighting its potential to transform decision-making by offering evidence-based insights.

Intersection of Big Data with Artificial Intelligence (AI), Machine Learning (ML), and Socio-economic Policy Modeling

The intersection of big data with artificial intelligence (AI), machine learning (ML), and socio-economic policy modeling represents a transformative domain that redefines how decisions are made, policies are designed, and insights are derived. At its core, big data provides the massive volumes, variety, and velocity of data that are necessary for training AI and ML models and enabling robust socio-economic analysis.

AI and machine learning thrive on large datasets. With the ability to process and analyze vast amounts of structured and unstructured data, these technologies uncover hidden patterns, predict trends, and generate actionable insights. For instance, natural language processing (NLP), a subset of AI, can analyze social media sentiments or government policy documents to understand public opinion or legislative focus. Meanwhile, ML algorithms, particularly deep learning models, rely on the availability of big data to improve their accuracy in tasks such as image recognition, speech processing, and predictive modeling (Russell & Norvig, 2021). In socio-economic contexts, such models have been instrumental in analyzing the economic impacts of urbanization, tracking income inequality, or optimizing healthcare delivery systems.

Big data's integration into socio-economic policy modeling goes beyond just data availability; it introduces new paradigms for evidence-based policymaking. With the fusion of geospatial data, census information, and satellite imagery, policymakers can model socio-economic dynamics at granular levels. For example, urban planners use geospatial big data to monitor land use changes and their effects on housing markets and infrastructure demands. This approach helps align development strategies with sustainable growth objectives (Batty, 2024). Similarly, econometric models now incorporate real-time big data streams, such as mobility data from smartphones, to predict unemployment trends or assess the effectiveness of fiscal stimulus packages.

AI and ML also facilitate socio-economic policy modeling by making predictive analytics more accessible and precise. Techniques such as random forests, neural networks, and support vector machines excel in identifying relationships between variables, even in complex, nonlinear datasets. For instance, an ML model could analyze climate data and agricultural production to predict food security challenges, helping governments develop timely interventions (Goodfellow et al., 2016). The integration of big data in such models allows for continuous updates, ensuring that predictions remain accurate as new data flows in.

Moreover, the intersection of these fields supports interdisciplinary research aimed at solving global challenges, such as poverty alleviation, climate change adaptation, and economic resilience. Big data enables a holistic approach by combining data sources, including socio-economic surveys, satellite-derived environmental data, and even social media activity. For instance, integrating remote sensing data with socio-economic variables can help policymakers identify communities vulnerable to natural disasters, enabling targeted disaster preparedness and recovery efforts.

Despite these advancements, challenges persist in the ethical and practical application of big data in these domains. Issues of data privacy, algorithmic bias, and data quality must be addressed to ensure equitable outcomes and trustworthy systems. Nonetheless, as computational capabilities grow and data governance frameworks improve, the synergy between big data, AI, ML, and socio-economic policy modeling is poised to become even more impactful in addressing pressing societal issues.

2.7 Applications of Data Types and Scales in Social Sciences

Market Research

Categorical data plays a significant role in market research. It is used to divide consumers into different groups based on various characteristics, such as their preferences, age, or geographical region. This type of data helps businesses understand their target audience more clearly. By identifying these groups, companies can create marketing strategies that are specifically designed to meet the needs and desires of different consumer segments. For example, a business might create separate marketing campaigns for different age groups or regions, ensuring that each group receives the most relevant message. This data-driven approach helps businesses make informed decisions that can lead to more effective marketing and higher customer satisfaction.

Medical Research

In medical research, ordinal scales are often used to assess the severity of diseases. These scales rank diseases or conditions based on their severity, such as mild, moderate, or severe. Healthcare providers rely on these scales to categorize patient conditions, which is crucial for prioritizing treatment. By understanding the severity of a condition, doctors can determine which patients need urgent care and which can wait. This helps ensure that limited medical resources are used most effectively. Ordinal scales provide a systematic way to manage patient care and make critical decisions about treatment plans, improving overall healthcare delivery.

Environmental and Climate Studies

Continuous data is essential for environmental and climate studies. It helps researchers track climate variables, such as temperature, rainfall, and atmospheric pressure, over time. This type of data allows scientists to observe long-term trends and monitor how the climate is changing globally. For example, continuous data can reveal whether temperatures are rising or if rainfall patterns are shifting. This information is vital for understanding the impact of climate change and assessing the effectiveness of environmental policies. By collecting and analyzing continuous data, scientists can make informed predictions about future climate conditions and guide policy decisions aimed at mitigating environmental damage.

Economic and Business Analysis

Binary data is often used in economic and business analysis to measure success or failure. For example, binary data can indicate whether a policy or intervention has been successful or not, based on clear outcomes such as "yes" or "no." This simplifies the evaluation process, as it provides a straightforward way to measure whether objectives have been met. In business, binary data can be used to analyze whether a product launch has succeeded or whether a marketing campaign has reached its goals. By using binary data, businesses and policymakers can quickly assess the effectiveness of their actions, allowing them to make timely adjustments and improve future decisions.

Environmental Economics

In environmental economics, data types and scales play a critical role in assessing the economic impacts of environmental changes and in valuing natural resources. For instance, spatial data derived from remote sensing, often measured on ratio scales, can quantify changes in land use, such as deforestation or urban sprawl. These data are then combined with socio-economic data—like income or agricultural productivity—measured on ratio scales, to evaluate the economic costs of environmental degradation. Nominal data, such as land cover classifications, are also used to analyze patterns of resource use and to propose optimal land management strategies. For example, linking satellite-derived measurements of mangrove deforestation to fishermen's income in coastal communities provides insights into the socio-economic consequences of ecological loss, aiding in the design of policies for sustainable development (Barbier, 2007).

Public Policy

Public policy research leverages data types and scales to assess and design interventions that address societal challenges. Nominal and ordinal scales are often used to classify and rank variables like policy priorities or public health outcomes, while interval and ratio scales are employed to measure changes in variables such as crime rates, education levels, or public expenditures. A notable interdisciplinary example involves the use of Geographic Information Systems (GIS) to evaluate urban green space distribution and its impact on public health. By overlaying spatial data on green spaces (measured on ratio scales) with health outcome data (e.g., ordinal rankings of health status or ratio measurements of healthcare access), researchers can identify inequities in green space access and propose evidence-based policy reforms (Jennings et al., 2016).

Easy to Digest Box

In data science, ***data type*** *and* ***measurement scale*** *are ways of organizing and understanding information. A* ***data type*** *is like the "kind" or "type" of data. It tells us what kind of information we're working with. While* ***a measurement scale*** *is how we measure or organize data. It helps us understand what we can do with the data.*

In *simple words,* ***data types*** *are what kind of data you have (numbers, words, yes/no), and* ***measurement scales*** *tell us how we can measure or compare that data.*

2.8 Summary of Key Points

- Data structure is a collection of data values, the relationships among them, and the functions or operations that can be applied to the data.
- Metadata is data about data. It provides additional information about a specific set of data.
- Data can be in categorical/nominal data, ordinal data, numerical/continuous data, and binary data.
- In data science, a data type is a classification that specifies which type of value a variable has and what type of mathematical, relational, or logical operations can be applied to it without causing an error.

- Discrete data consists of specific values that can be counted, while continuous data can take on any value within a range and is often measured. The type of data can influence the types of statistical analysis that can be used.
- Data type and measurement scale can impact the type of statistical analysis and affect how data is visualized and interpreted.
- Data transformation techniques may be required to handle different data types.
- It's important to carefully design and implement rating scale techniques to ensure valid and reliable data collection.
- The "Five Vs" of big data, which are Volume, Velocity, Variety, Veracity, and Value, are key characteristics that define the unique nature of big data and the challenges associated with it.

2.9 Hands-on Experience

Working with RStudio

Creating a New Project

In RStudio, creating a new project is an essential step to organize your work. Projects allow you to keep related files, scripts, and datasets in one place, reducing confusion and improving workflow. To start a new project, go to the **"File"** menu, select **"New Project,"** and choose whether you want to create it in a new directory, an existing directory, or from a version control system like Git. Structuring your work this way is especially useful for larger projects or collaborative tasks.

Understanding Different Data Types

Data in R can be stored in various forms, including vectors, matrices, data frames, and lists. Each type serves a specific purpose. For example, data frames allow you to handle datasets with multiple variables of different types. Understanding the differences and knowing when to use each type is crucial for effective data analysis. RStudio provides tools and commands to check and manipulate data types, such as **class()**, **typeof()**, and **str()**.

Looking for Datasets

Finding suitable datasets is a key step in any data analysis project. Many datasets are publicly available through online repositories like Kaggle (https://www.kaggle.com/datasets), UCI Machine Learning Repository (https://archive.ics.uci.edu/), Our World in Data (https://ourworldindata.org/), Disaster Data (https://public.emdat.be/data), or government websites. R also offers built-in datasets, accessible through the datasets package, and external datasets can be imported from sources such as CSV files, Excel sheets, and databases. By exploring these resources, you can identify data that aligns with your analysis objectives.

Creating and Importing Datasets

Once you have identified your data source, you can either create a dataset manually or import an existing one into RStudio. To create a dataset, you can use R commands like **data.frame()** or **matrix()** to define data structures directly in your script. For importing, functions like **read.csv()** and **read_excel()** allow you to load files into RStudio effortlessly. The interface also provides an "**Import Dataset**" menu under "**File**", enabling users to upload data without writing code. Ensuring the data is correctly imported is vital for smooth analysis.

Evaluating Datasets

After importing or creating datasets, evaluating their quality and structure is the next critical step. Functions such as **head(), summary(),** and **str()** provide insights into the dataset's content, structure, and any potential issues, such as missing or inconsistent values. Visualizing the data using plots or tables can also help identify trends or anomalies. Evaluating datasets thoroughly ensures that your analysis is based on reliable and accurate information.

Practice 2

Learning Objectives

Understand RStudio Basics

- Explain the purpose of setting a working directory in RStudio.
- Differentiate between built-in datasets and imported datasets in R.
- Describe common data formats (CSV, Excel, JSON) and how to load them into R.

Loading Data into R

- Use functions like `read.csv()` to load CSV files.
- Install and use packages `(readr, readxl, jsonlite)` for handling data in different formats.
- Practice setting the working directory and loading data with or without specifying file paths.

Exploring and Summarizing Data

- Use exploratory functions like `head()`, `summary()`, `str()`, and `dim()` to understand datasets.
- Explain the importance of data exploration in preparing for analysis.

Generating Random Data for Practice

- Generate random numeric data using functions like `sample()` and `rnorm()`.
- Create and populate data frames with simulated data.

- Save generated data to a file using `write.csv()`.

Data Cleaning and Preprocessing

- Identify and handle missing data using `na.omit()`
- Detects and removes duplicate rows with `duplicated()`.
- Convert data types using functions like `as.Date()` for date variables.
- Apply the `dplyr` package to filter, select, rename, and group data efficiently.

Creating and Visualizing Spatial Data

- Differentiate between spatial objects (points, lines, polygons) and their applications.
- Use the `sf` package to create spatial data objects.
- Visualize spatial data using `ggplot2`, with attention to map aesthetics (axes, labels, and legends).

Creating Text Data for Analysis

- Simulate character data for text processing tasks.
- Install and load R packages (`tm, SnowballC, tidyverse`) required for text analysis.

Package Management in R

- Install and load multiple R packages for specialized tasks.
- Understand the importance of library management for extending R's functionality.

Improving Reproducibility

- Use `set.seed()` to ensure reproducibility in generating random data.
- Save and document workflows for sharing and collaboration.

Practical Applications of R

- Apply learned techniques to real-world data analysis scenarios, such as cleaning raw datasets, generating synthetic data, or creating spatial visualizations.
- Demonstrate the ability to process and visualize tabular, spatial, and text data in R.

When working with RStudio, the first step is to set your working directory and load your dataset. There are several ways to load data into R, depending on the type of data source you are using. You can work with built-in datasets that R provides, import data from external files such as CSV or Excel, or even connect to a database to retrieve data.

For example, if you want to load data from a CSV file, you can use the `read.csv()` function. This function reads a CSV file and loads it into a data frame.

For basic or quick usage, use ***read.csv****. But if you're loading extra libraries and handling large datasets, use* ***read_csv****.*

A data frame is a common data structure in R used for storing and manipulating tabular data. Here's how you can use it:

```
# Check the current working directory
getwd()

# Set working directory
setwd("/path/to/your/folder") # Replace with your
directory

# Load your data
data <- read.csv("path/to/yourfile.csv")
```

In the above code, "`path/to/yourfile.csv`" is the path to your CSV file, and the data variable will store the contents of that file in a data frame. But since you have set your working directory, you can also directly type the file's name as follows:

```
# Load your data
data <- read.csv("yourfile.csv")
```

If you're working with other file types, such as Excel files, you can use the `readxl` package to read Excel files, or the `jsonlite` package to handle JSON files. Before using these packages, you need to install them once. You can do this by running the following code in RStudio:

```
install.packages("readr")
install.packages("readxl")
install.packages("jsonlite")
```

After installing these packages, you can load data from Excel files using `read_excel()` or from JSON files using `fromJSON()`, depending on the format you're working with.

```
# Load the required package
library(readxl)
# Read Excel file
excel_data <- read_excel("path/to/file.xlsx", sheet
= "Sheet1")
# Load the required package
library(jsonlite)
# Read Excel file
json_data <- fromJSON("path/to/file.json")
```

Once you have loaded your dataset, it's time to explore the data. This will help you understand the structure and contents of the dataset. In R, there are several useful functions for this:

head(): This function shows the first few rows of the dataset. It's useful for getting a quick preview of the data.

```
head(data)
```

summary(): This function provides summary statistics for each column, such as the minimum, maximum, mean, and other statistical measures. It's a great way to get an overview of the data.

```
summary(data)
```

str(): This function displays the structure of the dataset, including the data types of each column and the number of observations. It helps you understand how the data is organized.

```
str(data)
```

dim(): This function returns the dimensions of the dataset, including the number of rows and columns. It gives you a quick look at the size of the data.

```
dim(data)
```

Using these functions, you can start to get a feel for the data you're working with and decide how to proceed with analysis. Whether you're cleaning the data, performing statistical analysis, or visualizing it, exploring the dataset thoroughly is an essential first step.

Creating Random Data for Analysis

To start generating random data, we first need to install some libraries to help us. These libraries are called "random" and "data.table". We can easily install them by using the following command in R:

```
install.packages(c("random", "data.table")) #
install multiple packages
```

Once the libraries are installed, we load them into our R environment so that we can use their functions. This is done with the `library()` function:

```
library(random)
library(data.table)
```

Next, we set a seed using the `set.seed()` function. The seed ensures that the random data generated will be the same every time we run the code. This is important for reproducibility, especially if we want others to get the same results as we did.

```
set.seed(123)
```

Now, we can begin generating the random data. We decided to create data for 15 people, so we set *n* to 15, which is the number of rows of data we want. Here's how we generate each variable:

Age: We create a random sample of ages between 18 and 65 for the 15 people. The `sample()` function is used to randomly pick these ages.

```
n <- 100 # Define the number of samples
age <- sample(18:65, n, replace = TRUE)
```

Gender: We generate random genders for each person, choosing between "Male" and "Female". Again, we use the `sample()` function for this.

```
gender <- sample(c("Male", "Female"), n, replace =
TRUE)
```

Height: We generate random heights using a normal distribution with a mean of 170 cm and a standard deviation of 10 cm. The `rnorm()` function is used here, and we round the results to two decimal places using the `round()` function.

```
height <- round(rnorm(n, mean = 170, sd = 10), 2)
```

Weight: Similarly, we generate random weights using a normal distribution with a mean of 70 kg and a standard deviation of 10 kg. We round these values as well.

```
weight <- round(rnorm(n, mean = 70, sd = 10), 2)
```

Commute Type: We also create a random sample of how each person commutes. The options are "Public transportation", "Car", or "Walking".

```
commute_type <- sample(c("Public transportation",
"Car", "Walking"), n, replace = TRUE)
```

Once all the data is generated, we put everything into a data frame. A data frame is like a table where each row represents one person, and each column represents a different attribute (e.g., age, gender, height, etc.).

```
data <- data.frame(Age = age, Gender = gender,
Height = height, Weight = weight, Commute_Type =
commute_type)
```

You can view the data by using the `View()` function, which will open a table in new tabs within RStudio:

```
View(data)
```

Output:

Filter

	Age	Gender	Height	Weight	Commute_Type
1	48	Male	183.77	80.92	Walking
2	32	Female	168.20	71.60	Walking
3	31	Male	154.32	97.08	Walking
4	20	Female	167.39	72.86	Car
5	59	Female	179.62	69.67	Public transportation
6	60	Female	178.54	60.10	Public transportation
7	54	Female	174.19	72.12	Walking
8	31	Female	173.40	60.28	Car
9	42	Female	175.96	75.49	Car
10	43	Female	188.71	59.51	Walking

Finally, if you want to save the generated data to a file, we can write it to a CSV file using the `write.csv()` function. This file can be opened in other programs, such as Excel, for further analysis:

```
write.csv(data, file = "random_data.csv", row.names
= FALSE)
```

This creates a CSV file called "random_data.csv" that contains the data we just generated. The `row.names = FALSE` part ensures that row numbers are not included in the CSV file.

Clean and Preprocess the Data

Data cleaning is a crucial first step in any data analysis process. When working with raw data, you will often encounter issues such as missing values, duplicate entries, or inconsistent formats. These problems need to be addressed before you can begin meaningful analysis. If these issues are not handled, they can lead to incorrect conclusions or biased results.

The first task in data cleaning is often dealing with missing values. Missing values are common in datasets, and there are different ways to handle them. One simple approach is to remove rows that contain missing values. In R, the `na.omit()` function can be used to drop rows with missing data. Here is an example of how you can use it:

```
cleaned_data <- na.omit(raw_data)
```

This line of code removes any rows from the dataset `raw_data` that contain missing values and stores the result in `cleaned_data`.

Next, you may need to check for duplicate rows. Duplicates can distort analysis and lead to overrepresentation of certain data points. To identify duplicates, you can use the `duplicated()` function in R, which returns a logical vector indicating whether each row is a duplicate of a previous row:

```
duplicates <- duplicated(raw_data)
```

This will return TRUE for rows that are duplicates and FALSE for unique rows. You can then remove duplicates using the `!duplicated()` function:

```
unique_data <- raw_data[!duplicated(raw_data),]
```

This will keep only the unique rows in the dataset.

In addition to missing values and duplicates, data may also need to be converted into the appropriate types for analysis. For example, a variable that represents dates might be read as text. You can use R's `as.Date()` function to convert it into a date format:

```
raw_data$Date <- as.Date(raw_data$Date, format =
"%Y-%m-%d")
```

Finally, the dplyr package in R is a powerful tool for manipulating data. It provides functions such as `filter()`, `select()`, and `mutate()` to help you clean and transform your data efficiently. For example, if you want to remove rows based on a condition, you can use the `filter()` function:

```
library(dplyr)
filtered_data <- filter(raw_data, Value > 10)
```

This code filters out all rows where the value is less than or equal to 10, keeping only the rows that meet the condition.

In addition, the following are samples of code to filter, select, rename, or group your dataframe.

```
 # Filter row based on condition
filtered_df <- df % > % filter(column_name > 0)

# Select specific columns
selected_cols <- df % > % select(column_name1,
column_name2)

 # Rename columns
Renamed_df <- df % > % rename(new_column_name =
old_column_name)

# Group by a column and summarise data
summarized_df <- df % > % group_by(column_name) % >
% summarise(avg_value = mean(value))
```

Creating Spatial Data

To create spatial data in RStudio, you need to work with different types of geographical objects, such as points, lines, and polygons. These objects are the basic building blocks of spatial data, and you can use them to represent real-world features like locations, roads, or areas.

Creating Point Data

In RStudio, a point is a simple representation of a specific location on a map. For example, you might want to represent the location of a school or a hospital. To create point data, you can use the sf package, which provides simple features for spatial data handling. Below is an example code to create a point:

```
# Install and load the necessary packages
install.packages(c("sf", "ggplot2"))
library(sf)
library(ggplot2)

# Create a point with coordinates (longitude,
latitude)
point <- st_sfc(st_point(c(139.6917, 35.6895)), crs
= 4326)

# Convert to a data frame for ggplot2
point_df <- st_as_sf(point)

# Plot the point using ggplot2 with axes and a
legend
ggplot(data = point_df) +
 geom_sf() +
 theme_minimal() +
          labs(title = "Point Location (Longitude,
Latitude)",

  subtitle = "Tokyo",
  caption = "Source: Your Data") +

 theme(axis.text.x = element_text(angle = 45, hjust
= 1), # Rotate x-axis labels for clarity

  axis.text.y = element_text(angle = 45, hjust =
  1)) +

 scale_x_continuous(name = "Longitude") +
 scale_y_continuous(name = "Latitude") +
     theme(legend.position = "none") # No legend is
needed for a single point
```

Output:

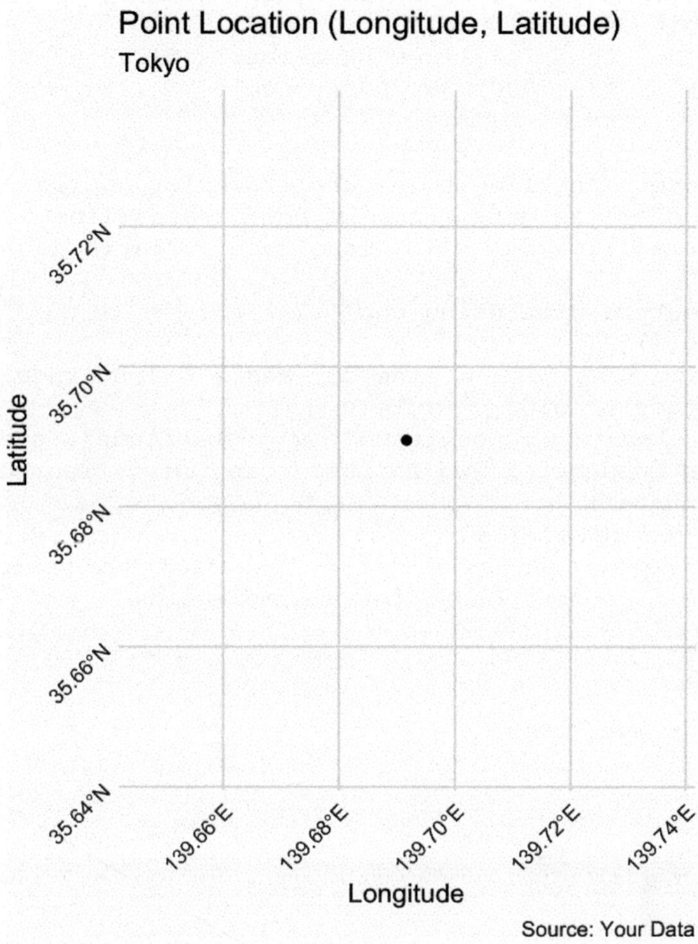

In this example, the point represents the coordinates of Tokyo (longitude 139.6917 and latitude 35.6895). The `st_sfc()` function creates a simple feature collection, and `st_point()` creates a single point. The coordinate reference system (CRS) is set to 4326, which is the standard coordinate based on World Geodetic System 1984.

Creating Line Data

A line is used to represent linear features, such as roads or rivers. To create a line, you can use multiple points connected in a sequence. Here's how you can create line data in RStudio:

```
# Create a line by connecting two points
(longitude, latitude)
line <- st_sfc(st_linestring(matrix(c(139.6917,
35.6895, 139.7000, 35.7000), ncol = 2, byrow =
TRUE)), crs = 4326)

# Convert the line to a data frame for ggplot
line_df <- as.data.frame(st_coordinates(line))
colnames(line_df) <- c("longitude", "latitude")

# Create a plot using ggplot2
ggplot() +
   geom_line(data = line_df, aes(x = longitude, y =
latitude), color = "blue") +
      labs(x = "Longitude", y = "Latitude", title =
"Line Connecting Two Points", caption = "Source:
Your Data") +
 theme_minimal() +
    theme(legend.position = "none") # Remove legend
since it's not needed for a simple line
```

Output:

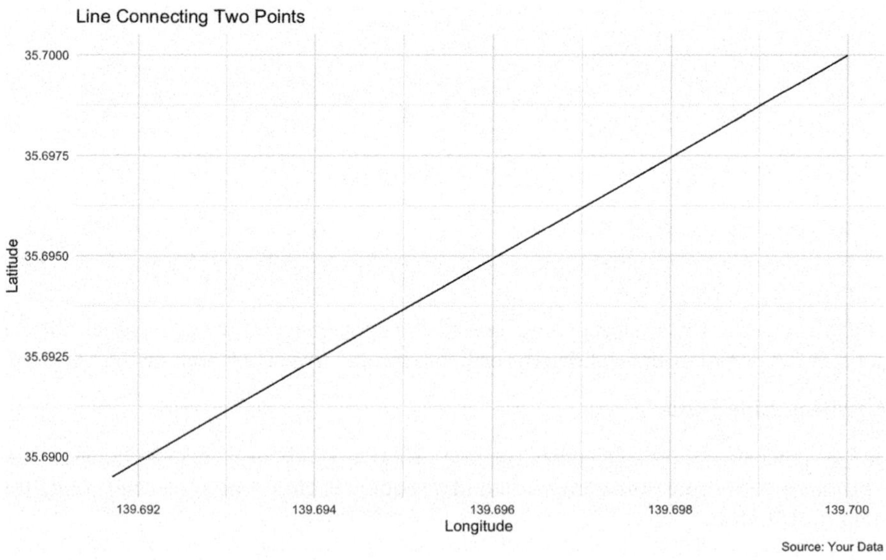

In this example, the `st_linestring()` function creates a line connecting two points: the first one in Tokyo and the second one in a nearby location. Again, the CRS is set to 4326 for coordinates.

Creating Polygon Data

A polygon represents an area, such as a park or a building boundary. You can create a polygon by defining multiple points that form a closed shape. Here's an example of creating a polygon:

```
# Create a polygon by connecting a series of points
polygon <- st_sfc(st_polygon(list(cbind(c(139.6917,
139.6950, 139.6970, 139.6980, 139.6917), c(35.6895,
35.6920, 35.6900, 35.6880, 35.6895)))), crs = 4326)

# Convert the polygon to a data frame for ggplot
polygon_df <- st_as_sf(polygon)

# Plot using ggplot2
ggplot() +
     geom_sf(data = polygon_df, aes(fill = "Polygon
Area"), color = "blue") +
     scale_fill_manual(values = "lightblue", name =
"Legend") +
 labs(title = "Polygon Plot with Axes and Legend",

     x = "Longitude",
     y = "Latitude",
     caption = "Source: Your Data") +

 theme_minimal() +
 theme(legend.position = "topright")
```

Output:

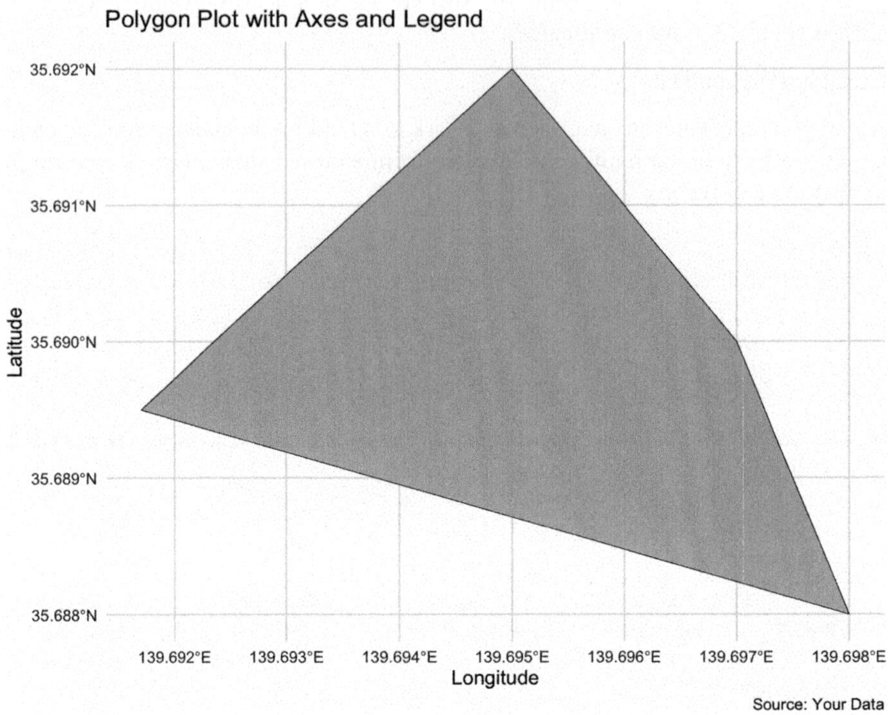

In this example, `st_polygon()` creates a polygon using four points, which form a free polygon. The points are defined in a `cbind()` function to combine the coordinates into pairs of longitude and latitude. The polygon will represent a closed area.

Creating spatial data in RStudio using points, lines, and polygons is a simple process that allows you to represent real-world features on a map. By using the sf package, you can easily manipulate and visualize these spatial objects. Whether you're mapping locations, connecting roads, or outlining areas, RStudio provides a powerful tool for working with spatial data straightforwardly. Chapter 7 of this book will discuss more detail about spatial data.

Creating Character Data

Follow the code below to create sample data. A vector named `customer_reviews` is defined with various customer feedback statements. These reviews include positive and negative comments like "The product is amazing!" and "The quality is poor." The data will be used for text processing later.

```
# Creating sample data
```

```
customer_reviews <- c("The product is amazing!",
                          "I'm very happy with my
   purchase.",
                          "The quality is poor.",
                          "It's a great value for
   money.",
                          "I would highly recommend
   it.",
                          "I'm disappointed with the
   service.",
                          "The product arrived
   damaged.")
```

Then installs and loads several R packages required for text analysis. These include:

- **tidyverse**: A collection of tools for data manipulation and visualization.
- **tm**: For text mining tasks like cleaning and processing text data.
- **SnowballC**: For stemming, which reduces words to their base form (e.g., "running" to "run").
- **wordcloud**: To create visually appealing word clouds.
- **RColorBrewer**: For generating color palettes used in word clouds.

If these packages are not already installed, the `install.packages()` function will add them to your R environment.

```
# Install and load necessary packages
install.packages("tidyverse")
install.packages("tm")
install.packages("SnowballC")
install.packages("wordcloud")
install.packages("RColorBrewer")

# Load the necessary libraries
library(tidyverse)
library(tm)
library(SnowballC)
library(wordcloud)
library(RColorBrewer)
```

Next, a `data.frame` is created to store a set of comments and unique IDs. This represents customer feedback, with each comment as a row. A corpus (a collection of text documents) is created from the comment column of the `data.frame` for further text analysis.

```
# Read the data
data <- data.frame(id = c(1, 2, 3, 4, 5, 6, 7, 8),
                   comment = c("Great product! I
  love it.",
                               "The service was
    terrible.",
                               "This is an awesome
    book.",
                               "I'm not satisfied
    with the quality.",
                               "The food was
    delicious.",
                               "What a great
    product!",
                               "This is great!",
                               "Awesome, I am
    satisfied"))

# Create a corpus of the comments column
corpus <- Corpus(VectorSource(data$comment))
```

Text preprocessing is performed to clean the data. This includes:

- **Removing punctuation**: Gets rid of symbols like "!" and ".".
- **Converting to lowercase**: Standardizes all words to lowercase.
- **Removing stopwords**: Removes common words (e.g., "and," "the") that don't add value to analysis.
- **Stripping whitespace**: Removes unnecessary spaces.

These steps ensure the text is clean and ready for analysis.

```
# Preprocess the text
corpus <- tm_map(corpus, removePunctuation)
corpus <- tm_map(corpus, tolower)
corpus <- tm_map(corpus, removeWords,
stopwords("english"))
corpus <- tm_map(corpus, stripWhitespace)
```

A **Term-Document Matrix (TDM)** is created, where rows represent words, and columns represent documents. The TDM helps quantify the frequency of each word across all comments. The matrix is then inspected and converted to a standard format for further analysis.

```
# Create a term document matrix
tdm <- TermDocumentMatrix(corpus)

# Inspect the document-term matrix
inspect(tdm)

# Convert the tdm to a matrix
m <- as.matrix(tdm)
```

The following code calculates the frequency of each word by summing up the values in the matrix. It then sorts the words by frequency in descending order and stores the results in a `data.frame`.

```
# Get the frequency of each word
v <- sort(rowSums(m), decreasing = TRUE)

# Create a dataframe with the words and their
frequency
df <- data.frame(word = names(v), freq = v)
```

Finally, the next code is used to generate the most frequently used words in the text data (word cloud). The code sets parameters such as the minimum frequency, the number of words to display, and rotation options for the words. A color palette from `RColorBrewer` is used to enhance the visual appeal of the word cloud.

```
set.seed(1234) # for reproducibility

# Plot the word cloud
wordcloud(words = df$word, freq = df$freq,
min.freq = 1, relative_scaling = 1,
          max.words = 200, random.order = FALSE,
  rot.per = 0.35,
          colors = brewer.pal(8, "Dark2"))
```

Output:

By running this code, you can process text data, analyze word frequencies, and create a word cloud that visually highlights keywords from the comments. This approach helps summarize textual information and identify patterns in feedback.

Image Processing

Image processing can be done in R using the **imager** package, which provides a range of functions for working with images. Below is a step-by-step explanation and code to process an image by converting it to grayscale, inverting it, and saving the processed image.

First, we need to load the imager package. If you haven't installed it, you can do so using the following code.

```
install.packages("imager")
# Load required packages.
library(imager)
```

To process an image, you first need to load it into R. Replace "`image.jpg`" with the path to your image file.

```
# Load image
image <- load.image("image.jpg")
```

Before making any changes, you can visualize the original image using the `plot()` function.

```
# Display the original image
plot(image)
```

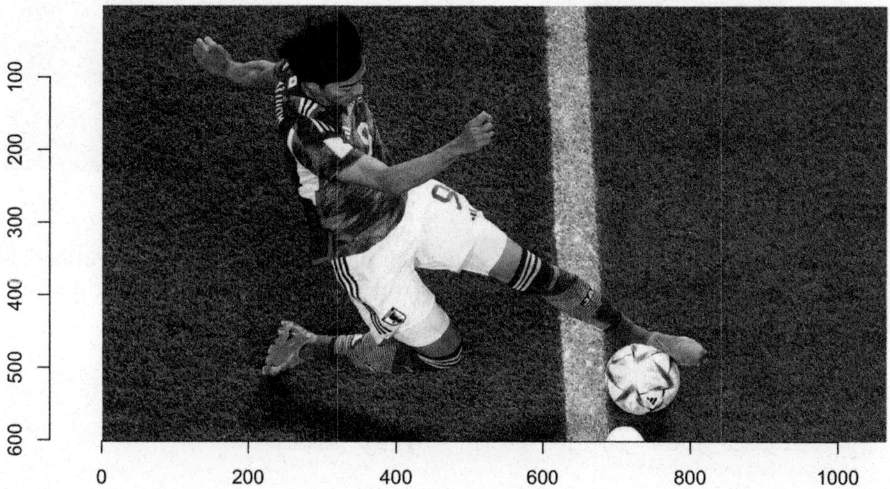

Converting the image to grayscale simplifies the data by removing color information while retaining intensity. Use the `grayscale()` function to achieve this.

```
# Convert image to grayscale
gray_image <- grayscale(image)
```

You can also display the grayscale image to see the result.

```
# Display grayscale image
plot(gray_image)
```

Image inversion flips the brightness of each pixel, creating a negative effect. To invert a grayscale image, subtract its values from 1 (since pixel values in R typically range from 0 to 1).

```
# Invert grayscale image
inverted_gray_image <- 1 - gray_image
```

Display the inverted image to observe the changes.

```
# Display inverted grayscale image
plot(inverted_gray_image)
```

Finally, save the inverted grayscale image to your computer. Specify the file name and desired location.

```
# Save inverted grayscale image
save.image(inverted_gray_image, "inverted_gray_
image.jpg")
```

Notes for Mac Users

If you're using macOS and encounter issues with the imager package, you may need to install **XQuartz**. XQuartz allows cross-platform applications that use X11 for graphical user interfaces to run on macOS.

1. Download XQuartz from XQuartz official website: https://www.xquartz.org/
2. Follow the installation instructions.
3. If problems persist, you can consult this Stack Overflow discussion for troubleshooting tips.

Practice with Different Datasets

To improve your proficiency in R programming, one of the most effective strategies is practicing with a variety of datasets. Different types of datasets can expose you to a broad range of data structures, formats, and analytical challenges.

Working with datasets of varying sizes and complexities is particularly valuable. Smaller datasets are ideal for beginners as they help build foundational skills, such as data cleaning, transformation, and visualization. On the other hand, larger and more complex datasets introduce advanced concepts like data wrangling, statistical modeling, and machine learning algorithms. These practices can significantly enhance your problem-solving abilities and confidence in handling real-world data challenges using R.

Seek Help and Learn from Others

R is supported by a large and active community of users and developers, making it an excellent environment for collaborative learning. If you face difficulties or have questions, don't hesitate to seek help. The R Documentation and resources like R-bloggers offer comprehensive tutorials and insights. Additionally, online forums such as Stack Overflow and R-related Reddit communities provide platforms for troubleshooting and exchanging ideas.

Participating in data analysis competitions, such as those hosted on Kaggle, is another excellent way to learn. These competitions challenge you with real-world problems and expose you to diverse approaches from other participants. Similarly, collaborating with other R users—whether through workshops, hackathons, or study groups—enables you to exchange techniques and discover creative solutions. By engaging with the R community, you can continuously improve your skills and stay updated with the latest tools and best practices.

Leveraging AI Tools to Enhance Learning

Modern AI tools such as ChatGPT, Gemini, BlackboxAI, and Copilot can further support your learning journey in R. These tools can assist in generating code snippets, debugging, and brainstorming solutions for analytical problems. However, the most critical factor remains your own **curiosity and the quality of your questions and prompts**. Combining these tools with thoughtful practice and collaboration will ensure steady progress in mastering R programming.

By adopting these practices, you can build a strong foundation in R, gain confidence in data analysis, and prepare yourself for increasingly complex challenges in the field of data science.

References

Barbier, E. B. (2007). Valuing ecosystem services as productive inputs. *Economic Policy, 22*(49), 177–229. https://doi.org/10.1111/j.1468-0327.2007.00174.x

Batty, M. (2024). *Inventing future cities*. MIT Press. ISBN 9780262548656

Boyd, D., & Crawford, K. (2012). Critical questions for big data: provocations for a cultural, technological, and scholarly phenomenon. *Information, Communication & Society, 15*(5), 662–679. https://doi.org/10.1080/1369118X.2012.678878

Chen, H., Chiang, R. H., & Storey, V. C. (2014). Business intelligence and analytics: from big data to big impact. *MIS Quarterly, 36*(4), 1165–1188. https://doi.org/10.2307/41703503

Gandomi, A., & Haider, M. (2015). Beyond the hype: big data concepts, methods, and analytics. *International Journal of Information Management, 35*(2), 137–144. Available at https://www.sciencedirect.com/science/article/pii/S0268401214001066

Goodfellow, I., Bengio, Y., & Courville, A. (2016). *Deep learning*. MIT Press. ISBN 9780262035613

Janssen, M., van der Voort, H., & Wahyudi, A. (2017). Factors influencing big data decision-making quality. *Journal of Business Research, 70*, 338–345. https://doi.org/10.1016/j.jbusres.2016.08.007

Jennings, V., Larson, L., & Yun, J. (2016). Advancing sustainability through urban green space: cultural ecosystem services, equity, and social determinants of health. *International Journal of Environmental Research and Public Health, 13*(2), 196. https://doi.org/10.3390/ijerph13020196

Kitchin, R. (2014). *The data revolution: big data, open data.* SAGE Publications.

Lazer, D., Pentland, A., Adamic, L., Aral, S., Barabasi, A. L., Brewer, D., Christakis, N., et al. (2009). Computational social science. *Science, 323*(5915), 721–723. https://doi.org/10.1126/science.1167742

Russell, S., & Norvig, P. (2021). *Artificial intelligence: A modern approach* (4th ed.). Pearson. ISBN 9780137505135

Wickham, H., & Grolemund, G. (2017). *R for data science.* O'Reilly Media. Available at https://www.oreilly.com/library/view/r-for-data/9781492097396/

Chapter 3
Data Exploration, Preprocessing, and Modeling

Abstract This chapter focuses on data exploration and preprocessing—key steps for ensuring data quality and accuracy. These tasks are iterative and often require repetition, utilizing techniques such as summary statistics, data visualization, and data profiling. The discussion extends to data modeling, including the creation and application of models to enhance understanding of observed data. Additionally, the chapter provides an overview of the differences between artificial intelligence, machine learning, and deep learning, highlighting widely used and effective algorithms. The second part includes practical exercises with a dataset on "Annual Working Hours vs. GDP per Capita," covering tasks such as handling missing values, identifying outliers, addressing data quality issues, filtering data, standardizing it, and creating plots—all within the RStudio environment.

Relation to other chapters: Directly supports Chap. 4 (statistics) and later chapters on machine learning and visualization (Chaps. 5 and 6).

3.1 Introduction

Data science offers invaluable tools for studies in various fields, enabling rigorous, data-driven insights into societal trends, behaviors, and issues. By using data science techniques, researchers can analyze large datasets from multiple sources, such as government records, census data, and social media, to uncover patterns and correlations related to income distribution, education levels, employment, and health outcomes.

Combining data science and machine learning algorithms, researchers can build predictive models to identify areas with high levels of inequality and predict the future impact of different policies. These models can incorporate diverse data points, such as demographic information, geographic location, and economic indicators, to understand how different factors interact and influence inequality. Additionally, text mining techniques can analyze public discourse from social media or news articles

F. Ramdani, *Data Science: Foundations and Hands-on Experience*,
https://doi.org/10.1007/978-981-96-4683-8_3

to track the public's sentiment on policies aimed at reducing inequality, offering insights into social attitudes and the effectiveness of communication strategies.

However, before those advanced tools and techniques can be applied, it is important to explore, preprocess and evaluate the model of the data. Because, by effectively employing techniques for data exploration, preprocessing, and modeling, we can harness raw data to uncover patterns that drive understanding and inform policy. This chapter provides a foundation for each of these essential steps, emphasizing their significance, methodologies, and best practices, particularly in the context of social studies.

3.2 Data Exploration

Data exploration involves looking closely at the raw data to understand its features, patterns, and connections. This step helps us spot potential problems like missing information, unusual data points, or other quality issues. By carefully exploring and cleaning the data, we ensure it is reliable and accurate. This not only helps in fixing data problems but also makes the models we build work better and easier to understand. Without proper data exploration and preparation, it is difficult to create useful and trustworthy models.

Data exploration techniques include *summary statistics*, *data visualization*, *data profiling*, and *outlier detection*. The details are explained as follows:

1. Summary statistics
   Summary statistics calculate central measures (mean, median) and variability indicators (standard deviation, variance) and offer insight into the data's overall structure and central tendencies. For example, exploring income distribution across regions can highlight disparities and guide hypotheses about socio-economic inequalities.

   Figure 3.1 illustrates the summary statistics of `mtcars` dataset, a built-in dataset in R. It contains information about various car models from the 1974 Motor Trend magazine. It is widely used for practicing data analysis and visualization techniques. The dataset includes 32 observations (rows), each representing a specific car model, and 11 variables (columns). The variables in the `mtcars` dataset are as follows:

   - **mpg (Miles/(US) gallon)**:
     - A measure of fuel efficiency, indicating how many miles a car can travel per gallon of fuel.
   - **cyl (Number of cylinders)**:
     - The number of cylinders in the engine, it is typically 4, 6, or 8.

```
> print(summary_stats)
      mpg             cyl             disp             hp             drat             wt       
 Min.   :10.40   Min.   :4.000   Min.   : 71.1   Min.   : 52.0   Min.   :2.760   Min.   :1.513  
 1st Qu.:15.43   1st Qu.:4.000   1st Qu.:120.8   1st Qu.: 96.5   1st Qu.:3.080   1st Qu.:2.581  
 Median :19.20   Median :6.000   Median :196.3   Median :123.0   Median :3.695   Median :3.325  
 Mean   :20.09   Mean   :6.188   Mean   :230.7   Mean   :146.7   Mean   :3.597   Mean   :3.217  
 3rd Qu.:22.80   3rd Qu.:8.000   3rd Qu.:326.0   3rd Qu.:180.0   3rd Qu.:3.920   3rd Qu.:3.610  
 Max.   :33.90   Max.   :8.000   Max.   :472.0   Max.   :335.0   Max.   :4.930   Max.   :5.424  
      qsec             vs               am              gear            carb      
 Min.   :14.50   Min.   :0.0000   Min.   :0.0000   Min.   :3.000   Min.   :1.000  
 1st Qu.:16.89   1st Qu.:0.0000   1st Qu.:0.0000   1st Qu.:3.000   1st Qu.:2.000  
 Median :17.71   Median :0.0000   Median :0.0000   Median :4.000   Median :2.000  
 Mean   :17.85   Mean   :0.4375   Mean   :0.4062   Mean   :3.688   Mean   :2.812  
 3rd Qu.:18.90   3rd Qu.:1.0000   3rd Qu.:1.0000   3rd Qu.:4.000   3rd Qu.:4.000  
 Max.   :22.90   Max.   :1.0000   Max.   :1.0000   Max.   :5.000   Max.   :8.000  
```

Fig. 3.1 Summary statistics of the `mtcars` dataset

- **disp (Displacement in cubic inches)**:
  - The total volume of all the cylinders in the engine, represents engine size.
- **hp (Gross horsepower)**:
  - The power output of the engine.
- **drat (Rear axle ratio)**:
  - A measure of the gear ratio in the rear axle of the car.
- **wt (Weight in 1000 lbs)**:
  - The weight of the car (in thousands of pounds).
- **qsec (1/4 mile time in seconds)**:
  - The time it takes for the car to travel a quarter mile, indicates acceleration performance.
- **vs (Engine type)**:
  - A binary variable where:
    1. `0` represents a V-shaped engine.
    2. `1` represents a straight (or inline) engine.
- **am (Transmission type)**:
  - A binary variable where:
    1. `0` represents an automatic transmission.
    2. `1` represents a manual transmission.
- **gear (Number of forward gears)**:
  - The number of forward gears in the transmission.

- **carb (Number of carburettors)**:
  - The number of carburettors in the engine.

2. Data Visualization
   Visualizations such as histograms, box plots, and scatter plots are powerful tools to detect patterns and anomalies. Box plots can highlight outliers, scatter plots can show correlations (e.g., income vs. education), and histograms can reveal data distributions. Interactive visualizations, such as dashboards, can also allow dynamic examination of social datasets. Figure 3.2 shows the box plot of variables of the `mtcars` dataset.

3. Data Profiling
   Data profiling involves examining the frequency, range, and distribution of values across variables. In social studies, profiling may reveal unique patterns or anomalies, such as non-response rates in survey data or unusual spikes in certain demographics. Profiling can also help identify categorical values and detect data errors, which are crucial for developing accurate data quality assessments. Figure 3.3 shows the correlation heatmap of variables as one of the profiling output analysis of the `mtcars` dataset.

4. Outlier Detection
   Outlier detection is the process of spotting data points or observations that stand out because they are extremely high or extremely low from the rest of the dataset. These unusual points could represent errors, rare events, or important findings. Detecting them is crucial in many areas like finance, where it helps to find unusual market behavior; healthcare, where it can identify rare medical conditions; and fraud detection, where it is used to uncover suspicious activities. Recognizing outliers helps improve data quality and provides valuable insights for decision-making.

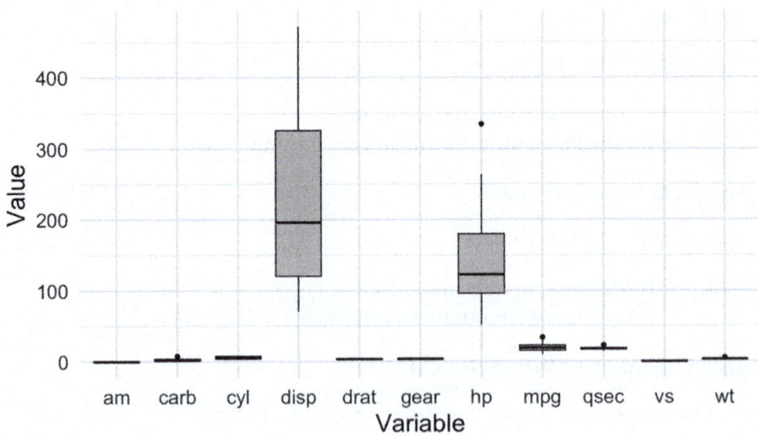

Fig. 3.2 Box plot of variables of the `mtcars` dataset

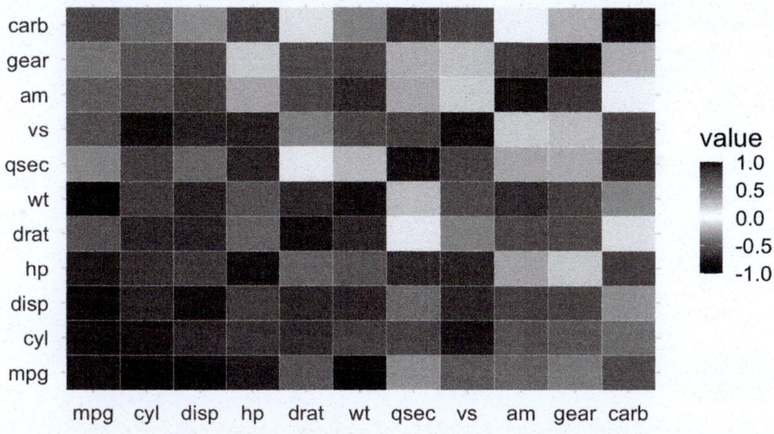

Fig. 3.3 Correlation heatmap of variables as one of the profiling output analysis of the `mtcars` dataset

There are several common techniques used for outlier detection:

Z-Score: The Z-score is a statistical tool used to measure how far a data point is from the average (mean) of all the data, measured in terms of standard deviations. In simpler terms, it tells us if a data point is unusually high or low compared to the rest of the data. If a data point is more than a certain number of standard deviations away from the average, it is considered an outlier or an exception. Figure 3.4 shows the plot of outliers of miles per gallon (`mpg`) variables using `mtcars` dataset.

Interquartile range (IQR): The IQR is a way to understand how spread out the data is (Fig. 3.5). It is calculated by subtracting the value at the first quartile (25% mark) from the value at the third quartile (75% mark). The IQR tells us the range within which most of the data points fall. If a data point is far outside this range, it is considered an outlier.

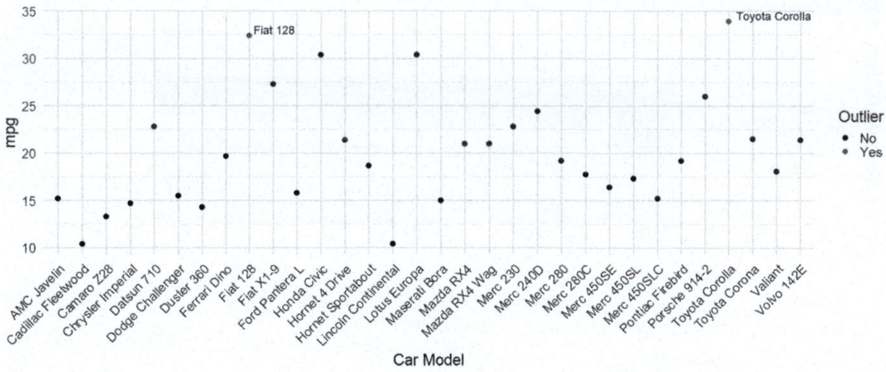

Fig. 3.4 Plot of outliers detection using Z-Score method of mpg variables of mtcars dataset

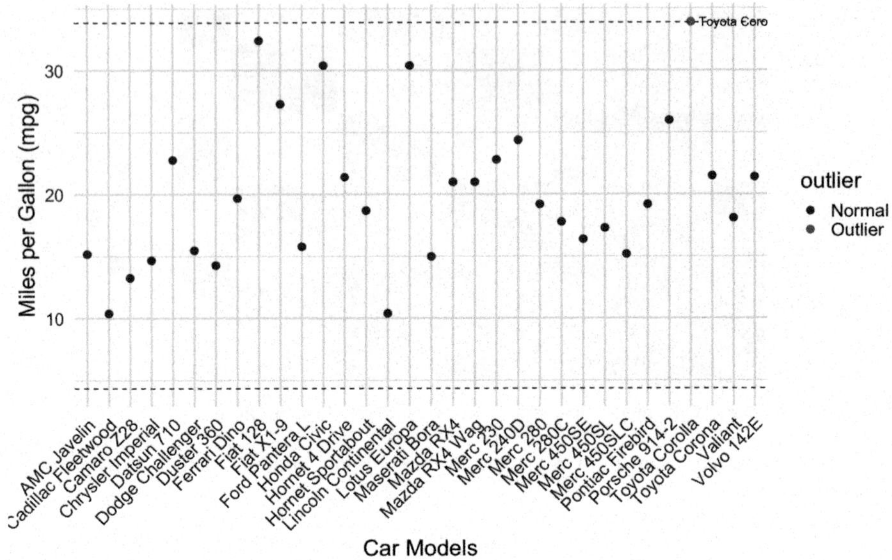

Fig. 3.5 Plot of outliers detection using IQR method of mpg variables of mtcars dataset

Box plot: A box plot is a visual way to represent how data is distributed. It shows us the middle value (median), the range of the middle 50% of the data (quartiles), and any outliers that fall outside of this range (Fig. 3.6). A box plot is helpful for quickly spotting patterns, extremes, and the general spread of data.

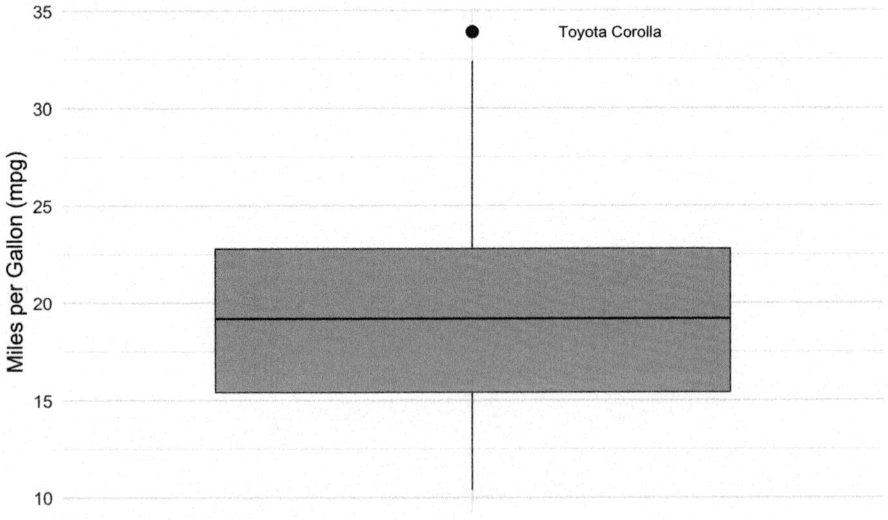

Fig. 3.6 Boxplot of outliers detection using IQR method of mpg variables of mtcars dataset

DBSCAN: DBSCAN stands for Density-Based Spatial Clustering of Applications with Noise. It is an algorithm used to group data points into clusters based on how closely packed they are (Fig. 3.7). If a data point is far away from others, in a region with low density, DBSCAN will label it as an outlier.

Isolation forest: The isolation forest algorithm is a machine learning technique used to detect outliers. It works by randomly selecting data features and creating a series of decision trees that "isolate" each point. Outliers are easier to isolate because they stand apart from the rest of the data, while normal data points tend to be grouped together (Fig. 3.8).

Local outlier factor (LOF): LOF is a method for detecting outliers by comparing the density of a data point to the density of its neighbors. If a data

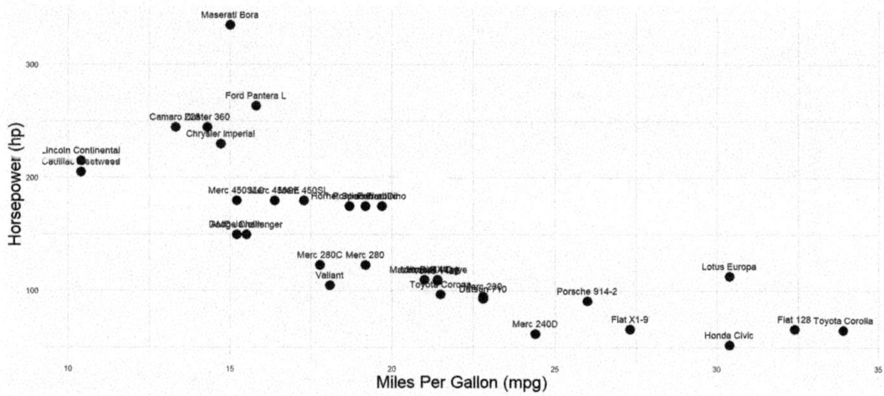

Fig. 3.7 Plot of outliers detection using DBSCAN method of mpg and horse power variables of mtcars dataset

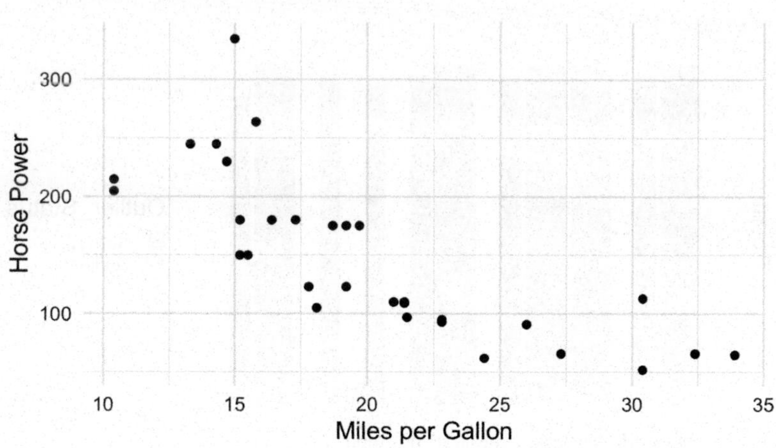

Fig. 3.8 Plot of outliers detection using isolation forest method of mpg and horse power variables of mtcars dataset

point is in a low-density area compared to its neighbors, it is considered an outlier (Fig. 3.9). This method is useful when you need to find outliers in data that has varying density, as it looks at the local neighborhood around each point.

These techniques can be used individually or in combination to detect outliers in data. Figure 3.10 shows the plot of outliers count per variable of the mtcars dataset.

When it comes to outlier detection methods, the choice of method depends on the type of data, the problem at hand, and the desired level of sensitivity. DBSCAN is particularly effective in detecting outliers in spatial data, like the distribution of geographical points. In contrast to traditional methods like Z-scores, DBSCAN does

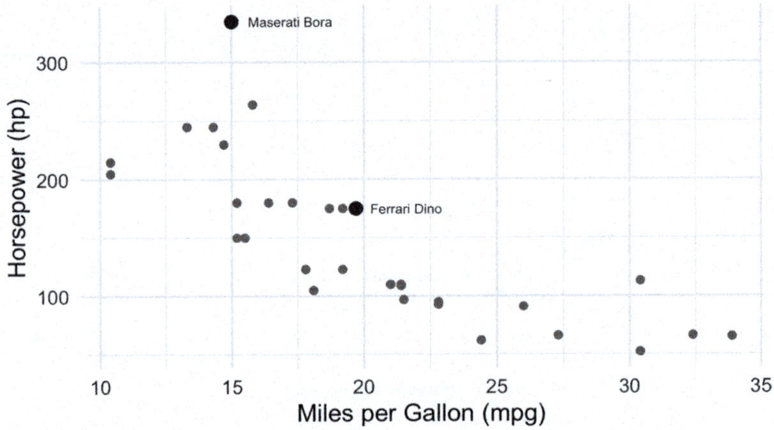

Fig. 3.9 Plot of outliers detection using LOF method of mpg and horsepower variables of mtcars dataset

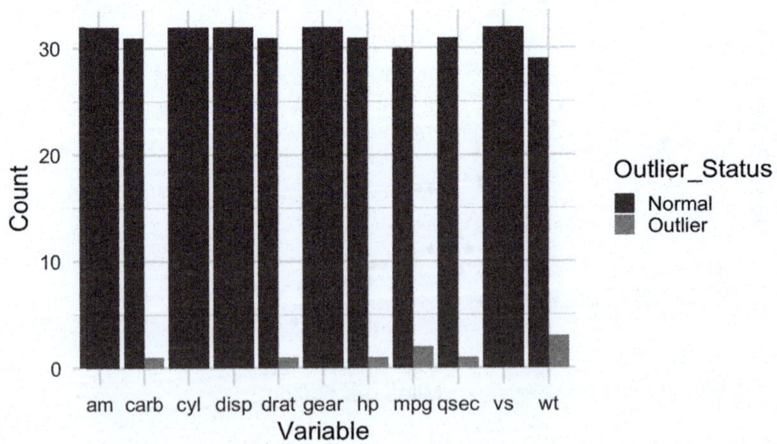

Fig. 3.10 Plot of outliers count per variable of the `mtcars` dataset

not require specifying the number of clusters in advance and can identify data points that do not belong to any cluster—i.e., outliers—based on their density relative to surrounding points.

The reason DBSCAN works well for spatial data is that it looks for areas of high data density and labels points in less dense regions as noise, which can be outliers. This is very useful when dealing with geographic data, where natural clusters of points (e.g., cities, towns, or other features) may form, and points that don't fit into these clusters might be considered anomalies or errors. Traditional statistical methods like Z-scores are based on global measures like the mean and standard deviation, which might not effectively capture the local structure in data, particularly in spatially distributed datasets.

In contrast, for other types of data, like those with more uniform or linear relationships, methods such as IQR might be more appropriate, as they are simpler and well-suited to univariate or small-scale datasets. In the context of social science research, choosing the correct outlier detection method ensures that the analysis accurately reflects the real-world patterns in the data and avoids misleading conclusions, especially when the data involves complex spatial or hierarchical relationships.

3.3 Data Preprocessing

Data preprocessing is a critical step where raw data is cleaned, organized, and transformed to make it ready for analysis. This stage involves various tasks to address common issues like missing values, inconsistencies, and redundancies, which ultimately improve the quality of the data.

Since data preprocessing is an ongoing process, it may need to be repeated multiple times as new insights or problems arise during model development and testing. It is important to handle challenges like data bias, inconsistencies, and noise carefully, as these can negatively affect the accuracy and reliability of the final model.

Additionally, data preprocessing is key to feature engineering, which includes selecting and creating the most relevant features or variables that help improve the performance of the model. Domain knowledge and a deep understanding of the data, gained through exploration, are essential for making informed decisions in a data science project.

The process also plays a significant role in validating and evaluating models by providing insights into their performance and helping identify potential errors or biases. Lastly, data preprocessing is vital for ensuring data privacy and security. By identifying and handling sensitive information appropriately—such as anonymizing or de-identifying data—it helps protect individual privacy. Below are some of the essential steps involved in data preprocessing.

1. Data cleaning

Data often has missing values, which can happen for various reasons like people not responding to surveys, mistakes during data entry, or inconsistent reporting. There are different ways to deal with these missing values.

One option is **deletion**, where you remove the rows that have missing values. While this method is straightforward, it can result in losing important information and may introduce bias, especially if the missing data is not random.

Another option is **imputation**, which involves filling in the missing values with estimated numbers. This can be done by using simple statistics like the mean or median, or by applying more advanced techniques, such as machine learning methods like regression or k-nearest neighbors. Imputation helps keep the dataset intact, preventing data loss while maintaining its overall integrity.

2. Data integration
   Various studies often involve merging datasets from diverse sources (e.g., census data with survey results). Data integration tools like `dplyr` and `data.table` packages in R help standardize formats and merge data tables effectively, enabling seamless and complex data fusion. Proper integration ensures a unified dataset that preserves the context of research variables.
3. Data transformation and standardization
   Feature scaling is a crucial step in preparing data for machine learning. It involves adjusting the scale of all the features so they fall within a similar range of values. This step is important because many machine learning algorithms assume that all features are on the same scale. If some features have much larger or smaller values than others, they might overpower the model's learning process, leading to biased or inaccurate results.

   When analyzing data with multiple variables, it is essential to transform the data to a common scale. If the features are on different scales, it can distort the training of the model, leading to poor performance. There are several techniques used to scale features, including:

- **Standardization (Z-score normalization):** This method involves rescaling the data so that the mean of the feature becomes 0 and the standard deviation becomes 1. This method is commonly used when you want to transform features to be comparable in terms of their variance. Standardization is particularly useful when you are dealing with data where different features have different units or different magnitudes. For example, in a dataset containing both height (in centimeters) and weight (in kilograms), standardizing both features would allow them to be compared directly, as both would have a mean of 0 and a standard deviation of 1. Standardization is also useful when the data follows a Gaussian distribution or when models like linear regression, logistic regression, or support vector machines (SVMs) are being used, as these models typically assume that the features are centered around zero and have the same variance. The formula for standardization is:

$$X_{\text{standard}} = \frac{X - \mu}{\sigma}$$

where:

- X is the original value.
- μ is the mean of the feature.
- σ is the standard deviation of the feature.
- X_{standard} is the standardized value.

- **Min–max scaling**: This method is used to normalize data to a fixed range, typically between 0 and 1. This technique is most useful when the data is on different scales, and you want to bring them into a uniform range. For instance, if you have a dataset where one feature is in the range of 1–1000 (e.g., income) and another feature is in the range of 0 to 1 (e.g., proportion of time spent on a task), min–max scaling will adjust both features so that they fall within the same range. However, this method is sensitive to outliers. If there are extreme values in the data, min–max scaling can distort the transformed values, making it less suitable when outliers are present in the dataset. The formula for min–max scaling is:

$$X_{\text{scaled}} = \frac{X - \min(X)}{\max(X) - \min(X)}$$

where:

- X is the original value.
- *min*(X) is the minimum value of the feature.
- *max*(X) is the maximum value of the feature.
- X_{scaled} is the scaled value.

- **Log transformation**: This technique is often applied when the data has a skewed distribution, especially in the case of right-skewed data. This technique is useful when the data spans several orders of magnitude, as it helps compress large values and expand smaller ones, making the distribution more symmetric. For example, if you have a dataset on household income, where most households earn relatively low incomes but a few earn extremely high amounts, applying a log transformation will help reduce the impact of those extreme values, making the distribution more normal. It is particularly effective for dealing with exponential growth data or when data includes values that span several orders of magnitude, such as financial data, population counts, or biological measurements. The formula for log transformation is:

$$X_{\text{log}} = \log(X)$$

where:

- X is the original value.
- X_{log} is the log-transformed value.

It is important to remember that min–max scaling is useful when you need to scale the data to a specific range and preserve the relationships between values. It is suitable for algorithms that are sensitive to the scale of the data, such as neural networks and KNN, standardization should be applied when the data is normally distributed or when the features have different units or scales, and log transformation is best used when the data has a skewed distribution or contains extreme outliers that can affect model performance. It is commonly used with financial data or data where growth is exponential.

Another important preprocessing step is **feature selection**, which is the process of choosing a smaller set of relevant features from a larger set. The aim is to improve the model's performance and reduce the amount of data the model has to process. Feature selection helps make the model simpler and faster, while still keeping the most important information.

There are several methods for feature selection:

- **Filter methods**: These methods select features based on their statistical relevance to the target variable. Examples include using statistical tests like the chi-square test, calculating correlations, measuring information gain, or setting a threshold for variance.
- **Wrapper methods**: These methods assess the performance of different subsets of features by using a learning algorithm. Recursive Feature Elimination (RFE) is a popular wrapper method that repeatedly removes the least important features until the desired number of features is left. It ranks features based on how useful they are for the model and eliminates the least relevant ones. RFE can be used with linear models like logistic regression or support vector machines (SVM), as well as nonlinear models like decision trees and random forests. The advantage of RFE is that it helps reduce overfitting while improving the model's accuracy.
- **Embedded methods**: These methods perform feature selection during the model training process. Examples of embedded methods include lasso regression, ridge regression, and decision trees.
- **Hybrid methods**: These methods combine two or more feature selection techniques. For instance, a filter method might first remove irrelevant features, and then a wrapper method can be used to select the best subset of features.

Feature selection is an essential step in building machine learning models because it can boost the model's performance while reducing the time and resources needed for training. In Chap. 6, we will explore this topic in more depth.

Figure 3.11 illustrates data cleaning techniques for handling missing values, data integration, and data transformation/standardization using synthetic data.

3.4 Dealing with Missing Data

Missing data is a common challenge when working with datasets, and there are various strategies to address it. Here are a few of the most commonly used methods:

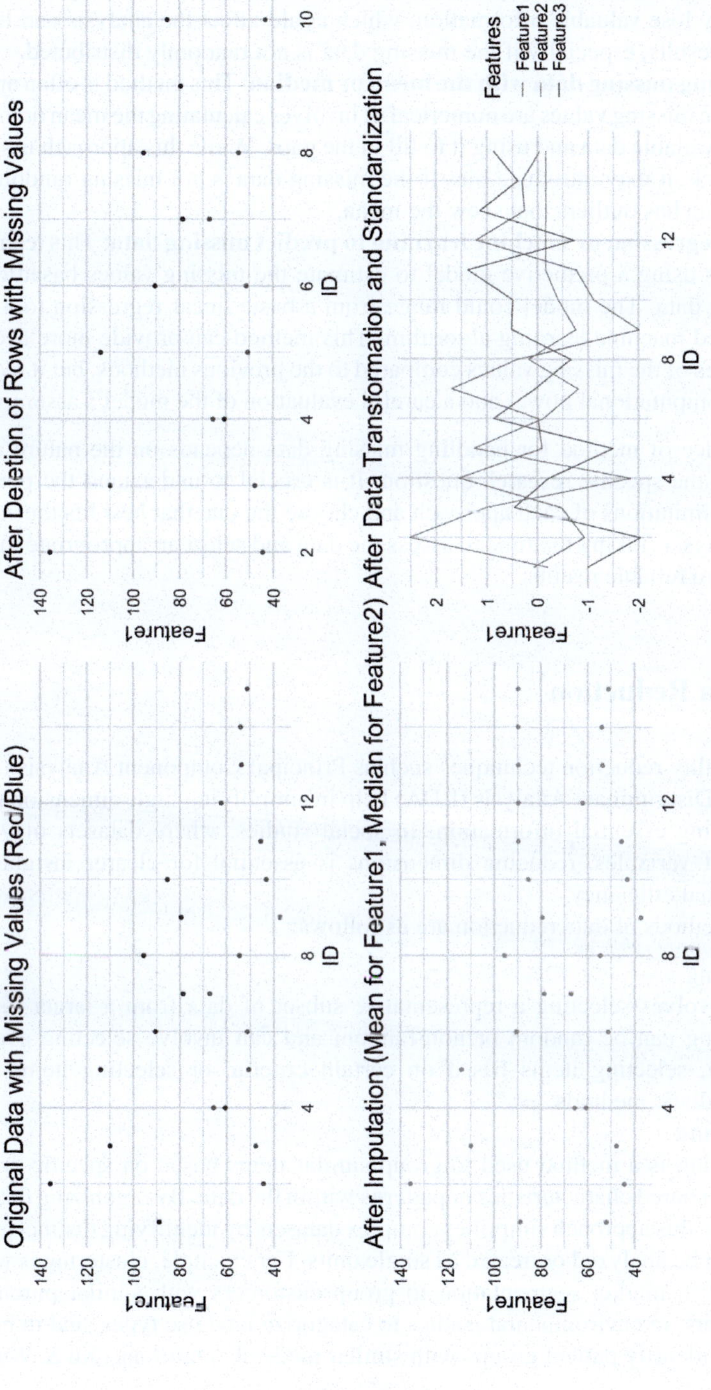

Fig. 3.11 Illustration of data cleaning, transformation, and standardization using synthetic data

1. **Removing rows with missing data**: This is the easiest approach, but it can create problems if a significant portion of the data is missing. By removing these rows, you may lose valuable information, which could affect the analysis and lead to biased results, especially if the missing data is not randomly distributed.
2. **Replacing missing data with the mean or median**: This method is often applied when the missing values are numerical. It involves calculating the mean or median of the available data and using it to fill in the gaps. While this approach is simple and quick, it may introduce bias if the missing data is not missing randomly or if the data has outliers that skew the mean.
3. **Using regression or machine learning to predict missing data**: This technique involves using a predictive model to estimate the missing values based on the existing data. The model could range from a basic linear regression to a more advanced machine learning algorithm. This method can provide more accurate estimates of the missing values compared to the previous methods, but it requires more computational power and a careful evaluation of the model's assumptions.

The choice of method for handling missing data depends on the nature of the dataset and the specific research question. It is crucial to understand the potential biases and limitations of each approach and choose the one that best fits the context of your analysis. Taking the time to assess the data and select an appropriate method ensures more reliable results.

3.5 Data Reduction

Dimensionality reduction techniques such as Principal Component Analysis (PCA) and Linear Discriminant Analysis (LDA) help in simplifying high-dimensional data without losing essential information. In social studies, where datasets may have hundreds of variables, reducing dimensions is essential for clearer insights and computational efficiency.

Some methods of data reduction are as follows:

A. Sampling
This involves selecting a representative subset of data from a larger dataset. Sampling can be random or non-random and can involve selecting every *n*-th item, selecting items based on certain criteria, or selecting items using probabilistic methods.

B. Clustering
Clustering is a method used to group similar items based on specific criteria, such as shared characteristics or patterns within the data. By organizing data into clusters, this approach simplifies complex datasets by identifying distinct groups that can be analyzed or treated as single units. For example, clustering is widely applied in market segmentation to group customers with similar purchasing behaviors, in environmental studies to categorize land use types, and in health-care to identify patient groups with similar medical conditions (Xu & Wunsch,

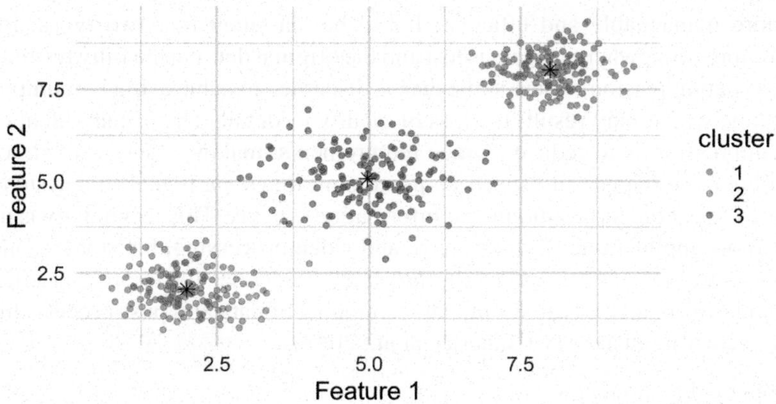

Fig. 3.12 Clustering for data reduction, where data points grouped into clusters with centroids

2005). This technique is particularly valuable in data science, as it helps uncover hidden patterns and reduces the overall complexity of analyzing large datasets. Figure 3.12 shows the clustering for data reduction, where data points grouped into clusters with centroids.

C. Feature selection

This involves identifying the most important features or variables in a dataset that have a strong influence on the outcome while removing the less relevant or redundant ones. Feature selection (Fig. 3.13) can be done through manual methods, where the researcher makes decisions based on their knowledge of the data, or by using automated techniques, such as algorithms that evaluate the importance of each feature and select the best ones. By removing irrelevant or less important features, feature selection can help reduce the complexity of the model, increase computational efficiency, and ultimately improve the accuracy and generalization ability of predictive models (Chandrashekar & Sahin, 2014).

D. Data compression

This involves using mathematical algorithms to reduce the size of a dataset without losing important information. Data compression is a technique commonly used in computer science and information technology to make data

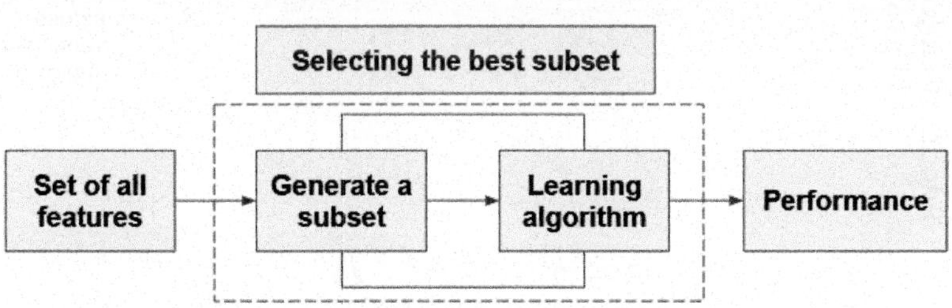

Fig. 3.13 Feature selection process

more manageable and efficient. It can be classified into two types: lossless compression, where no data is lost and the original data can be fully restored, and lossy compression, where some data is discarded to achieve higher compression ratios, which may result in a loss of quality or detail. The primary goal of data compression is to reduce storage requirements, making it easier to store large volumes of data and to speed up processing times, particularly in systems that need to handle large amounts of information quickly. This technology is used in various applications, such as image and video processing, file storage, and data transmission, where minimizing file size is essential for improving efficiency and performance or for storing large amounts of data and post-process this data for scientific discovery (Banerjee et al., 2022).

E. Principal Component Analysis (PCA)
PCA is a widely used statistical technique that helps uncover patterns in complex datasets by simplifying them. It works by reducing the number of variables in a dataset while retaining as much important information as possible. This is achieved by transforming the original variables into a smaller set of new variables, called principal components, which capture the most significant features or variations within the data. PCA is particularly useful in fields like machine learning, data analysis, and image processing, where handling high-dimensional data efficiently is essential (Jolliffe & Cadima, 2016). Figure 3.14 illustrates the PCA plot, where arrows are used to indicate the directions of the first and second principal components (PC1 and PC2).

F. Linear Discriminant Analysis (LDA)
LDA is a supervised dimensionality reduction technique designed to find a linear combination of input features that maximizes the separation between predefined classes. By projecting the data onto a lower-dimensional space, LDA enhances class separability, making it easier to classify or analyze the data. This method

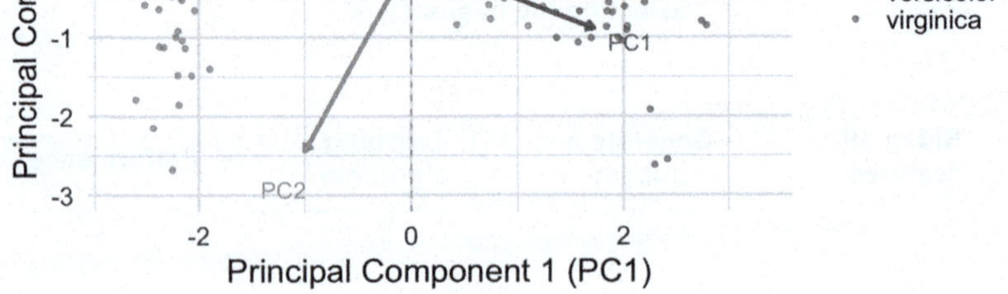

Fig. 3.14 Illustration of PCA using `iris` dataset

is widely applied in pattern recognition tasks, such as face recognition, and in machine learning applications, including classification problems and feature selection. Its effectiveness lies in its ability to balance class separation while minimizing within-class variance, which is essential for improving model performance. Figure 3.15 illustrates the top terms per topic in the LDA model and document-topic distribution. The `AssociatedPress` dataset is used, and a subset of 100 documents is selected.

G. t-distributed stochastic neighbor embedding (t-SNE)
It is a nonlinear method used for dimensionality reduction, especially effective in visualizing complex, high-dimensional datasets in a simpler, low-dimensional space. This technique transforms the high-dimensional data into a two- or three-dimensional space while maintaining the local relationships and structure of the data, making it easier to identify patterns, clusters, or trends. Unlike linear methods like Principal Component Analysis (PCA), t-SNE excels at capturing nonlinear relationships in the data, which is particularly useful in fields such as bioinformatics, image recognition, and natural language processing. Its ability to group similar data points while separating dissimilar ones has made it a popular tool for exploring datasets with complex underlying structures. The technique was introduced by Van der Maaten and Hinton (2008) in their seminal work, which demonstrated its ability to preserve the local structure of data and reveal meaningful patterns in various applications. Figure 3.16 shows the plot of t-SNE using the `iris` dataset.

How to choose the method for data reduction? It depends on the specific requirements and characteristics of the dataset. Simple sampling is effective for drawing a small, representative sample from a large dataset without analyzing the entire dataset. For instance, a company with thousands of customer transactions could randomly sample 100 transactions to gain insights into customer behavior. Clustering is useful for grouping similar data points, reducing complexity. In market research, clustering can group customers based on buying patterns, enabling businesses to target specific customer segments instead of analyzing individual transactions.

Feature selection reduces the number of variables in a dataset by retaining only the most relevant ones. For example, in healthcare data, predicting patient outcomes might involve keeping critical features like age, medical history, and vital signs while discarding irrelevant variables. Data compression reduces the size of data for storage or transmission without significant information loss. Large image files, for instance, can be compressed using algorithms like JPEG to reduce file size while maintaining acceptable quality.

Principal Component Analysis (PCA) is effective for datasets with many variables, simplifying them into fewer dimensions without significant information loss. In finance, PCA can simplify complex stock market data by focusing on key trends or factors influencing stock prices. Linear Discriminant Analysis (LDA) is suited for classification tasks where dimensionality reduction emphasizes differences between classes. In face recognition, LDA reduces facial features to a few key dimensions, distinguishing individuals.

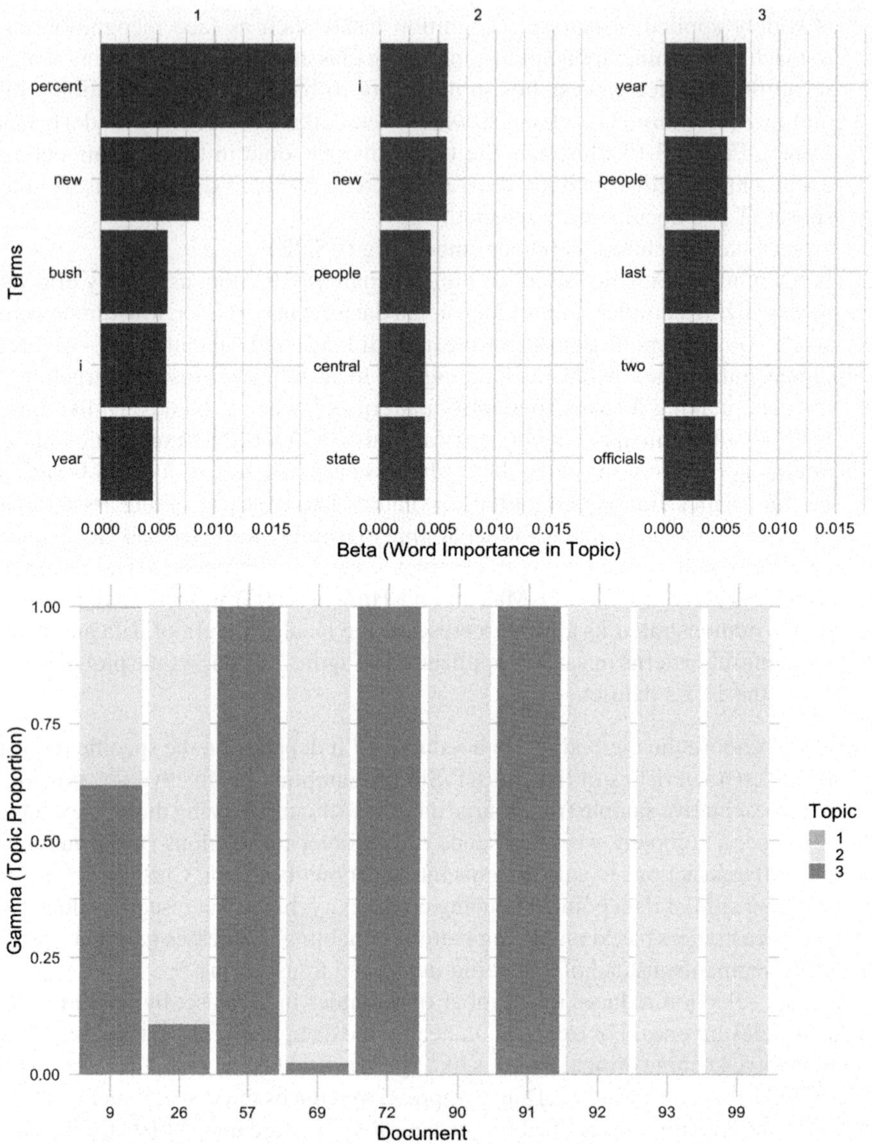

Fig. 3.15 Illustration of the top terms per topic in the LDA model and document-topic distribution

t-SNE is a powerful tool for visualizing high-dimensional data by mapping it to 2D or 3D space. In bioinformatics, t-SNE visualizes genetic data by placing similar genetic profiles close together, making patterns easier to identify. In geoinformatics, t-SNE aids in visualizing hyperspectral data from earth observation imagery by plotting similar spectral values together, uncovering hidden patterns.

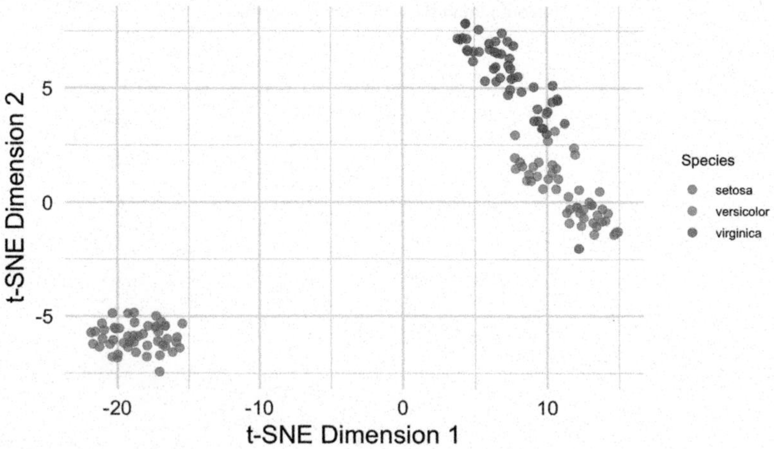

Fig. 3.16 t-SNE plot of `iris` dataset

3.6 Splitting Data

Creating a machine learning model requires testing its ability to work with new, unseen data to ensure accurate predictions on data not used during training. This process assesses the model's generalization capability. A common approach involves splitting the data into two parts: one for training the model and the other for testing it. This method, known as the "train-test split," randomly divides the data into two groups. One group is used to train the model, while the other evaluates its performance. This approach provides insight into how the model is likely to handle real-world data not encountered during training.

A. Holdout method

The holdout method is one of the simplest and most commonly used ways to split data into training and testing sets (Fig. 3.17). In this approach, we randomly divide the dataset into two parts: one part is used to train the model, and the other is used to test how well the model performs. Usually, around 70–80% of the data is set aside for training, while the remaining 20–30% is used for testing. This method is popular because it is easy to understand and implement, making it a convenient choice for many data science tasks. However, a limitation of the holdout method is that the results can vary significantly depending on how the data is randomly split. This means that different random splits could lead to different outcomes, which can be problematic when we need consistent and reliable results. To reduce this variability and improve the stability of model performance, techniques like cross-validation are often used. Cross-validation helps provide a more reliable and consistent evaluation of the model by testing it multiple times on different splits of the data.

B. Cross-validation

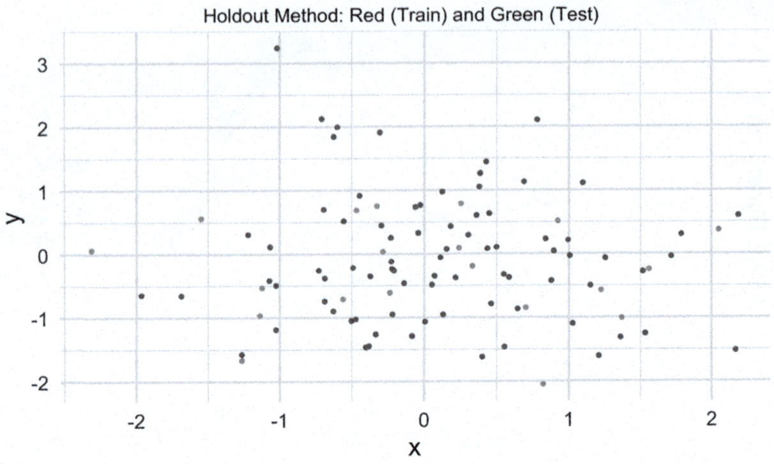

Fig. 3.17 Illustration of holdout method where the training data is plotted in red, and the test data is plotted in green

In cross-validation, we break the data into *k* equal parts, called folds, as shown in Fig. 3.18. The model is trained *k* times, with each fold acting as the test set once, while the other *k-1* folds are used to train the model. After training on each combination of training and test data, we check how well the model performs and then calculate the average performance across all folds. This approach helps us get a more accurate estimate of how well the model will perform on new, unseen data, as it ensures that every data point is used for both training and testing. By using each data point in different situations, this method reduces the chance of the model becoming too closely fitted to specific data, which is known as overfitting. It also gives a more reliable evaluation compared to just splitting the data once into a training and testing set. Cross-validation is widely used because it provides a stronger, more dependable way to assess the model's true performance across various datasets.

C. Leave-one-out cross-validation (LOO-CV)
   It is a specific type of cross-validation where the number of folds, k, is set equal to the total number of samples in the dataset. In each iteration, the model is trained using all but one sample, and the remaining sample is used as the test data. This process is repeated for every sample in the dataset, ensuring that each sample serves as the test point exactly once. Although this method requires a lot of computational power because the model needs to be trained repeatedly, it provides a very precise estimate of how the model will perform on new, unseen data. Figure 3.19 shows the LOO-CV plot. The main advantage of LOO-CV is that it reduces bias in the model's evaluation, but this comes at the cost of higher computational demands.

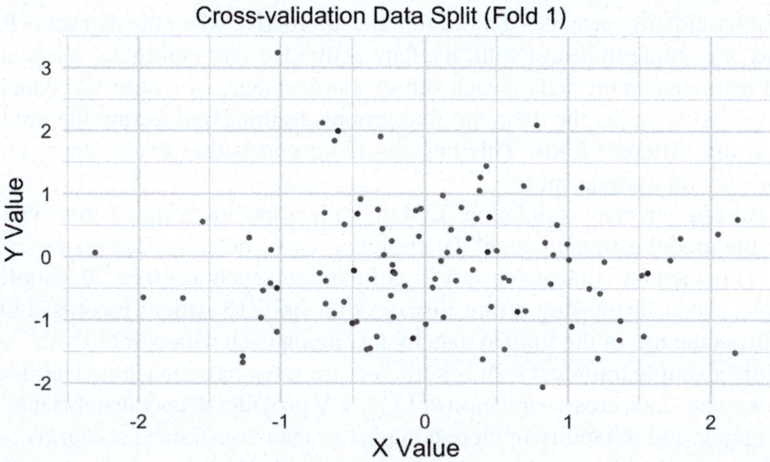

Fig. 3.18 Illustration of cross-validation data slit, showing the training data in blue and testing data in red

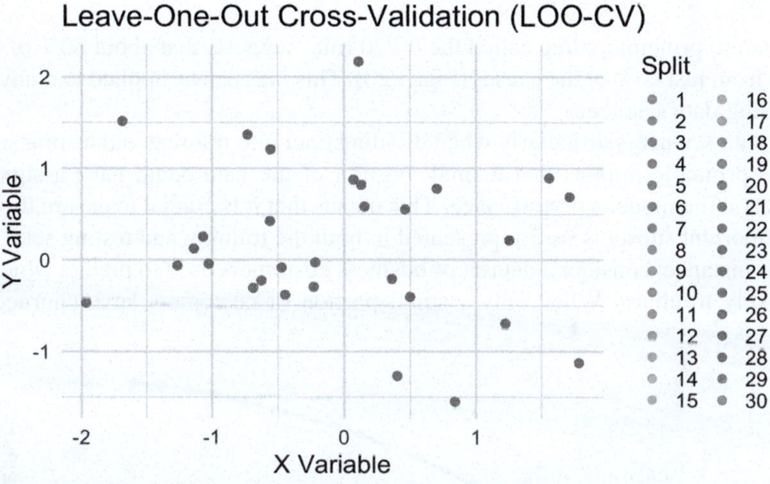

Fig. 3.19 LOO-CV plot showing the LOO-CV process with different colors representing each split

The choice of method for splitting data into training and testing depends on the size of the dataset, the computational resources available, and the desired accuracy of the performance estimate.

The holdout method is a straightforward approach used when dealing with a large dataset. The data is split into two parts: one for training the model and the other for testing it. For example, when predicting house prices using a dataset of 10,000 homes, 80% of the data could be used for training and the remaining 20% for testing. This method is fast, but performance can vary based on how the data is split

Cross-validation provides a more reliable alternative when the dataset is limited. Instead of a single train-test split, the data is divided into multiple subsets, and the model is trained and tested on each subset. For instance, with only 100 data points, cross-validation splits the data into five groups, training and testing the model five times using different folds. This ensures more consistent performance, reducing dependency on a single split.

Leave-one-out cross-validation (LOO-CV) is a specific form of cross-validation where the model is trained on all data points except one and tested on the excluded point. This method is ideal for very small datasets, such as 10 or 20 samples. For example, when diagnosing a rare disease with only 15 patient records, LOO-CV maximizes the use of the limited data by testing on each data point exactly once.

While a simple train-test split is sufficient for most basic machine learning tasks with abundant data, cross-validation or LOO-CV provides deeper insights into model performance and reliability in more complex or data-constrained scenarios.

3.7 What is the Pareto Principle?

The Pareto principle, often called the 80/20 rule, suggests that about 80% of results come from just 20% of the causes (Fig. 3.20). This idea can be applied to many areas, including data science.

In data science, particularly when dividing data into training and testing sets, the Pareto principle implies that a small portion of the data could have a significant impact on the model's performance. This means that it is crucial to ensure this small but important subset is well-represented in both the training and testing sets.

For instance, consider a dataset of business customers used to predict which ones are likely to churn. When only a small portion of customers have churned, it is

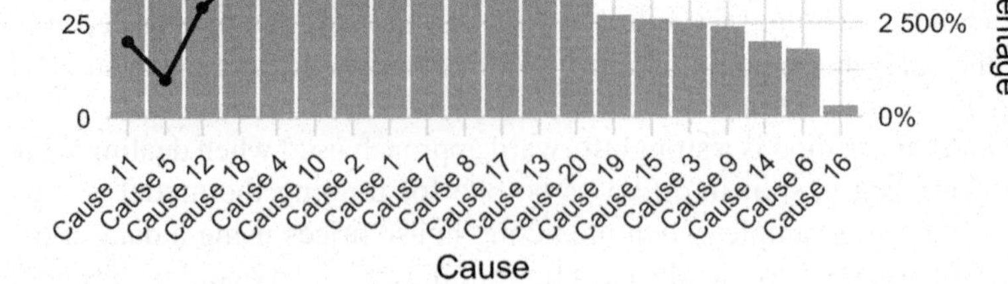

Fig. 3.20 Illustration of Pareto principle

essential to ensure that this group is equally represented in both the training and testing datasets. Without balanced representation, the model may struggle to predict churn effectively for these customers.

To address this, stratified sampling can be applied when dividing the data. This method ensures that the small group of churned customers is proportionally represented in both the training and testing sets.

Incorporating the Pareto principle during data splitting helps the model learn to make accurate predictions across all groups, not just the majority, resulting in improved overall performance.

3.8 Data Modeling and Processing

The execution time of a program implemented with a certain algorithm varies greatly depending on the input data. For example, it is easy to imagine that 10 data items can be processed in an instant, but 10,000 data items will take a long time to process.

At this time, it is important to consider how much the processing time will change depending on the number of inputs. If the amount of data increases 10 times or 100 times, will the processing time also double or 100 times, or will it increase 100 times or 10,000 times? Even in data analysis, if the processing time is not measured before analysis, the processing may take an enormous amount of time.

When creating a program called an algorithm, which is a procedure or calculation method for solving a problem, it is necessary to consider not only the algorithm but also the data structure, and how to store the data.

Create a model and apply it to the observed data to understand the phenomenon. It is called modeling. Useful information can be obtained by visualizing things that cannot be understood just by looking at the data, using graphs, etc., and predicting the results of unknown data.

At this time, even the same data can be interpreted and used differently depending on what kind of model the analyst creates. There is no such thing as **"the absolutely correct model,"** but the analyst must choose the right model.

Modeling is the core of data science where researchers use algorithms to capture patterns and make predictions. In social studies, modeling can reveal latent trends, forecast events, and test hypotheses on large datasets.

In reality, there are many models developed by researchers around the world, so it is common for researchers to select an appropriate model for the problem they are working on, and use it after correcting and fine-tuning it.

Clustering

Data clustering is a technique used in machine learning and data analysis to group data points with similar characteristics into clusters. These clusters are formed based on how alike or different the data points are from each other in terms of specific features or attributes. The main goal of clustering is to uncover hidden patterns and structures within a dataset that might be hard to spot at first glance. By doing so, clustering helps in drawing useful insights that can guide further analysis or decision-making.

There are several methods for clustering data such as hierarchical clustering, K-means clustering, and density-based clustering. Clustering algorithms assign data points to groups based on a similarity or distance measure. The specific method for calculating similarity depends on the nature of the data and the problem at hand.

For example, in a marketing scenario, businesses may use clustering to group customers based on shared traits like age, spending habits, or interests. This allows businesses to target specific customer groups with personalized marketing efforts, which can improve engagement and customer retention.

Clustering is a versatile tool that can be used in many fields, such as image analysis, natural language processing, and bioinformatics. The success of clustering depends on factors like the chosen algorithm, the quality of the data, and how the results are interpreted. Below are some common types of clustering methods:

1. **Hierarchical clustering**: This approach builds a hierarchy of clusters starting from individual data points and gradually merging them into larger clusters. The result is a tree-like diagram called a *dendrogram*, which shows how clusters are related (Fig. 3.21). There are two types of hierarchical clustering: agglomerative and divisive. In agglomerative clustering, each data point starts as its own cluster, and the closest clusters are merged together step by step until one cluster remains. In divisive clustering, the process is reversed: the whole dataset starts as one cluster and is split into smaller ones until each point forms its own cluster.
2. **K-means clustering**: This is a widely used method where the data is divided into k number of clusters. The algorithm starts by randomly placing k centroids (central points of the clusters). Then, each data point is assigned to the closest centroid, and the centroids are recalculated until the clusters stabilize. While efficient and scalable, K-means requires the number of clusters to be determined in advance.
3. **Density-based clustering**: This method groups data points based on their density, assuming that clusters are regions where data points are closely packed together, separated by regions with fewer points. A popular example is Density-Based Spatial Clustering of Applications with Noise (DBSCAN). DBSCAN identifies clusters by setting a minimum number of points required to form a cluster and measuring the distance between points. This method is useful for finding irregularly shaped clusters and handling noise in the data.

These clustering methods can be applied in various scenarios, including customer analysis, image processing, medical research, and more, offering valuable insights by organizing complex data into manageable groups.

The choice of clustering method depends on the data and the problem at hand. Hierarchical clustering is useful for visualizing the relationships between clusters, while K-means is effective for partitioning data into a specified number of clusters. Density-based clustering is useful for identifying clusters with arbitrary shapes and can handle noise in the data.

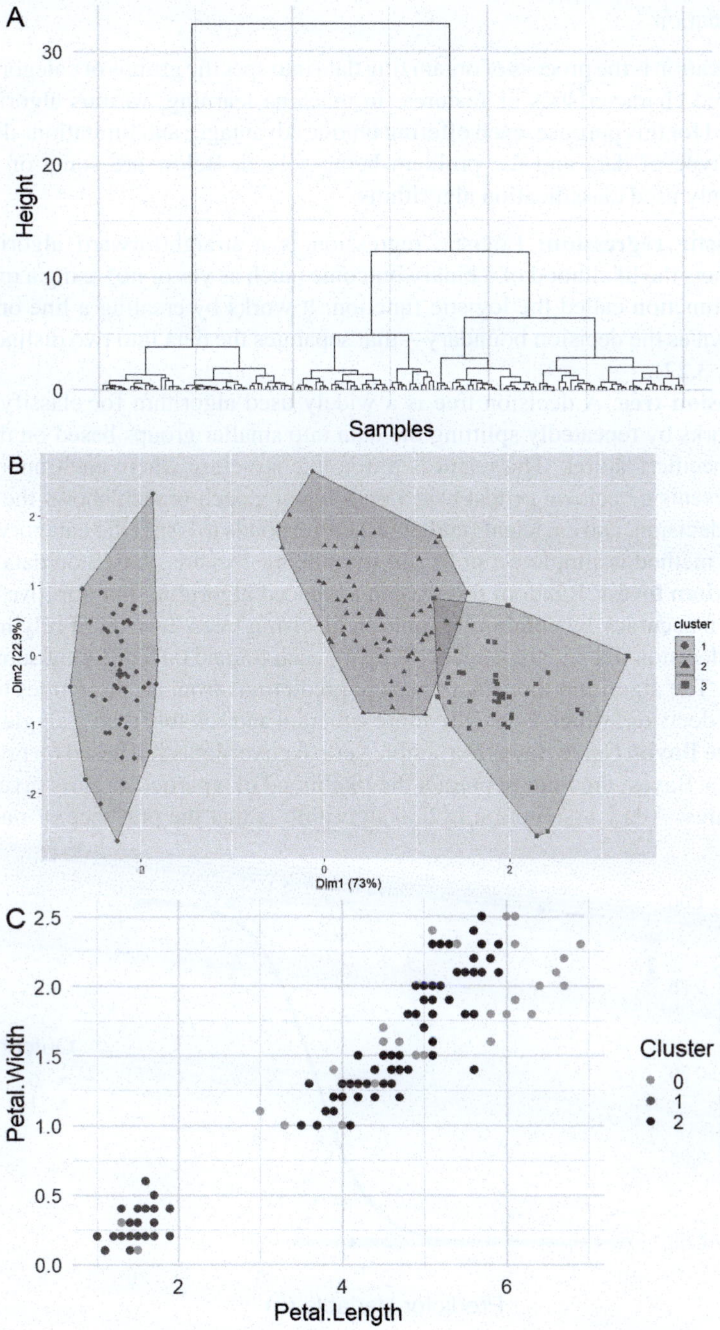

Fig. 3.21 Hierarchical clustering (A), K-means (B), and density-based clustering (C) using the `iris` dataset

Classification

Classification is the process of organizing data into specific groups or categories based on shared characteristics or features. In machine learning, various algorithms are designed for this purpose, each offering unique advantages and limitations depending on the type of data and the problem being solved. Below are some of the most commonly used classification algorithms:

- **Logistic regression:** Logistic regression is a straightforward algorithm that predicts the likelihood of a binary outcome (such as yes or no) using a mathematical function called the logistic function. It works by creating a line or curve—known as the decision boundary—that separates the data into two distinct classes (Fig. 3.22).
- **Decision tree**: A decision tree is a widely used algorithm for classifying data. It works by repeatedly splitting the data into smaller groups based on the values of specific features. The result is a tree-like structure where each internal node represents a decision or test based on a feature, each branch shows the result of that decision, and each leaf (end point) corresponds to a specific category or class. This method is simple yet powerful for making decisions based on data.
- **Random forest**: Random forest is an advanced algorithm that improves classification accuracy by combining multiple decision trees. Instead of relying on just one decision tree, it builds many of them, each trained on a different subset of the data. The algorithm then combines the predictions from all these trees to make a final decision, which is usually more accurate and reliable than a single tree.
- **Naive Bayes**: Naive Bayes is a simple yet effective algorithm based on probability. It uses Bayes' theorem to predict the likelihood of a particular class given certain features. A key assumption in this algorithm is that the presence of one feature

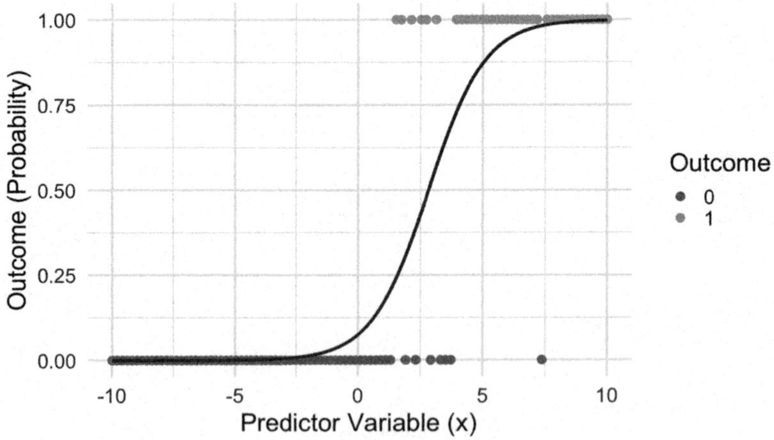

Fig. 3.22 Illustration of logistic regression

is independent of the presence of others. Despite this "naive" assumption, the algorithm often works surprisingly well in practice.

- **Support vector machines (SVM)**: SVM is another popular classification algorithm that focuses on finding the best-dividing line (or hyperplane) to separate data into distinct groups. Its goal is to maximize the distance between this boundary and the nearest data points from each class, ensuring clear and accurate separation. This makes SVM particularly effective for tasks with complex data distributions.

You will learn more details about these classification algorithms in Chap. 6.

3.9 Model Evaluation and Validation

Evaluating a model is a key step in the machine learning process because it shows how well the model can handle new, unseen data. There are different methods to evaluate a model's performance, and the method you choose depends on the type of problem you're solving and the data you are working with. Below are some common approaches:

- **Train/test split**: This is one of the simplest ways to evaluate a model. The data is divided into two sets: one for training the model and the other for testing its performance. By training the model on one set and evaluating it on the other, you can check how well it performs on data it has not seen before.
- **Cross-validation**: In this approach, the data is divided into smaller subsets, or "folds." The model is trained on all but one fold and tested on the fold left out. This process is repeated so that every fold gets a chance to be the test set. Finally, the performance results are averaged to give an overall assessment. This method is more reliable than a simple train/test split because it uses all the data for both training and testing systematically.
- **Leave-one-out cross-validation (LOO-CV)**: This is a special case of cross-validation where the number of folds equals the number of data points. Each data point is used as a test set exactly once, while the rest of the data is used for training. The results are then averaged to evaluate the model. This method is very thorough but can be computationally expensive for large datasets.
- **Bootstrapping**: This technique involves creating multiple random samples (called "bootstrap samples") by sampling the data with replacement. The model is trained on these samples, and its performance is tested on the original dataset. Bootstrapping helps assess the variability and robustness of the model.
- **Evaluation metrics**: To measure how well a model performs, we use metrics such as accuracy (how many predictions are correct), precision (how many positive predictions are correct), recall (how many actual positives are identified), F1 score (a balance between precision and recall), and ROC-AUC score (which shows how well the model distinguishes between classes). The choice of metric depends on the specific problem, such as whether false positives or false negatives are more critical. More details will be discussed in Chap. 6.

Selecting the right evaluation method and metric is crucial for getting not just an accurate picture of the model's performance, but also fair, reliable, and ready for real-world decision-making.

Train/test split is often used when we have a large dataset, like studying the effects of different teaching methods on student performance. We split the data into two parts: one to train the model and the other to test its predictions. For example, you might use 80% of the data to train the model and 20% to test how well it predicts student outcomes in new classrooms.

Cross-validation is useful when we want to get a more reliable estimate of model performance. Instead of relying on just one train-test split, we divide the data into multiple parts. Each part gets a chance to be the test set, ensuring that all data is used both for training and testing. This technique is common when evaluating the impact of a social program, like assessing the effectiveness of a job training program across different communities. It ensures the model is not biased by just one subset of the data.

LOO-CV is a specific form of cross-validation where each data point gets its turn to be the test set. This is particularly useful when data is scarce, like analyzing the impact of a new policy in a small town, where every individual in the dataset is important. It helps maximize the information we can extract from limited data.

Bootstrapping involves repeatedly sampling from the data with replacement to estimate the variability of a model's predictions. It is useful when we have data that might have inherent uncertainty, like estimating voter behavior from a sample survey. By resampling the data multiple times, we get a better sense of the model's robustness and how it might perform with different sets of data.

Evaluation metrics like accuracy, precision, recall, and F1 score are used to assess how well a model is performing. For example, when predicting crime rates in certain neighborhoods, accuracy alone might not be enough, especially if some areas have very low crime rates. In such cases, metrics like recall and F1 score help ensure the model correctly identifies areas with high crime, even if they make up a small portion of the total dataset.

Model evaluation and validation ensures the model is neither too simple (underfitting) nor too complex (overfitting) and can handle real-world data effectively.

3.10 Overfitting and Underfitting

Overfitting happens when a machine learning model learns the training data too well, including its random noise, instead of focusing only on the important patterns. This means the model "memorizes" the training data rather than learning to apply its knowledge to new, unseen data. Overfitting often occurs when the model is overly complex, with too many parameters, making it flexible enough to capture even irrelevant details in the training set. As a result, the model performs poorly when tested on new data.

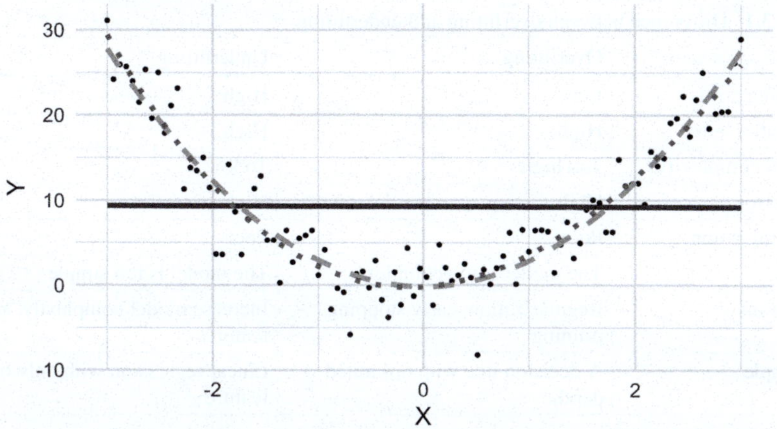

Fig. 3.23 Illustration of overfitting and underfitting using synthetic data and polynomial regression models. Where the linear model (blue) is expected to underfit, the quadratic model (green) is expected to be a good fit, and the cubic model (red) is expected to overfit

Underfitting occurs when a model is too simple to capture the key patterns in the data. This leads to poor performance on both the training data and any new data it encounters because the model fails to learn enough from the dataset. Figure 3.23 illustrates the overfitting and underfitting using synthetic data and polynomial regression models.

To address overfitting, you can use strategies like regularization, which adds constraints to simplify the model; early stopping, which halts training before the model becomes overly specialized; or pruning, which removes unnecessary components of the model. These techniques reduce the model's complexity and help it focus on meaningful patterns rather than noise.

To fix underfitting, you can increase the model's complexity by using a more advanced algorithm or adding additional features to the dataset. This allows the model to better capture the hidden relationships within the data.

The key to building effective machine learning models is finding the right balance between overfitting and underfitting. If the model is too simple, it will underfit the data, failing to learn enough. If it is too complex, it will overfit, losing its ability to generalize. The goal is to create a model that performs well on new, unseen data by accurately identifying the underlying patterns while ignoring irrelevant details. Table 3.1 summarizes the difference between overfitting and underfitting.

Table 3.1 Difference between overfitting and underfitting

	Overfitting	Underfitting
Training error	Low	High
Validation error	High	High
Model complexity	Too high	To low
Test error	High	High
Generalization	Poor	Poor
Cause	The model is too complex	The model is too simple
Solutions	Regularization, early stopping, pruning	Increase model complexity, add features
Example	A decision tree with unlimited depth	Linear regression with only one feature

3.11 Advanced Topics: Machine Learning in Social Studies

Models can be created using artificial intelligence (AI), machine learning (ML), and deep learning (DL). AI is a branch of computer science and engineering that focuses on designing machines capable of performing tasks that typically require human intelligence. These tasks include understanding spoken or written language, recognizing patterns in images, and making decisions based on data.

ML, a subset of AI, involves creating algorithms that can learn from data and make predictions or decisions without being explicitly programmed. These algorithms can uncover patterns and relationships in data automatically, enabling them to draw insights and provide solutions.

DL, a more advanced branch of ML, specializes in analyzing complex and unstructured data such as text, images, and audio. By using neural networks with multiple layers, DL is particularly effective for tasks like image recognition, speech processing, and predictive modeling. It is increasingly being used in social studies to analyze social media trends, visualize intricate networks, and simulate human behavior. Figure 3.24 illustrates the relationship between AI, ML, and DL, highlighting their interconnected roles.

ML in social studies is a way of using computer programs to find patterns in data that can help us understand human behavior, social trends, and societal issues. Social studies typically include subjects like economics, sociology, geography, and political science, and machine learning can analyze large amounts of data from these fields to help researchers make better predictions, decisions, and policies.

For example, in economics, ML can analyze financial data to predict market trends or the economic impact of certain events. In sociology, ML can help study how social media influences public opinion or how people interact in different communities. In geography, it can track population changes, land use, or environmental impacts.

Here is a simple example to understand it: imagine you want to predict how likely people are to vote based on their age, income, and education level. A machine

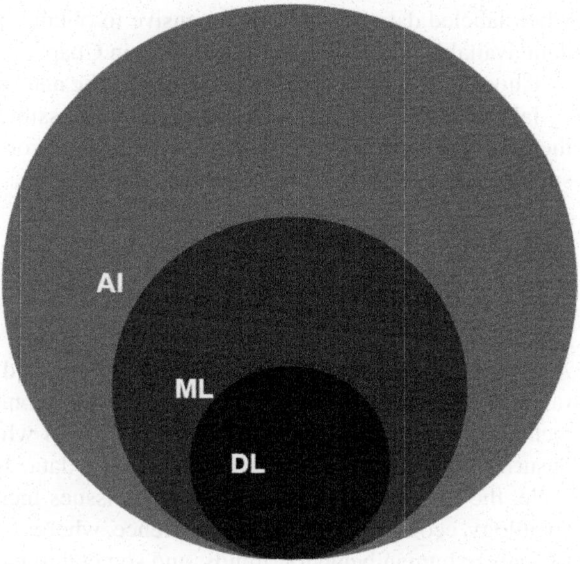

Fig. 3.24 Where are the positions of AI, ML, and DL?

learning model could look at historical data of past elections to learn the patterns of voting behavior and then predict how likely different groups of people are to vote in future elections.

In machine learning, there are three main approaches to classification: supervised learning, unsupervised learning, and semi-supervised learning. Each method has its unique characteristics and is suited to different scenarios.

Unsupervised learning involves training an algorithm on data that does not have any labels or predefined categories. In this approach, the algorithm works independently to explore the data, identifying patterns, groupings, or underlying structures. Since no specific target outcome is provided, the algorithm uncovers relationships within the data on its own. This approach is commonly applied in tasks such as clustering (grouping similar data points) and dimensionality reduction (simplifying data while retaining its essential features).

Supervised learning, on the other hand, is used when labeled data is available. Here, the algorithm is provided with input features along with their corresponding target outcomes. By analyzing the relationship between these inputs and outputs, the algorithm learns how to predict the correct target for new, unseen data. Supervised learning is frequently used for tasks like classification (assigning categories to data) and regression (predicting numerical values).

Semi-supervised learning serves as a middle ground between the two methods. It is particularly useful when only a small portion of the data is labeled, while the rest remains unlabeled. The algorithm initially examines the unlabeled data to detect patterns and structures, much like in unsupervised learning. It then uses the labeled data to refine its understanding and improve its accuracy. This approach is valuable when labeled data is scarce or expensive to obtain, but there is plenty of unlabeled data available. We will learn more detail in Chap. 6.

Choosing the right approach depends on the nature of the task and the availability of labeled data. If labeled data is readily accessible, supervised learning is often the best option. However, if labels are unavailable or limited, unsupervised or semi-supervised learning can offer effective alternatives.

3.12 Challenges and Considerations

As social studies data becomes more complex and abundant, it brings with it a range of challenges that require careful consideration. These challenges span ethical, technical, and methodological concerns, each of which plays an important role in ensuring the integrity and usefulness of the data. In particular, as data grows in scale, the importance of addressing these issues increases, especially in fields like sociology, economics, and political science, where social studies data is heavily used to analyze human behavior, trends, and societal dynamics.

Ethics and privacy

One of the key concerns when working with social studies data is ethics, particularly when it involves sensitive information about individuals or communities. Ethical considerations are vital to ensuring that the data is collected, stored, and used responsibly. Social studies often require access to personal data such as income, health, or family details, which could be exploited if not handled carefully. Ensuring data privacy involves anonymizing sensitive information to make it impossible to trace back to any individual. Data anonymization tools, along with data masking techniques, are essential in this process. These tools help remove or obscure personally identifiable information, reducing the risk of misuse or unauthorized access. We will discuss ethics in more detail in Chap. 10 of this book.

Data quality and bias

Another significant challenge in social studies data is maintaining data quality and addressing potential biases. Social data can be biased due to various factors, including the way samples are collected, measurement errors, or even biases introduced by the researchers themselves. For example, a survey that only includes participants from urban areas may not accurately represent rural populations. Bias in data can lead to incorrect conclusions and flawed policy recommendations. To minimize these biases, researchers employ data preprocessing techniques, such as normalization, which adjusts data to a standard scale, and careful variable selection, which ensures that only relevant factors are included in the analysis. While these techniques are helpful, they are not enough on their own to eliminate bias. Researchers must also exercise caution when interpreting results, ensuring transparency about their methods and being clear about the limitations of the data. Being upfront about potential biases allows others to better understand and evaluate the findings.

Interdisciplinary collaboration

Finally, interdisciplinary collaboration is crucial when working with social studies data, especially in the realm of data science. Social studies data often requires input from experts in other fields to fully understand its context and implications. For example, sociologists can offer valuable insights into human behavior and societal trends, which can guide decisions about which variables to include in an analysis. This collaboration helps to create a more robust framework for interpreting the data, ensuring that findings are not only statistically sound but also meaningful and relevant to real-world issues. Working with domain experts also helps ensure that data is interpreted within the correct cultural, historical, and social contexts, which enhances the impact and applicability of the findings.

Easy to Digest Box

Data exploration

This is like looking at your books or clothes to see what you have before deciding what to do with them. In data science, we look at the data to understand what kind of information it has. For example, if you have a list of students' test scores, you might check to see if any scores are missing or if any numbers are too high or low.

Example*: If you are looking at how many apples, bananas, and oranges are in a basket, you would count each type and see how many of each there are. This is exploring your data.*

Data preprocessing

This is like cleaning up and organizing your books before reading them. In data science, you make the data ready by fixing problems like missing information or organizing it in a way that makes sense. This step is important because bad or messy data can give wrong answers.

Example*: If some students forgot to write their test scores, you might guess or add a note saying "missing," or if some numbers are too strange, you could fix them.*

Data modeling

This is like making a plan or a rule about how to play with your toys. In data science, you create a model, which is like a "smart guess," to help you understand what might happen next. The model looks at all the data you have to try to predict future things.

Example*: If you know that students who study for an hour usually get higher scores, you could make a rule (model) that says, "If a student studies for an* *hour, they will probably get a high score." Then, you can use this model to guess future scores.*

Putting it all together

Imagine you want to predict how well kids do in a game based on how much they practice. First, you'd ***explore*** *their past scores (data exploration), then you would* ***organize*** *the scores if any are missing or wrong (data preprocessing), and finally, you would make a rule or prediction about how practicing more helps them win (data modeling).*

3.13 Summary of Key Points

- Data exploration and preprocessing are crucial for ensuring data quality and accuracy.
- Data exploration and preprocessing are iterative processes that may need to be repeated multiple times.
- Data exploration techniques include summary statistics, data visualization, and data profiling.
- The choice of outlier detection method depends on the type of data, the problem at hand, and the desired level of sensitivity.
- The choice of feature scaling technique depends on the distribution of the features and the requirements of the machine learning algorithm being used.
- Data preprocessing techniques include data cleaning, data integration, data transformation, and data reduction.
- Domain knowledge and data understanding obtained through data exploration are crucial for effective data science projects.
- Data exploration and preprocessing are essential for maintaining data privacy and security.
- Modeling is creating a model and applying it to the observed data to understand the phenomenon.
- The choice of technique used for model evaluation will depend on the specific problem being addressed and the nature of the data.
- A model that is too simple will underfit the data, while a model that is too complex will overfit the data.

3.14 Hands-on Experience

Working with RStudio

Dealing with missing values, outliers, and data quality problems.

Data analysis often begins with cleaning and preparing data to ensure it is suitable for analysis. One common issue is missing values, which occur when certain data points are absent. In R, missing values are represented as NA. To handle these, you can either remove the rows or columns containing missing values using functions like `na.omit()` or fill in the gaps using techniques such as mean or median imputation (`dplyr::mutate()` with `replace_na()` is useful for this). For example, when analyzing numerical data, you might replace missing values with the average of the available values to maintain consistency.

Outliers, which are extreme values that deviate significantly from the rest of the data, can distort your analysis. To identify outliers, you can use visualizations like boxplots (`boxplot()` function) or statistical methods like the interquartile range (IQR). Once identified, you may decide to remove or adjust outliers depending on their context and relevance to your study. Similarly, addressing data quality problems such as inconsistent formatting or erroneous values often involves standardizing or correcting errors using functions like `stringr::str_replace()` for text data. Data cleaning is a crucial first step in ensuring reliable results in any analysis.

Now we will work using data from https://ourworldindata.org/grapher/annual-working-hours-vs-gdp-per-capita-pwt look for the download icon and click it. A new window will open then go to "data" scroll down and select "download full data." It will come in zip format so you need to unzip it. Inside the unzipped folder there will be three files:.CSV,.JSON, and.md. We will use.CSV data for practice in this chapter also in Chap. 4.

When working with R, it is important to organize your workspace properly to avoid errors and confusion. One of the first things you should do before starting your analysis is to **check and set your working directory**. The working directory is the folder on your computer where R will look for files to load and save. If your working directory is not set correctly, R will not be able to find the data files you need, and this could lead to frustrating errors.

Next, after setting your working directory, you will need to **load the data** you want to analyze. You have already downloaded and extracted the data from a compressed.zip file, it should now be in your working directory. Once the data is loaded into R, it is a good idea to **view it** to ensure it has been imported correctly. By doing this, you can familiarize yourself with the structure of your dataset, such as the number of rows, columns, and the types of data it contains.

PRACTICE 3

Learning Objectives

Understand basic directory operations in R

- Learn how to check the current working directory using `getwd()`.
- Set a specific working directory using `setwd()` to manage data files effectively.

Install and use R libraries

- Gain familiarity with installing libraries (install.`packages()`) and loading them using `library()` for extended functionality.

Data loading and initial exploration

- Load datasets in CSV format using `read_csv()` from the readr package.
- View the structure of datasets using `head()` and `View()` for quick exploration.

Data cleaning techniques

- Handle missing values in the dataset using the `na.omit()` function.
- Rename columns of a dataset to improve readability and usability.

Data subsetting and selection

- Learn to extract specific rows based on conditions (e.g., filter data for a single country).
- Practice removing unnecessary columns to focus on relevant data using indexing.

Introduction to data visualization

- Understand the importance of visualizing data to identify patterns and trends.
- Create simple line graphs using the ggplot2 package to represent time-series data.

Advanced data manipulation using dplyr

- Filter data for multiple countries using `filter()` and the %in% operator.
- Combine multiple data cleaning steps to prepare datasets for analysis.

Visualizing data for comparative analysis

- Generate comparative line graphs to analyze trends between different groups (e.g., countries).
- Customize graphs with meaningful labels, legends, and color schemes.

Addressing challenges in data analysis

- Apply the learned techniques to analyze and visualize data from a real-world dataset (e.g., GDP by country).
- Develop critical thinking to solve challenges like identifying top-performing or underperforming countries based on GDP growth.

Enhance analytical skills

- Use bar charts and line charts to summarize and communicate findings effectively.
- Compare multiple entities (e.g., countries) and draw insights from data visualizations.

Below is a step-by-step example in R to help you deal with missing values, outliers, and data quality problems. Follow this code to practice setting the working directory, loading the data, and viewing it:

```
# Check your current working directory
getwd()

# Set your working directory (replace the path with
your folder location)
setwd("/Your/path/annual-working-hours-vs-gdp-per
-capita-pwt")

# Install and load the library
install.packages("readr")
library(readr)

# Load your data (assuming it is a CSV file named
"data.csv")
AWH < - read_csv("annual-working-hours-vs-gdp-per-
capita-pwt.csv")

# View the first few rows of your data
head(AWH)

# Open the data in a spreadsheet-like viewer
View(AWH)
```

After you open the data in a spreadsheet-like, you will see there are so many NA cells. To remove these cells, you can use the following code

```
# Removing NA values
AWH < - na.omit(AWH)
View(AWH)
```

Now all NA values have been removed, but the header name is still too long. We can rename the header using the following code.

```
# Rename only the 1st, 4th to 6th column names
colnames(AWH)[c(1,4,5,6)] <- c("Country", "WH",
"GDP", "POP")
View(AWH)
```

Subsetting data

Subsetting involves selecting specific portions of a dataset to focus on relevant information or reducing the size of the data for easier analysis. R provides multiple ways to subset data, such as using base R functions like `subset()` or indexing with brackets (`[,]`). For instance, you can select rows where a variable meets a certain condition (e.g., selecting only data from a specific year). In the dplyr package, functions like `filter()` and `select()` make subsetting data more intuitive and readable. For example, filter(`data, year == 2023`) allows you to extract rows where the year is 2023. These methods are particularly helpful when working with large datasets, as they allow you to focus only on the relevant portion for analysis.

From the AWH data, we will subset data only for Japan; you can use the following code:

```
# Subset single data
df_japan <- subset(AWH, Country = = "Japan")
View(df_japan)
```

If you only need population data, you can use this code:

```
# Delete columns
df_japan < - df_japan[,-c(4,5,7)] # Delete column
4, 5, and 7 from the dataframe
View(df_japan)
```

Visualizing data

Data visualization is an important part of data analysis. It helps us understand patterns, trends, and relationships in data. In R, one of the most popular tools for creating beautiful and informative visualizations is the `ggplot2` package. This package allows users to create a wide variety of plots, such as scatter plots, bar charts, and line graphs, with just a few lines of code.

The strength of `ggplot2` lies in its flexibility. You can layer different elements on a plot, customize colors, and adjust labels to make the plot easy to interpret. For beginners, `ggplot2` is easy to start with, but it is also powerful enough for advanced users.

Using data from df_japan, we will plot using a line graph (Fig. 3.25) using the following code:

```
# Install and load the library
install.packages("ggplot2")
library(ggplot2)
# Plot the graph
ggplot(df_japan, aes(x = Year, y = POP, color =
Country)) + geom_line() + labs(x = "Year", y =
"Population", color = "Country")
```

The plot will be shown in the plots tabs within RStudio as follows:

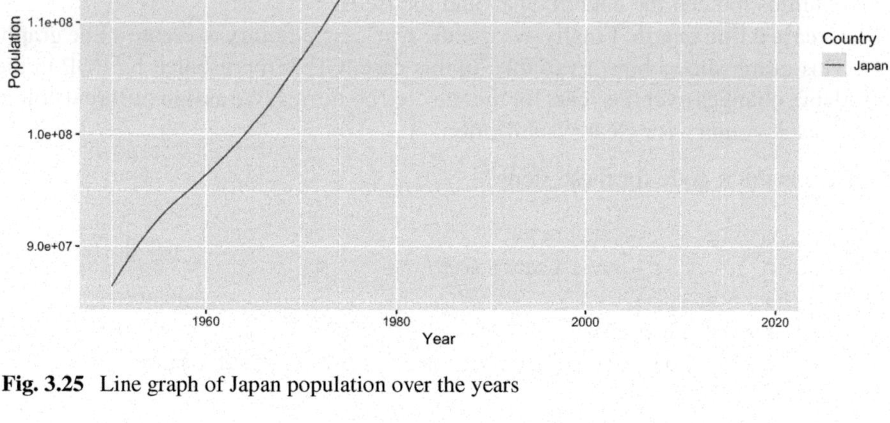

Fig. 3.25 Line graph of Japan population over the years

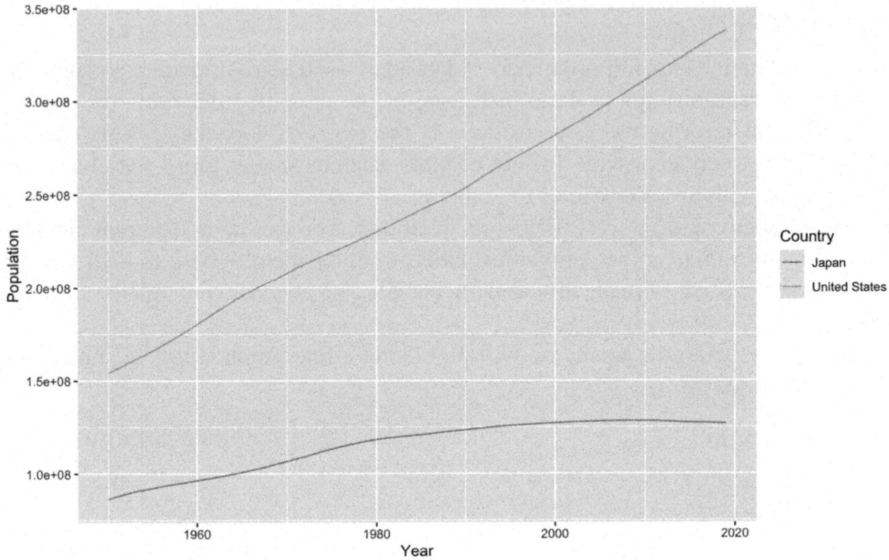

Fig. 3.26 Line graph of Japan and United States population over the years

Analyze data for multiple countries

This example demonstrates how to analyze data for multiple countries using R. The process involves selecting specific countries from a dataset, cleaning the data, and visualizing the results with a line graph using the `ggplot2` library. Here is how you can achieve this step by step:

1. **Load required library**: First, we use the dplyr library for data manipulation. This library simplifies filtering and selecting specific data from large datasets.
2. **Subset the data**: To analyze specific countries, we filter the dataset (AWH) to include only rows for "Japan" and "United States." This is achieved with the `filter()` function and the %in% operator. After filtering, we remove unwanted columns to keep the dataset clean and focused.
3. **Create a line graph**: Finally, we use the `ggplot2` library to create a line graph. This graph shows how a variable, in this case, GDP (represented by POP in the data), changes over the years for the selected countries. We assign different colors to each country for clear visualization.

Here is the R code for these steps:

```
# Load necessary libraries
library(dplyr)
library(ggplot2)
# Step 1: Subset data for multiple countries
```

```
multi_country <- AWH % > %
filter(Country %in% c("Japan", "United States")) #
Filter for Japan and United States
multi_country <- multi_country[,-c(4,5,7)] # Remove
unnecessary columns (columns 4, 5, and 7)

# Step 2: Create a ggplot line graph
ggplot(multi_country, aes(x = Year, y = POP, color
= Country)) +
 geom_line() + # Add a line for each country's data
        labs(x = "Year", y = "Population", color =
"Country") # Label the axes and legend
```

What does the code do?

- The `filter(Country %in% c("Japan", "United States"))` line selects only the rows where the Country column matches "Japan" or "United States."
- The `multi_country[,-c(4,5,7)]` line removes columns 4, 5, and 7 from the dataset. This step helps focus the analysis on relevant data.
- The `ggplot()` function creates a plot, where:
  - `aes(x = Year, y = POP, color = Country)` specifies the aesthetics of the plot, such as the x-axis (`Year`), y-axis (`POP`), and the line color by `Country`.
  - `geom_line()` adds the line graph to the plot.
  - `labs()` customizes the axis labels and legend title.

When you run the above code, you will get a clean and visually appealing line graph showing the GDP trends for Japan and the United States over the years (Fig. 3.26). This graph helps compare the economic performance of the two countries.

Challenges

Using the "GDP By Country 1999–2022" data from: https://www.kaggle.com/datasets/alejopaullier/-gdp-by-country-1999-2022?resource=download

- Show the GDP growth (mean) of Japan using line chart plot
- Compare the GDP growth (mean) of China, India, and Japan. Plot using line chart
- Show the top ten lowest GDP growth rate (mean) countries using bar chart
- Show the top ten highest GDP growth rate (mean) countries using bar chart

Expected results:

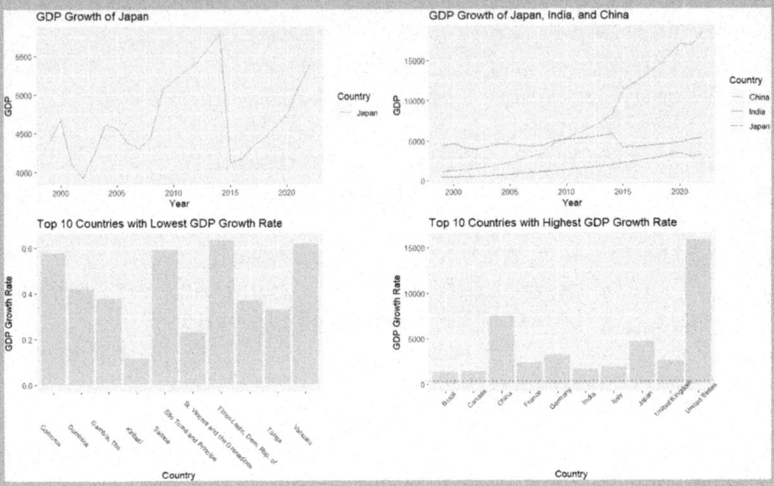

References

Banerjee, T., Choi, J., Lee, J., Gong, Q., Chen, J., Klasky, S., Rangarajan, A., & Ranka, S. (2022). *Scalable hybrid learning techniques for scientific data compression.* https://arxiv.org/abs/2212.10733

Chandrashekar, G., & Sahin, F. (2014). A survey on feature selection methods. *Computational Intelligence and Neuroscience., 40*(1), 16–28. https://doi.org/10.1016/j.compeleceng.2013.11.024

James, G., Witten, D., Hastie, T., & Tibshirani, R. (2013). *An introduction to statistical learning.* Springer. Available at https://link.springer.com/book/10.1007/978-1-0716-1418-1

Jolliffe, I. T., & Cadima, J. (2016). Principal component analysis: A review and recent developments. *Philosophical Transactions of the Royal Society a: Mathematical, Physical and Engineering Sciences, 374*(2065), 20150202. https://doi.org/10.1098/rsta.2015.0202

Van der Maaten, L., & Hinton, G. (2008). Visualizing data using t-SNE. *Journal of Machine Learning Research, 9*, 2579–2605. Available at https://jmlr.org/papers/v9/vandermaaten08a.html

Xu, R., & Wunsch, D. (2005). Survey of clustering algorithms. *IEEE Transactions on Neural Networks, 16*(3), 645–678. Available at https://ieeexplore.ieee.org/document/1427769

Chapter 4
Statistics Descriptive and Inferential

Abstract This chapter explains the difference between descriptive and inferential statistics. The first part of this chapter covers the concept of a hypothesis, the process of developing one, and methods for testing it. The discussion includes graphs that simplify statistical findings for better understanding. Additionally, the chapter introduces parametric and non-parametric statistics, along with common methods such as the t-test, ANOVA, and regression analysis. The second part demonstrates hypothesis testing using statistical methods in RStudio, focusing on the hypothesis: "Working hours are similar in developing and developed countries." The section concludes with presenting results through histograms and scatterplots.

Relation to Other Chapters: This chapter builds on the modeling from Chap. 3 and prepares readers for visual and machine learning analysis in Chaps. 5 and 6.

4.1 Introduction

Statistics plays a crucial role in social science research by offering tools to gather, analyze, interpret, and share data effectively. It helps researchers understand complex data, uncover patterns, test ideas, and make informed decisions based on evidence. By using statistical methods, social scientists can describe trends, predict outcomes, identify relationships, and evaluate theories. This chapter provides an introduction to the basics of descriptive and inferential statistics, explaining how they are used to solve real-world problems and answer important questions in social science.

F. Ramdani, *Data Science: Foundations and Hands-on Experience*,
https://doi.org/10.1007/978-981-96-4683-8_4

4.1.1 Definition and Uses of Statistics in Data Science

What is Statistics?

Statistics, a fundamental branch of mathematics, focuses on gathering, analyzing, interpreting, presenting, and organizing data. It leverages mathematical models, tools, techniques, and algorithms to extract insights from data, enabling meaningful conclusions and informed decision-making in both academic and practical applications. Statistics plays a crucial role in understanding complex phenomena by uncovering patterns and trends, testing hypotheses, and making predictions.

This discipline is widely applied across various fields, such as business, medicine, social sciences, engineering, environmental science, and more. For instance, businesses use statistics to analyze market trends and improve decision-making, while in medicine, it supports clinical trials and public health research. Similarly, social scientists rely on statistical methods to explore human behavior, and engineers apply them in quality control and system optimization.

Statistics has two primary branches: **descriptive statistics** and **inferential statistics**. Descriptive statistics summarize and visualize data using measures like mean, median, standard deviation, and graphical representations, making it easier to understand large datasets. Inferential statistics, on the other hand, extends beyond the immediate data, enabling researchers to make predictions or draw conclusions about a broader population based on a representative sample. For example, pollsters use inferential methods to predict election outcomes, while scientists use them to test theories with limited experimental data.

Why Use Statistics in Data Science?

Understanding statistics is a cornerstone of data science, as it offers the tools and methodologies needed to analyze and interpret complex datasets effectively. By applying statistical techniques, data scientists can uncover meaningful patterns, derive actionable insights, and make data-driven decisions in a wide range of fields, including healthcare, finance, environmental science, and social research (Crawley, 2015; McKinney, 2022).

Statistics provides a systematic approach to summarizing data, identifying trends, and predicting future outcomes. For example, descriptive statistics, such as mean, median, standard deviation, and range, help summarize and describe data concisely. Inferential statistics, on the other hand, enable scientists to conclude a larger population based on the analysis of a smaller sample, often using techniques like hypothesis testing, confidence intervals, and regression analysis (Field, 2018).

Moreover, statistics empowers data scientists to evaluate the reliability and accuracy of their analysis. Through an understanding of statistical inference, they can test hypotheses, determine the significance of their results, and quantify the confidence levels of their predictions. This process ensures that insights derived from data are both credible and actionable, reducing the risk of errors or misinterpretation (Montgomery et al., 2019).

A solid knowledge of statistics is indispensable for data scientists, as it underpins their ability to transform raw data into meaningful knowledge. Whether assessing trends, building predictive models, or validating findings, statistical methods are foundational tools that enable impactful, evidence-based decisions in an increasingly data-driven world.

4.2 Comparison Between Descriptive and Inferential Statistics

Descriptive Statistics.

Descriptive statistics involve summarizing and organizing data to highlight its key characteristics, providing a clear snapshot of the information. This branch of statistics employs tools such as measures of central tendency, measures of dispersion, and data visualization techniques to present data effectively. While descriptive statistics are invaluable for identifying patterns, and trends, and summarizing datasets, they do not enable researchers to make predictions, infer conclusions about a broader population, or establish causation.

The following are methods that are commonly used in descriptive statistics:

- **Measures of Central Tendency**

  Measures of central tendency summarize the center or typical value of a dataset, providing an anchor point for understanding the distribution of data. The three common measures are:

  Mean: Also known as the arithmetic average, the mean is calculated by dividing the sum of all data points by the total number of data points. It is the most widely used measure of central tendency but is sensitive to extreme values, such as outliers, which can distort its representation of the data.

  Median: The median represents the middle value in a sorted dataset, dividing it into two halves. Unlike the mean, the median remains unaffected by outliers, making it a more reliable measure in skewed datasets.

  Mode: The mode is the most frequently occurring value in a dataset. Unlike the mean and median, the mode is particularly useful for nominal or categorical data, where values represent categories rather than numbers. For example, in a survey of favorite colors, the mode reveals the most popular choice. Figure 4.1 illustrates the mean, median, and mode in a histogram.

- **Measures of Dispersion**

  Dispersion refers to how much the values in a dataset vary or spread out from the central point, such as the mean. Understanding the spread of data is crucial for

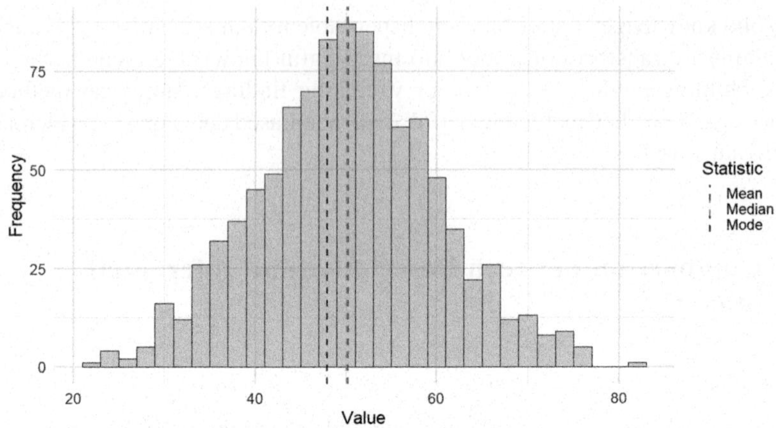

Fig. 4.1 Illustration of mean, median, and mode in a histogram

interpreting patterns and making predictions. There are several common ways to measure dispersion, and three of the most widely used methods are:

Range: The range is the simplest measure of dispersion, calculated by subtracting the lowest value in the dataset from the highest value. While it provides a quick sense of the spread, it has a major limitation: It is heavily influenced by outliers. This means that if there is an unusually high or low value, the range may give a misleading impression of the data's overall variability. The range does not tell us anything about the distribution of values between the minimum and maximum.

Variance: Variance measures how much each data point differs from the mean of the dataset. It is computed by taking the average of the squared differences between each data point and the mean. This gives a sense of how much the data values deviate from the average. However, the variance can be sensitive to extreme values, as squaring large differences amplifies their effect. Though useful, variance is not always intuitive because its units are squared, making it harder to directly interpret in the context of the original data.

Standard Deviation: The standard deviation is simply the square root of the variance. It brings the units of measurement back to the original scale of the data, making it easier to understand in practical terms. The standard deviation gives a clear picture of how spread out the data points are around the mean. It is generally less affected by extreme values compared to variance and is often preferred because it provides a more interpretable measure of variability. Figure 4.2 shows the range, variance, and standard deviation of three different variables.

Skewness and Kurtosis: These statistical measures help to describe how data is distributed, as shown in Fig. 4.3. Skewness measures the asymmetry of the data. When skewness is zero, the data is symmetrical and follows a normal distribution, known as a mesokurtic distribution. Positive skewness suggests that the data is

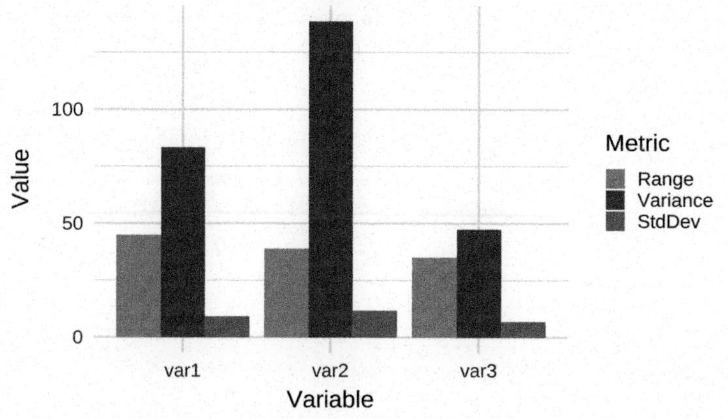

Fig. 4.2 Range, variance, and standard deviation (StdDev) of three different variables

stretched more toward the right, creating a right-skewed or leptokurtic distribution, while negative skewness indicates that the data leans to the left, creating a left-skewed or platykurtic distribution. On the other hand, kurtosis measures the "peakedness" or "flatness" of a distribution. A kurtosis of zero indicates a mesokurtic distribution, meaning that the data has a moderate peak, similar to a normal distribution. Positive kurtosis reflects a distribution that is more peaked than a normal distribution, while negative kurtosis indicates a distribution with a flatter shape compared to the normal distribution.

- **Data Visualization Techniques**

It refers to the graphical representation of data. Three common types of visualizations are:

i. **Histograms:** Histograms are bar graphs that show the frequency distribution of a dataset (Fig. 4.4). They are particularly useful for showing the shape of the distribution, such as whether it is symmetrical or skewed.
ii. **Boxplots:** Boxplots are used to show the distribution of a dataset by depicting the five-number summary of the data: the minimum and maximum values, the median, the first and third quartiles, and outliers (Fig. 4.5). They are particularly useful for comparing the distribution of different datasets.
iii. **Scatterplots:** Scatterplots are used to show the relationship between two different variables (Fig. 4.6). They are particularly useful for identifying trends or patterns in the data. Each point in the scatterplot is an observation.

   Furthermore, a scatterplot can be used to illustrate three types of relationships: "negative correlation," "no correlation," and "positive correlation," each of which provides insights into the nature of the data's association, as shown in Fig. 4.7.

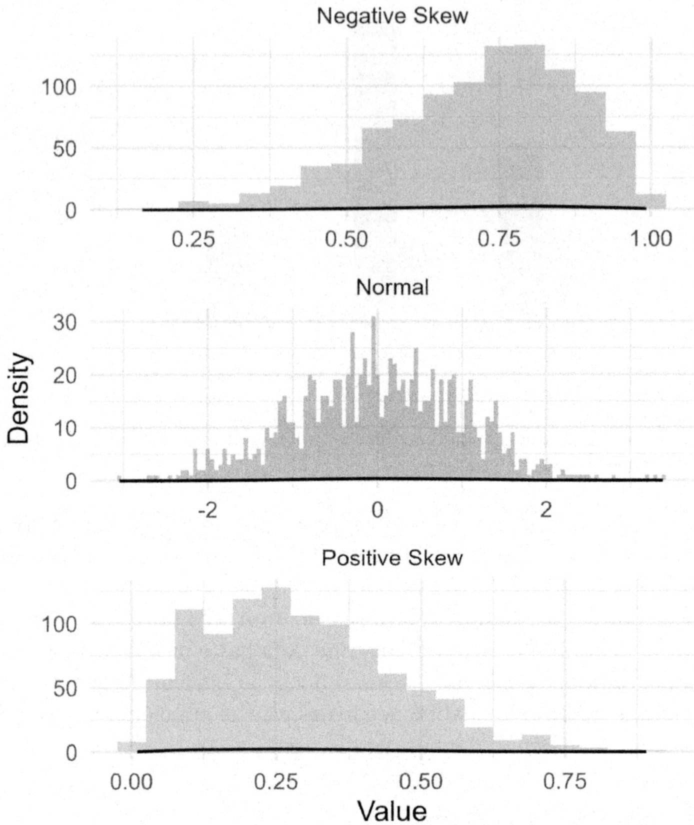

Fig. 4.3 Illustration of negative, normal, and positive skewness

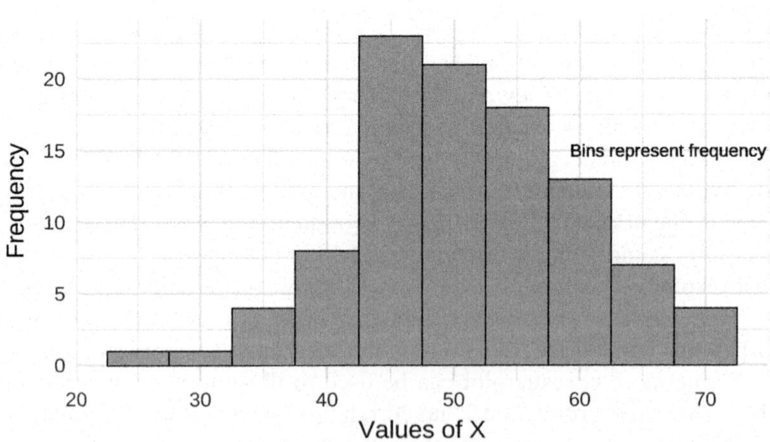

Fig. 4.4 Histograms

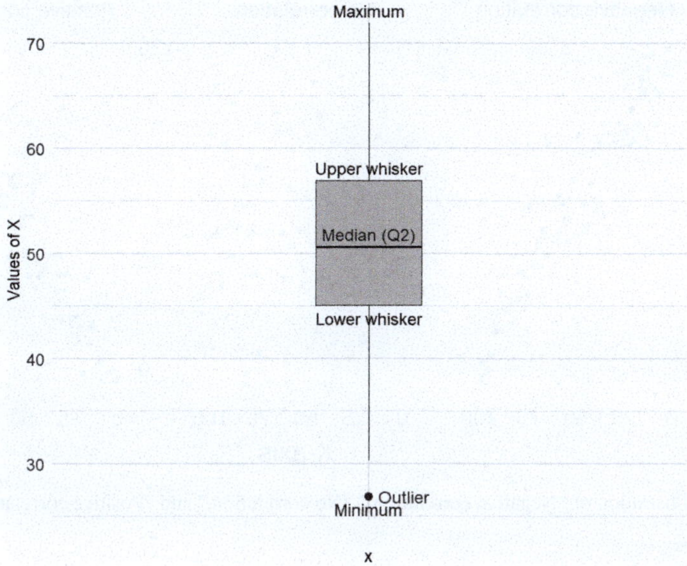

Fig. 4.5 Boxplot

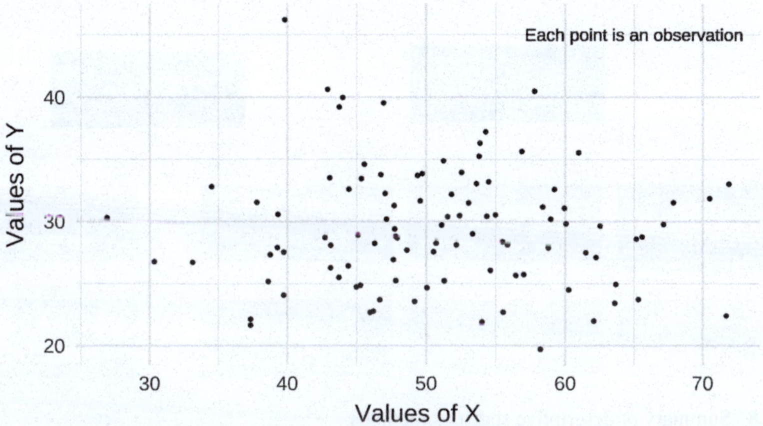

Fig. 4.6 Scatterplot

We can also categorize descriptive statistical methods based on data types. For continuous data, methods such as central tendency, dispersion, and distributional analysis are appropriate. For discrete data, frequency analysis is commonly used. Figure 4.8 provides a summary of this approach.

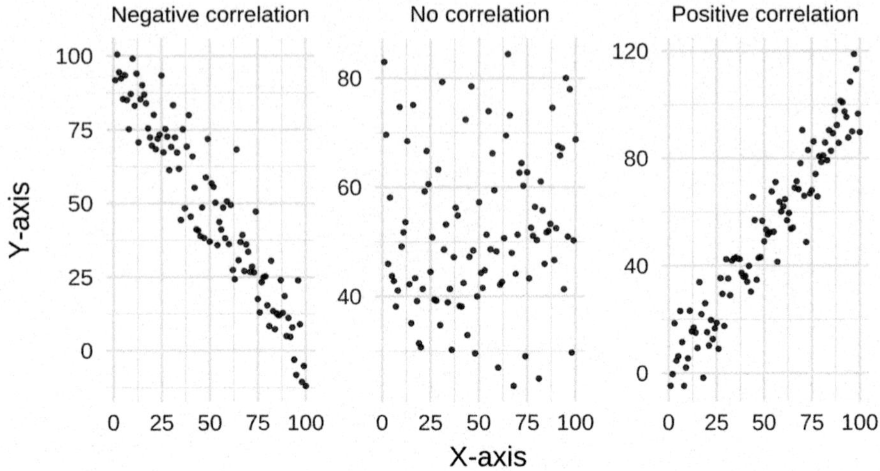

Fig. 4.7 Illustration of "Negative correlation," "No correlation," and "Positive correlation"

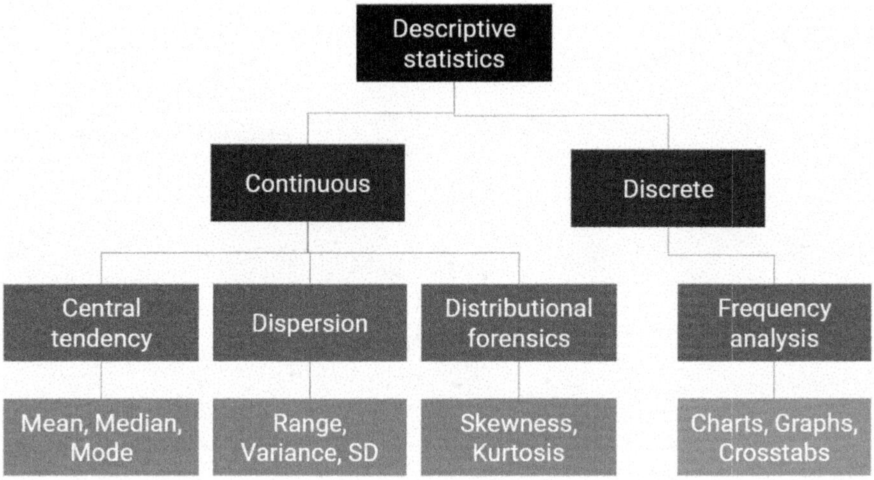

Fig. 4.8 Summary of descriptive statistics methods

Inferential Statistics

Inferential statistics allow researchers to make predictions or draw conclusions about a population based on a sample. This branch is essential for hypothesis testing, estimating population parameters, and making predictions.

The goal is to test hypotheses, estimate parameters, or make predictions about a population. For the datasets, inferential statistics are typically based on a sample of data that is used to make inferences about a larger population.

The measures used include hypothesis tests, confidence intervals, correlation coefficients, and regression analysis. These methods assume that the sample is representative of the population and that the data is independent and identically distributed. However, there are limitations, as these methods can be affected by sampling error or bias and may not generalize to the entire population. Common use cases are in research and scientific studies, where they are applied to test hypotheses and make predictions about populations.

The following are common methods used in inferential statistics:

- **Probability Distributions**

  Understanding probability distributions is fundamental in inferential statistics, as they describe how data points are expected to be distributed within a population.

  i. The **Normal Distribution**, also called the **Gaussian distribution**, is a continuous probability distribution that takes the shape of a symmetrical bell curve (Fig. 4.9). It is widely used to represent data that naturally follows a pattern of variation around a central value, like human heights, body weights, or IQ scores. The distribution is characterized by two main parameters: the **mean**, which represents the average value, and the **standard deviation**, which measures how spread out the values are around the mean. In many cases, data that is normally distributed tends to cluster near the center, with fewer values further from the center, creating the bell shape.

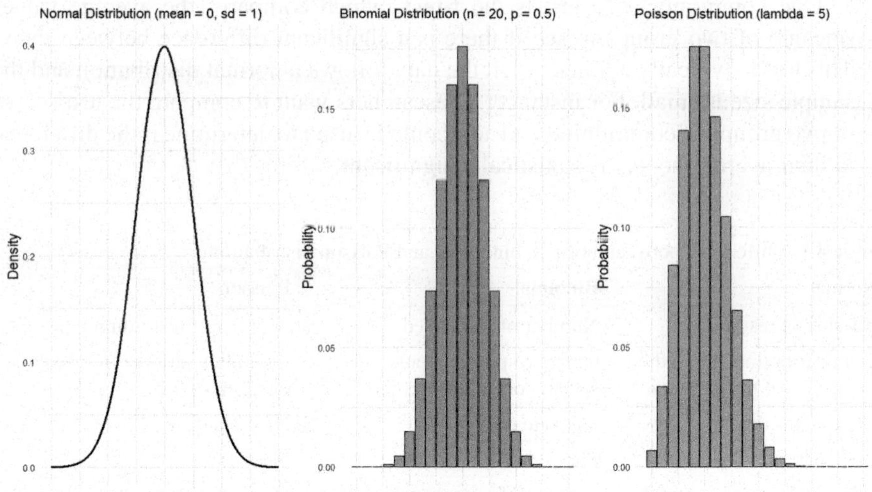

Fig. 4.9 Illustration of the normal distribution, binomial distribution, and Poisson distribution

ii. The **Binomial Distribution** is a discrete probability distribution that describes the number of successes in a fixed number of independent trials, where each trial has two possible outcomes: success or failure. It is often used in situations where we want to predict the probability of a certain number of successes out of a set number of trials, such as flipping a coin or testing whether a drug is effective. The binomial distribution is defined by two parameters: the number of trials (**n**) and the probability of success on each trial (**p**).

iii. The **Poisson Distribution** is another discrete probability distribution, but it describes the probability of a given number of events happening in a fixed period or space, where the events occur independently and at a constant average rate. For example, it might be used to model the number of phone calls received by a call center in an hour or the number of accidents at a particular intersection in a day. The Poisson distribution is determined by a single parameter: the average number of events per unit of time or space (often denoted as λ, lambda). Table 4.1 summarizes the difference between normal, binomial, and Poisson distribution.

- **Hypothesis Testing**

 Hypothesis testing is a fundamental component of inferential statistics, which helps us assess whether there is enough evidence to support a particular claim or hypothesis about a population. In other words, it helps determine if an observed effect or relationship is likely to be real or just due to random chance. Several statistical tests are commonly used for hypothesis testing, each serving a specific purpose depending on the type of data and research question.

 One commonly used test is the **t-test**, which compares the average values (means) of two groups to see if there is a significant difference between them. This test is typically applied when the data follows a normal distribution and the sample size is small. For instance, if researchers want to compare the test scores of two groups of communities, a t-test could be used to determine if the difference in their average scores is statistically significant.

Table 4.1 Difference between normal, binomial, and Poisson distribution

Normal	Binomial	Poisson
Number of test infinite	Number of tests fixed	Number of test infinite
The distribution is based on the values of the datasets	Only two possible outcomes: success or failure	Unlimited number of possible outcomes
Continuous data	Discrete data	Discrete data
Bell-shaped	Skewed	Skewed
Natural phenomena, heights, weights, errors	Number of successes in a fixed number of trials (coin toss)	Rare events, count data (printing mistakes, script typo)

Another important test is analysis of variance (**ANOVA**), which is used when comparing the means of three or more groups to see if any of them are significantly different from one another. Like the t-test, ANOVA assumes that the data is normally distributed, but it is especially useful when dealing with large sample sizes. For example, an ANOVA could be used to compare the average expenditure of households across different regions to see if the differences in their expenditure are statistically significant.

The **Chi-square test** is used for categorical data to determine if there is a significant relationship between two variables. This test compares the observed frequencies of data points in categories with what would be expected if there was no relationship between the variables. A typical example might involve testing whether there is a significant association between gender and preference for a certain type of sport.

These tests are crucial in research because they help us identify whether the differences observed between groups are due to actual effects or simply due to random chance. By using these statistical methods, researchers can make evidence-based decisions rather than relying on subjective judgment or anecdotal information. Table 4.2 provides a summary of these tests and their differences.

*In data science, we use **statistics** to understand and make sense of numbers. there are two main types: **descriptive statistics** and **inferential statistics**.*

1. ***Descriptive Statistics**: This helps us summarize and describe important details about data. For example, imagine you want to know how tall your classmates are. You can measure their heights and then use **descriptive statistics** to find:*

   - ***Average Height**: The middle point of all the heights.*
   - ***Biggest Height**: The tallest person in the class.*
   - ***Smallest Height**: The shortest person in the class.*

   This helps us see what the data looks like, just like looking at a picture to understand it better
2. ***Inferential Statistics**. This helps us make guesses or predictions about a bigger group using a smaller group of data. For example, imagine you ask*

Table 4.2 Difference between t-test, ANOVA, and Chi-square

Test	Number of groups compared	Type of data	Sample size	Type of analysis
T-test	2	Interval/ratio/continuous	Small	Means
ANOVA	3 or more	Interval/ratio/continuous	Large	Means
Chi-square	2	Nominal/categorical	Any	Association

just a few people in your school how much they like a new snack, and based on their answers, you guess how much everyone in the whole school might like it. ***Inferential statistics*** *helps you make these kinds of guesses with numbers.*

Why Do We Need Both?

- ***Descriptive statistics*** *help us understand the data we already have, like how tall people in your class are.*
- ***Inferential statistics*** *help us make predictions about a larger group, like how all students on the campus might feel about the food in the cafeteria.*

4.3 Hypothesis in Statistics

In social studies, a hypothesis is a tentative explanation or prediction about a phenomenon or relationship between two or more variables. It is an educated guess or an assumption that researchers make before conducting a study, which is then tested and either accepted or rejected based on the evidence gathered.

Examples of Hypotheses in Social Studies

- "Individuals who experience higher levels of stress will have a greater likelihood of developing depression than those who experience lower levels of stress."
- "Increased parental involvement in children's education leads to improved academic achievement."
- "Employees who receive feedback from their supervisors will have higher levels of job satisfaction and organizational commitment than those who do not receive feedback."

In each of these examples, the hypothesis provides a tentative explanation for the relationship between two or more variables. The researcher would then gather data to test the hypothesis and draw conclusions about whether the data supports or refutes the hypothesis.

In social studies, hypotheses provide a framework for research and help us focus on specific questions that we want to answer. They guide our research by providing a clear direction and a set of expectations for what we might find. Hypotheses also allow us to test our assumptions and determine whether our findings support or refute our initial ideas.

Always remember that assumptions need to be supported by references or literature. In academia, we often use the idiom "standing on the shoulders of giants," which means that every theoretical or conceptual framework—sometimes also called the research mechanism—must be grounded in established scientific theories.

Hypotheses are used in social studies in various ways, including:

- **As Part of the Research Design:** Hypotheses can be used to guide the selection of research methods, the design of experiments, and the sampling of participants.
- **As a Basis for Data Analysis:** Hypotheses can be used to guide the analysis of data collected from surveys, experiments, or observational studies.
- **To Conclude:** Hypotheses can be used to draw conclusions about the relationships between variables and to determine whether there is a significant difference between groups.

In hypothesis testing, we aim to conclude a population parameter based on a sample statistic. However, there are various types of errors that can occur in the process.

The two types of errors that can occur in hypothesis testing. A **Type I Error** happens when we mistakenly reject the null hypothesis, even though it is true. Essentially, we incorrectly conclude that there is a significant difference or effect when, in fact, there isn't one. This type of error is commonly referred to as a "false positive." The likelihood of making a Type I error is represented by the symbol alpha (α), and researchers often set this value at 0.05 or 0.01, meaning that there is a 5% or 1% chance, respectively, of making this mistake in a statistical test.

On the other hand, a **Type II Error** occurs when we fail to reject the null hypothesis, even though it is false. In this case, we overlook a real significant difference or effect that actually exists. This is known as a "false negative." The probability of making a Type II error is represented by the symbol beta (β). Unlike Type I error, the probability of a Type II error depends on various factors, including the sample size, the effect size, and the chosen significance level. A comparison of these errors can be found in Table 4.3, which provides a clearer understanding of how they differ. While Fig. 4.10 illustrates these errors, so we can have a better understanding of them.

Each type of error has different implications: a Type 1 error can cause temporary stress or confusion, often leading to unnecessary medical consultations. However, these are generally short-term effects that can be clarified with additional testing.

Table 4.3 Difference between Type I and II errors

Null hypothesis is	True	False
Rejected	Type I error False positive Probability $= \alpha$	Correct decision True positive Probability $= 1 - \beta$
Accepted	Correct decision True negative Probability $= 1 - \alpha$	Type II error False negative Probability $= \beta$

Fig. 4.10 Illustration of Type I and II errors

On the other hand, a Type 2 error, particularly in a pregnancy context, could delay essential prenatal care, potentially affecting the health of both mother and baby.

In business, Type 2 errors often have more significant consequences than Type 1 errors, as they can result in missed risks, such as fraud or market shifts, that could damage a company's finances and reputation. Similarly, failing to detect shifts in customer needs—a Type 2 error in customer retention—can reduce loyalty and market share. Thus, effective risk management prioritizes minimizing Type 2 errors to address potential threats proactively before they escalate into critical issues.

Type I and Type II errors are critical concepts in hypothesis testing, especially in social studies where decisions can significantly impact societies and economies. These errors occur when researchers draw incorrect conclusions from their data, either by rejecting a true null hypothesis (Type I error) or failing to reject a false null hypothesis (Type II error). Practical examples from fields like economics, public policy, and market research highlight the real-world implications of these errors. A Type I error, also known as a false positive, occurs when we conclude there is an effect or relationship when none exists. For instance, imagine a government study that concludes that a new tax policy significantly reduces income inequality. If this result is incorrect, the government may implement the policy nationwide, redirecting substantial resources to an ineffective intervention. Similarly, in public health policy, a campaign might be deemed effective in reducing smoking rates due to a Type I error, leading policymakers to invest heavily in an initiative that fails to yield real benefits. In market research, a company might mistakenly believe a new product feature enhances customer satisfaction. Acting on this false conclusion, the company could spend millions promoting the feature, only to discover later that it provides no value to consumers.

On the other hand, a Type II error, or a false negative, occurs when we fail to detect an effect or relationship that actually exists. In economic policy, for example, a central bank may fail to recognize a significant link between interest rates and inflation due to a Type II error. This oversight could delay necessary interventions, exacerbating an economic crisis. In public policy, a social program aimed at reducing youth unemployment might be prematurely abandoned if its effectiveness is underestimated. This not only deprives young people of potential opportunities but also prevents the program from being scaled up to help more communities. Similarly, in market research, a company may conclude that a new marketing strategy has no impact on sales when, in fact, it does. Missing this insight could result in a lost competitive edge, allowing rivals to capitalize on similar strategies.

Balancing Type I and Type II errors is a complex but essential task in social research. The consequences of these errors differ depending on the context. Type I errors often lead to wasted resources on ineffective policies or strategies, while Type II errors can result in missed opportunities to address critical societal challenges or market demands. For example, in evaluating a poverty alleviation program, a Type I error might lead policymakers to continue investing in a program that has no real effect, draining funds that could be better used elsewhere. Conversely, a Type II error might cause them to abandon a program that could have significantly reduced poverty, leaving vulnerable populations without support.

Minimizing these errors requires thoughtful study design and robust methodologies. Adjusting the significance level, for instance, can help manage Type I errors, although this often increases the risk of Type II errors. Increasing sample sizes can improve the reliability of results, reducing the likelihood of both error types. Employing advanced statistical methods, such as econometric modeling or machine learning, can also help researchers uncover subtle patterns and relationships, providing more accurate insights.

4.4 Population Versus Sample

Population refers to the entire group of individuals or objects that interest the researcher or analyst. It is the complete set of all possible observations that meet the criteria for inclusion in the study. For example, if a researcher is interested in studying the average height of all the students in a particular school, then the population would be all the students in that school.

While a sample is a subset of the population. It is a smaller group of individuals or objects selected from the population. Samples are used in statistical analysis when it is not feasible to study the entire population due to practical or financial limitations. For example, if a researcher wants to study the average height of all the students in a school, they might randomly select a sample of students from the school to participate in the study. Figure 4.11 illustrates the concept of population and sample.

Calculating Sample Size

The sample size required for a study depends on several factors, such as the size of the population, the confidence level, the margin of error (also called the confidence interval), and the expected proportion or variability within the population. There are two methods to calculate the sample size, and it is explained as follows:

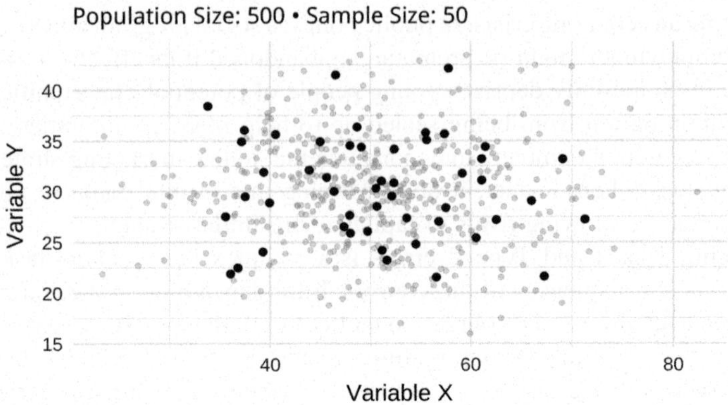

Fig. 4.11 Illustration of population and sample

1. If the Population Size is Known

When the population size N is known, the sample size n can be calculated using the following formula:

$$n = \frac{N \cdot Z^2 \cdot p(1-p)}{(N-1) \cdot E^2 + Z^2 \cdot p \cdot (1-p)}$$

where:

- n: Sample size.
- N: Total population size.
- Z: Z-score, which corresponds to the desired confidence level (e.g., $Z = 1.96$ for 95% confidence).
- p: Estimated proportion of the population (e.g., 0.5 if unknown for maximum variability).
- E: Margin of error (e.g., $\pm$ 5%, or 0.05).

This formula adjusts the sample size based on the size of the population, ensuring that the sample is proportionate to the population and accounts for finite population corrections (FPC). The formula is widely used in statistical sampling and originates from principles established in survey methodology. While it doesn't have a single attributable source, it is commonly found in research methodology textbooks and guidelines for sample size determination.

While Yamane (1967) introduced a simplified formula for determining sample size, assuming a 95% confidence level and maximum variability ($p = 0.5$):

$$n = \frac{N}{1 + Ne^2}$$

where

- n Sample size.
- N Total population size.
- e: Margin of error (e.g., 0.05 for $\pm$ 5%).
- If the Population Size Is Unknown or Very Large

Cochran (1977) developed a widely used formula. When the population size N is unknown or considered infinite (e.g., very large populations), the simplified formula for sample size is:

$$n = \frac{Z^2 \cdot p \cdot (1 - p)}{E^2}$$

where:

- n: Sample size.
- Z: Z-score, as explained above.
- p: Estimated proportion of the population.
- E: Margin of error.

This formula assumes that the population size is large enough that the finite population correction is unnecessary. It's commonly used in large-scale studies or when the population size is difficult to determine.

Steps to Calculate Sample Size:

1. **Decide on the Confidence Level**:
   - Common values are 90, 95, or 99%.
   - For 90% confidence, $Z = 1.645$.
   - For 95% confidence, $Z = 1.960$.
   - For 99% confidence, $Z = 2.576$.
2. **Estimate the Expected Proportion** p:
   - Use 0.5 if you don't have prior knowledge (maximum variability assumption).
3. **Set Your Margin of Error** E:
   - Typically 5% (0.05) for surveys or studies.
4. **Insert Values into the Formula**:

   For known N, use the first formula.
   For unknown N, use the second formula.

Example of Calculation:

Suppose you want to calculate a sample size with:

- Confidence level: 99% ($Z = 2.58$).
- The margin of error: 5% ($E = 0.05$).
- Expected proportion: 50% ($p = 0.5$).

For Known Population:

If the population $N = 10{,}000$:

$$n = \frac{10,000 * 2.58^2 * 0.5 * (1 - 0.5)}{(10,000 - 1) * 0.05^2 + 2.58^2 * 0.5 * (1 - 0.5)} = \frac{16641}{25 + 0.96} = 641.025$$

So, $n \approx 641$.

For Unknown Population:

$$n = \frac{2.58^2 * 0.5 * (1 - 0.5)}{0.05^2} = \frac{6.6564 * 0.25}{0.0025} = 665.64$$

So, $n \approx 666$.

Confidence Intervals and Errors

Confidence intervals are a key concept in statistics that helps us estimate the range of values where we believe a population parameter, like the average or proportion, which is likely to fall. This estimate is based on data collected from a sample and is linked to a certain level of confidence, which indicates how sure we are about the estimate. For instance, **a 95% confidence interval** is commonly used in research. This means that if we were to repeat the process of taking samples 100 times, about 95 of those intervals would contain the true value of the parameter, assuming that the sampling process is not biased. In simpler terms, it gives us an idea of how precise our estimate is. Figure 4.12 illustrates the confidence interval and error where the confidence interval is shown in red and the standard error is shown in green.

For example, in a survey estimating the average income of a region's population, a 95% confidence interval of **($50,000 to $55,000)** suggests that researchers can

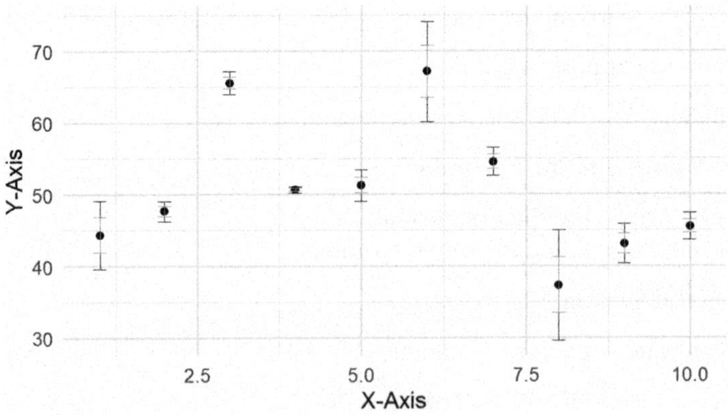

Fig. 4.12 Illustration of confidence interval and errors

be 95% confident that the true average income falls within this range. This confidence level does not imply certainty but reflects the **probability based on repeated sampling** under the same conditions.

Errors, particularly the **margin of error**, play a critical role in determining the width of the confidence interval. The margin of error depends on factors such as the **sample size**, **variability of the data (standard deviation)**, and the chosen confidence level. Larger sample sizes and lower variability generally result in narrower confidence intervals, improving precision.

For instance, in public opinion polls, confidence intervals account for sampling errors. A reported approval rating of **50 ± 3%** with a 95% confidence level means that the true approval rating is likely between 47 and 53%. However, increasing the confidence level to 99% would make the interval wider (e.g., 45–55%) because higher confidence requires more margin for uncertainty.

The trade-off between precision (narrow intervals) and confidence (wider intervals) is a key consideration in research. Confidence intervals should not be confused with **statistical errors** like Type I errors (false positives) or Type II errors (false negatives), which are related to hypothesis testing but can influence confidence interval interpretation indirectly.

In practice, confidence intervals are widely used across disciplines, such as:

- **Healthcare**: Estimating the effectiveness of a new drug where the confidence interval for recovery rates might be 75% to 85%.
- **Economics**: Forecasting GDP growth rates with an interval of 2.5–3.5%.
- **Environmental Studies**: Predicting annual rainfall based on climate models with intervals that reflect uncertainties.

4.5 Regression Analysis

Regression analysis is a statistical method used to explore how one or more independent variables are related to a dependent variable. In simple terms, it helps us understand how changes in one or more factors (the independent variables) can affect another factor (the dependent variable). This technique is often used to make predictions—for example, to estimate the value of the dependent variable based on known values of the independent variables.

There are different types of regression analysis, each suited for specific types of data or research questions. For example, linear regression is used when the relationship between variables is straight-line (linear), while logistic regression is used for binary outcomes, like yes/no answers. Multiple regression is used when there are several independent variables affecting the dependent variable.

The choice of which type of regression analysis to use depends on the nature of the data and the research objectives. Understanding the specific context of your study, such as whether your variables are continuous, categorical, or binary, will guide you in selecting the most appropriate regression model.

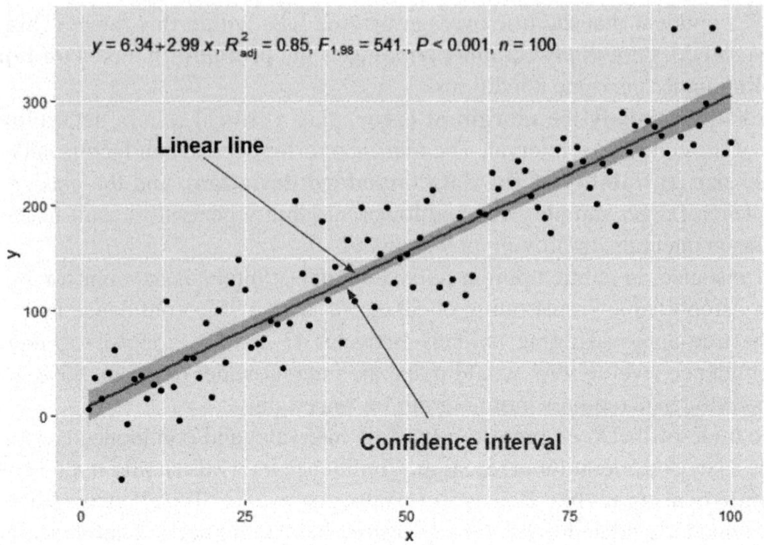

Fig. 4.13 Scatterplot of regression analysis

In regression analysis, we generate a scatterplot as shown in Fig. 4.13. It is a scatter plot with a linear regression line and confidence interval overlayed. Following is a breakdown of each component:

1. **Scatter Plot Points (Black Dots)**: Each dot represents an individual data point in the dataset, plotting the relationship between two variables (one on the x-axis and the other on the y-axis).
2. **Linear Regression Line (Blue Line)**: This line represents the best-fit linear relationship between the two variables. It shows how the dependent variable (*y*-axis) changes concerning the independent variable (*x*-axis). The equation of this line is given at the top of the plot:

$$y = 6.34 + 2.99x.$$

   This equation indicates that for each unit increase in x, the predicted y value increases by approximately 2.99 units. The intercept (6.34) is the expected y value when x is 0.
3. **Confidence Interval (Shaded Area)**: The shaded region around the regression line is the confidence interval, which provides a range in which we expect the true regression line to lie with a certain level of confidence (often 95%). Wider regions indicate more uncertainty.

4. **Statistical Information**:

- Radj2 = 0.85: This is the adjusted R-squared value, indicating that 85% of the variability in the dependent variable can be explained by the linear relationship with the independent variable.
- F1, 98 = 541: The F-statistic and associated degrees of freedom (1 and 98) are from an ANOVA test that assesses the overall significance of the model.
- $P < 0.001$: This is the p-value, indicating that the relationship is statistically significant, meaning that it's highly unlikely that this linear association is due to random chance.
- $n = 100n$: The sample size for this analysis indicates that there are 100 data points in total.

This plot shows a strong positive linear relationship between the two variables, supported by a high R-squared value and a significant p-value. The confidence interval indicates the precision of this estimate.

4.6 Parametric Versus Non-parametric

Parametric statistics assume that the data **follows a specific distribution**, typically the normal distribution and that the parameters of this distribution are either known or can be estimated. These methods are used in statistical tests such as t-tests, analysis of variance (ANOVA), and regression analysis. For these tests to be valid, certain assumptions must be met, including normality of the data (data points are symmetrically distributed around the mean) and homogeneity of variances (similar spread in the data across groups).

In contrast, **non-parametric statistics do not assume any specific distribution** of the data. These methods are useful when the data does not meet the assumptions of normality and homogeneity of variances, or when the underlying distribution is unknown. Non-parametric tests are often called "distribution-free" tests because they do not rely on these assumptions. Commonly used non-parametric tests include the Wilcoxon rank-sum test, Mann–Whitney U test, Kruskal–Wallis test, and Spearman's rank correlation coefficient. Although non-parametric tests are generally less powerful than parametric tests, they are more flexible and robust to violations of assumptions.

The choice between parametric and non-parametric methods depends on the type of data and whether the assumptions of normality and homogeneity of variances can be justified. When the assumptions of normality and equal variances are met, parametric methods are typically preferred for their greater statistical power. However, when these assumptions are violated or when there is limited knowledge about the distribution of the data, non-parametric methods are a more appropriate choice.

4.7 Advanced Statistics

Advanced statistics refers to the application of complex statistical methods and techniques to solve problems in various fields, such as science, engineering, business, medicine, and social studies. It involves the use of sophisticated mathematical models and algorithms to analyze and interpret data, make predictions, and test hypotheses.

Some examples of advanced statistical methods include structural equation modeling (SEM), time series analysis, factor analysis, cluster analysis, and item response theory (Table 4.4). These methods are used to gain deeper insights into the relationships between variables, identify patterns and trends in data, and make accurate predictions about future outcomes.

Advanced statistics is particularly important in fields where data is complex and high-dimensional, such as genomics, finance, and social network analysis. It can help researchers and practitioners make better decisions by providing them with more accurate and reliable information about the phenomena they are studying.

Easy to Digest Box

Imagine you have a big basket of fruits, and you want to learn about them. Descriptive statistics is like looking at the basket and counting: "There are 50 fruits—10 apples, 15 bananas, 20 oranges, and 5 mangoes." It helps you describe and organize what's in the basket.

Inferential statistics is like being a detective. If someone gave you a small sample of fruits from the basket, you could use that to guess what the rest of the basket might look like. It's about making smart predictions based on a small part.

In data science, we use these two ideas together: describing what we see and predicting what we don't. Computers help with big datasets, but it's just like learning about fruits in a basket!

Table 4.4 Description of advanced statistical methods

Method	Description
Factor analysis	A method for identifying underlying factors that explain the variance in a set of observed variables
Cluster analysis	A method for grouping similar cases or observations into clusters based on their similarity
Structural equation modeling (SEM)	A method for testing and estimating complex relationships between variables
Time series analysis	A method for analyzing data that is collected over time
Item response theory (IRT)	A method for modeling data that has a hierarchical structure, such as individuals nested within groups or regions

4.8 Summary of Key Points

- Descriptive statistics describe the characteristics of the population or sample, while inferential statistics make predictions and draw conclusions about the population based on data from a sample.
- Skewness measures the degree of asymmetry in a dataset, while kurtosis measures the degree of peakedness or flatness of a distribution.
- In social studies, a hypothesis is a tentative explanation or prediction about a phenomenon or relationship between two or more variables.
- Assumptions need to be supported by references/literature.
- Population refers to the entire group of individuals or objects of interest, while the sample is a subset of the population.
- A confidence interval is a range of values that is likely to contain the true population parameter with a certain degree of confidence.
- Regression analysis is a statistical technique used to examine the relationship between a dependent variable and one or more independent variables.
- Advanced statistics refers to the application of complex statistical methods and techniques to solve problems in various fields. It involves the use of sophisticated mathematical models and algorithms to analyze and interpret data, make predictions, and test hypotheses.
- Parametric tests assume that the data comes from a normal distribution, while non-parametric does not assume any specific distribution of the data.

4.9 Hands-on Experience

Working with RStudio

Run RStudio as Administrator.

To avoid any permission or access issues, it is recommended to always run RStudio as an administrator. The following explains how to proceed:

- **Windows**:
  1. Right-click on the RStudio icon.
  2. Select **More**.
  3. Click **Run as administrator**.
- **Mac:**
  1. Locate the RStudio application.
  2. Hold down the **Control** key on your keyboard and click on the app.
  3. From the context menu, select **Open** while still holding the **Control** key.
- If prompted, enter your administrator credentials.

Practice 4

Learning Objectives

Installing and Activating Required Packages

- Learn how to install and load necessary R packages like ggplot2, dplyr, and readr for data analysis.
- Understand package management in R for efficient workflow.

Importing and Cleaning Data

- Practice importing datasets into R using both manual and code-based methods.
- Perform data cleaning tasks such as renaming columns, updating values, and handling missing data using R functions and packages like countrycode.

Performing Statistical Calculations

- Calculate key descriptive statistics, including mean, median, mode, range, variance, and standard deviation.
- Interpret these statistics to understand the dataset.

Visualizing Data

- Create various histograms, density, and scatter plots to visualize data distributions and relationships.
- Use advanced visualization techniques like adding labels for extreme values with geom_text_repel.

Analyzing Data Distributions

- Understand and compute measures of skewness and kurtosis to analyze data distribution properties.
- Perform hypothesis testing (e.g., Jarque–Bera test) to evaluate normality.

Summarizing Data

- Explore methods to generate summary statistics, including basic summaries, custom summary tables, and formatted tables using skimr, flextable, and janitor.

Creating Bubble and Box Plots

- Visualize complex relationships between variables (e.g., GDP, working hours, population) using bubble plots.
- Summarize data distributions by group using box plots to identify trends and outliers.

Filtering and Grouping Data

- Group data by categories (e.g., continent) and extract subsets based on specific criteria (e.g., top/bottom countries by GDP or working hours).
- Combine and clean grouped datasets for further analysis.

Interpreting Data Visualizations and Outputs

- Extract meaningful insights from visualizations (e.g., trends, outliers, and relationships among variables).
- Relate statistical results and visual outputs to socio-economic phenomena, such as working hours and GDP.

Applying Inferential Statistics

- Formulate and test hypotheses about data properties (e.g., normality assumptions).
- Interpret *p*-values and test results to conclude population-level characteristics.

Create a New R Script

When starting a new project, always check and set your working directory. This ensures your data, and outputs are saved in the correct location. Use the following code to set your working directory:

```
# Check your current working directory
getwd()

# Set your working directory (replace the path with
your folder location)
setwd("/Your/path/annual-working-hours-vs-gdp-per-
capita-pwt")
```

Activate Required Packages.

Ensure that all required packages are installed and loaded into your R environment. If a package is not installed yet, you can install it using the following code:

```
# Install required packages
install.packages(c("ggplot2", "dplyr", "readr"))
```

After installation, load the packages:

```
# Load required packages
library(ggplot2)
library(dplyr)
library(readr)
Import Dataset
```

For this exercise, use the dataset annual-working-hours-vs-gdp-per-capita-pwt.csv from the previous chapter. You can import it manually or using the code:

- **Manual Import:**

  1. Go to File > Import Dataset > From Text (readr).

- Follow the prompts to load your dataset.
- Code to Check Working Directory and Import:

```
# Import dataset
AWH< - read.csv("annual-working-hours-vs-gdp-per
-capita-pwt.csv")
```

Data Cleaning

After importing the dataset, clean and preprocess it:

1. **Rename Columns:** Adjust column names to be more descriptive.
2. **Update Column "Continent":** Update the continent based on countries' name.
3. **Remove NA Values:** Filter out missing values:

```
# Rename only the 1st, 4th to 7th column names
colnames(AWH)[c(1,4,5,6,7)]<- c("Country", "WH",
"GDP", "POP", "Continent")

# Update column "Continent" since it is empty
install.packages("countrycode")
library(countrycode)

# Use countrycode to map countries to continents
AWH$Continent<- countrycode(AWH$Country,
"country.name", "continent")
```

```
# View the updated dataframe
View(AWH)

# Remove NA values
AWH<- na.omit(AWH)
```

Perform Statistical Calculations

Now, calculate essential statistical measures for analysis:

1. Mean, Median, and Mode:

```
# Calculate mean, median, and mode
mean_GDP<- mean(AWH$GDP)
median_GDP<- median(AWH$GDP)
mode_GDP<- names(table(AWH$GDP))
  [which.max(table(AWH$GDP))]
```

2. Range, Variance, and Standard Deviation

```
# Calculate range, variance, and standard deviation
range_GDP<- range(AWH$GDP)
variance_GDP<- var(AWH$GDP)
sd_GDP<- sd(AWH$GDP)

# Print the result into the console
mean_GDP
median_GDP
mode_GDP
range_GDP
variance_GDP
sd_GDP.
```

Output:

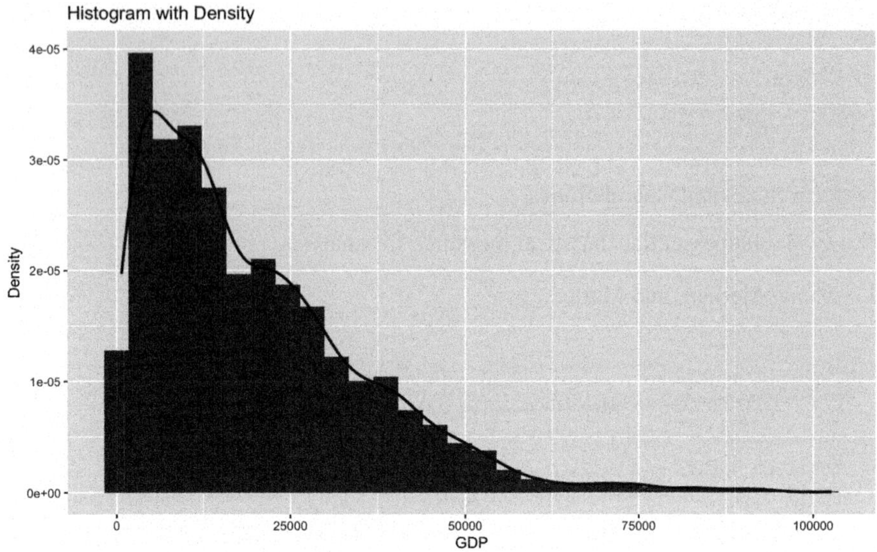

3. Draw Histogram with Density:

```
# Draw histogram
ggplot(AWH, aes(x=GDP))+
  geom_histogram(aes(y=..density..), bins=30,
fill="blue", alpha=0.7)+
  geom_density(color="red", size=1)+
  labs(title="Histogram with Density", x="GDP",
y="Density")
```

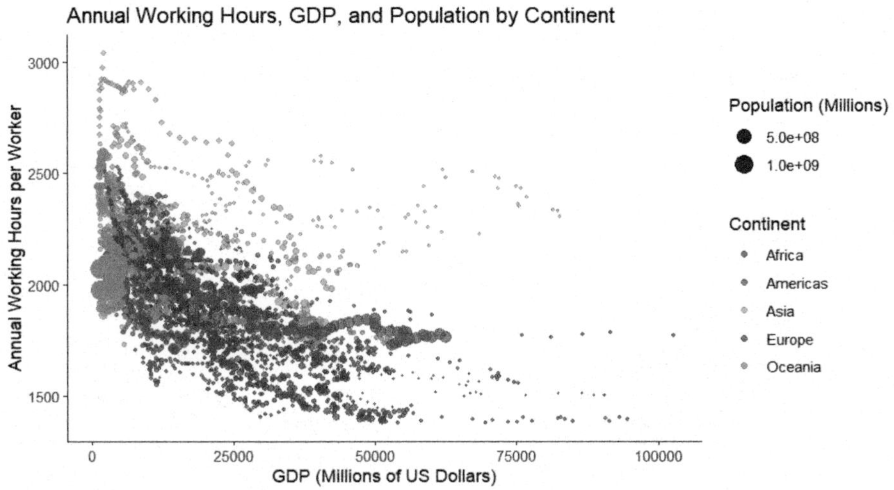

4. Calculate Skewness and Kurtosis:

```
# Install and load e1071 package for skewness and
kurtosis
install.packages("e1071")
library(e1071)
# Calculate skewness and kurtosis
skewness_GDP<- skewness(AWH$GDP)
kurtosis_GDP<- kurtosis(AWH$GDP)

# Print the result into the console
skewness_GDP
kurtosis_GDP
```

Output:

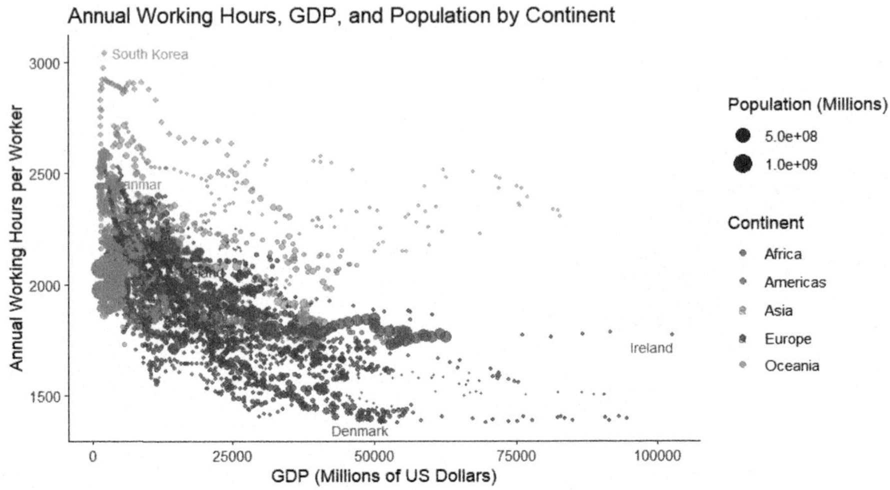

Interpretation

- **Positive Skewness:** Indicates a right-skewed distribution (longer tail on the right).
- **Positive Kurtosis:** Means a more peaked distribution, while negative kurtosis means a flatter one. A kurtosis greater than + 2 suggests a peaked distribution, while less than -2 indicates a too-flat one. When skewness and kurtosis are close to zero, it's considered a normal distribution.

Different Methods to Create Descriptive Summary Statistics

1. Basic Summary:

```
# Example 1: Basic summary
summary(AWH)
```

Output:

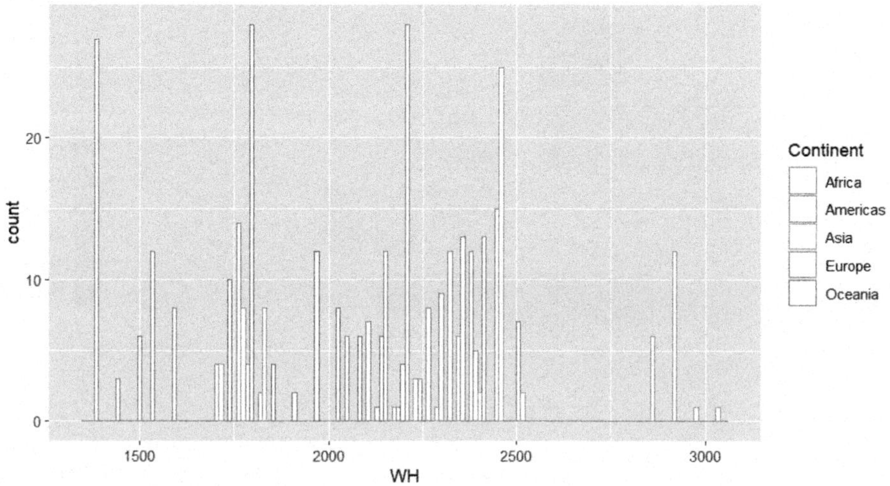

2. Custom Summary Table:

```
# Example 2: Create custom summary table
summary_stats<- data.frame(
  Mean=sapply(AWH[, c("WH", "GDP", "POP")], mean),
  Median=sapply(AWH[, c("WH", "GDP", "POP")],
median),
  SD=sapply(AWH[, c("WH", "GDP", "POP")], sd),
  Min=sapply(AWH[, c("WH", "GDP", "POP")], min),
  Max=sapply(AWH[, c("WH", "GDP", "POP")], max)
)
# Print the summary table
print(summary_stats)
```

Output:

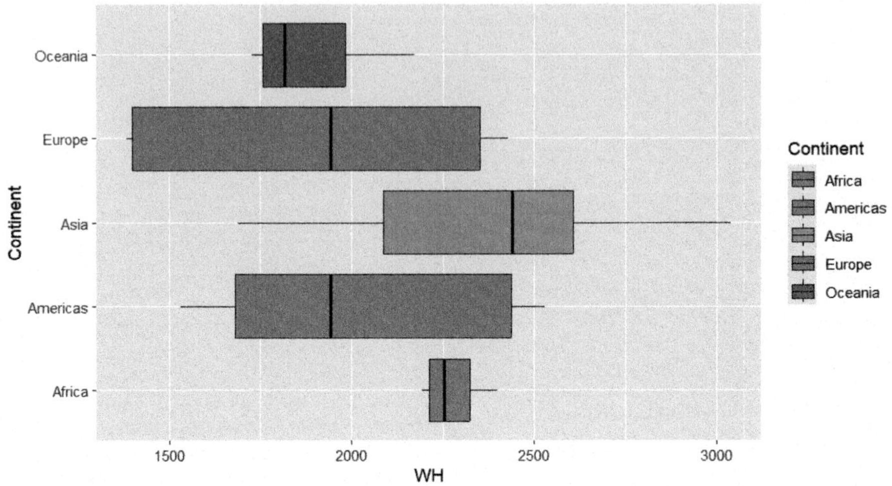

3. Using skimr Package:

```
# Example 3: Using skimr
install.packages("skimr")
library(skimr)
skim(AWH)
```

Output:

```
> skim(AWH)
— Data Summary ————————————————————————
                           Values
Name                       AWH
Number of rows             3457
Number of columns          7
_______________________
Column type frequency:
  character                3
  numeric                  4
________________________
Group variables            None

— Variable type: character ————————————————————————————————————————
  skim_variable n_missing complete_rate min max empty n_unique whitespace
1 Country               0             1   4  19     0       69          0
2 Code                  0             1   3   3     0       69          0
3 Continent             0             1   4   8     0        5          0

— Variable type: numeric ——————————————————————————————————————————
  skim_variable n_missing complete_rate      mean          sd     p0      p25       p50
1 Year                  0             1     1991.        18.9   1950     1976      1993
2 WH                    0             1     1984.        282.   1381.    1787.     1970.
3 GDP                   0             1    19648.      15796.    715.    7400.    15433.
4 POP                   0             1 67881408. 184814265. 189043  5917969  15572194
        p75         p100 hist
1      2006         2019 ▂▃▅▇▇
2     2167.        3040. ▂▇▅▂▁
3    28073.      102622. ▇▂▁▁▁
4 55594838   1423520354  ▇
```

4. Using flextable and janitor:

```
# Example 4: Pretty tables with flextable and
janitor
install.packages(c("flextable", "janitor"))
library(flextable)
library(janitor)

AWH %>%
  tabyl(Continent, Year) %>%
  adorn_totals(where="col") %>%
  adorn_percentages(denominator="col") %>%
  adorn_pct_formatting() %>%
  adorn_ns(position="front") %>%
  flextable::flextable() %>%
  flextable::autofit().
```

Output:

Continent	1950	1951	1952	1953	1954	1955	1956	1957	1958	1959	1960
Africa	0 (0.0%)	0 (0.0%)	0 (0.0%)	0 (0.0%)	0 (0.0%)	0 (0.0%)	0 (0.0%)	0 (0.0%)	0 (0.0%)	0 (0.0%)	0 (0.0%)
Americas	7 (29.2%)	8 (29.6%)	8 (29.6%)	8 (28.6%)	8 (28.6%)	8 (28.6%)	8 (28.6%)	8 (28.6%)	8 (28.6%)	8 (28.6%)	8 (26.7%)
Asia	1 (4.2%)	2 (7.4%)	2 (7.4%)	3 (10.7%)	3 (10.7%)	3 (10.7%)	3 (10.7%)	3 (10.7%)	3 (10.7%)	3 (10.7%)	5 (16.7%)
Europe	15 (62.5%)	16 (59.3%)	16 (59.3%)	16 (57.1%)	16 (57.1%)	16 (57.1%)	16 (57.1%)	16 (57.1%)	16 (57.1%)	16 (57.1%)	16 (53.3%)
Oceania	1 (4.2%)	1 (3.7%)	1 (3.7%)	1 (3.6%)	1 (3.6%)	1 (3.6%)	1 (3.6%)	1 (3.6%)	1 (3.6%)	1 (3.6%)	1 (3.3%)

You can click on "Zoom" icon to check all the data.

Inferential Statistics

Inferential statistics allow us to make conclusions about a population based on data from a sample. In this case, we are testing whether the dataset's properties (skewness and kurtosis) align with a normal distribution.

- **Null Hypothesis (H_0):** The dataset has skewness and kurtosis that match a normal distribution.
- **Alternative Hypothesis (H_1):** The dataset has skewness and kurtosis that do not match a normal distribution.

To evaluate this, we calculate the *p*-value for the test. We reject the null hypothesis if the p-value is less than the significance level ($\alpha = 0.05$).

```
# Install the package
install.packages("tseries")

# Load required library
library(tseries)

# Test the hypotheses
jarque.bera.test(AWH$WH)
```

Output:

```
> jarque.bera.test(AWH$WH)

        Jarque Bera Test

data:  AWH$WH
X-squared = 59.162, df = 2, p-value = 1.422e-13
```

In this case, since the p-value is **less than 0.05**, we can reject the null hypothesis. This means that there is enough evidence to conclude that the dataset has skewness and kurtosis that are different from a normal distribution. In simpler terms, the test results do not suggest that the dataset is consistent with a normal distribution.

Bubble Plot Analysis

We are now visualizing relationships within the dataset using bubble plots. The following questions will guide our interpretation:

1. **Which countries work longer or shorter hours?**
2. **Which countries have higher or lower GDP?**
3. **How significant are these trends?**
4. **Are there any outlier countries?**

We create a bubble plot to explore the relationship between GDP, working hours (WH), population (POP), and continent.

```
# Create the bubble plot
ggplot(AWH, aes(x=GDP, y=WH, size=POP,
color=Continent))+
  geom_point(alpha=0.7)+
  scale_color_manual(values=c("#E41A1C", "#377EB8",
"#4DAF4A", "#984EA3", "#FF7F00", "#FFFF33",
"#A65628", "#F781BF"))+
  scale_size(range=c(0.5, 6))+
  labs(title="Annual Working Hours, GDP, and
Population by Continent",
      x="GDP (Millions of US Dollars)",
      y="Annual Working Hours per Worker",
      size="Population (Millions)",
      color="Continent")+
 theme_classic()
```

Output:

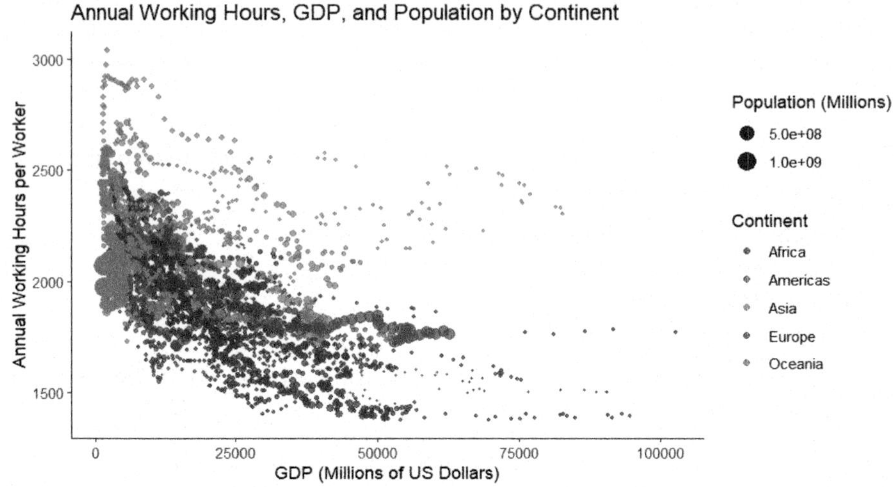

However, this plot does not visualize the countries' names with extreme values (outliers). To highlight countries with extreme values in your plot, you can use the geom_text_repel function from the ggrepel package, which avoids text overlap. Here's the updated code:

```
library(ggplot2).
library(ggrepel).

# Define the conditions for extreme values.
extreme_values<- AWH %>%
  filter(
WH==max(WH) | WH==min(WH) |
      GDP==max(GDP) | GDP==min(GDP) |
      POP==max(POP) | POP==min(POP).
  )

# Updated plot with country labels for extreme
values.
ggplot(AWH, aes(x=GDP, y=WH, size=POP,
color=Continent))+
  geom_point(alpha=0.7)+
  geom_text_repel(data=extreme_values,
aes(label=Country), size=3)+
```

```
  scale_color_manual(values=c("#E41A1C", "#377EB8",
"#4DAF4A", "#984EA3", "#FF7F00", "#FFFF33",
"#A65628", "#F781BF"))+
  scale_size(range=c(0.5, 6))+
  labs(
    title="Annual Working Hours, GDP, and
Population by Continent",
    x="GDP (Millions of US Dollars)",
    y="Annual Working Hours per Worker",
    size="Population (Millions)",
    color="Continent".
  )+
  theme_classic().
```

Output:

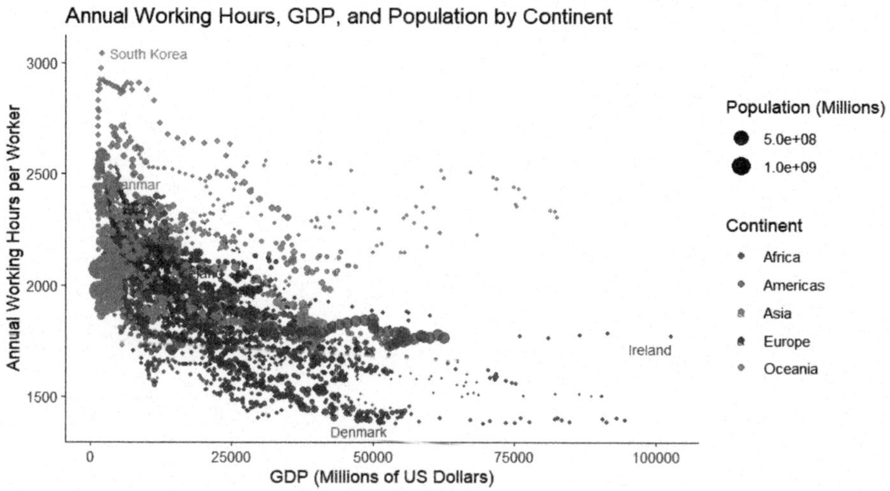

What Does the Code Do?

- **Load Libraries**: It loads the ggplot2 and ggrepel libraries for data visualization and creating readable labels.
- **Identify Extreme Values**: It creates a subset of data (extreme_values) from the AWH dataset where the values for Annual Working Hours (WH), Gross Domestic Product (GDP), or Population (POP) are at their maximum or minimum.
- **Create Scatter Plot**: It creates a scatter plot with:

  X-axis: GDP.
  Y-axis: Annual Working Hours (WH).
  Size of Points: Population (POP).
  Color of Points: Continent.

- **Add Labels for Extreme Values**: It uses geom_text_repel to add country labels for the extreme values identified earlier, ensuring that they do not overlap.
- **Customize Plot Appearance**:

  Custom color palette for continents.
  Size scaling for population points.
  Title and axis labels.
  A classic theme for a clean plot.

Filtering and Grouping Data

We analyze the dataset by grouping it by continent and selecting countries based on their GDP and working hours.

```
# Group the data by continent and select the top 20
countries by GDP.
big_gdp<- AWH %>%
#  filter(Year==2019) %>%
  group_by(Continent) %>%
  arrange(desc(GDP)) %>%
  slice_head(n=20)

# Group the data by continent and select the bottom
20 countries by GDP.
low_gdp<- AWH %>%
#  filter(Year==2019) %>%
  group_by(Continent) %>%
  arrange(GDP) %>%
  slice_head(n=20).

# Group the data by continent and select the top 20
countries by working hours
long_working_hours<- AWH %>%
#  filter(Year==2019) %>%
  group_by(Continent) %>%
  arrange(desc(WH)) %>%
  slice_head(n=20)

# Group the data by continent and select the bottom
20 countries by working hours.
short_working_hours<- AWH %>%
#  filter(Year==2019) %>%
  group_by(Continent) %>%
  arrange(WH) %>%
```

```
  slice_head(n=20)

# Combine the selected data into a single data
frame
selected_data<- bind_rows(big_gdp, low_gdp, long_
working_hours, short_working_hours)
selected_data<- na.omit(selected_data)
# Remove duplicate rows
#selected_data<- selected_data[!duplicated(selected_
data),]
```

Histogram

A histogram helps us visualize the distribution of working hours across continents.

```
# Create histogram.
ggplot(selected_data, aes(x=WH, color=Continent))+
  geom_histogram(fill="white", position="dodge").
```

Output:

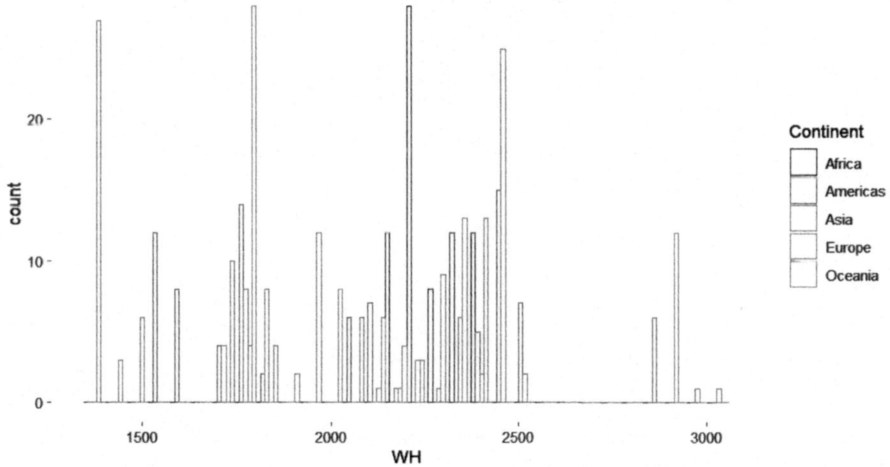

Boxplot

A boxplot summarizes the distribution of working hours for each continent, highlighting the median, quartiles, and potential outliers.

```
# Create boxplot.
ggplot(selected_data, aes(x=Continent, y=WH,
fill=Continent))+
  geom_boxplot()+
  coord_flip().
```

Output:

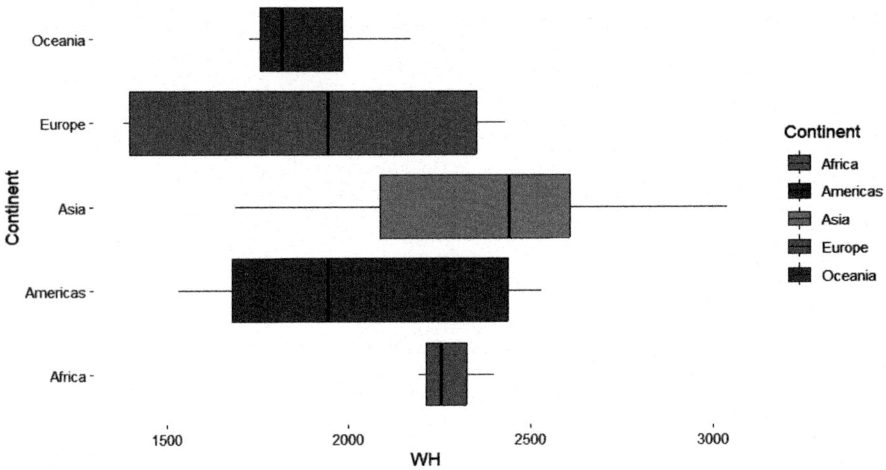

References

Cochran, W. G. (1977). *Sampling Techniques* (3rd ed.). Wiley. Available at https://fsapps.nwcg.gov/gtac/CourseDownloads/IP/Cambodia/FlashDrive/Supporting_Documentation/Cochran_1977_Sampling%20Techniques.pdf

Crawley, M. J. (2015). *Statistics: An introduction using R*. Wiley. Available at https://minerva.it.manchester.ac.uk/~saralees/statbook4.pdf

Field, A. (2018). *Discovering statistics using IBM SPSS statistics*. Sage. ISBN 978-9351500827

McKinney, W. (2022). *Python for data analysis: Data wrangling with Pandas, NumPy, and Jupyter*. O'Reilly Media. ISBN 9781491957660

Montgomery, D. C., Peck, E. A., & Vining, G. G. (2019). *Introduction to linear regression analysis*. Wiley.

Yamane, T. (1967). *Statistics: An introductory analysis* (2nd ed.). Harper and Row.

Chapter 5
Data Visualization and Uncertainty

Abstract This chapter covers data visualization and uncertainty, highlighting examples of effective and poor visualization practices. The first part explains key visualization objectives, including exploration, synthesis, presentation, and analysis. Different visualization types are described, such as graphical, visual encoding, and hybrid methods. A detailed focus is given to visualizing uncertainty, ranging from 1 to 3D representations. Strategies for effectively representing uncertainty are outlined, along with practical examples to enhance understanding of data visualization and its complexities. This part concludes with a discussion on human perception, cognitive biases, and heuristic biases in data visualization. The second part includes a practical exercise creating a fan chart to visualize population projections and their uncertainty, using total population data (combined for both sexes) provided by the Population Division of the United Nations Department of Economic and Social Affairs.

Relation to Other Chapters: This chapter complements the statistical insights from Chap. 4 and lays the groundwork for handling spatial and machine learning data in Chaps. 6 and 7.

5.1 Introduction

Data visualization transforms complex data into graphical representations, allowing patterns, insights, and relationships within the data to be easily understood. Effective data visualization bridges the gap between raw data and meaningful insights by turning abstract information into visual forms that simplify interpretation and analysis. As data science gains prominence in decision-making, the need to visualize uncertainty—reflecting the degree of confidence or doubt associated with data points or predictions—becomes crucial. Uncertainty can arise from data limitations, model assumptions, or inherent randomness in the data, impacting how results should be communicated to avoid over interpretation or misrepresentation.

F. Ramdani, *Data Science: Foundations and Hands-on Experience*,
https://doi.org/10.1007/978-981-96-4683-8_5

5.2 Data Visualization and Its Uncertainty

Data visualization is the process of displaying information or data in a graphical or visual format to communicate complex information in an easy-to-understand manner. The purpose of data visualization is to make it easier to interpret, analyze, and communicate insights and patterns in the data.

Uncertainty in data science refers to the degree of doubt or lack of confidence in the accuracy of a particular data point or model prediction. In other words, it represents the level of confidence that one can have in the results of a data analysis or machine learning algorithm. Uncertainty can arise due to various factors such as incomplete or inaccurate data, model limitations, or variability in the data.

Data visualization can help to address the issue of uncertainty in data science by providing a way to visually represent the uncertainty in the data. One approach is to use visual cues such as color, size, or transparency to indicate the level of uncertainty in the data. For example, a scatter plot with data points colored by the degree of uncertainty can help to identify areas of high and low confidence in the data.

Another approach is to use visualizations to explore the sensitivity of the results to changes in the underlying assumptions or parameters of the model. This can be carried out by creating interactive visualizations that allow users to explore different scenarios and see how the results change based on different assumptions.

Data visualization plays a crucial role in data science by enabling analysts and decision-makers to explore and communicate complex data in an intuitive and easily understandable way.

By incorporating visualizations that convey uncertainty, data scientists can help to ensure that their results are not overinterpreted and that the limitations of their models are clearly communicated.

Visualizing Uncertainty is Regarded as One of The Unsolved Problems in The Data Visualization Community (Yu, 2018)

Many reasons are causing this problem, such as:

- ***First**, the gap between the scientific visualization community and other domains such as news agencies, and consulting companies. In the scientific community, researchers have a systematic way to deal with visualizing uncertainty but they are not accessible to non-experts outside of the scientific community. That is partly because the science researchers proposed the methodologies to deal with visualizing uncertainty but they did not connect them to the problems the general public care about*
- ***Second**, the traditional methods for visualizing uncertainty are limited. For example, the box plot cannot reflect the true distribution of data. In addition, traditional ways to visualize uncertainty usually do not consider*

visual cognition and perception. They often require the users to have an understanding of statistics to understand the visualization (Yu, 2018)

5.3 Bad Data Visualization

One of the most challenging aspects of data visualization is the visualization of uncertainty. When we see a data point drawn in a specific location, we tend to interpret it as a precise representation of the true data value.

Poorly designed data visualizations can lead to misinterpretations and confusion. One common issue is the distortion of the x- or y-axis, which can exaggerate or downplay trends, misleading viewers about the data's actual behavior. Additionally, missing axis legends or labels often leave audiences unsure about what each axis represents, making it difficult to understand the context or scale.

The choice of shapes and colors plays a crucial role in visualization effectiveness, yet poor color schemes or confusing shapes can distract from the data or even evoke unintended emotional responses. A lack of consideration for the phenomenon being represented can lead to an incomplete or inaccurate portrayal of complex realities, failing to capture the nuances of real-world situations.

Inappropriate color choices, such as using clashing or indistinguishable shades, can hinder comprehension and accessibility, especially for viewers with color vision deficiencies. These and other issues contribute to poor data visualizations, which ultimately obscure the data's true message rather than clarifying it. Figure 5.1 shows the example of a bad data visualization.

5.4 Data Visualization and Its Objectives

Data visualization serves several core objectives, each essential to transforming data into actionable insights:

1. **Exploration**: Data visualization helps analysts explore data to detect patterns, outliers, or anomalies. For example, a scatter plot with residuals can highlight unexpected deviations.
2. **Synthesis**: Visualization combines different data elements into a cohesive story, providing a holistic view. For instance, synthesizing economic data with crime statistics helps reveal correlations that might inform policy.
3. **Presentation**: Data visualization enables the clear delivery of insights to stakeholders. Effective presentations tailor visuals to the needs of specific audiences, ensuring accessibility across formats (e.g., printed, digital, mobile).

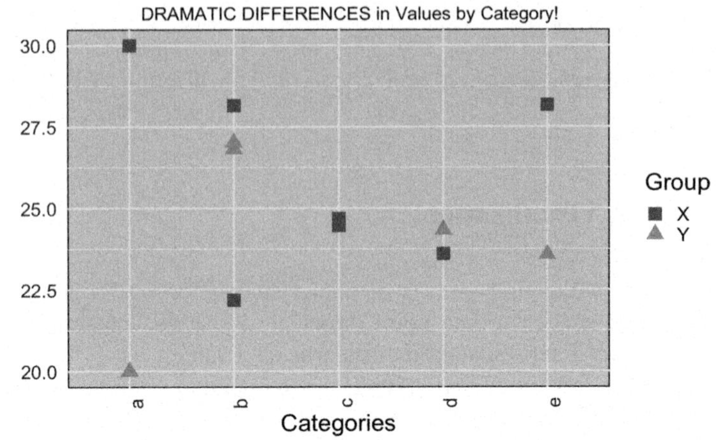

Fig. 5.1 Example of bad data visualization demonstrating several flaws including a distorted *Y*-axis that exaggerates differences, clashing red and bright green colors, a distracting bright yellow background, a misleading title that overemphasizes the data, a rotated *x*-axis label, a missing *y*-axis legend, and a *y*-axis that does not start at zero

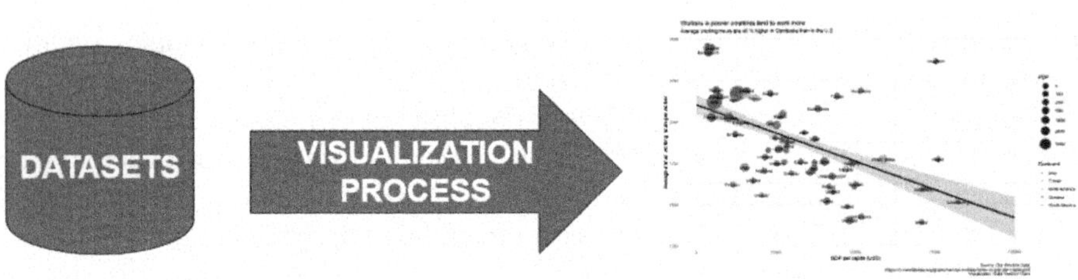

Fig. 5.2 Visualization process as grammar

4. **Analysis**: Detailed visualizations support in-depth examinations, such as identifying measurement trends over time or comparing model outputs to assess accuracy.

The visualization process functions like a grammar, guiding the translation of raw data into forms suitable for communication (Fig. 5.2). This transformation requires balancing the "how," "to whom," and "for what purpose" of the visualization.

5.5 Techniques and Theory for Visualizing Uncertainty

Data visualization experts have proposed three primary categories for representing uncertainty, each with its strengths and applications:

1. **Graphical Annotations**: Techniques such as confidence intervals, error bars, and distributional moments visually represent uncertainty around specific values (Fig. 5.3). For instance, a confidence interval around an estimated mean conveys possible fluctuations in the actual value.
2. **Visual Encoding Channels**: Adjusting visual elements (e.g., color, size, transparency) can denote uncertainty (Fig. 5.4). Using colors that fade with increasing uncertainty or enlarging symbols in regions with low confidence is examples of this approach.
3. **Hybrid Approaches**: Combining visual encodings with graphical annotations creates layered representations of uncertainty. Hybrid techniques, like contour box plots and interval plots, integrate aspects of both graphical annotations and visual encoding channels to represent confidence in complex datasets (Fig. 5.5) (Table 5.1).

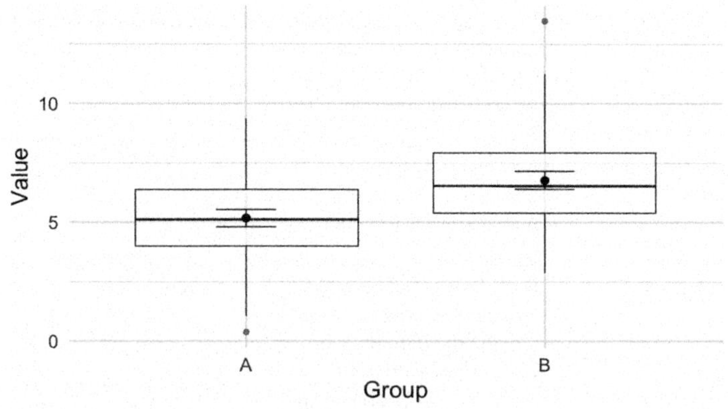

Fig. 5.3 Illustration of a boxplot with the distribution of values in each group, with mean values represented as blue dots and error bars to represent the confidence interval

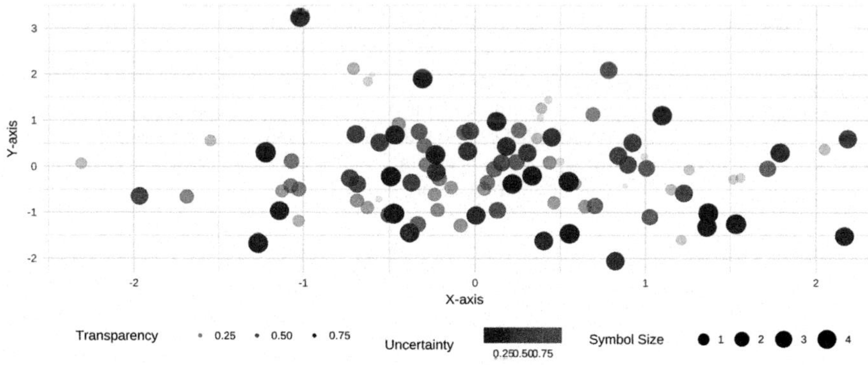

Fig. 5.4 Illustration of the visual encoding channels

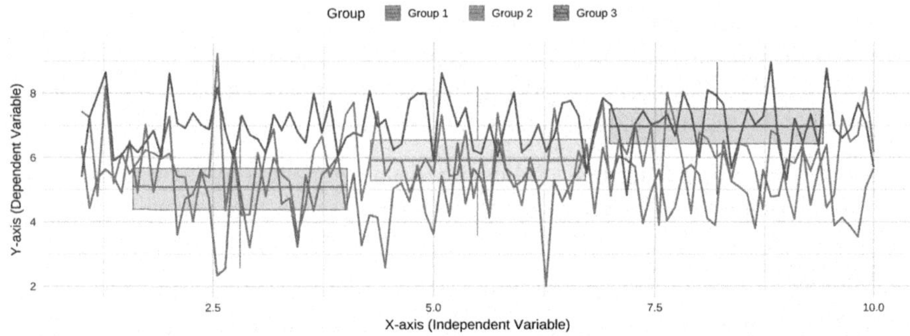

Fig. 5.5 Illustration of the hybrid approaches, combining graphical annotations and visual encodings, providing a clear representation of uncertainty and confidence intervals in the data

Table 5.1 Summarizes the theory in uncertainty visualization

Theory	Summary	Visualization techniques
Frequency framing	Uncertainty is more intuitively understood in a frequency framing (1 out of 10) than in a probabilistic framing (10%)	Icon array, quantile dotplot, hypothetical outcome plot
Attribute substitution–deterministic construal error	If given the opportunity, viewers will mentally substitute uncertainty information for data that are easier to understand	Hypothetical outcome plots
Visual boundaries = cognitive categories	Ranges that are represented by boundaries lead people to believe that data inside and outside the boundary is categorically different	Ensemble display, error bar alternatives
Visual semiotics	Some encoding techniques naturally map onto uncertainty	Fuzziness, transparency, location, value-suppressing color pallet
Aleatory uncertainty (statistical uncertainty)	Natural variability is inherent in a system or process and cannot be reduced through additional data collection or modeling	Error bars, histograms, box plots, density plots, and heatmaps
Epistemic uncertainty (lack of knowledge)	Lack of knowledge or understanding about a system or process that can be reduced through additional data collection or modeling	Sensitivity analysis, model averaging, Bayesian inference, and ensemble methods

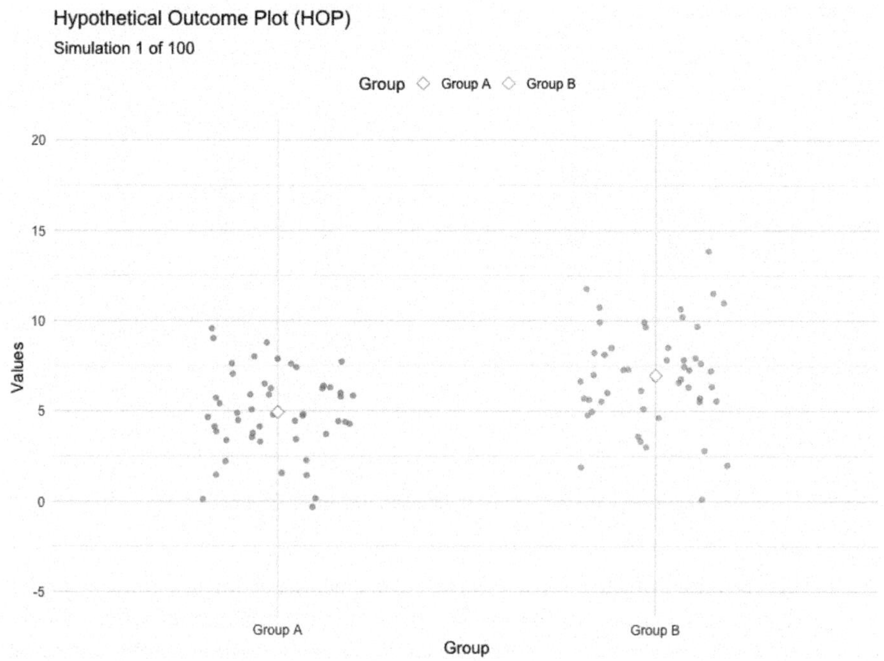

Fig. 5.6 Hypothetical outcome plots (HOPs). For animation, the GIF file is available here https://x.gd/wONoc

In recent years, researchers have begun exploring innovative approaches to make uncertainty visualization more accessible and easier to understand. One notable example is the development of hypothetical outcome plots (HOPs), a technique that uses visualization and animation to represent data with uncertainty (Fig. 5.6). By animating potential outcomes, HOPs allow users to "experience" uncertainty dynamically, providing a more intuitive understanding of complex data. Studies suggest that HOPs are more effective in helping users grasp uncertainty compared to traditional static methods of uncertainty visualization (Hullman et al., 2015). This advancement has the potential to transform how uncertainty is communicated in fields like science, policymaking, and education.

5.6 Uncertainty Visualization in Various Dimensions

1. 1D to 4D Within Scientific Community

   Uncertainty visualization techniques are adapted to the dimensionality of the data:

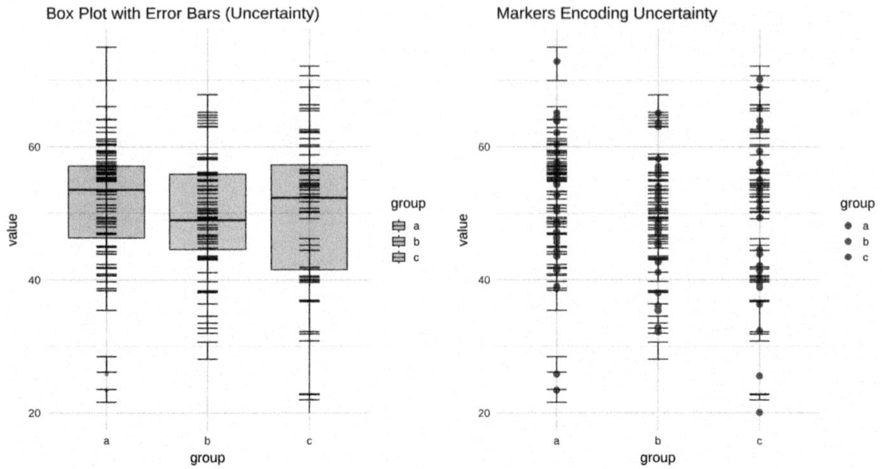

Fig. 5.7 1D representations with variations of data and uncertain data points

a. **1D Representations**: Uncertainty in data can arise from variations or unclear data points. There are different ways to visualize this uncertainty, two of which are commonly used in scientific research. The first method involves box plots and error bars, which show the spread of data and help highlight potential errors or variations in measurements. The second method uses markers to represent uncertainty. These markers can visually encode the level of uncertainty, providing a clear understanding of the reliability of the data. In scientific visualization, markers are particularly useful for indicating uncertainty (see Fig. 5.7). Both of these visualization techniques play a crucial role in communicating the reliability and variability of data in a way that is easy to understand for researchers and audiences alike.

In Figure 5.7, the uncertainty is represented by creating lower and upper bounds around the observed value. These bounds simulate variability or uncertainty in the data. Error bars are drawn to visually represent the range of uncertainty for each point (or group in the box plot). Data points are plotted as markers, and error bars are used to encode the uncertainty visually around the points.

2D Representations: Bivariate extensions of the boxplot allow for visualizing the relationship between two variables, extending the traditional boxplot from one dimension to two. These enhanced boxplots display how two variables are related to one another, providing a more comprehensive view of the data. Bivariate boxplots can help identify correlations, outliers, and variations between the two variables. There are four common types of bivariate boxplots, each offering a different way to explore the interactions between two datasets:

i. **Rangefinder boxplot** consists of six line segments, where the center cross lines intersect at the median values, while the other lines indicate the interquartile range of the data.
ii. **2D boxplot** is made up of three components: a median point, an inner box that includes 50% of the data, and an outer box that marks the separation of outliers from the main dataset.
iii. **Bagplot,** similar to the 2D boxplot, a bagplot also has three main parts: a "bag" (the dark gray area) containing 50% of the data points, a "loop" (the gray area) indicating points outside the bag, and a "fence" that helps distinguish inliers from outliers.
iv. **Quel and Rel plots** resemble other bivariate boxplots and also follow the same structure with three key elements: a center, an interior hinge containing 50% of the data, and a fence that separates inliers from outliers. These visual representations are all illustrated in Fig. 5.8.

c. **3D and 4D Representations:** Uncertainty visualization techniques, such as glyphs, image discontinuity, and attribute modification, are commonly used to test algorithms, assess data quality, and perform similar evaluations. These methods have become increasingly complex compared to earlier versions (see Fig. 5.9). For instance, some examples include:

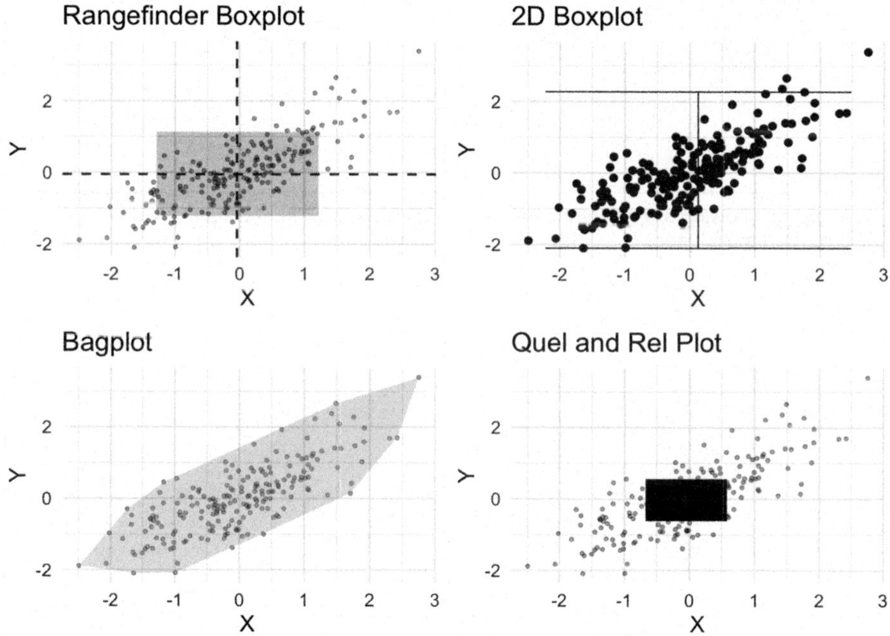

Fig. 5.8 Rangefinder boxplot, 2D boxplot, bagplot, and Quel and Rel plot

i. Spherical glyphs are scaled according to radiosity differences, which represent variations in light intensity across a surface.
ii. Line glyphs that display particle positions along streamlines are calculated using two different integration methods.
iii. Uncertainty vector glyphs over Monterey Bay, California, were used to represent directional uncertainty in the data.
iv. Line glyphs that highlight the differences between surfaces interpolated using bilinear and multiquadric methods.
v. Uncertainty isosurfaces, which depict regions of constant uncertainty values.

These techniques provide a clearer understanding of uncertainty in data, enhancing the ability to interpret complex spatial phenomena.

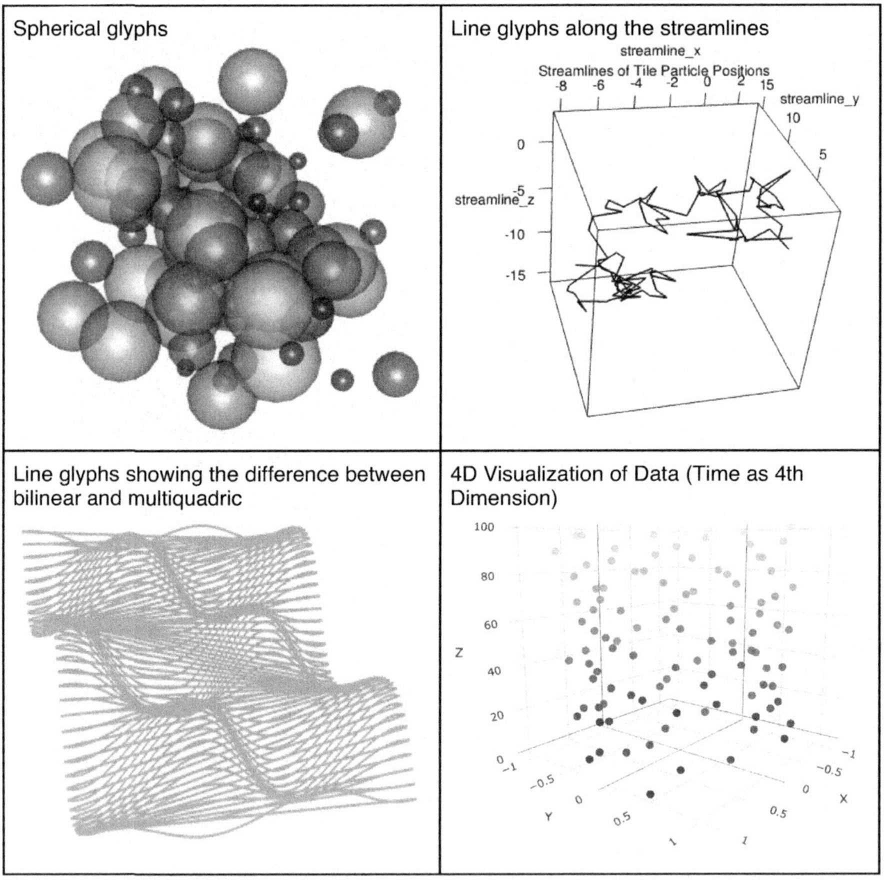

Fig. 5.9 3D and 4D representations

2. Visualizing the Uncertainty Outside the Scientific World

   a. The Tendency and Forecast

      This category typically displays data or predictions about one or more observed objects. To represent uncertainty and its possible trends, it often uses lines. A common approach in this category is showing the regression of uncertain data, which can also be illustrated through lines. Some of the common types of uncertainty visualizations in this category are watercolor regression, fan charts (as shown in Figure 5.10), and probability intervals.

   b. The Spreadsheet of Uncertainty

      This method of uncertainty visualization takes a straightforward approach by presenting the numerical values of uncertainty directly within a spreadsheet format, as shown in Figure 5.11. By using a tabular layout, it allows users to clearly and efficiently interpret the data without requiring complex graphical representations. Such an approach is particularly useful for audiences who prefer precise numerical insights over visual abstractions. This type of visualization aligns with best practices for presenting quantitative data, as described in studies emphasizing clarity and accessibility in data communication.

   c. Statistic Summary of Uncertainty

      This approach to uncertainty visualization relies on conventional statistical methods to provide a clear and concise summary of uncertainty. By applying techniques such as confidence intervals, standard deviations, or probability distributions (Figure 5.12) it aims to make complex data more interpretable and actionable for decision-makers. Traditional statistical tools are widely used in

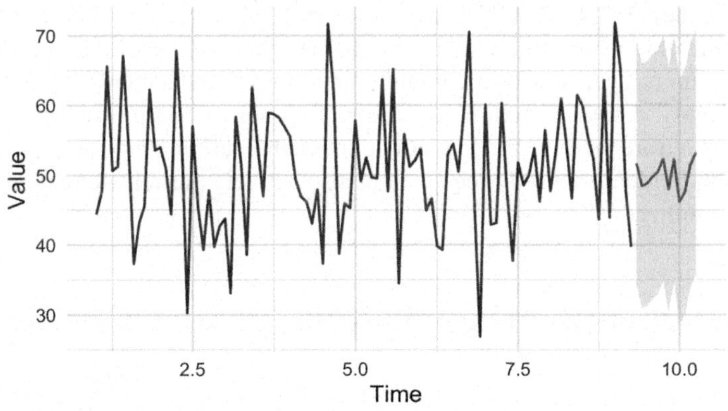

Fig. 5.10 Forecast with uncertainty intervals

Fig. 5.11 Spreadsheet of uncertainty (showing numbers) of Fig. 5.10

```
> print(tail(forecast_table, 10))
         Time Observed Forecast    Lower    Upper
103  9.500000       NA 48.81570 31.25042 66.38098
104  9.583333       NA 49.78492 32.21964 67.35020
105  9.666667       NA 50.45922 32.89394 68.02450
106  9.750000       NA 52.34632 34.78104 69.91160
107  9.833333       NA 48.01623 30.45095 65.58151
108  9.916667       NA 52.28612 34.72084 69.85140
109 10.000000       NA 46.21613 28.65085 63.78141
110 10.083333       NA 47.64179 30.07651 65.20707
111 10.166667       NA 51.49229 33.92701 69.05757
112 10.250000       NA 53.21409 35.64881 70.77937
```

Fig. 5.12 Basic summary statistics of the uncertainty (forecast intervals) of Fig. 5.10

```
> print(summary_stats)
           Statistic     Value
1               Mean 50.036593
2 Standard Deviation  2.213934
3       95% CI Lower 32.471312
4       95% CI Upper 67.601874
```

this context because they offer a well-established framework for quantifying and communicating variability or potential errors in data.

d. Simulation of Uncertainty

This kind of uncertainty visualization is typically interactive and dynamic, allowing users to actively engage with the content. For example, a chart might display a compass for each region, where the color area within each compass represents the likelihood of a particular political party winning. By clicking a button like "SPIN AGAIN," the results will often change, demonstrating the unpredictable nature of the data (Fig. 5.13). This type of simulation helps users engage more deeply with the content and aids in understanding the concept of uncertainty. Another example could involve users selecting categories to group data, which are then color-coded for better visualization. Through these visualizations, individuals not only see data but also actively participate in understanding its variability.

5.7 Classification of Uncertainty Visualization Techniques

Kinkeldey et al. (2014) provide a comprehensive review of various studies on how uncertainty is visualized, offering a classification of visualization techniques based on three key theoretical contrasts. First, the **coincident/adjacent** dichotomy distinguishes between visualizations where uncertainty is represented alongside the information (coincident) and those where uncertainty is shown separately from the main

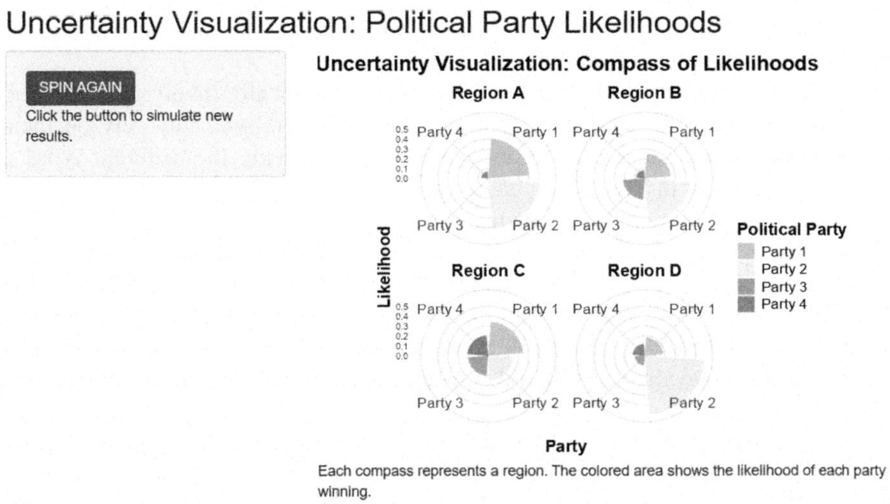

Fig. 5.13 Simulation of uncertainty. The animation is available at https://x.gd/PSYFR

data (adjacent). Second, the **intrinsic/extrinsic** contrast separates visualizations that alter existing graphical elements (intrinsic) from those that add new elements, such as grids, glyphs, or icons, to represent uncertainty (extrinsic). Finally, the **static/dynamic** distinction refers to whether the visualization remains fixed or changes over time, such as through animation or interactive features.

In a similar vein, Matthews et al. (2008) categorize uncertainty visualization techniques into four levels: **alteration**, **addition**, **animation**, and **interaction**. The first category, alteration, involves modifying the visual properties of data—such as color, size, position, clarity, and transparency—to reflect uncertainty. In the addition category, extra static elements, like labels or icons, are incorporated into the visualization to represent uncertainty. The third category, animation, introduces time-based changes where uncertainty is reflected in animation characteristics, including speed, duration, and range of motion. Lastly, the interaction category allows users to explore uncertainty through interactions, such as mouse-over events that trigger additional information.

5.8 Strategy for Uncertainty Visualization

There is no single "best" method or framework for visualizing uncertainty. Instead, how uncertainty is visualized should be approached in a way that considers each specific situation, and it must be supported by thorough empirical research. This means that designing effective uncertainty visualizations requires expertise from multiple disciplines. The suitability of different techniques often depends heavily on the context, but our current understanding of which factors are most relevant in each case is still incomplete (Tufte, 2001).

Therefore, creating effective visualizations should ideally involve close collaboration among researchers, designers, and the end-users who will rely on them. The foundation for such collaboration involves identifying the different types of uncertainty present in a particular case study.

Without reliable methods to evaluate the effectiveness of uncertainty visualizations, there is a risk of creating visually appealing designs that do not provide the necessary decision support. Poorly designed visualizations can even hinder decision-making by slowing it down or introducing biases (Cleveland, 2009). Self-reported feedback from users is not a reliable method for assessing the effectiveness of these visualizations, so evaluations should be conducted using objective and reproducible methods.

Users who interact with uncertain information have diverse needs and capabilities, and there is currently no widely accepted theory that addresses how to account for these differences in specific cases. This is important because the way uncertainty is visualized cannot be separated from the way it is interpreted and reasoned about. Consequently, effective uncertainty visualization should not just convey information; it should also promote and sometimes teach appropriate ways to interpret and reason about that information (Santucci et al., 2020).

Just as literacy must be learned, graphical literacy—the ability to understand and use visual data—also needs to be developed and taught (Tufte, 2001).

While there are certainly challenges in visualizing uncertainty for decision-making, the potential benefits are significant. The range of techniques and methods for uncertainty visualization is expanding, and as these methods become more refined, they can improve the communication and understanding of uncertainty across various decision-making contexts (Bertini et al., 2021). Over time, a more robust and case-specific methodology for uncertainty visualization will likely enhance its role in decision-making.

However, it is important to recognize that visualization may not always be the best tool for conveying uncertainty. In some situations, words or numbers might be more effective for a particular type of uncertainty or for a specific audience (Few, 2006). Even when uncertainty visualization is not the primary focus, understanding the visual aspects of a decision—such as how information is presented or interpreted visually—can help manage the uncertainty involved in the decision-making process (Kosslyn, 2006).

5.9 12-Step Strategy for Designing Uncertainty Visualizations

Uncertainty visualization is particularly important in fields like data science, decision-making, and scientific research, where data might not always be complete, exact, or reliable. Understanding and visualizing uncertainty help users interpret data more accurately, avoid overconfidence in findings, and make informed decisions.

Lapinski (2009) proposed a 12-step strategy for designing visualizations that effectively communicate uncertainty, based on the Uncertainty Visualization Development Strategy (UVDS) as follows:

1. **Identify the Task**: Start by figuring out exactly what you need to show in the visualization.
2. **Understand the Data**: Take time to know the data. Ask why it is important to visualize this data.
3. **Reason for Visualizing**: Think about why it is useful to show this uncertain information.
4. **User and Purpose:** Identify who will use the visualization and how it will help them.
5. **Choose the Type of Uncertainty**: Decide which kind of uncertainty you want to focus on (e.g., unknown outcomes, variability in data).
6. **Define Uncertainty**: Make a clear definition of what "uncertainty" means for your data.
7. **Causes of Uncertainty**: Understand what specific things make the data uncertain.
8. **Categories of Uncertainty**: Group the causes of uncertainty into broader categories.
9. **Requirements**: List what you need to create the visualization properly.
10. **Prepare the Data**: Organize or process the data to make it ready for visualization.
11. **Design the Visualization**: Start creating the visualization by trying different design techniques to show uncertainty.
12. **Get Feedback**: Test the visualization with an audience. If needed, go back and make improvements to steps 10 or 11.

The process begins by identifying the visualization task. Here, the designer needs to clarify what exactly they aim to communicate through the visualization, specifically focusing on the aspect of uncertainty within the data. Next, they work to understand the data itself, which involves asking why this data should be visualized, and what value it brings to the audience. In steps three and four, designers consider the context and purpose by identifying why the uncertainty needs to be shown and determining who the intended user is. Knowing the audience and the ways this visualization could benefit them is crucial in shaping how the data is represented.

After setting the groundwork, the designer must decide which type of uncertainty to highlight (step five) and provide a clear definition of what "uncertainty" means within this specific context (step six). This involves understanding whether the uncertainty arises from measurement errors, missing information, unpredictable outcomes, or other factors. By focusing on a particular type of uncertainty, the visualization remains clear and purposeful rather than overwhelming or confusing the viewer with multiple, undefined sources of uncertainty.

The next stage, steps seven and eight, dives deeper into the sources and categories of uncertainty. Designers examine the root causes, identifying specific factors that make the data uncertain, such as sampling limitations or variability in measurements. These causes are then organized into broader causal categories, which may include randomness, incomplete knowledge, or model assumptions. This categorization aids in structuring the visualization to address each type of uncertainty appropriately.

In step nine, the designer outlines the specific requirements needed for creating the visualization. This includes technical needs like software, data processing tools, or design elements that will help represent uncertainty accurately. With the requirements in mind, step ten involves preparing the data, processing it, and possibly transforming it into a format suitable for visualization.

Only after these steps are completed does the visual design phase begin in step eleven. At this stage, the designer experiments with various techniques to represent uncertainty visually. Techniques might include color coding, transparency, error bars, or confidence intervals, depending on the type and level of uncertainty. The objective is to convey the uncertainty clearly, so users can interpret the data correctly without misinterpreting the reliability or accuracy of the information.

Finally, step twelve involves gathering feedback on the visualization. Audience feedback helps assess whether the design successfully communicates uncertainty. If the feedback suggests that the visualization could be improved, the designer may go back to steps ten or eleven to adjust the data preparation or design. This iterative process ensures that the final product is both accurate and user-friendly.

By following these steps, designers can create uncertainty visualizations that not only depict data but also communicate the nuances of reliability and variability within it. This systematic approach helps build visualizations that are informative and cautious, enabling users to make decisions with a clearer understanding of data limitations.

Research suggests that representations involving hue, value, and transparency worked best. In addition to transparency, value, and hue, graphical attributes that were found useful in representing uncertainty include resolution, fuzziness, and blurring (Kinkeldey et al., 2014) as shown in Fig. 5.14.

Some studies have suggested using side-by-side representations of the variable and uncertainty relating to the variable (Deitrick & Wentz, 2015) as shown in Fig. 5.15.

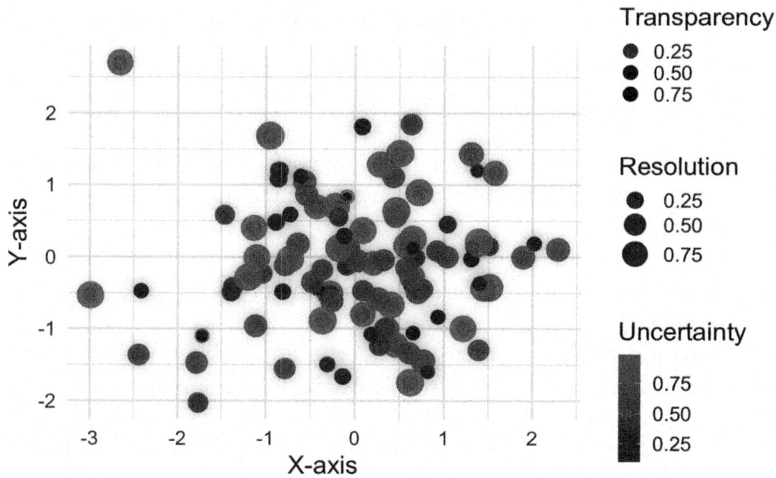

Fig. 5.14 Representations involving hue, value, and transparency, in addition with resolution, fuzziness, and blurring

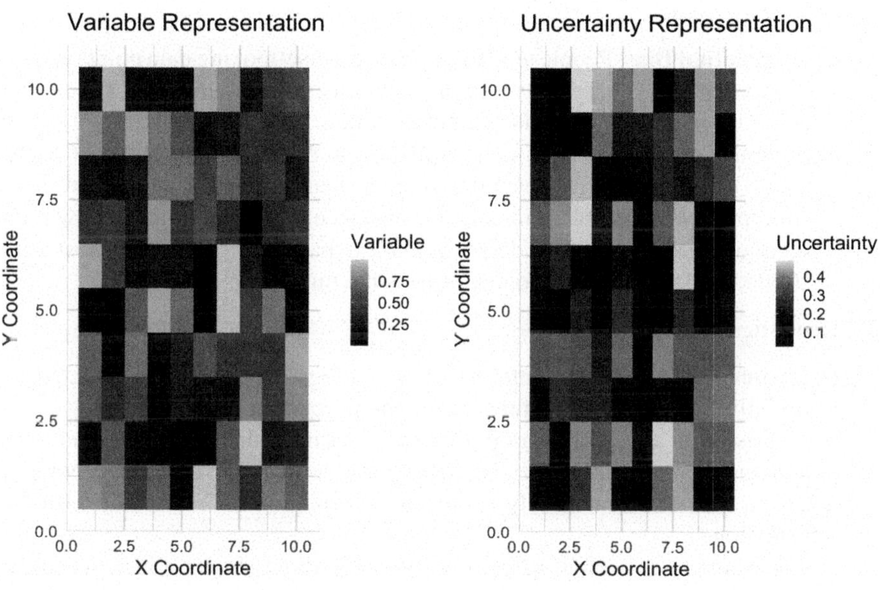

Fig. 5.15 Variable and uncertainty are shown side-by-side

5.10 Challenges in Uncertainty Visualization

Visualizing uncertainty effectively remains a challenging area in data visualization, with limitations stemming from gaps between scientific methods and practical applications in other fields. Traditional methods, like box plots, often fail to capture the true data distribution or are hard for non-experts to interpret due to their reliance on statistical understanding.

Uncertainty representation is not easily separable from interpretations of value, and thus, individual and group differences (cultural, political, social, linguistic, etc.) play an important role.

Visual variables influence the visualization user's perception in different ways. What is perceived depends on the human capacity to see or perceive.

Additionally, cognitive biases and human perception significantly affect how uncertainty is understood. Users may misinterpret visual cues or fail to recognize uncertainty if it is presented in an overly complex or ambiguous manner.

1. Human Perception and Cognitive Biases

   Data scientists must consider human perception in uncertainty visualization. Key concerns include:

   a. **Perceptual Bias**: People tend to perceive precise-looking data points as accurate, even when uncertainty is high. Techniques like fading colors or softening lines can help mitigate this misinterpretation.
   b. **Cognitive Bias**: Decision-makers often rely on recent information (recency bias) or oversimplified mental shortcuts (heuristic bias), which can distort interpretations of uncertain data. For instance, a fan chart might show future economic projections, but decision-makers may focus on only the most recent trend, neglecting the full range of possible outcomes.

2. Heuristics Biases

   Heuristics refers to reflex patterns of reasoning that are widely attested and apparently "deep-seated" features of human psychology.

   Heuristics is a mental shortcut that relies on immediate examples that come to a given person's mind when evaluating a specific topic, concept, method, or decision. Humans tend to rely on recent information far more than historical information.

   For example, a person watches a TV show about sharks. Later, when they go to the beach, they feel afraid of sharks, even though shark attacks are rare. Because they just saw sharks on TV, they think a shark attack is more likely than it is. This shows how what we see or hear about recently can influence our thoughts, even if it is not that common or dangerous.

   In the case of uncertainty visualization, heuristic biases play a significant role in shaping human perception, especially in situations involving uncertainty. In uncertainty visualization—like maps showing probabilities of natural disasters or data projections—heuristics affect how people interpret and respond to the information presented. Here is how heuristic biases impact human perception in uncertainty visualization:

1. **Simplifying Complex Information**: When people encounter complex visualizations, they often rely on mental shortcuts, or heuristics, to make quick judgments. For example, if a map shows high-probability areas for earthquakes, people might overestimate the likelihood of experiencing one because it stands out visually, even if the overall probability is low.
2. **Availability Heuristic**: This bias specifically causes people to assess risk based on what easily comes to mind. If a person recently heard about a flood, they may feel more anxious about flood risks when looking at a flood probability map, even if their area is statistically safe. The vividness of recent information can skew their interpretation of the visualization, leading them to overestimate risks.
3. **Confirmation Bias**: Heuristic biases also contribute to confirmation bias, where people interpret data in a way that supports their existing beliefs. For instance, if someone believes that climate change will lead to more extreme weather events, they might interpret weather probability maps as evidence, even if the visualization does not actually confirm this.
4. **Impact of Visual Design**: Design choices, like color intensity or the use of alarming symbols, can amplify heuristic biases. Bright colors or exaggerated symbols may cause users to perceive certain risks as greater than they are. This can be problematic in uncertainty visualization, as people might not accurately interpret the actual probabilities or risk levels being communicated.
5. **Misinterpretation of Uncertainty**: Heuristic biases can lead people to misunderstand probabilistic information. For example, they might see a 30% chance of rain and interpret it as more likely than it is, especially if recent weather has been rainy. Depending on the data being visualized, this can lead to overconfidence or unwarranted fear.

Heuristic biases shape how people perceive and respond to uncertainty visualizations. Because people rely on mental shortcuts to simplify complex or uncertain information, they may misinterpret probabilities or risks based on their recent experiences, emotions, or the visual design of the information itself. Effective uncertainty visualization should therefore account for these biases by using clear, balanced visuals and avoiding design elements that might unnecessarily amplify fears or overconfidence.

Cognitive biases and heuristics often influence how people interpret data, so thoughtful visualization design can help minimize their effects. For example, recency bias—where people give undue weight to recent information—can be addressed by emphasizing long-term trends in a dataset. This could involve displaying a clear timeline that highlights patterns across a broad period rather than focusing on just the most recent data points. Smoothing data in a graph, such as with moving averages, can also help shift attention from short-term fluctuations to the overall trajectory.

To counter confirmation bias, which leads people to focus on information that aligns with their preexisting beliefs, visualizations should present balanced and comprehensive data. For instance, you might juxtapose contrasting data points or use neutral colors and labels to avoid implying one outcome is better than another. Including interactive features that allow users to explore alternative scenarios or filter data by different variables can encourage them to consider multiple perspectives.

Clear, concise, and unbiased visual elements—such as appropriate scales, accurate labeling, and annotations explaining key takeaways—can guide users toward objective interpretations. By designing with these principles, visualizations can help people focus on the data's full story rather than their mental shortcuts.

A Real-World Case Study

One real-world case study demonstrating how effective uncertainty visualization influenced decision-making comes from the public health response to the COVID-19 pandemic. Early in the pandemic, governments and public health officials relied on models to predict how the virus might spread under different scenarios, such as implementing or delaying lockdowns. These models often came with a high degree of uncertainty due to limited data and the evolving nature of the virus.

A notable case involved the work of the Institute for Health Metrics and Evaluation (IHME), which presented its projections of COVID-19 cases, hospitalizations, and deaths using uncertainty bands on their graphs (IHME, 2020). These bands—shaded regions around the central prediction line—showed the range of possible outcomes, from best-case to worst-case scenarios. By visualizing this uncertainty, decision-makers could see not just what might happen but how much confidence they could have in each prediction.

This visualization had a significant influence on decision-making. For instance, policymakers in some regions used the worst-case scenario from these models to prepare healthcare systems for surges in hospitalizations. At the same time, the best-case scenarios gave hope and showed the potential impact of early interventions like mask mandates and social distancing. The clear communication of uncertainty helped leaders strike a balance between caution and optimism, making better-informed decisions without over-or under-reacting to the available data.

By presenting uncertainty visually, the IHME models empowered public health officials to plan for a range of possibilities, communicate risks effectively to the public, and adjust strategies as new data emerged—all of which were critical in managing the crisis (Ioannidis et al., 2020).

Easy to Digest Box

Data Visualization *is like turning numbers and facts into pictures or charts so we can easily understand them. Imagine you have a lot of candy of different colors, and you want to show how many candies of each color you have. Instead of just writing down the numbers, you could draw a picture of each color candy to make it easier to see which color you have the most of. That is what data visualization does —it turns boring numbers into colorful pictures or graphs!*

For example:

- ***Bar Chart****: If you have 10 red candies, 5 blue candies, and 2 green candies, you can use a bar chart with three bars, showing how tall each bar is for the different colors*
- ***Pie Chart****: You can draw a big circle (like a pizza) and divide it into slices. Each slice shows how much of each color candy you have, so you can quickly see which color is the biggest slice*

Uncertainty in Data *means that sometimes the information we have is not 100% certain or perfect. It is like when you guess how many candies are in a jar, but you are not sure because you cannot see inside the jar. The number you guessed might be close, but it might not be exactly right. In data science, uncertainty happens when there is not enough information, or the information we have might not be completely accurate*

For example:

- ***Weather Prediction****: A weather forecast might say there is a 70% chance of rain tomorrow. That means they are not 100% sure if it will rain, but there is a good chance. The 30% chance is the uncertainty —it might not rain at all!*

In simple words, data visualization helps us understand information better, and uncertainty reminds us that sometimes things are not completely clear.

5.11 Summary of Key Points

- Data visualization is the process of displaying information or data in a graphical or visual format to communicate complex information.
- The visualization process is like a kind of "grammar" that allows for the optimal design and production for the use of the visualization, depending on the application.
- The main objective of visualization is to (1) explore, (2) synthesis, (3) present, and (4) analysis.
- Uncertainty in data science refers to the degree of doubt or lack of confidence in the accuracy of a particular data point or model prediction.
- There are three broad categories of uncertainty visualization techniques: (1) graphical annotations, (2) visual encoding channels, and (3) hybrid.
- Research suggests that representations involving transparency, value, and hue, plus graphical attributes work best.
- Be careful with (1) human perceptions, (2) cognitive bias, and (3) heuristic bias.
- Just like literacy, graphical literacy needs to be taught and developed.
- Readers' decisions are strongly affected by the way information is visualized.

- Whether and how we choose to represent the uncertainty also can make a major difference in how accurately our audience perceives the meaning of the data.

5.12 Hands-on Experience

Working with RStudio

Create a Fan Chart

This practice demonstrates creating a **fan chart** in R using population projection data. A fan chart is a graphical representation showing the range of probable outcomes (prediction intervals) over time. Below are the detailed steps to prepare the dataset, analyze it, and create the visualization.

Practice 5

Learning Objectives

Data Downloading and Organization:

- Learn how to download datasets from the United Nations World Population Prospects website
- Understand how to store datasets in an organized manner within a working directory for easy access

Environment Setup in R

- Understand how to install and load necessary R packages for data analysis (tidyverse, ggtext, readxl, grid, janitor)
- Learn how to check and set the working directory in R for consistent file path management:

Data Import and Cleaning:

- Gain proficiency in importing Excel data into R using the readxl package
- Learn how to clean and preprocess data using the janitor and dplyr packages to tidy the datasets
- Learn how to filter, rename, and reshape datasets into a long format for easier analysis

Data Transformation and Merging:

- Understand how to merge and combine different data sources, including probabilistic projections and demographic indicators
- Learn how to subset data for specific countries and filter out unnecessary rows or columns

- Understand the concept of prediction intervals and how to handle them in datasets

Creating Visualizations:

- Learn how to create a fan chart using ggplot2 to visualize demographic projections and uncertainties
- Understand the use of geom_ribbon() to represent prediction intervals and geom_line() to plot actual data
- Gain skills in customizing ggplot visualizations, such as adding annotations, adjusting color schemes, and formatting axis labels

Chart Interpretation and Customization:

- Interpret the significance of the fan chart in terms of demographic trends and uncertainty
- Learn how to customize plots with specific text, curves, and annotations to convey insights
- Understand how to use ggsave() to export visualizations as image files

Exploring Further Analysis:

- Apply knowledge to add other countries of interest (e.g., Indonesia) and include them in the fan chart
- Explore how adjusting the data and visualization parameters can enhance insights into population projections and uncertainties

Application of Concepts to Real-World Data:

- Understand how population projections can inform policy decisions and future planning
- Learn how to communicate complex data and predictions in an accessible and informative visual format.

Downloading Data.

1. Select "Data Download Files" in the United Nations World Population Prospects website: https://population.un.org/wpp/.
2. Under "**Standard Projections (Estimates and Projection scenarios),**" click **Complete (estimates and all projection scenarios)**.
3. Under "**Probabilistic Projections (PPP scenarios)**" (top left menu), click **Population - Both Sexes**.
4. Save both files into the **same working folder or directory** on your computer.

Setting Up Your Environment

Make sure the required R packages are installed. The code snippet below will install, load the necessary libraries, and set up the working directory.

```
# Install required packages at once
install.packages(c("tidyverse", "ggtext", "readxl",
"grid", "janitor")) # Only do it once!
# Load required libraries
library(tidyverse)
library(ggtext)
library(readxl)
library(grid)
library(janitor)
# Check the current working directory
getwd()
# Set working directory
setwd("/path/to/your/folder") # Replace with your
directory
```

Import and Clean Data

The following code imports the two datasets, cleans them, and transforms them into a tidy format. **Pay attention to the ".xlsx" file name**, since they always update the data. Most likely, the files' names will change again in future.

```
# Import dataset: Probabilistic Projections (PPP
scenarios)
file < - "UN_PPP2024_Output_PopTot.xlsx"
View(file)
# Extract sheet names excluding notes
sheet_names < - excel_sheets(file)
sheet_names < - sheet_names[sheet_names ! =
"NOTES"]
# Load data from all sheets
projections < - map_dfr(sheet_names, ~ read_
xlsx(file, sheet = .x, skip = 16,.name_repair =
janitor::make_clean_names))
# Filter and rename columns
projections < - projections % > %
filter(type ! = "Label/Separator") % > %
rename(entity = region_subregion_country_or_area)
# Transform data to long format
projections_long < - projections % > %
pivot_longer(cols = x 2024: x 2100, names_to =
"year", values_to = "value",
```

```
names_transform = function(x) as.numeric(str_
remove(x, "x")),
values_transform = as.numeric)
# Import dataset: Standard Projections
file_path < - "WPP2024_GEN_F01_DEMOGRAPHIC_
INDICATORS_FULL.xlsx"
indicators < - read_excel(file_path, skip =
16,.name_repair = janitor::make_clean_names)
# Clean and rename columns
indicators < - indicators % > %
rename(entity = region_subregion_country_or_area) %
> %
mutate(across(total_population_as_of_1_january_
thousands:net_migration_rate_per_1_000_population,
as.numeric))
# Combine median projections with indicators
indicators_projection_median_combined < -
indicators % > %
filter(entity %in% c("China", "India", "Nigeria"))
% > %
select(entity, year, value = total_population_as_
of_1_january_thousands) % > %
bind_rows(
projections_long % > %
filter(entity %in% c("China", "India", "Nigeria"),
variant = = "Median PI") % > %
select(entity, year, value)
)
# Subset projection data for selected countries
projections_subset < - projections_long % > %
pivot_wider(names_from = "variant", values_from =
"value") % > %
filter(entity %in% c("China", "India", "Nigeria"))
# Rename columns for prediction intervals
colnames(projections_subset)[c(11, 12, 14, 15)] <
- c("Lower.95.PI", "Lower.80.PI", "Upper.80.PI",
"Upper.95.PI")
# Subset indicators for selected countries
indicators_subset < - indicators_projection_median_
combined % > %
filter(entity %in% c("China", "India", "Nigeria"))
```

Creating the Fan Chart

This code generates the fan chart to visualize the population projections.

```
# Create the fan chart
ggplot(projections_subset, aes(x = year)) +
geom_ribbon(aes(ymin = Lower.95.PI, ymax =
Upper.95.PI, fill = entity), alpha = 0.22) +
geom_ribbon(aes(ymin = Lower.80.PI, ymax =
Upper.80.PI, fill = entity), alpha = 0.44) +
geom_line(data = indicators_subset, aes(y = value,
color = entity), size = 1.25) +
annotate("text", x = c(1950, 1965, 1980), y =
c(7.2e5, 4.2e5, 2.2e5),
label = c("China", "India", "Nigeria"), col =
c("China" = "#EE1C25", "India" = "#FF9933",
"Nigeria" = "#008,000"),
hjust = 0, family = "Fira Sans Condensed Medium")
+
annotate("richtext", x = c(2023, 2023), y =
c(1.89e6, 2.08e6),
label = c("80% prediction interval", "95%
prediction interval reflects the spread < br > in
the distribution of outcomes and provides < br > an
assessment of the uncertainty"),
hjust = 0, family = "Fira Sans", size = 2.5,
label.size = 0, fill = NA) +
annotate("curve", x = c(2052, 2059), xend =
c(2063, 2070), y = c(1.87e6, 2.01e6),
yend = c(1.75e6, 1.95e6), linewidth = 0.2,
curvature = 0.2,
arrow = arrow(angle = 20, length = unit(1.5,
"mm"), type = "closed")) +
geom_vline(aes(xintercept = 2022), linetype =
"dashed", linewidth = 0.25) +
annotate("text", x = 2024, y = 1.5e5, label =
"Projection \U2192", hjust = 0, family = "Fira
Sans Condensed") +
scale_y_continuous(labels = scales::label_
number(scale = 1e-3, suffix = "m")) +
scale_color_manual(values = c("China" = "#EE1C25",
"India" = "#FF9933", "Nigeria" = "#008,000"),
aesthetics = c("fill", "color")) +
```

```
guides(col = "none", fill = "none") +
labs(title = " < span style = 'color:#FF9933'
> India < /span > has overtaken < span style =
'color:#EE1C25' > China < /span >,
while < span style = 'color:#008,000' > Nigeria < /
span > will overtake India in the future",
subtitle = "Probabilistic population projections
based on the UN World Population Prospects 2024",
caption = "Data: United Nations, World Population
Prospects 2022. Visualisation: Data Science Class",
x = NULL, y = "Population in million") +
theme_minimal(base_family = "Fira Sans Condensed")
+
theme(
panel.grid = element_blank(),
panel.grid.major.y = element_line(size = 0.3,
color = "#DAD9D9"),
plot.background = element_rect(color = NA, fill =
"white"),
text = element_text(),
axis.line.x = element_line(color = "black",
linewidth = 0.3),
axis.ticks.x = element_line(color = "black",
linewidth = 0.3),
axis.ticks.length.x = unit(2, "mm"),
axis.title = element_text(family = "Fira Sans
Condensed Medium"),
legend.position = "top",
legend.justification = "left",
legend.text = element_markdown(),
plot.title = element_markdown(face = "bold"),
plot.title.position = "plot",
plot.subtitle = element_markdown(margin = margin(b
= 8), lineheight = 1),
plot.caption = element_markdown(
hjust = 0, size = 5, family = "Fira Sans Condensed
Light"),
plot.caption.position = "plot")
```

Save the Chart.

Save the fan chart as an image file.

```
ggsave("fanchart-china-india-nigeria.png", width =
7, height = 6)
```

The chart shows how **India** has surpassed **China** in population and how **Nigeria** is projected to overtake both countries in future.

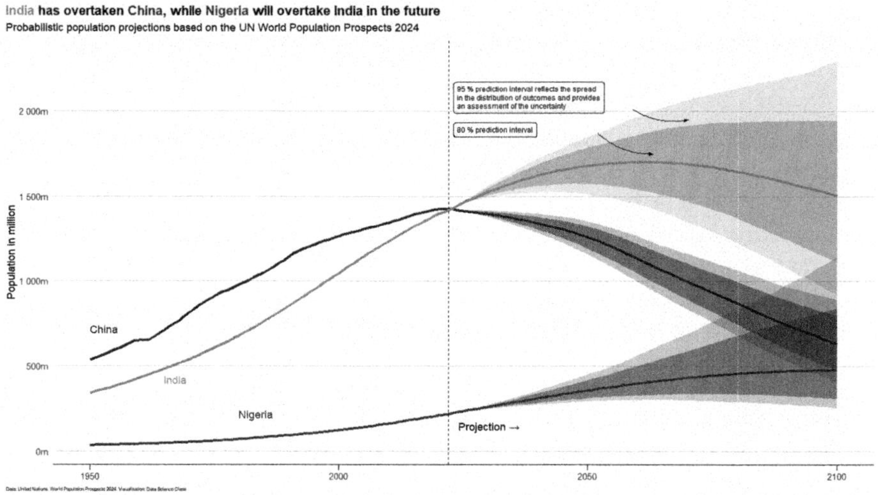

From the figure we know that India's population growth has been remarkable, steadily increasing since 1950. Around 2024, India's population surpasses China's, marking a significant demographic milestone. The projection suggests that India's population will continue growing slightly before stabilizing around the mid-twenty-first century and eventually declining in the latter half of the century.

China, which experienced rapid population growth in the second half of the twentieth century, is now on a declining trajectory. The red line shows that China's population reached its peak before 2024 and has begun to decrease. This decline is attributed to low fertility rates, an aging population, and the long-term effects of policies like the one-child policy. The projected population for China shows a continuous decrease throughout the century.

Nigeria's population, on the other hand, has been growing at an accelerated rate. While its population was much smaller than China's and India's in the past, the green line reveals a steep upward trend. Projections indicate that Nigeria will surpass India's population later in the century, making it one of the most populous countries in the world.

The shaded areas around the lines represent prediction intervals, illustrating the level of uncertainty in future estimates. The wider shaded regions (95% prediction intervals) reflect greater variability in outcomes, while the narrower areas (80% prediction intervals) offer more confidence in the predictions. These intervals emphasize that while trends can be estimated, future demographic changes depend on various factors, including policies, healthcare, and societal changes.

What Does the Code Do?

- **Creates a plot** with ggplot() using the projections_subset data, mapping year on the x-axis.
- **Displays two layers of ribbons** to represent uncertainty in the projections:
- A 95% prediction interval (lower and upper bounds) with geom_ribbon() and 22% opacity.
- An 80% prediction interval (lower and upper bounds) with 44% opacity.
- **Adds a line** (geom_line()) representing the actual population data (indicators_subset), with color based on the country.
- **Annotates country labels** for China, India, and Nigeria at specific years (1950, 1965, 1980) with different colors.
- **Includes rich text annotations** about the 80% and 95% prediction intervals.
- **Adds curved arrows** to highlight future projections from 2052 to 2070.
- **Draws a vertical dashed line** at the year 2022 to separate historical data from projections, with a label pointing to the future.
- **Customizes axis labels** to display population in millions using scale_y_continuous().
- **Sets custom colors** for China, India, and Nigeria using scale_color_manual().
- **Removes the legend** and adjusts text, title, subtitle, and caption styles.
- **Uses a minimal theme** with custom adjustments to grid lines, plot background, and axis lines.

Challenges
Add your home country or any other country of interest, for example "Indonesia" and plot into your fan chart!
Expected results:

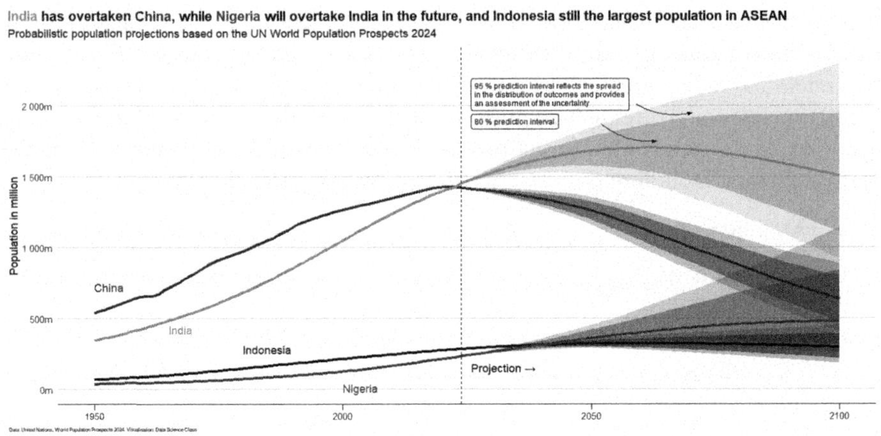

References

Bertini, E., et al. (2021). Uncertainty visualization in decision-making. *Proceedings of the IEEE Symposium on Visualization.*

Cleveland, W. S. (2009). *The Elements of Graphing Data.* Hobart Press.

Deitrick, S., & Wentz, E. A. (2015). Developing implicit uncertainty visualization methods motivated by theories in decision science. *Annals of the Association of American Geographers, 105*(3), 531–551. https://doi.org/10.1080/00045608.2015.1012635

Few, S. (2006). *Information Dashboard Design.* O'Reilly Media.

Hullman, J., Resnick, P., & Adar, E. (2015). Hypothetical outcome plots outperform error bars and violin plots for inferences about reliability of variable Ordering. *PLoS ONE, 10*(11), e0142444. https://doi.org/10.1371/journal.pone.0142444

IHME. (2020). COVID-19 Projections. Institute for Health Metrics and Evaluation. Retrieved from https://www.healthdata.org/research-analysis/diseases-injuries/covid

Ioannidis, J. P. A., Cripps, S., & Tanner, M. A. (2020). Forecasting for COVID-19 has failed. *International Journal of Forecasting, 36*(3), 741–744. https://doi.org/10.1016/j.ijforecast.2020.08.004

Kinkeldey, C., MacEachren, A. M., & Schiewe, J. (2014). How to Assess Visual Communication of Uncertainty? A Systematic Review of Geospatial Uncertainty Visualisation User Studies. *The Cartographic Journal, 51*(4), 372–386. https://doi.org/10.1179/1743277414Y.0000000099

Kosslyn, S. M. (2006). *Graph Design for the Eye and Mind.* Oxford University Press.

Lapinski, Anna-Liesa S. (2009). A strategy for uncertainty visualization Design. Technical Memorandum, Defence R&D Canada (2009). Available at https://users.cs.utah.edu/~miriah/uncertainty/Lapinski.pdf

Tufte, E. R. (2001). The visual display of quantitative information. Graphics Press. Available at https://archive.org/details/visualdisplayofq0000edwa

Yu, Z. Y. (2018). *Visualizing uncertainty : What we talk about when we talk about uncertainty.* Northeastern University. https://doi.org/10.17760/D20290236

Chapter 6
Machine Learning, Measuring Uncertainty, and Forecasting

Abstract This chapter dives into the fundamentals of machine learning, exploring its brief history, underlying logic, major types, popular algorithms, and both advantages and limitations. The important topic of measuring uncertainty in data science is addressed, with methods such as the confusion matrix, receiver operating characteristic curve, and Monte Carlo simulations, which help assess model accuracy and performance. Strategies for reducing uncertainty are also included. Forecasting methods are examined, covering definitions, types, algorithms, applications, and the benefits and drawbacks of using these techniques. The next section explores forecasting with Japanese cherry blossom datasets and building effective storytelling, an essential skill in data science.

Relation to other chapters: Expands on the machine learning introduction in Chap. 3.

6.1 Introduction

Machine learning (ML) is a transformative branch of artificial intelligence (AI) that develops algorithms and models allowing computers to autonomously learn from data. Unlike conventional programming, ML does not rely on hardcoded instructions; instead, it identifies patterns within data to make predictions or decisions. Its applications are vast, ranging from automated translations to complex decision-making systems in economics and environmental studies. The ability to use ML techniques in social studies is becoming increasingly important due to the growing abundance, variety, and value of data.

F. Ramdani, *Data Science: Foundations and Hands-on Experience*,
https://doi.org/10.1007/978-981-96-4683-8_6

6.2 Brief History and Key Terminology

Brief history

The foundation of ML was laid in the mid-twentieth century, with Alan Turing's seminal 1950 paper Computing Machinery and Intelligence, which introduced the "Turing Test." This marked the early conceptualization of machines exhibiting learning capabilities. In 1959, Arthur Samuel coined the term "machine learning" while developing a program to play checkers, demonstrating that machines could improve performance through experience. Breakthroughs like the introduction of backpropagation algorithms for neural networks (Rumelhart et al., 1986) and ensemble methods (Dietterich, 2000), followed by the deep learning revolution in the 2010s. These advancements have made it possible to analyze unstructured data, such as social media content and satellite imagery, for socio-economic insights.

Key terminology

In machine learning, several key terms are frequently used. These terms help in understanding how algorithms process data and make predictions. Below are some of the most important concepts:

- **Feature**: In machine learning, a feature refers to an input variable or attribute that is used by the model to make predictions or decisions. For example, in a poverty prediction model, features could include household income, education level, or employment status. In a land use classification task, features might include reflectance values from satellite images. Features can take different forms, such as numerical data (e.g., income), categorical data (e.g., urban or rural), or binary data (e.g., yes or no). Features are critical because they provide the model with the necessary information to make accurate predictions.
- **Label**: The label is the output or target variable in supervised learning. It represents the value that the model is trying to predict or classify. In a poverty prediction model, for example, the label could be the poverty level, such as "low," "medium," or "high". In land use classification, the label might correspond to specific land types, such as "forest," "urban," or "agriculture". Labels are sometimes referred to as "targets" or "annotations" in various literature. The goal of the model is to learn the relationship between features and labels during the training process.
- **Training set**: The training set is a subset of data that is used to train a machine learning model. This dataset consists of input–output pairs, where the input is a feature and the output is the corresponding label. During the training process, the model learns the relationship between the features and the labels, allowing it to make predictions. A good training set is essential for the model to generalize well to new, unseen data.
- **Validation**: The validation set is a separate subset of data used to tune the hyperparameters of the machine learning model. Hyperparameters are the settings that control the training process, such as learning rate or the number of layers in a neural network. The validation set helps in assessing how well the model performs during

training and ensures that it does not overfit or underfit. It also provides insight into how the model might perform on unseen data.

- **Test set**: The test set is a final subset of data that is used to evaluate the performance of the trained model. It consists of examples that the model has never seen during the training process. The test set allows for an unbiased evaluation of the model's accuracy and generalization ability. After the model is trained and validated, it is tested on this set to measure how well it can predict outcomes on new, unseen data.
- **Accuracy**: Accuracy is a common performance metric in machine learning that measures how often the model makes correct predictions. It is calculated as the proportion of correct predictions out of the total number of predictions. For example, if a model correctly predicts the label for 80 out of 100 data points, the accuracy would be 80%. Accuracy is useful for assessing a model's overall performance but may not always reflect the model's true effectiveness, especially when dealing with imbalanced datasets.
- **Precision**: Precision is another important performance metric that focuses on the accuracy of the positive predictions made by the model. It measures the proportion of true positives (correctly identified positive instances) out of all the instances the model predicted as positive. For example, in a spam email detection system, precision measures how many of the emails identified as spam are actually spam. High precision is important when false positives (incorrectly labeling something as positive) are costly or undesirable.
- **Overfitting**: Overfitting is a common problem in machine learning where a model performs well on the training data but fails to generalize to new, unseen data. This happens when the model becomes too complex and starts to capture not only the true underlying patterns but also the noise or irrelevant details in the training data. As a result, the model performs poorly on the test set because it has memorized the training data rather than learning generalizable patterns. Regularization techniques, such as adding constraints or simplifying the model, are often used to prevent overfitting.
- **Underfitting**: Underfitting occurs when a machine learning model is too simple and fails to capture the underlying patterns in the data. It happens when the model does not have enough complexity or flexibility to learn from the training data, resulting in poor performance on both the training set and test set. Underfitting can be addressed by using a more complex model, adding more features, or increasing the training time to allow the model to learn better.

These terms are fundamental to understanding how machine learning models work and how their performance is evaluated. Each concept plays a crucial role in the training, evaluation, and refinement of machine learning algorithms. As the field of ML continues to grow, understanding these basic terms is essential for developing more accurate and effective models.

6.3 Types of Machine Learning

ML can be classified into three main categories based on the nature of the input data and learning objectives:

Supervised learning

In supervised learning, the model is trained on labeled data, where the desired output is known. The algorithm learns the relationship between the input variables (features) and the corresponding output variables (labels) to make predictions or classify new, unseen data. It is widely used in applications where the desired output is known. There are two basic types of supervised learning: regression and classification.

Regression can be used for predicting continuous outcomes. For example, predicting life expectancy based on healthcare spending and socio-economic indicators. Or predicting income inequality (dependent variable) using independent variables like education levels, healthcare access, and geographic factors.

Classification can be used for categorizing observations into discrete classes, such as classifying citizens into income brackets or identifying crime types in metropolitan areas based on incident reports and demographic data.

In the context of machine learning, Fig. 6.1 represents a concept of *supervised learning*. Here is how the boy's understanding of the three cats relates to machine learning:

1. **Training phase**: The boy has likely been taught (or has learned) to recognize what a "cat" looks like. In machine learning, this would be the phase where a model is trained on labeled data (images of cats labeled as "cat"). The boy, in this case, could have been shown many images of cats in the past, along with

Fig. 6.1 Concept of supervised learning

their labels ("cat"), which helps him learn to identify the distinguishing features of a cat.
2. **Pattern recognition**: When the boy sees the three cats, his brain processes the features of the animals (e.g., fur, ears, whiskers, body shape) and matches them to the patterns he has learned. Similarly, in machine learning, a trained model uses features extracted from images (like edges, shapes, and textures) to classify them based on patterns learned from previous training data.
3. **Inference**: The boy can immediately classify the animals as cats based on the learned patterns, similar to how a machine learning model, after being trained, makes an inference on new data. For example, once a convolutional neural network (CNN) is trained with many images of cats, it can infer whether a new image contains a cat or not by analyzing the features.

The boy understands that the animals are cats because of previous experiences (training) and the ability to recognize patterns (inference), just like how a machine learning model classifies objects based on learned features.

Unsupervised learning

Unsupervised learning deals with unlabeled data, where the algorithm aims to discover patterns, structures, or relationships within the data. It does not have predefined outputs, so the algorithm learns to represent the data in a meaningful way. Techniques like clustering are valuable for grouping urban regions based on socio-economic similarities. Another example is clustering neighborhoods based on income, housing quality, and public service access to identify zones for targeted policy action.

Figure 6.2 represents a concept of *unsupervised learning*. In the context of unsupervised learning, the computer is not given explicit labels (such as "banana" or "papaya") for the images. Instead, it tries to understand patterns and structure from the data by grouping similar things together based on their features, without being told what those features represent.

Then how does the computer understand that there is a banana in the picture? The computer will need the following parameters:

1. **Feature extraction**: The computer first looks for important features in the image, such as shapes, textures, and colors. For example, it might detect the shape of the banana and papaya, as well as its texture or color pattern.
2. **Clustering**: Using these features, the computer can apply clustering algorithms (e.g., K-means, hierarchical clustering) to group similar images together. The clustering algorithm identifies similarities between the images of the banana and papaya, and since the banana has different features from the papaya (e.g., size, shape, or color), it might end up in its own distinct group.
3. **Dimensionality reduction**: To make sense of the data in a simpler form, the computer might use dimensionality reduction techniques like Principal Component Analysis (PCA) or t-SNE (t-distributed stochastic neighbor embedding) to map the high-dimensional feature space into a lower-dimensional one. This can

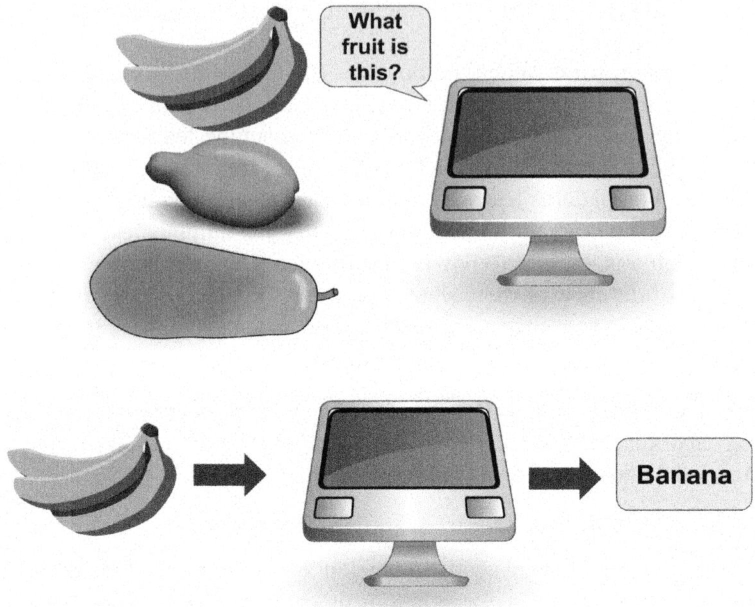

Fig. 6.2 Concept of unsupervised learning

help visualize the similarities and differences between the banana and papaya more clearly.

4. **Pattern recognition**: If the computer has been trained on many images of bananas and papayas beforehand (even without labels), it can recognize common patterns for each species, such as specific features of a banana's shape compared to a papaya's. These patterns can help the system separate the banana from the papaya, even if it doesn't know what a "banana" or "papaya" is in human terms.

In unsupervised learning, the computer does not directly "know" it is a banana—it just detects and clusters patterns based on the input data, distinguishing the banana from papayas by the unique features it identifies.

Reinforcement learning

Reinforcement learning (RL) involves an agent that learns to interact with an environment to maximize a reward signal. The agent takes action, receives feedback from the environment, and adjusts its actions based on the rewards and penalties it receives. Over time, the agent learns to make optimal decisions. Applications include resource allocation and policy optimization in public administration. For instance, an agent learns to allocate limited budgets for public infrastructure development efficiently by trial-and-error in simulated urban environments.

Figure 6.3 represents a concept of *reinforcement learning*. The scenario involving a dog as an agent and a girl as an environment illustrates how the agent learns

Fig. 6.3 Concept of reinforcement learning

to perform tasks through interactions and feedback. Following are the breakdown process:

1. **Agent (dog)**: The dog is the agent, which is the decision-maker in the RL system. The dog's goal is to perform a specific task (e.g., fetching a stick, sitting when instructed) by taking actions that lead to favorable outcomes.
2. **Environment (girl)**: The girl represents the environment, which is everything the agent interacts with. In this case, the girl might give commands, provide feedback, or set obstacles, shaping the agent's experience.
3. **State**: The state refers to the situation the agent is in at any given time. For example, the state could be the position of the dog, whether it's sitting or standing, or its proximity to the stick.
4. **Action**: The action is what the dog (agent) chooses to do at any moment. This could involve sitting, jumping, moving toward the stick, or responding to a command.
5. **Reward**: After the agent takes an action, the environment (girl) provides a reward or punishment. If the dog successfully fetches the stick, the girl might reward it with praise or a treat. If the dog fails, it might not receive any reward or could be given negative feedback.
6. **Observation**: The observation is what the dog perceives about its current state. This could be visual (seeing the stick), auditory (hearing the girl's voice), or tactile (feeling the leash)

While the following is the learning process:

- **Trial-and-error**: The agent (dog) repeatedly interacts with the environment (girl) by performing actions. After each action, the dog receives feedback in the form of rewards or punishments. This helps the dog learn which actions lead to positive outcomes and which ones should be avoided.
- **Policy**: Over time, the dog develops a policy, which is a strategy or a set of rules for deciding which action to take in a given state. Initially, the dog may take random

actions, but as it accumulates experience (repeated trial-and-error), it begins to favor actions that lead to higher rewards.

- **Value function**: The dog learns to estimate the long-term value of being in a certain state. If sitting when instructed is often rewarded with treats, the dog will learn that sitting is a valuable state and will be more likely to choose that action in similar future states.
- **Exploration vs. exploitation**: The dog might explore new actions to discover even better ways to perform the task (exploration). However, as it learns which actions are rewarding, it will start exploiting those known actions to maximize rewards (exploitation).

In this analogy, the dog represents an RL agent, and the girl provides the environment that shapes the learning process through feedback. The dog gradually learns the optimal behavior (policy) through interactions, aiming to maximize the cumulative reward over time.

Semi-supervised learning

Semi-supervised learning combines elements of supervised and unsupervised learning by leveraging both labeled and unlabeled data. This approach is particularly useful when labels are difficult or expensive to obtain, but unlabeled data is available in large quantities. For example, in image classification, only a small subset of images may have labels (e.g., labeled "banana" or "papaya"), while the rest are unlabeled. The model uses the labeled data for initial learning and the unlabeled data to refine its understanding of patterns in the data.

In the context of semi-supervised machine learning, we can think of a young girl as the trainer, a computer as the machine learning model, and a collection of bananas and papayas as the dataset to be used (Fig. 6.4). Semi-supervised machine learning is an approach in which the model is trained using a combination of labeled and unlabeled data.

First, the girl provides the computer with a small subset of labeled data. For example, she shows the computer some bananas and papayas and labels them, such as "This is a banana" or "This is a papaya." This labeled data helps the computer

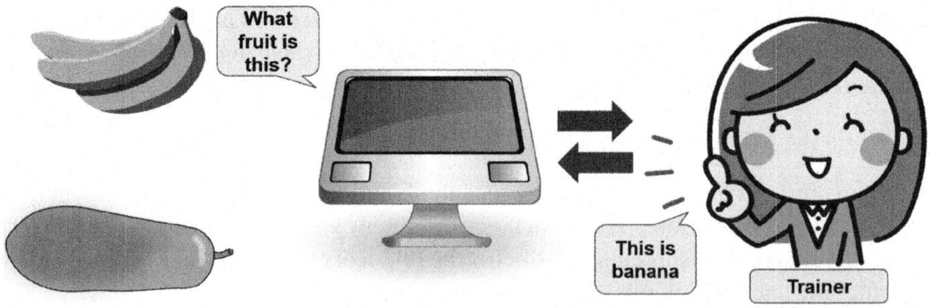

Fig. 6.4 Illustration of the concept of semi-supervised learning

understand basic characteristics of the two types of fruit, such as color, shape, or texture.

The computer is then presented with a much larger, unlabeled dataset—other fruits that are not told whether they are bananas or papayas. This is where semi-supervised learning comes into play. The computer uses the prior knowledge it gained from the labeled data to try to classify the unlabeled data. For example, it can use an algorithm like clustering to group fruits based on shared features. If the computer already knows that bananas are typically yellow and curved, while papayas tend to be oval and orange, it will try to identify the unlabeled fruit based on these patterns.

The girl can help again by reviewing the computer's classification results. If there are any errors, she can provide feedback, such as flagging that a fruit that was incorrectly classified as a banana is actually a papaya. This feedback improves the computer model, making it more accurate at distinguishing between bananas and papayas.

With this approach, the computer can learn to recognize bananas from papayas even though most of the available data is unlabeled. Semi-supervised methods are particularly useful when labeled data is difficult or expensive to obtain, but unlabeled data is available in large quantities. This process illustrates how semi-supervised learning allows for more efficient use of data while minimizing the need for manual labeling.

Semi-supervised learning is widely used in facial recognition, text analysis, and biomedical applications where collecting labels requires specialized expertise.

6.4 Algorithms in Machine Learning

ML encompasses a range of algorithms, each suited to specific tasks. In this book, it will be classified into two big groups, that is linear and nonlinear. In linear, we try to model a linear relationship between two variables using a straight line. While in nonlinear we try to model a nonlinear relationship between two variables using a curve. Nonlinear regression is more flexible than linear regression and can model complex relationships, such as exponential growth, decay, saturation, oscillation, and logistic growth.

In both linear and nonlinear regression, the goal is to make the sum of the squares as small as possible. The sum of squares is calculated by finding the difference between the mean and each data point.

We can tell if a relationship is linear or nonlinear by looking at a scatterplot of the data. If the points generally follow a straight path, the relationship is linear. If the points do not generally follow a straight path, the relationship is nonlinear.

Nonlinear algorithms in machine learning are techniques that model complex relationships between variables in data. These algorithms capture intricate interactions and patterns in data that linear models can't represent as well. They can be used to predict outcomes and identify decision boundaries in classification problems.

Linear models

Linear regression is a basic algorithm often used in regression tasks. It establishes a straight-line relationship between input features (independent variables) and the target variable (dependent variable). This means that linear regression assumes a direct, proportional relationship between the inputs and the output. For example, it can be used to predict housing prices based on factors like square footage, number of rooms, and location. Linear regression is easy to understand and interpret, making it a common choice for many basic predictive modeling problems.

Logistic regression is another widely used technique, but it is specifically designed for binary classification problems. It is used when the target variable has two possible outcomes, such as yes or no, true or false. For example, logistic regression could be applied to predict whether a person will default on a loan based on factors like income, credit score, and loan amount. The model outputs a probability, which is then converted into one of the two categories. Logistic regression is a simple but effective tool for many practical classification tasks in fields like finance and healthcare. For the illustration you may refer to Fig. 3.22 in Chap. 3.

Nonlinear models

There are many nonlinear algorithms in machine learning, such as decision trees, random forest (RF), classification and regression trees (CART), Naive Bayes, support vector machines (SVM), neural networks (NN), k-nearest neighbors (k-NN), convolutional neural networks (CNN), gradient boosting machines (GBM), Gaussian mixture model (GMM), Minimum Distance, Maximum Likelihood, spectral angle mapping (SAM), and multi-layer perceptron (MLP). Each of the algorithms will be discussed briefly as follow:

Decision trees

Decision trees are a type of model that uses a tree-like structure to make decisions based on the values of input features. Each node of the tree represents a decision rule, and branches represent possible outcomes. Decision trees can handle both regression (predicting continuous outcomes) and classification tasks (predicting discrete categories). One key advantage of decision trees is their simplicity and interpretability, as they provide a visual representation of decision-making. However, they can be prone to overfitting, meaning they may perform well on training data but poorly on unseen data. Figure 6.5 illustrates the decision tree based on the well-known iris dataset.

Random forest (RF)

RF is an ensemble learning method that combines many decision trees to improve prediction accuracy. By averaging the results of multiple trees, random forests reduce the risk of overfitting and provide more robust and reliable predictions. This method is particularly useful in complex tasks, such as predicting customer behavior or classifying large datasets. Random forests are widely used in fields like finance, medicine, and marketing due to their high accuracy and ability to handle large datasets. Figure 6.6 illustrates the error rate and variable of importance of RF model

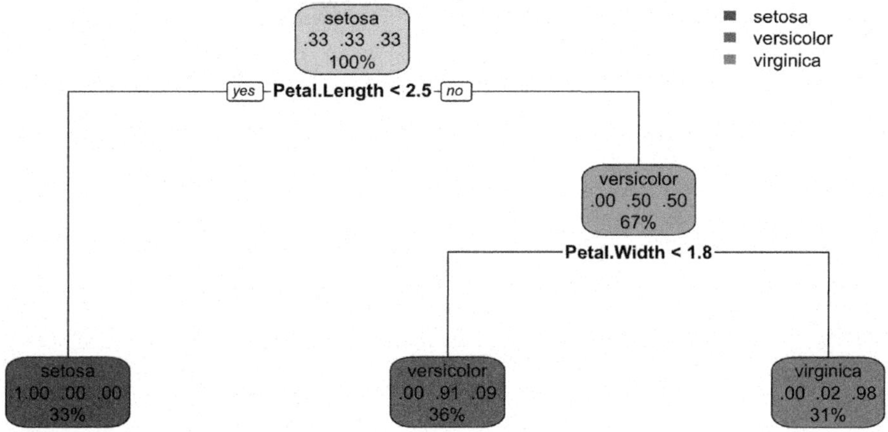

Fig. 6.5 Decision tree of iris dataset

from iris dataset. The error rate in a random forest is the proportion of incorrect predictions made by the model. For example, if a random forest predicts 90 out of 100 instances correctly, it has an error rate of 0.1. A variable of importance in a random forest is a measure of how important a variable is in classifying data. It shows how much accuracy is lost when a variable is excluded from the model, or how much accuracy is gained when a variable is included.

Classification and regression trees (CART)

CART is a machine learning algorithm that uses decision trees to create models for two types of tasks: classification and regression. A decision tree is a structure that looks like a flowchart, where each internal node represents a decision based on a specific feature or attribute, and each leaf node represents the outcome or prediction. Classification is a task where the goal is to categorize data into predefined classes or labels. For example, CART can be used to predict whether an email is spam or not based on its features such as subject line, sender, and keywords. In this case, the decision tree will classify emails into two categories: spam or not spam. Regression, on the other hand, involves predicting continuous values rather than categories. For example, CART can be used to predict house prices based on factors like the size of the house, its location, number of rooms, and other relevant features. In regression, the tree outputs a numerical value, such as the predicted price of the house. CART builds a binary tree structure, which means each decision splits the data into two groups based on a feature's value. The internal nodes of the tree represent decisions made on the input features, while the leaf nodes contain the outcome: class labels in classification or predicted values in regression. Figure 6.7 illustrates the CART model. We will practice using CART to classify earth observation satellite images in Chap. 7.

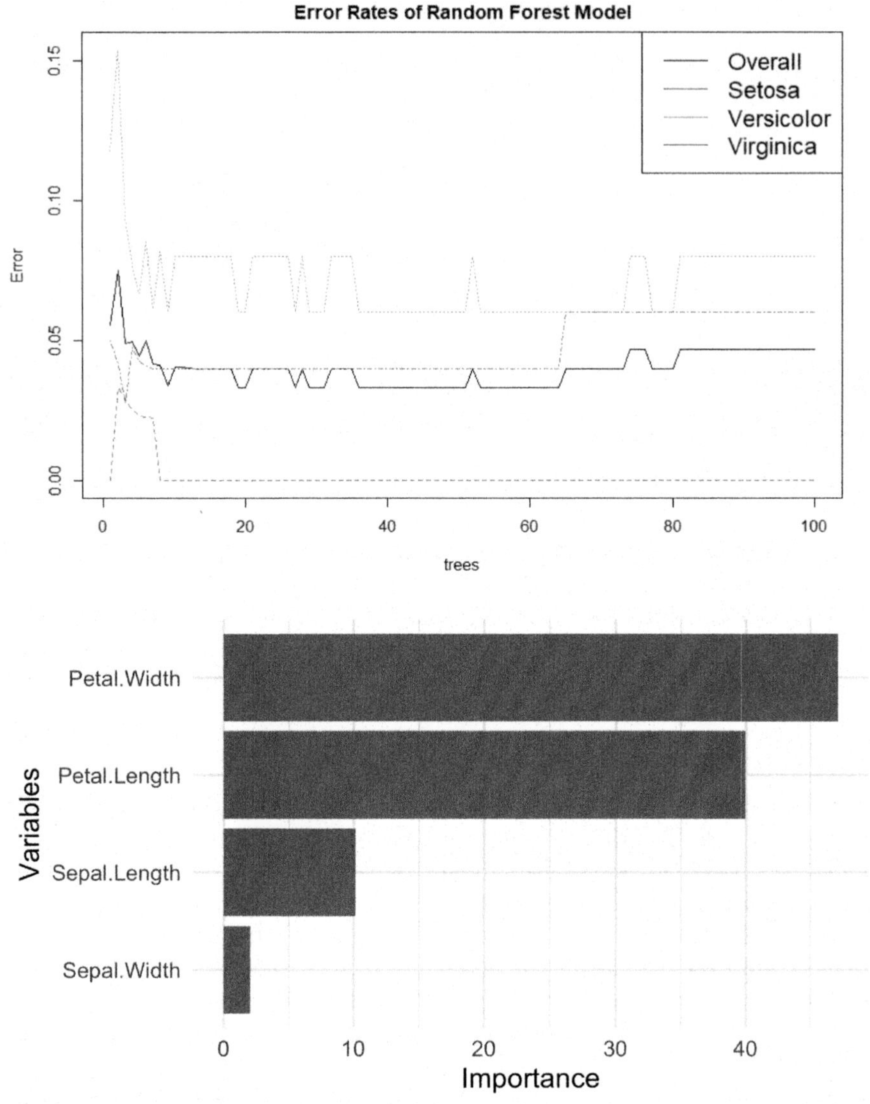

Fig. 6.6 Error rates and variable of importance of random forest model using iris dataset

Support vector machines

SVM is another popular algorithm used for both classification and regression tasks. SVM works by finding the optimal hyperplane, which is a boundary that best separates different classes or predicts continuous values in regression tasks. SVM is known for its ability to handle high-dimensional spaces and works well in situations where there is a clear margin of separation between classes. It is commonly used in

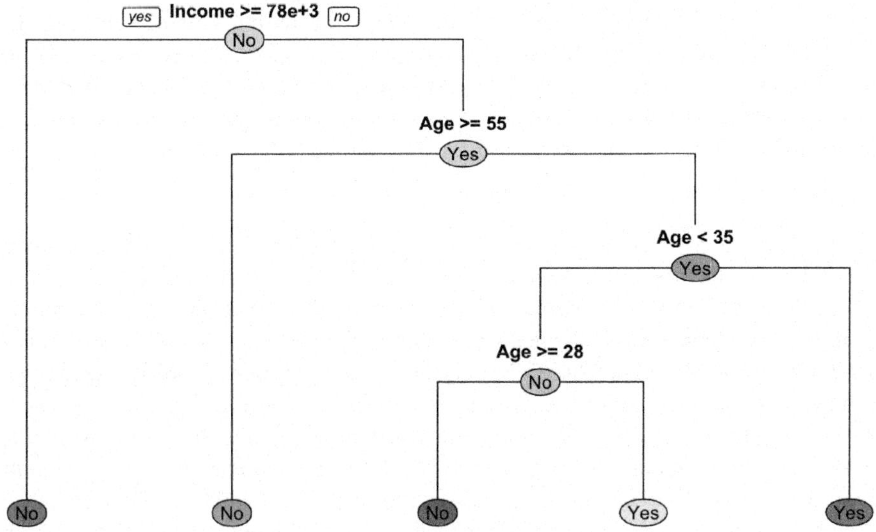

Fig. 6.7 CART model

text classification, image recognition, remote sensing, and geoinformatics. Figure 6.8 illustrates the SVM decision boundary.

A solid blue line represents the decision boundary that the SVM algorithm has learned. This boundary separates the two classes and is the optimal hyperplane that maximizes the margin between the two classes. Two dashed red lines represent the margins of the SVM classifier. These lines show the boundaries within which

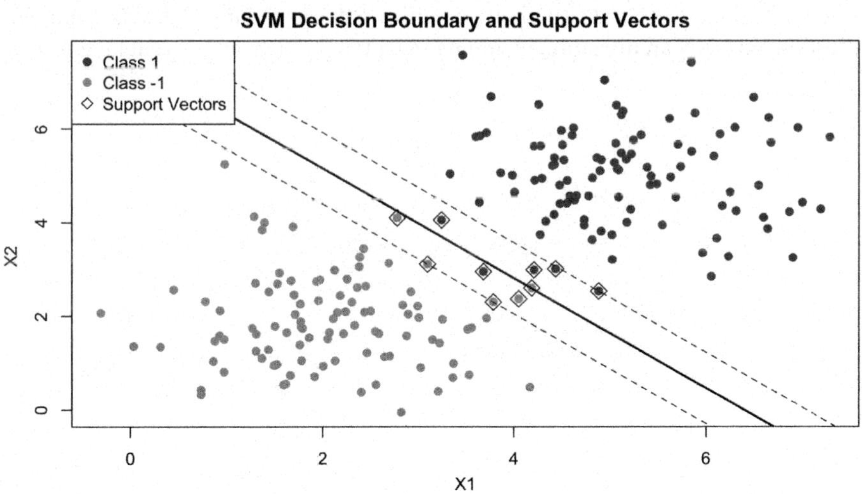

Fig. 6.8 SVM decision boundary

no data points are located, while the margin is the region between the decision boundary and these red lines. The support vectors lie on these margins. Points that are support vectors (the most critical data points for defining the decision boundary) are highlighted as purple diamonds. These support vectors are the points closest to the decision boundary and are crucial for training the SVM model.

Naive Bayes

Naive Bayes is a simple yet powerful probabilistic algorithm that relies on Bayes' theorem to make predictions based on prior knowledge and observed data. The algorithm operates under the assumption that the presence (or absence) of a particular feature in a dataset is independent of the presence (or absence) of other features, given the class label. This "naive" independence assumption simplifies the computation, making Naive Bayes highly efficient, especially for large datasets. Despite its simplicity, it is widely used in applications such as spam detection, sentiment analysis, and document classification, where its performance often rivals more complex algorithms. Figure 6.9 shows two groups of points (Class 1 and Class 2), with a decision boundary dividing the space. The background is shaded to indicate the regions where the Naive Bayes classifier predicts each class.

Neural networks

NN are a class of algorithms inspired by the human brain's structure. These networks consist of layers of nodes, or neurons, which process information and pass it on to the next layer. Neural networks are particularly effective in solving complex problems, such as recognizing patterns in images or understanding natural language. A subset of neural networks, known as deep learning neural network (DNN), has gained significant attention in recent years for its ability to solve problems in fields like image and speech recognition. Deep learning models often consist of many hidden layers, allowing them to learn highly complex patterns in large datasets. Figure 6.10 illustrates the NN architecture, including the input, hidden, and output layers, as well

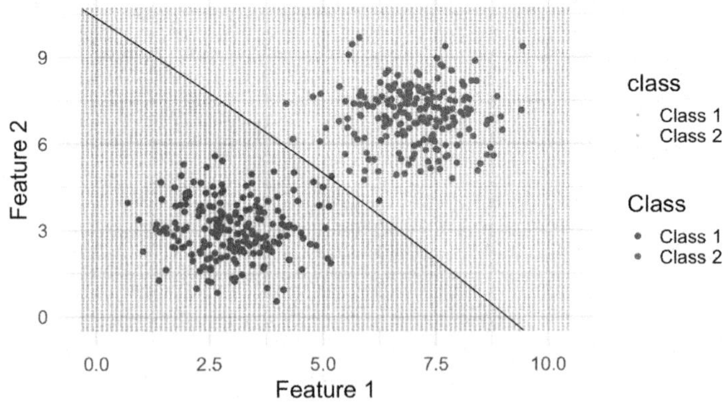

Fig. 6.9 Illustration of Naive Bayes

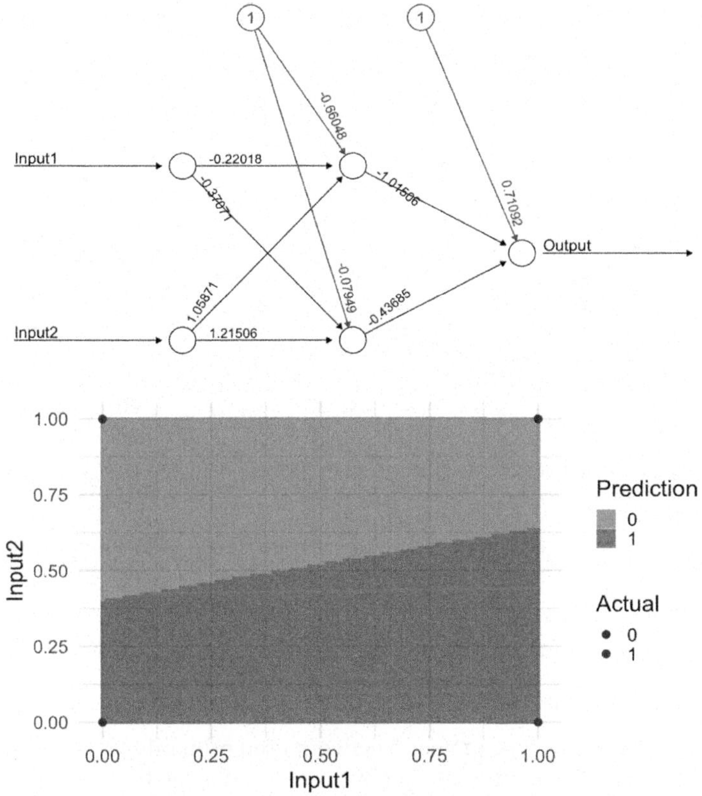

Fig. 6.10 Neural network architecture and its decision boundary

as the learned weights for each connection (weights initialization is shown in blue) and its decision boundary.

k-nearest neighbors

k-nearest neighbors (k-NN) is a machine learning algorithm that uses proximity to classify or predict data points. It is a popular, simple, and supervised learning classifier that is used for both classification and regression tasks. KNN compares a data point to a set of data it has been trained on to make predictions. It assumes that similar points are close together and assigns a new data point to the majority class of its neighbors. KNN is a non-parametric algorithm, meaning it does not make any assumptions about the dataset. It is also known as a lazy learner because it only stores a training dataset and performs all computations when a prediction is made. However, KNN can become slower as the number of observations and independent variables increases. Figure 6.11 illustrates the KNN decision boundary of the synthetic 2D dataset with $k = 5$.

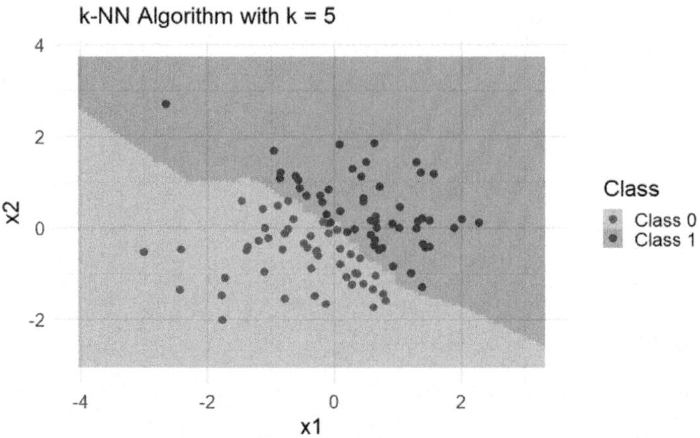

Fig. 6.11 KNN decision boundary of the synthetic 2D dataset

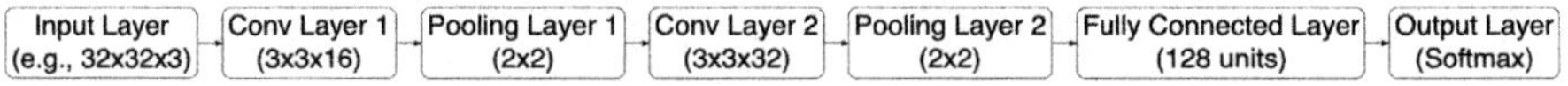

Fig. 6.12 CNN architecture

Convolutional neural networks

CNNs are a specialized type of neural network used primarily for image processing. In social science applications, CNNs have been used to analyze satellite images for tasks like identifying illegal deforestation. By learning patterns in pixel data, CNNs can identify features such as trees, roads, and buildings, making them valuable for monitoring environmental changes. These models have revolutionized fields like computer vision and remote sensing. Figure 6.12 illustrates the CNN architecture.

The figure visually demonstrates the standard workflow of a CNN. It begins with raw input data, applies feature extraction through convolutional layers, reduces dimensions with pooling layers, combines features using fully connected layers, and finally produces the classification probabilities in the output layer.

Gradient boosting machines

GBM combines multiple "weak learners," such as decision trees, to create a strong predictive model. GBM builds the model in stages, with each stage attempting to correct the errors made by the previous one. This iterative process results in a model that is highly accurate and robust. Gradient boosting is widely used in predicting economic trends, customer behavior, and other areas where predictive accuracy is crucial. It is especially effective when dealing with complex, nonlinear relationships in the data. Figure 6.13 illustrates the model's performance of GBM based on the Boston dataset that shows the relative influence of the predictors and the Partial Dependence Plots (PDP) for a specific variable, e.g., "lstat."

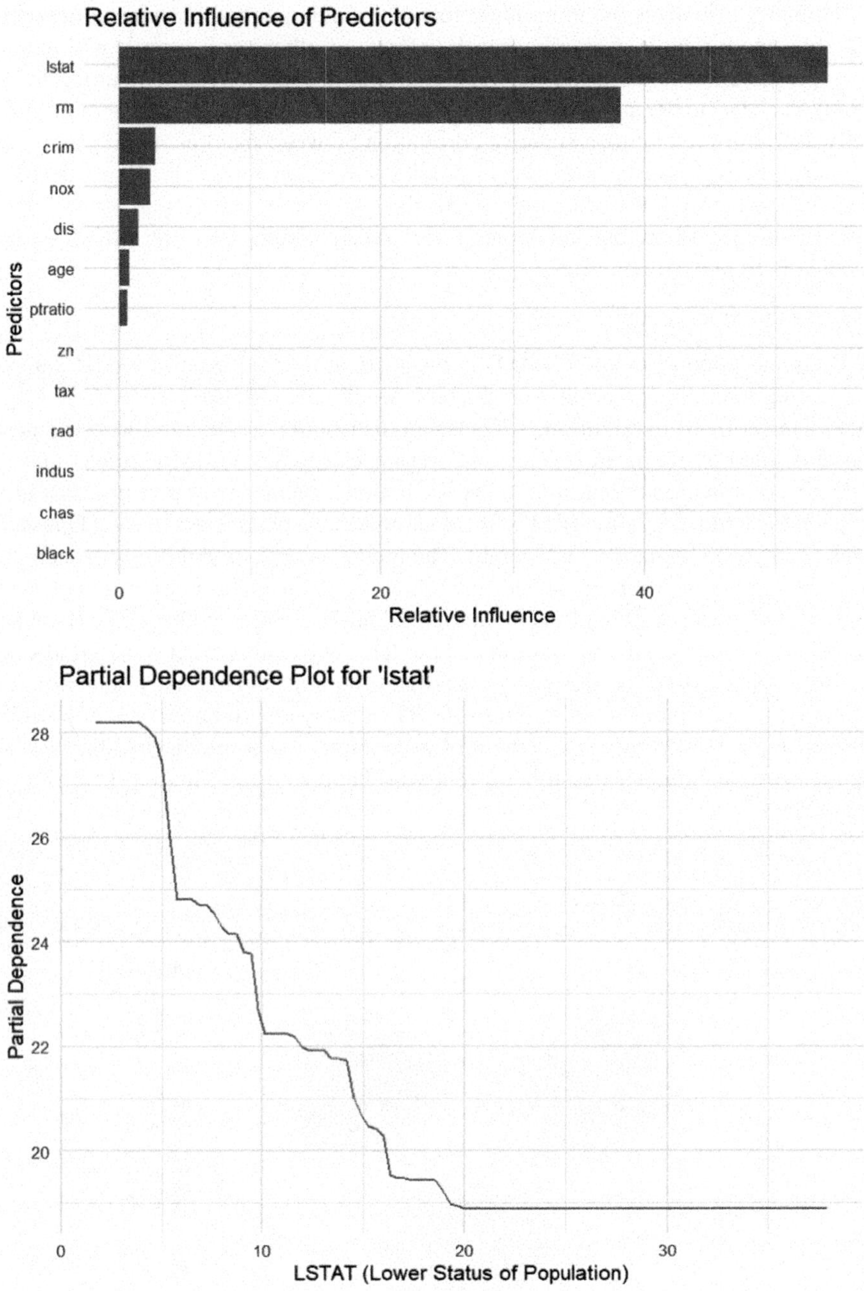

Fig. 6.13 GBM model's performance of the Boston dataset

This plot visualizes the marginal effect of a single predictor (lstat) on the target variable (medv) while averaging out the effects of other predictors. It will help us to understand the relationship between lstat and housing prices, as learned by the GBM. As lstat (lower status population) increases, medv (median house price) typically decreases, reflecting a negative correlation between socio-economic status and housing prices. The plot may reveal nonlinear relationships (e.g., sharp declines, plateaus), which GBMs can capture effectively. These plots are part of the model interpretation process and are crucial for understanding how the GBM utilizes predictors to make predictions.

Gaussian mixture model

A Gaussian mixture model (GMM) is a statistical method used to model datasets containing overlapping groups or clusters, where each group is represented by a Gaussian (normal) distribution. A Gaussian distribution is the familiar bell-shaped curve defined by its mean (center) and variance (spread). GMM assumes that the data is a combination of multiple such distributions. Using an iterative process called Expectation–Maximization (EM), GMM estimates the parameters of each Gaussian, such as its mean, variance, and weight. The model assigns probabilities to each data point belonging to different clusters and refines these estimates until the data is well-represented by the combination of Gaussians. Unlike simpler methods like K-means, GMM allows clusters to overlap and can model groups of different shapes and sizes. GMM is widely used for clustering, density estimation, and anomaly detection. For example, it can separate overlapping voices in a noisy environment or group similar customers in marketing. Practical implementations are available in libraries like Scikit-learn, making it accessible for real-world applications. Figure 6.14 illustrates the GMM.

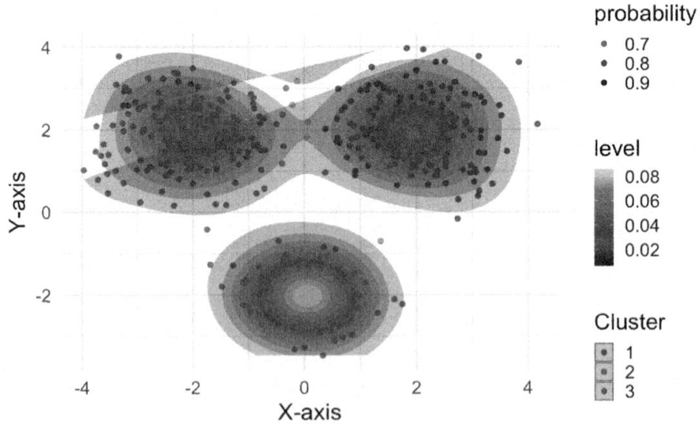

Fig. 6.14 Illustration of GMM

Minimum Distance

The Minimum Distance algorithm is a simple yet powerful approach in machine learning, especially for classification tasks. At its core, this algorithm works by finding the shortest distance between a data point that needs to be classified (called the "query point") and a set of predefined reference points or groups (also called "centroids"). These centroids typically represent the central or average location of each class of data points in a dataset. The algorithm assigns the query point to the class of the nearest centroid based on the computed distance. One of the most common distance measures used in the Minimum Distance algorithm is the Euclidean distance. This calculates the straight-line distance between two points in space. The Minimum Distance algorithm is computationally efficient and works well when the classes in the dataset are compact, distinct, and evenly distributed. However, it can struggle with more complex datasets where the class boundaries are irregular or where classes overlap significantly. In such cases, more advanced machine learning algorithms, like decision trees or neural networks, might perform better. This approach is widely used in pattern recognition, image processing, and remote sensing applications. For example, in remote sensing, the Minimum Distance algorithm can classify satellite images into classes like water bodies, forests, and urban areas by assigning each pixel to the closest spectral signature of these classes. Figure 6.15 shows the illustration of the Minimum Distance algorithm.

Maximum Likelihood

The Maximum Likelihood algorithm is a fundamental concept in statistics and machine learning used to estimate the parameters of a model. The basic idea is to find the set of parameters that make the observed data most likely under a given model. While the concept itself is rooted in statistics, it plays a significant role in nonlinear machine learning methods because it can adapt to complex patterns in

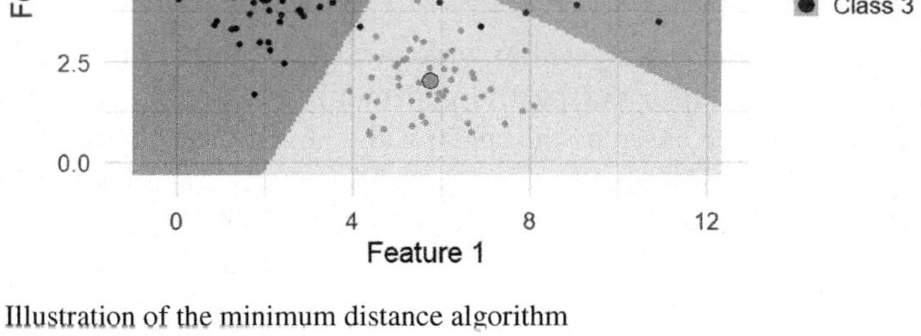

Fig. 6.15 Illustration of the minimum distance algorithm

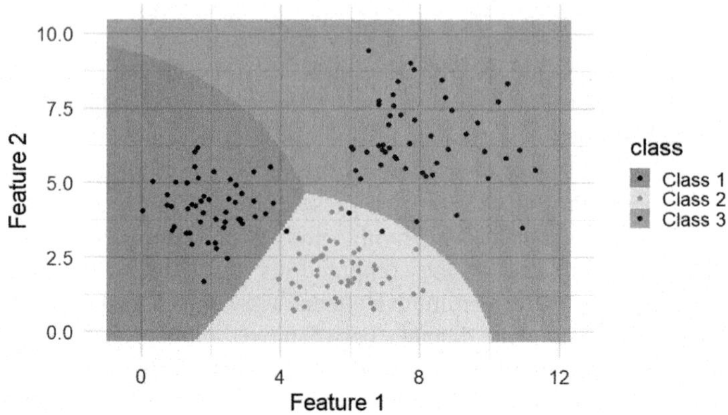

Fig. 6.16 Illustration of the maximum likelihood algorithm

data. The Maximum Likelihood classifier considers not only the cluster centers but also the shape, size, and orientation of the clusters. This is achieved by calculating a statistical distance based on the mean values and covariance matrix of the clusters. One of the most common distance measures used in the Maximum Likelihood algorithm is the Mahalonobis distance. It is a probability value that observation x belongs to a specific cluster. In the case of remote sensing, a cell of raster data is assigned to the class (cluster) to which it has the highest probability. Because that class has the smallest value in the units of Mahalonobis distance. Figure 6.16 shows the illustration of the Maximum Likelihood algorithm. Can you spot the difference between Maximum Likelihood and Minimum Distance algorithm?

One of the strengths of Maximum Likelihood is its flexibility. It can be used for both simple linear models and more complex, nonlinear ones, making it highly versatile in machine learning. However, it does have limitations. If the model is misspecified (i.e., it does not accurately represent the underlying data-generating process), the results can be biased or misleading. Additionally, Maximum Likelihood can be computationally expensive for nonlinear models with large datasets, as optimizing the likelihood function may involve evaluating complex mathematical expressions multiple times. For a more detailed discussion of the Minimum Distance and Maximum Likelihood algorithms, refer to the work by Bishop (2006).

Spectral angle mapping (SAM)

SAM is a machine learning algorithm widely used in the field of remote sensing, particularly for analyzing hyperspectral and multispectral data. This technique is designed to classify data based on the spectral signature of each pixel in an image. A spectral signature represents how a material reflects or absorbs light across different wavelengths, making it a unique identifier for various surface types such as vegetation, water, soil, or man-made materials. SAM operates by treating each spectral signature as a vector in a multi-dimensional space, where the dimensions correspond to the wavelengths of light in the data. The algorithm then measures the angle

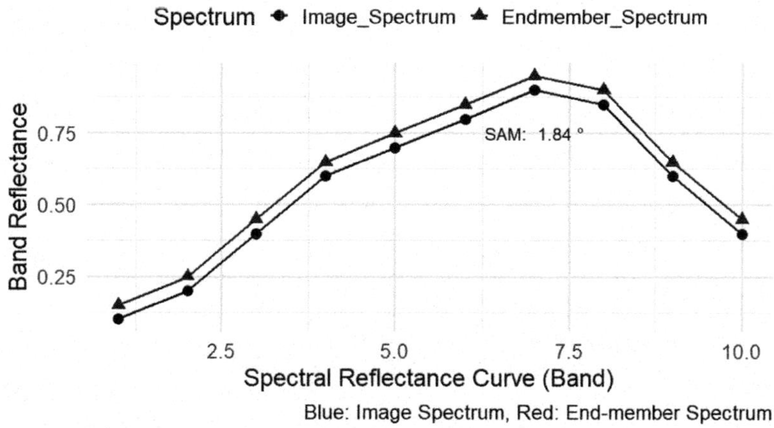

Fig. 6.17 Illustration of the SAM algorithm

between two spectral vectors: one from the pixel being analyzed and another from a reference material (or class). The key idea is that the smaller the angle between these vectors, the more similar their spectral characteristics are, meaning the pixel likely belongs to the same class as the reference material. By using angles rather than direct differences, SAM is relatively robust to variations in illumination or intensity, as it focuses on the shape of the spectral curve rather than its absolute values. Figure 6.17 shows the illustration of the SAM algorithm.

SAM is computationally efficient and straightforward, making it popular in applications like land cover classification and environmental monitoring. However, its accuracy depends on the quality of the reference spectra and the preprocessing of the data to remove noise or atmospheric interference.

Multi-layer perceptron (MLP)

MLP is a subset of neural network commonly used in machine learning, especially for solving nonlinear problems. The MLP is a deep learning algorithm consisting of layers of nodes, often referred to as neurons, which are inspired by how the human brain works. It has at least three layers: the input layer, one or more hidden layers, and the output layer. The input layer receives the raw data or features of a problem, like numbers or categories, and sends them to the next layer, the hidden layers. These hidden layers process the input through mathematical operations, including weights, biases, and activation functions (Fig. 6.18). The weights determine the importance of each input, while the biases shift the data to make the model more flexible. The activation function introduces nonlinearity into the model, allowing it to learn complex patterns.

The output layer gives the final prediction or result, which could be a classification label or a continuous value, depending on the problem. MLPs are trained using a method called backpropagation. This involves adjusting the weights and biases based on the error between the model's prediction and the actual outcome, which is

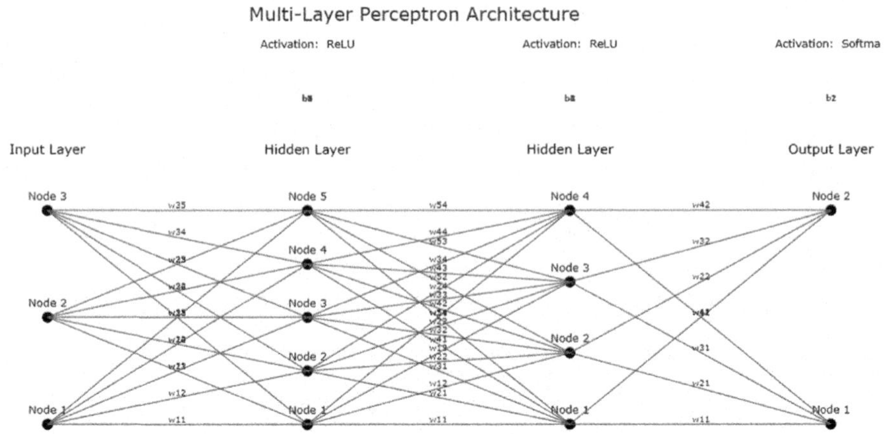

Fig. 6.18 Illustration of MLP architecture with four layers (input, hidden, hidden, output) and ReLU and softmax activation functions

calculated using a loss function. The adjustments are made through an optimization process, typically using gradient descent. This is the difference between MLP and NN algorithms, where the NN algorithm can contain loops while the MLP algorithm is only one-way or always feed-forward. The key strength of MLPs is their ability to model complex, nonlinear relationships in data, which makes them highly effective for a wide range of tasks like image recognition, speech processing, and even stock market predictions. However, MLPs require a lot of data and computational power, and if not properly tuned, they can overfit or underfit the data, meaning they might either memorize the data too well (overfitting) or fail to capture important patterns (underfitting).

6.5 Advantages and Disadvantages of Machine Learning

Advantages

Machine learning (ML) brings transformative capabilities to various domains by automating complex tasks, recognizing patterns, and deriving insights from large datasets. By streamlining processes that would otherwise be time-consuming or challenging for humans, ML enhances efficiency and productivity. Its ability to detect patterns and relationships in data provides valuable insights, enabling businesses to make informed decisions and optimize their strategies.

Additionally, ML excels in prediction and forecasting by analyzing historical data, and helping organizations with planning, risk assessment, and optimization. Personalization is another strength of ML, as it tailors recommendations, advertisements, and user experiences based on individual preferences and behavior. Furthermore,

ML's capacity to handle and analyze vast amounts of data uncovers hidden patterns and meaningful information, which would be nearly impossible for humans to extract manually. Together, these capabilities demonstrate ML's potential to revolutionize how we process and utilize information.

Disadvantages

Machine learning (ML) models face several critical challenges that impact their effectiveness and reliability. One major issue is their reliance on high-quality, diverse training data. When the data is biased, incomplete, or unrepresentative, the models can produce inaccurate or skewed predictions, limiting their utility. Compounding this is the lack of interpretability in many ML algorithms, particularly complex ones like deep neural networks. These models often operate as black boxes, making it difficult to understand their reasoning, explain their decisions, or build trust in their outputs.

Another common challenge is balancing a model's complexity. Overfitting occurs when a model performs well on training data but fails to generalize to new data, while underfitting happens when a model is too simplistic to capture important patterns. Striking the right balance is critical but often difficult. Adding to this is the need for large volumes of labeled data, especially for deep learning. Gathering and annotating such data can be time-consuming, costly, and impractical in certain fields.

ML also demands significant computational resources. Training complex models can strain processing power and memory, creating challenges for deployment, particularly in resource-limited environments. Ethical and legal concerns add another layer of complexity. Biases in training data can lead to discriminatory outcomes, while issues like privacy, data security, and accountability raise questions about responsible ML use.

The limitations of ML extend further. These models often lack domain-specific knowledge and common sense reasoning, relying solely on patterns from their training data. This can hinder their ability to handle novel or out-of-scope situations. Moreover, ML systems are vulnerable to adversarial attacks, where inputs are manipulated to deceive the model, posing risks in critical applications like autonomous vehicles or financial systems. Addressing these challenges is crucial to harnessing ML's full potential responsibly and effectively.

Its environmental impact is a growing concern, particularly in terms of energy efficiency. Running machine learning models often requires large amounts of computational resources, which, in turn, consume significant energy. For example, training deep learning models involves processing massive datasets and performing complex calculations, which demand high-performance hardware such as GPUs and TPUs. These hardware components are not only energy-intensive but also contribute to environmental degradation due to their production and operation.

One of the major challenges of ML is its "compute hunger." Advanced ML methods, especially deep learning algorithms, require thousands or even millions of iterations to optimize their performance. Each iteration consumes energy, and when multiplied over time and scaled across global usage, the energy demand becomes enormous. A report from the University of Massachusetts Amherst revealed that training a single large ML model could emit as much carbon dioxide as five cars over their entire lifespans. This highlights how energy-intensive ML processes contribute significantly to carbon emissions, exacerbating climate change (Strubell et al., 2019).

Strubell et al. (2019) ***discovered that training machine learning models can release over 626,000 pounds of carbon dioxide, which is almost five times the total emissions produced by an average car during its entire lifespan, including the car's production***

In addition to training, the deployment of ML models also consumes energy. Real-time applications, such as facial recognition, autonomous vehicles, and natural language processing tools, require constant processing power. These activities, running 24/7, strain energy systems further, particularly in data centers, which house thousands of servers running ML models. As demand for AI technologies grows, so does their environmental footprint, raising the need for more energy-efficient solutions.

Reducing the energy consumption of ML is critical for minimizing its environmental impact. Researchers and tech companies are exploring ways to address this issue, such as developing more efficient algorithms, using renewable energy sources to power data centers, and optimizing hardware to reduce energy requirements. However, the challenge remains significant, as the global adoption of ML technologies continues to expand rapidly.

6.6 Uncertainty in Data Science

Uncertainty is inherent in data analysis, affecting conclusions drawn from ML models. Recognizing and addressing these uncertainties is essential for ethical research.

As explained in Chap. 1, in the data science process there are six important stages: Define, plan, collect, analyze, interpret, and communicate. Each stage builds upon the previous one, forming a sequential workflow. However, as the process advances, the level of uncertainty increases. This increase in uncertainty reflects the accumulation of errors and challenges encountered during the transition between stages. The uncertainty can be categorized into three main types: Source error, process error, and use error.

Source error

The initial stages, define and plan, focus on establishing the research objectives, identifying data needs, and designing a methodology. Errors at this stage are labeled as Source Errors. These errors typically arise from poorly defined objectives, incomplete understanding of the research question, or inappropriate planning. For example, selecting irrelevant data sources or overlooking key variables can introduce significant uncertainties later in the process.

Process error

The next stages, collect and analyze, are where the data is gathered and processed. Errors here are classified as process errors and often result from inaccuracies during data collection or mistakes in analytical methods. These errors might stem from faulty instruments, data loss, improper statistical techniques, or biased analysis. Process errors can compound earlier source errors, leading to further uncertainty in results.

Use error

The final stages, interpret and communicate, focus on deriving meaning from the analyzed data and sharing the findings with stakeholders or the public. Errors in these stages are termed use errors and generally occur due to misinterpretation of results or ineffective communication. These errors might result in misinformed decisions or miscommunication of the research's implications.

Increasing uncertainty

As the process progresses from defining the research problem to communicating the results, the uncertainty becomes higher. This is because errors accumulate and propagate through each stage, making it increasingly difficult to manage their impact. For example, a small error in the planning stage may grow exponentially when compounded by process or use errors.

It is important to have careful planning, robust data collection, rigorous analysis, and clear communication to minimize errors and manage uncertainty throughout a data science process. It underscores the interconnected nature of each stage and the need to address potential sources of error early to ensure reliable and accurate outcomes.

Lego analogy

Figure 6.19 provides a visual analogy using LEGO blocks to explain the process of transforming raw data into actionable insights. It highlights different stages of data processing, evaluation, and utilization, with corresponding questions to assess the quality and certainty at each stage. It also shows that as data is refined through these stages, uncertainty is progressively reduced.

- **Data (raw)**: The first stage depicts a random pile of LEGO blocks, representing unprocessed, raw data. The key question here is, "*Is it acquired using valid methodology?*" This emphasizes the importance of collecting reliable and accurate data as the foundation for all subsequent steps. Poorly acquired data introduces a high level of uncertainty and compromises the entire process.
- **Sorted**: The second stage shows the LEGO blocks organized by color, representing data sorting and cleaning. The corresponding question, "*Is it sorted correctly?,*" addresses whether errors, inconsistencies, or irrelevant information

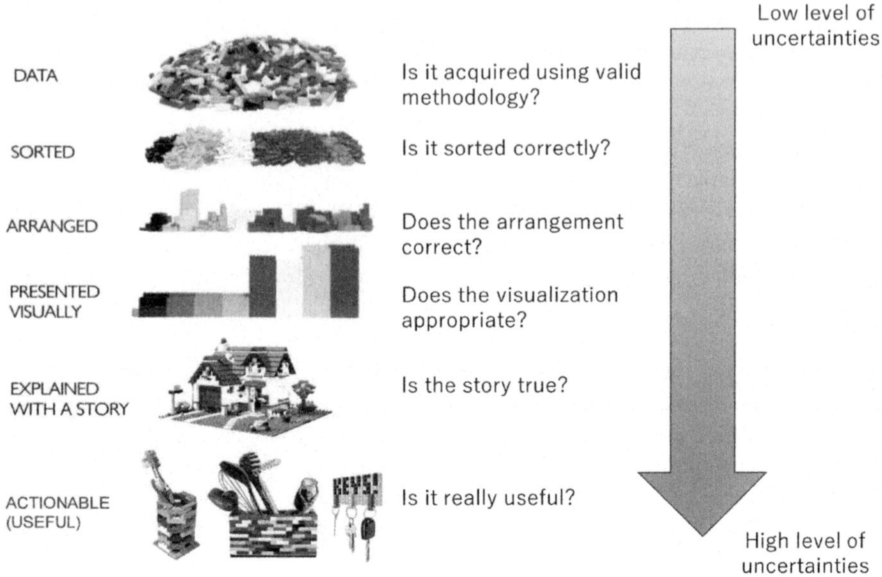

Fig. 6.19 Lego analogy to visualize the increasing uncertainty

have been removed. This step ensures the data is well-structured and ready for further analysis.

- **Arranged**: The third stage demonstrates the blocks arranged into specific patterns, symbolizing the arrangement of data into meaningful structures, such as tables or organized datasets. The question, "*Does the arrangement correct?,*" underscores the need to structure data accurately to support meaningful interpretation and analysis.
- **Presented visually**: In the fourth stage, the blocks are assembled into a recognizable visual form, akin to data visualization, such as charts, graphs, or maps. The question, "*Is the visualization appropriate?,*" stresses the importance of selecting appropriate and effective visualization techniques that convey insights clearly and accurately.
- **Explained with a story**: The fifth stage illustrates a detailed LEGO model of a house, symbolizing the storytelling aspect of data. At this stage, data insights are contextualized and narrated in a way that resonates with the audience. The question, "*Is the story true?,*" emphasizes the need for accuracy and integrity in how data-driven narratives are crafted.
- **Actionable (useful)**: Finally, the LEGO blocks are transformed into practical objects like a pen holder and key organizer, symbolizing actionable insights. The ultimate goal of the data process is to produce insights that can inform decisions or solve real-world problems. The question, "*Is it really useful?,*" challenges whether the results genuinely address the needs of stakeholders.

The figure demonstrates a clear flow from raw, unorganized data to actionable and practical outcomes, while highlighting the need to critically evaluate the quality and relevance of data at each stage. It underscores that achieving low levels of uncertainty and high utility requires careful attention to detail, methodology, and interpretation throughout the data lifecycle.

Machine learning is like teaching a computer to do things by showing it lots of examples, instead of giving it rules. For example, if you show a computer lots of pictures of cats and dogs, it can learn to tell the difference between them. It learns from the pictures, just like how you learn by seeing and practicing!

6.7 Quantifying Uncertainty

Basic calculation

To measure uncertainty, we can take multiple measurements. For example, suppose we want to calculate the time it takes to run 200 m. Let us say we recorded five measurements: 43 s, 52 s, 35 s, 29 s, and 49 s. The next step is to calculate the average by summing up all the measurements and dividing by the number of observations. The total is 208 s, and when divided by 5, the result is an average of 42 s.

Next, we calculate the variance of the measurements. For each measurement, subtract the average (42 s) and square the result. The variance is then computed as shown in the Table 6.1.

To calculate the standard deviation, we divide the total variance (368 s) by the number of observations (5), resulting in 73.6. The standard deviation is then simply the square root of 73.6, which is approximately 8.58.

Table 6.1 Calculating the variance

Subtraction	Variance	Square of variance
43–42	1	1
52–42	10	100
35–42	− 7	49
29–42	− 13	169
49–42	7	49
	Total	368

To express the final measurement with uncertainty, we present the average measurement along with the standard deviation. Thus, the final measurement is **42 ± 8.58 s.**

Intermediate calculation

1. Confusion matrix (for multiple classes)

Confusion matrix, sometimes also called confusion table, is a key evaluation tool in classification tasks in data science. It can evaluate the performance of a model by comparing predicted and actual classifications. Let us see a confusion matrix below:

	A	B	C	D	E	
A	**80**	4	0	15	7	106
B	2	**17**	0	9	2	30
C	12	5	**9**	4	8	38
D	7	8	0	**65**	0	80
E	3	2	1	6	**38**	50
Total	104	36	10	99	55	***304***

The matrix consists of five categories (A, B, C, D, E), displayed along both the rows (actual labels) and columns (predicted labels). Each cell contains the number of instances classified in a specific combination of actual and predicted labels.

The diagonal cells (highlighted with gray color) represent correct classifications where the predicted label matches the actual label. For instance, category A has 80 correct predictions, category B has 17, and so on. The off-diagonal cells reflect misclassifications, indicating how many instances were incorrectly predicted as another category. For example, 15 instances from category A were misclassified as D, and 12 instances from category C were misclassified as A.

The final row labeled "Total" sums the predicted instances for each category, while the last column provides the total number of actual instances per category. The bottom-right corner of the matrix, marked in black, indicates the overall total of all classifications, which is 304 in this case.

Then, to calculate the percent correctly classified (PCC) we can total all diagonal cells (correct classification) divided by the total of observations and times 100, which 209/304*100 = **68.8% (also known as "Overall Accuracy").** For land use and land cover classification using satellite images, this means there is a 68.8% chance that any given pixel is classified correctly. Alternatively, you could focus on the error rate, which shows a 31.2% chance that a pixel is classified incorrectly.

Actual class \ Predicted class	Positive	Negative	Also known as recall
Positive	True Positive (TP)	False Negative (FN)	Sensitivity TP/(TP+FN)
Negative	False Positive (FP)	True Negative (TN)	Specificity TN/(TN+FP)
	Precision TP/(TP+FP)	Negative Predictive Value TN/(TN+FN)	Accuracy TP+TN/(TP+TN+FP+FN)

Fig. 6.20 Confusion matrix

This matrix helps us to evaluate the accuracy and misclassification patterns of the model, offering insights into which categories are most often confused and where improvements may be necessary. However, this matrix can only be used to calculate the uncertainty of multiple classes such as the result of land use land cover classification from earth observation imagery.

2. Confusion matrix (for a single class)

The second method can be used to calculate the uncertainty of single classes such as the disaster-prone areas of volcanic eruptions, landslides, or flood events. Let us see a confusion matrix as Fig. 6.20:

The confusion matrix is organized into four main components based on the outcomes of the model's predictions:

True positive (TP): This is the number of instances where the model correctly predicted the positive class. For example, in a disaster-prone area model, TP would represent the number of locations actually affected by flood and were correctly identified by the model as positive.

False positive (FP): Also known as a "Type I error," this is the count of instances where the model predicted the positive class incorrectly. In the disaster-prone area, for example, FP would indicate a safe area incorrectly classified as a flood area.

True negative (TN): This represents cases where the model correctly predicted the negative class. In the disaster-prone area scenario, it corresponds to a safe area correctly identified as a flood area by the model.

False negative (FN): Also called a "Type II error," this refers to instances where the model failed to predict the positive class. These are cases where areas with flood were incorrectly classified as safe areas.

From the matrix, we then can calculate the precision, recall, specificity, negative predictive value, and accuracy. Following are the explanations:

Precision (TP/(TP + FP)): Precision measures the proportion of positive predictions that are actually correct. It is crucial in situations where false positives are costly, such as fraud detection.

Recall (TP/(TP + FN)): Also referred to as sensitivity, this metric evaluates the model's ability to identify positive cases. High recall is vital in cases like disease diagnosis, where missing a positive case (false negative) can be critical.

Specificity (TN/(TN + FP)): This metric measures the proportion of actual negative cases that are correctly predicted. Specificity is essential in applications where it is crucial to minimize false positives.

Negative predictive value (TN/(TN + FN)): This metric assesses how often a negative prediction is correct.

Accuracy (TP + TN)/(TP + TN + FP + FN): Accuracy measures the proportion of correctly classified instances (both positive and negative) out of all predictions.

Sometimes, we can also calculate the $F1$-score, which is a metric used in classification tasks to evaluate the accuracy of a model. It is the harmonic mean of **precision** and **recall**, providing a single measure that balances both. The formula is:

$$F1 - \text{score} = 2 \cdot \frac{\text{Precision . Recall}}{\text{Precision} + \text{Recall}}$$

Why do we use $F1$-score? Because it is useful when you need a balance between precision and recall and it is well-suited for imbalanced datasets, where one class has significantly more samples than the other. For example, if a model has **precision** value of 0.8 and **recall** value of 0.6, then the $F1$-score would be:

$$F1 = 2 \cdot \frac{0.8 \cdot 0.6}{0.8 + 0.6} = 2 \cdot \frac{0.48}{1.4} = 0.6857$$

This value provides a more comprehensive view of the model's performance compared to precision or recall alone. Each of these metrics provides insights into the strengths and weaknesses of a classification model, allowing researchers to make informed decisions about its suitability for specific applications. Table 6.2 summarizes these metrics.

Table 6.2 Summary of each metric

Metric name	Description	Value
Accuracy	Default metric for classification problems. Not the best for imbalance classes	0–1
Precision	High precision leads to less false positives	0–1
Recall	High recall leads to less false negatives	0–1
Specificity	High specificity means to low rate false positive	0–1
$F1$-score	Combination of precision and recall, usually a good overall metric for a classification model	0–1
Confusion matrix	When comparing prediction to truth labels to see where model gets confused. Can be hard to use with large number of classes	0–1

In social studies, we often deal with complex data where outcomes are uncertain, such as predicting whether a person will vote. For example, if we are predicting whether people will vote, the confusion matrix helps us understand how many people we correctly predicted would vote (true positives), how many we correctly predicted wouldn't vote (true negatives), how many we wrongly predicted would vote (false positives), and how many we wrongly predicted would not vote (false negatives). This matrix is useful because it quantifies the errors in the prediction, which helps us understand the uncertainty in our model's performance.

3. Receiver operator curve (ROC)

Another method to measure the uncertainty of a single-class classification model is the receiver operator curve (ROC). Different from the previous methods that use numbers to measure the uncertainty, the ROC method uses a graphical approach.

ROC is a graphical representation used to evaluate the performance of a binary classification model. The x-axis represents the false positive rate (1-specificity), while the y-axis shows the true positive rate (sensitivity). The curve plots the trade-off between these rates at different threshold settings of the classifier. An example of an ROC curve is presented in Fig. 6.21.

In the Figure, several curves are shown. The blue curve represents a "best classifier," which achieves 100% sensitivity with some false positives, shown as a point at the top-left of the plot. The green curve corresponds to a classifier that performs better than random, maintaining higher true positive rates for lower false positive rates. The orange curve represents a poorer classifier that approaches the performance of a random guess. The diagonal red dashed line indicates the performance of a random classifier, where the true positive rate equals the false positive rate, yielding no meaningful discrimination. Meanwhile, black curve represents a worse classifier.

ROC helps us see how well the model distinguishes between two categories, such as voters and non-voters. The closer the ROC curve is to the top-left corner, the better the model is at making correct predictions. In social studies, this can help

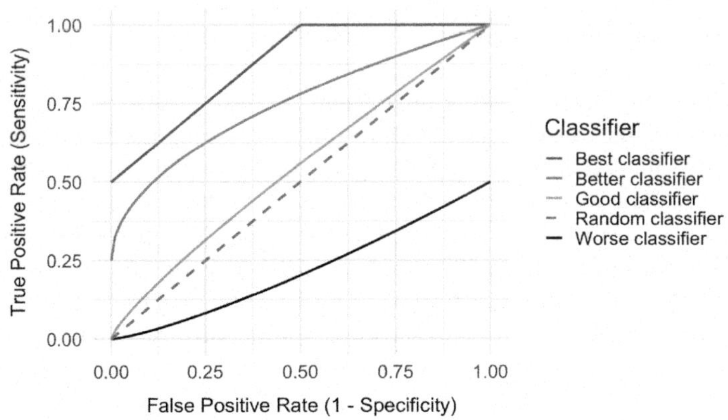

Fig. 6.21 ROC curve

determine the effectiveness of a model in predicting social outcomes, like identifying which communities are at risk of experiencing poverty or educational challenges. ROC curve provide practical ways to measure and understand the uncertainty in predictions, giving researchers better insights into how accurate their models are and where they may need to improve.

Advanced calculation

4. Monte Carlo approach

The Monte Carlo approach is a method for assessing model accuracy or performance by repeatedly running simulations with randomly sampled data, allowing for the estimation of a model's reliability and potential variations in predictions under different scenarios, essentially providing a more comprehensive understanding of how well the model performs across a range of possible inputs; it is particularly useful for evaluating uncertainty in predictions and assessing the impact of parameter variations.

There are some key points about the Monte Carlo approach to measure the uncertainty in data science projects, explained as follows:

Random sampling: The core principle is to repeatedly draw random samples from the data distribution to generate different input scenarios for the model.

Multiple simulations: By running the model on these random samples multiple times, you can gather a large set of predictions, providing a better picture of the model's overall performance.

Uncertainty quantification: This method helps estimate the range of possible outcomes and the associated probabilities, allowing you to quantify the uncertainty around the model's predictions.

So, how can we use Monte Carlo methods in practice? The first step is **hyperparameter tuning**. Monte Carlo simulations can explore various combinations of hyperparameters in a model, helping to identify the optimal settings for the best performance.

The next application is **sensitivity analysis**. By varying specific input parameters and running multiple simulations, we can evaluate how sensitive the model's predictions are to changes in those parameters.

Another important use is **model validation**. Comparing the model's predictions on randomly sampled data with actual target values provides a robust assessment of the model's accuracy.

Monte Carlo is a powerful method, but it requires careful consideration of two key factors: **computational cost** and **sampling strategy**. Running a large number of simulations can be computationally expensive, so optimizing the process based on the problem and available resources is essential. Additionally, the quality of the Monte Carlo simulation depends on the chosen sampling method, which should ensure that the data is representative of the problem being studied.

Figure 6.22 illustrates the Monte Carlo uncertainty testing shows the distribution of the sample means from the simulations. The red line represents the smoothed

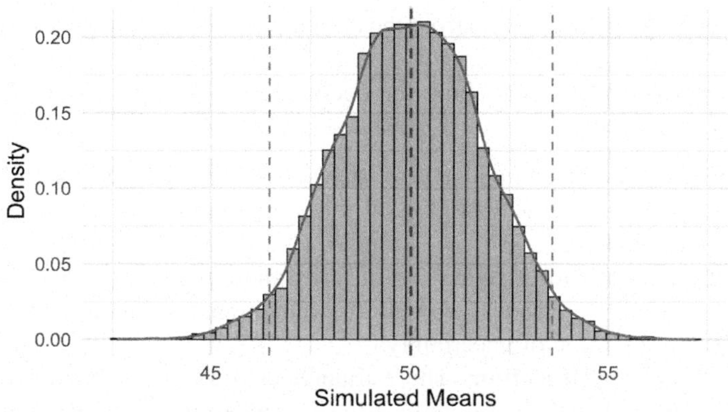

Fig. 6.22 Monte Carlo uncertainty testing shows the distribution of the sample means from the simulations

version of the histogram, showing the **estimated probability density function** of the simulated means. It helps to visualize the overall distribution and assess how well the means are concentrated around the central value. The blue dashed line indicates the **mean** of the simulated sample means, which is an estimate of the population mean. If the mean of the simulated sample means is close to the true population mean (50), it suggests that the simulation method is working well and that the sample means are accurate estimates of the true population mean. The width of the histogram and the density curve indicates the **variability or spread of the sample means**. A narrower distribution suggests lower uncertainty in estimating the population mean, while a wider distribution indicates higher uncertainty. While the green dashed lines represent the **95% confidence interval** for the sample means. The confidence interval gives you an estimate of the range within which the true population mean lies, based on the Monte Carlo simulation. If the interval is narrow, it suggests the estimation is precise, whereas a wider interval suggests higher uncertainty.

Monte Carlo simulations involve running thousands or even millions of scenarios by randomly varying inputs, such as economic growth rates or population trends, based on known probabilities. For example, when studying the impact of a new social policy, researchers might use Monte Carlo simulations to predict possible outcomes, like changes in employment rates or income distribution. By examining the range of results, they can identify the most likely outcomes and the risks of extreme scenarios. This approach is commonly used in public policy planning, urban development, and disaster management, where decisions must account for uncertainty in future events.

5. Deep ensembles

A "deep ensemble" technique is a method for estimating model uncertainty in machine learning by training multiple independent deep neural networks with slightly different architectures and initializations, then combining their predictions to gauge the overall uncertainty of the model on a given input; essentially, the disagreement between the different predictions from the ensemble indicates the level of uncertainty in the model's output.

There are some key points about the deep ensembles technique to measure the uncertainty in data science projects, explained as follows:

- **Multiple models**: The core idea is to train several separate deep neural networks on the same data, each with slightly different random initializations, creating an ensemble of models.
- **Diversity in predictions**: By having different models with diverse parameterizations, the ensemble produces a range of predictions for a given input, allowing for a better estimation of uncertainty.
- **Uncertainty quantification**: The variance or standard deviation across the predictions made by the ensemble is used as a measure of uncertainty.

Deep ensemble techniques are simple to implement, they are also easier to set up compared to more complex Bayesian methods because they can be built using standard deep learning tools. They are also effective when working with diverse or complex data. This makes them especially useful in situations where the input data varies a lot or has complicated patterns.

However, deep ensembles have some drawbacks. One major issue is the high computational cost. Training several independent models can require a lot of time and resources. Additionally, deep ensembles may sometimes struggle with calibration. This means they might not always give an accurate measure of uncertainty, and extra calibration steps could be needed to fix this.

Furthermore, deep ensembles use multiple machine learning models to make predictions while capturing uncertainty in complex datasets. In social studies, this can be applied to predict phenomena like crime rates or migration patterns. Each model in the ensemble is trained differently, and their predictions are averaged to improve accuracy. Importantly, deep ensembles also highlight areas where the models disagree, signaling higher uncertainty. For instance, when using satellite data and socio-economic indicators to predict poverty levels in different regions, deep ensembles can help policymakers understand not just the average prediction but also how confident the models are in their estimates.

Strategy to Suppress The Uncertainty

To maintain data quality and suppress the uncertainty in data science projects, several important steps should be followed:

First, never fully trust data that lacks clear metadata. Metadata provides essential details about the data, and without it, the data's reliability cannot be ensured. Avoid using data from sources that have a poor reputation, even if the source is an official government institution. The credibility of the data provider is crucial. Additionally, always ensure that the data has undergone and passed a proper quality control process

Second, use comparative data from trusted sources or authorities with high-quality standards. Comparing data from different reputable sources helps verify its accuracy and reliability. It is also essential to determine the specific requirements of the application being developed, including the type of users, the purpose of the data, and the decisions to be made based on the information

Third, carefully select and organize the data to ensure quality. This involves deciding on the data model to be used, the necessary hardware and software, and the expected final product. It's also vital to minimize potential errors by anticipating what problems may arise from using the data and planning solutions to address them. Always assess whether the quality of the data is acceptable

Finally, when making decisions based on the data, it is important to evaluate the level of uncertainty. Decide whether to accept or reject the uncertainty. If the quality is insufficient, consider revisiting the earlier steps to improve the data

Measuring uncertainty means figuring out how sure or unsure you are about something. In data science, this helps us understand if our predictions are accurate or if they could be wrong.

6.8 Forecasting

Forecasting in data science is the practice of predicting future trends or events by analyzing patterns and trends in historical data, essentially using past information to make informed guesses about what will happen in the future; in a data science project, forecasting is important because it allows you to proactively plan and make decisions based on anticipated outcomes, like predicting sales figures, customer behavior, or market trends, which can help businesses optimize operations and strategies.

Forecasting in data science involves using historical data to predict future outcomes. By analyzing past data, patterns and trends are identified, which can help forecast future values. This process is a key part of predictive analytics, where models are created to estimate what might happen in the future. In business, companies use forecasting to predict various things, such as sales, inventory levels, revenue, and customer churn. This helps businesses make better decisions about how to allocate resources, set prices, and develop marketing strategies.

Forecasting is important in data science projects because it supports informed decision-making. By predicting future trends, it helps businesses make proactive choices about resources, product development, and marketing. It also plays a role in risk mitigation by identifying potential problems or opportunities early, which helps businesses prepare and manage risks. Forecasting can improve performance by predicting changes in demand and adjusting production levels. Lastly, evaluating the accuracy of forecasting models is essential for assessing their effectiveness and making improvements.

Algorithms

There are different methods for forecasting that can help predict future outcomes based on historical data. These methods range from traditional statistical models to advanced machine learning algorithms. The choice of method often depends on the type of data available and the goal of the forecast. Some forecasting methods are well-known and widely used, such as moving average, exponential smoothing, regression analysis, and ARIMA. Each of these methods has its strengths and applications.

One common forecasting method is the **moving average** (Fig. 6.23). This technique involves calculating the average of past data points over a specific period. The idea is to use this average to predict the next value in the data series. It's a simple approach, often used when the data does not show a clear trend or seasonality. However, the moving average might not perform well in cases where there are significant changes or patterns over time.

Another popular method is **exponential smoothing** (Fig. 6.24). Unlike moving average technique, this technique gives more weight to recent data points, which makes it more responsive to current trends. By focusing more on the most recent observations, exponential smoothing helps capture short-term fluctuations and can be particularly useful for time series with a trend or seasonal pattern. This method can be more accurate in forecasting when there is a need to highlight more recent information.

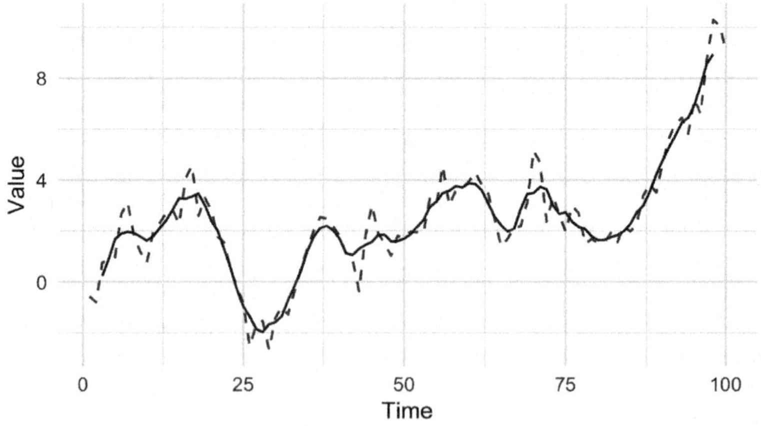

Fig. 6.23 Illustration of moving average, where original data is shown in dashed line while the forecasting data is shown in solid line

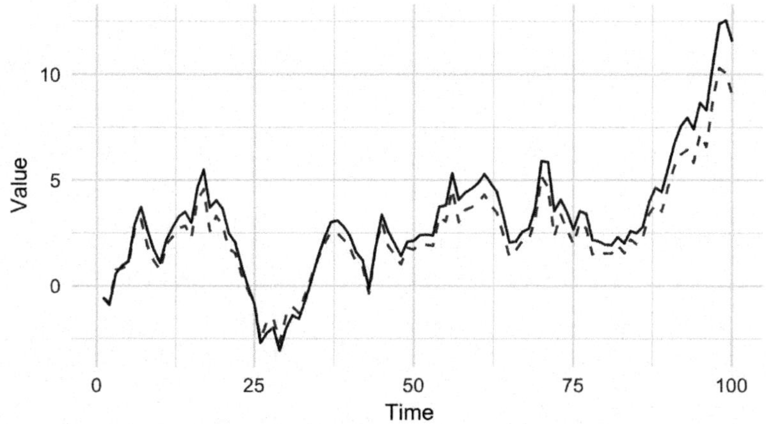

Fig. 6.24 Illustration of exponential smoothing, where original data is shown in dashed line while the exponentially smoothed data is shown in solid line

Regression analysis is another statistical method used in forecasting. This method looks for relationships between different variables (predictor and response) to predict how changes in one variable may affect another (Fig. 6.25). For example, in business forecasting, regression can be used to predict sales based on factors such as advertising expenditure or customer demand. By identifying these relationships, regression models provide insights that help make predictions based on how the variables are connected.

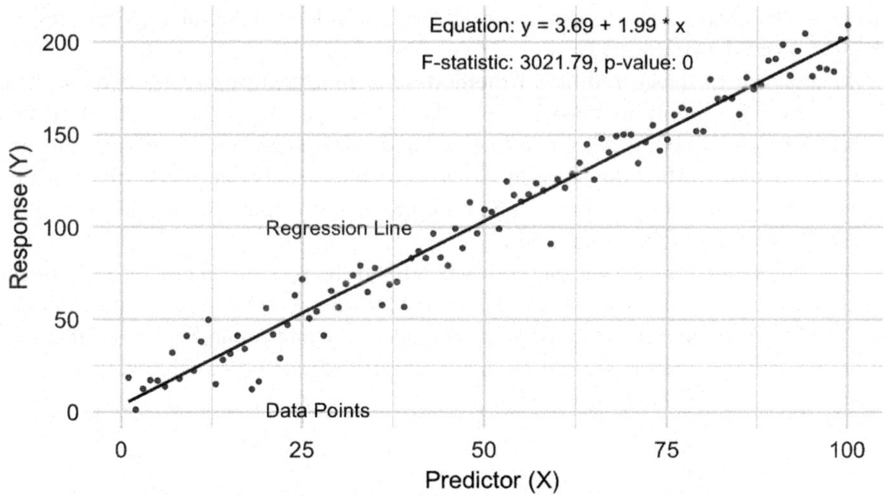

Fig. 6.25 Illustration of regression plot for forecasting

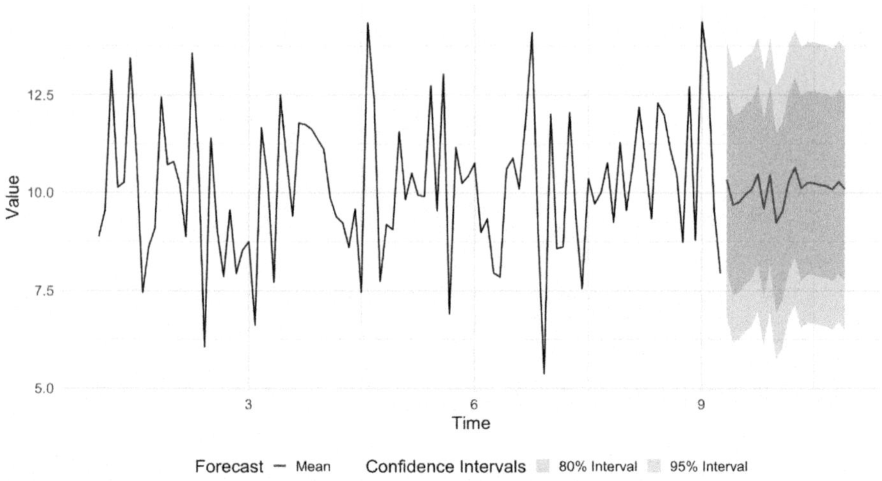

Fig. 6.26 Illustration of the ARIMA plot using synthetic data

ARIMA, or Autoregressive Integrated Moving Average, is a more advanced statistical technique often used for time-series forecasting. ARIMA is powerful because it combines three key elements: autoregression (using past values to predict future values), integration (differencing the data to make it stationary), and moving averages (smoothing the data to reveal trends). This method is particularly useful for analyzing data that changes over time, such as stock prices or weather patterns. ARIMA models can provide accurate forecasts when the time-series data exhibits trends, seasonality, or irregular patterns. Figure 6.26 shows the ARIMA plot using synthetic data, where blue for the mean forecast, orange for the 80% confidence interval, and light red for the 95% confidence interval.

In addition to these traditional methods, machine learning techniques such as **Prophet** are becoming increasingly popular for forecasting. Prophet, developed by Facebook (now Meta), is a flexible forecasting tool that can handle missing data and seasonal patterns. Machine learning algorithms like Prophet are particularly useful when working with large datasets and complex patterns that are difficult to capture using traditional statistical methods.

The choice of forecasting method depends on the specific characteristics of the data and the goals of the forecast. Each method has its advantages, and selecting the right one can significantly improve the accuracy and reliability of the forecast. It is important to carefully consider the nature of the data before choosing the most suitable method for the task at hand.

Types and Applications of Forecasts

There are two main types of forecasts used to predict future events: short-term forecasts and long-term forecasts.

Short-term forecasts are used to predict what will happen shortly, usually within a few days or weeks. These forecasts are important for businesses to make quick, responsive decisions. For example, businesses might use short-term forecasts to plan for upcoming demand or adjust marketing strategies.

Long-term forecasts are used to predict events that will happen further into the future, typically months or even years ahead. These forecasts help businesses plan for long-term growth, set goals, and make major investments, such as expanding operations or launching new products.

Forecasting has many important applications in business. For instance, in sales forecasting, companies predict future sales to help them plan production schedules, marketing campaigns, and staffing needs. By understanding future sales trends, businesses can avoid running out of products or overproducing.

In financial forecasting, companies predict their revenue, expenses, and cash flow over time. This helps them manage their budgets, plan for growth, and ensure financial stability.

Another key application is in supply chain management. Accurate forecasts help businesses manage their inventory by ensuring they have enough stock without overstocking. This improves efficiency and reduces costs. By forecasting future demand, businesses can prevent problems like stock shortages or excess inventory.

Advantages and Disadvantages of Forecasts

Forecasting helps businesses make better decisions. By predicting future trends, companies can plan for things like inventory and resource budgets. This allows them to adjust quickly to changing market conditions, ensuring they are always prepared for what's next. Forecasts also help businesses reduce risk. By knowing what might happen in the future, they can identify potential problems and find ways to avoid them. They can also take advantage of new opportunities before their competitors do. Additionally, forecasting improves efficiency. Accurate predictions allow companies to allocate resources more effectively, saving time and money, and ensuring their operations run smoothly.

Despite the benefits, forecasting has some drawbacks. One major issue is its dependence on data. If the data used in forecasting is inaccurate or incomplete, the predictions will be unreliable. This means forecasts may not always be accurate, especially for long-term predictions where uncertainties increase. Another challenge is unforeseen events, like economic crises or natural disasters. These unexpected events can completely disrupt forecasts and cause businesses to miss important shifts in the market. Lastly, some forecasting models are quite complex and require special knowledge to understand and interpret. This can make it difficult for businesses without expertise in data analysis to use forecasts effectively.

Easy to Digest Box

Machine learning is like teaching a computer how to recognize patterns or solve problems, just like a teacher helps students learn. For example, imagine you want to teach a computer how to tell the difference between pictures of cats and dogs. You show it many pictures of cats and dogs and tell it which is which. Over time, the computer learns to recognize the patterns that make a cat look like a cat and a dog look like a dog. Once it learns, it can look at a new picture and guess if it's a cat or a dog. That's how machine learning works—computers learn from examples!

Uncertainty means the computer is not completely sure about its guess. Uncertainty means the computer is not completely sure about its guess. Imagine you show the computer a picture of a fluffy animal it hasn't seen before. It might think, "This looks like a cat, but it's a little unusual, so I'm only 80% sure it's a cat." That percentage is a way of measuring how confident the computer is about its answer

Forecasting is when we try to predict what will happen in the future based on what we already know. It is like making a smart guess about what will happen next

For example, if you see the sky getting dark and you feel some raindrops, you might forecast that it will rain soon. Or, if you know it usually gets cold in winter, you can forecast that it will be cold in the near future.

6.9 Summary of Key Points

- ML is a subset of AI, it enables computers to analyze and interpret complex data, discover patterns, and make predictions or decisions based on that data.
- Types of ML include supervised, unsupervised, and reinforcement learning.
- Some keywords in ML includes feature, label, training and testing datasets, accuracy and precision, overfitting and underfitting.
- Despite the many benefits of ML, we must consider the disadvantages of ML such as legal and ethical issues.
- Uncertainty propagation begins from the source of data acquisition/collection and visualization is not an endpoint, but rather the start of an iterative process.
- There are three uncertainty categories which are (1) source, (2) process, and (3) use.
- Some methods to quantify uncertainty are confusion matrix, ROC, Monte Carlo and deep ensembles.
- Forecasting is the process of using historical data to predict future trends or events. It is the most wanted skill in the world of data science and becoming good at time series is a massive advantage.

6.10 Hands-on Experience

Working with RStudio

ARIMA forecast

This part demonstrates how to use R for ARIMA forecasting with historical data on cherry blossom bloom dates in Japan. The dataset is sourced from Kaggle: Japanese Cherry Blossom Data (https://www.kaggle.com/datasets/ryanglasnapp/japanese-cherry-blossom-data/data). You need to register before you can download the data. Data will come in.zip format, so you must unzip it first.

Below is the step-by-step process and the R code to clean, analyze, and forecast the data.

Practice 6

Learning Objectives

Importing and cleaning data:

- Import data from CSV files into R using read_csv() and handle missing values using na.omit()
- Identify and remove irrelevant columns to clean the data
- Rename columns and convert data types for further analysis (e.g., converting year columns to numeric)

Data transformation:

- Reshape data from wide format to long format using the gather() function for easier time-series analysis
- Extract and convert year, month, and date information from a date column
- Create a new column to represent the day of the year (DOY) for time-series analysis

Data visualization:

- Generate a simple time-series plot in R to visualize trends over time
- Create custom functions for shading specific months on a plot to highlight key periods
- Add annotations and custom labels to a plot to emphasize specific data points or trends
- Customize plots with different point shapes, sizes, and transparency levels using ggplot2
- Add linear regression lines and confidence intervals to visualize trends and uncertainty in the data
- Compare base R plots with ggplot2 for flexibility and customization options

Forecasting with ARIMA:

- Subset data for a specific site and prepare it for time-series forecasting
- Use the auto.arima() function to fit an ARIMA model for time-series data
- Forecast future values using the ARIMA model and plot the results
- Understand the concept of forecasting and its relevance in time-series analysis

Advanced visualization with ggplot2:

- Create scatterplots and line plots with ggplot2 to visualize time-series data for different variables
- Apply custom themes and improve the visual presentation of plots using ggplot2 functions
- Understand the application of linear regression and confidence intervals in scatterplots to identify trends and uncertainty

Practical application:

- Use the provided data to practice creating various plots such as line plots, scatterplots, and forecast plots
- Apply skills learned to forecast the Sakura full bloom dates for future years (2024–2030)
- Create multiple plots to explore trends and shifts in Sakura full bloom data

Setting up the environment

First, check and set your working directory to ensure that R can access the required files.

```
# Check the current working directory
getwd()

# Set working directory
setwd("/path/to/your/folder") # Replace with your
directory
```

Next, load the required libraries for data manipulation and visualization.

```
# Load libraries
library(ggplot2)
library(dplyr)
library(readr)
```

```
library(tidyr)
library(lubridate)
```

Importing and cleaning the data

The dataset is imported and cleaned to handle missing values and irrelevant columns.

```
# Import data
data < - read_csv("sakura_first_bloom_dates.csv")

# Handle missing values
data_cleaned < - na.omit(data)
summary(data_cleaned)

# Remove unnecessary columns
data_cleaned[, c('Currently Being Observed',
   '30 Year Average 1981-2010',
   'Notes')] < - list(NULL)

# Rename the first column
colnames(data_cleaned)[1] < - "Site"
summary(data_cleaned)
```

The columns representing years are identified and converted to numeric format for further analysis.

```
# Identify year columns
year_cols < - names(data_cleaned)[2:ncol(data)]
print(year_cols)

# Convert year columns to numeric
data_cleaned[, year_cols] < - lapply(data_cleaned[,
year_cols], as.numeric)
```

The data is then reshaped from a wide format to a long format for easier time-series analysis.

```
# Reshape data to long format
```

```
data_cleaned < - gather(data_cleaned, key = year,
value = value, -Site)
View(data_cleaned)
```

Additional processing is performed to extract year, month, and date information.

```
# Extract year, month, and date
data_cleaned$year < - substr(data_cleaned$value, 1,
4)
data_cleaned$month < - substr(data_cleaned$value,
6, 7)
data_cleaned$date < - substr(data_cleaned$value, 9,
10)

# Convert to numeric
data_cleaned$year < - as.numeric(data_cleaned$year)
ata_cleaned$month < - as.numeric(data_
cleaned$month)d
data_cleaned$date < - as.numeric(data_cleaned$date)

# Create a day-of-year (DOY) column
data_cleaned$doy < - yday(data_cleaned$value)
View(data_cleaned)
```

Visualizing the data

Now we will create three types of visualizations to analyze trends in the first bloom dates.

```
# Simple time-series plot
plot(data_cleaned$year, data_cleaned$doy,
  type = "l", main = "Sakura First Bloom Over
Time",
  xlab = "Year", ylab = "Day of Year", col =
"black")

# Function to shade a month and add text label
shade_month < - function(start_day, end_day, label,
color, text_x, text_y, label_color = rgb(0, 0.39,
0, 1)) {
```

```
 x_coords < - c(min(data_cleaned$year), max(data_
cleaned$year), max(data_cleaned$year), min(data_
cleaned$year))
 y_coords < - c(start_day, start_day, end_day, end_
day)
 polygon(x_coords, y_coords, col = color, border =
NA)
 text(x = text_x, y = text_y, labels = label, col
= label_color)
}

# Shade the area for April
shade_month(91, 121, "April", rgb(0.6, 1, 0.6,
0.5), 1960, 119)

# Shade the area for May
shade_month(121, 151, "May", rgb(1, 0.6, 0.6, 0.5),
1960, 136)

# Add additional text for earliest bloom
text(x = 2016, y = 110, labels = "The earliest
bloom at 2023", col = "black", cex = 0.7)
```

Output:

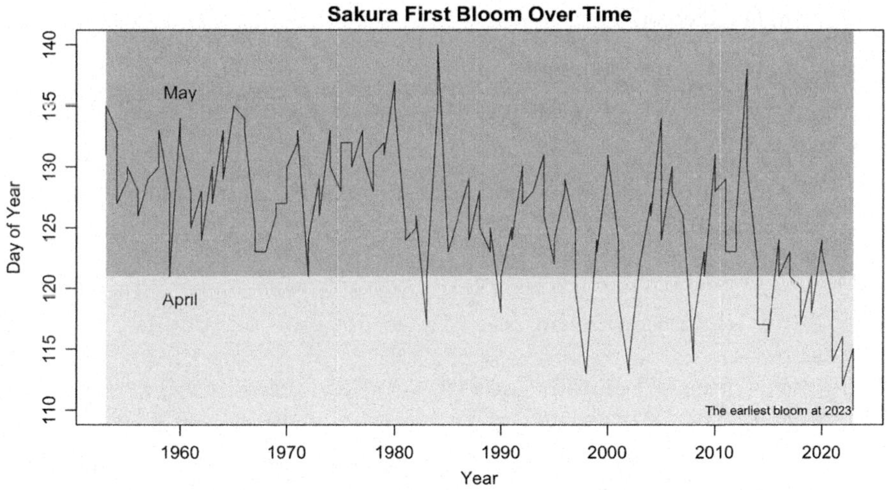

What does the code do?

- **Plotting time series**:

  plot(data_cleaned$year, data_cleaned$doy, type = "l", main = "Sakura First Bloom Over Time", xlab = "Year", ylab = "Day of Year", col = "black")

  This creates a line plot with years (data_cleaned$year) on the x-axis and the day of the year (data_cleaned$doy) on the y-axis, showing how the first bloom of Sakura changed over time.
  The line (type = "l") is colored black, and labels for the x and y axes are added.

- **Shading areas for specific months**:

  shade_month is a custom function to shade specific months in the plot.
  Inputs: The function takes the start_day and end_day of a month, a label for the month, a color for shading, and coordinates for placing the text label.
  The function uses polygon() to shade the specified area and text() to add the label.

  Shading Example for April:

  The function is called to shade from day 91 (March 31) to day 121 (April 30) with a light green color (rgb(0.6, 1, 0.6, 0.5)), and places the text "April" at the specified position on the plot.

  Shading Example for May:

  The function is similarly called to shade May (day 121 to day 151) with a light red color.

- **Adding text for specific points**:

  text(x = 2016, y = 110, labels = "The earliest bloom at 2023", col = "black", cex = 0.7)

  Adds custom text on the plot, indicating that the earliest bloom was at day 110 in 2023.

```
# Plot with month on x-axis and year on the fill
aesthetic
ggplot(data_cleaned, aes(x = year, y = doy)) +
 geom_point(aes(size = 3), alpha = 0.5) + # Adjust
point size and transparency
 geom_smooth(method = "lm", se = FALSE) + # Add a
linear regression line
```

```
  labs(title = "Shift in Asahikawa and Obihiro
Sakura First Blooms",
     x = "Year", y = "First Bloom Date") +
  theme_bw() # Apply a black and white theme
```

Output:

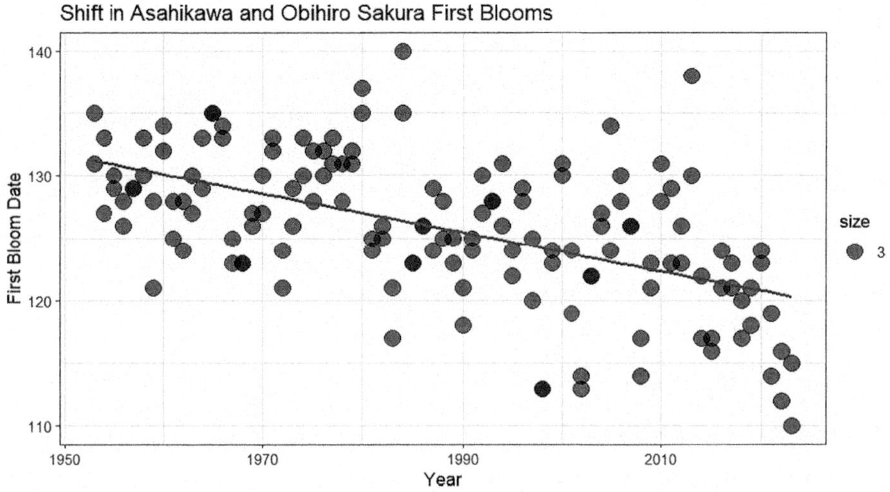

If you want to change the "circle" symbol into different symbol you can use following code.

```
# Plot with customized point style
ggplot(data_cleaned, aes(x = year, y = doy)) +
  geom_point(shape = 17, size = 3, alpha = 0.5) + #
Set shape, size, and transparency
  geom_smooth(method = "lm", se = FALSE) + # Add a
linear regression line
  labs(title = "Shift in Asahikawa and Obihiro
Sakura First Blooms",
     x = "Year", y = "First Bloom Date") +
  theme_bw() # Apply a black and white theme
```

Output:

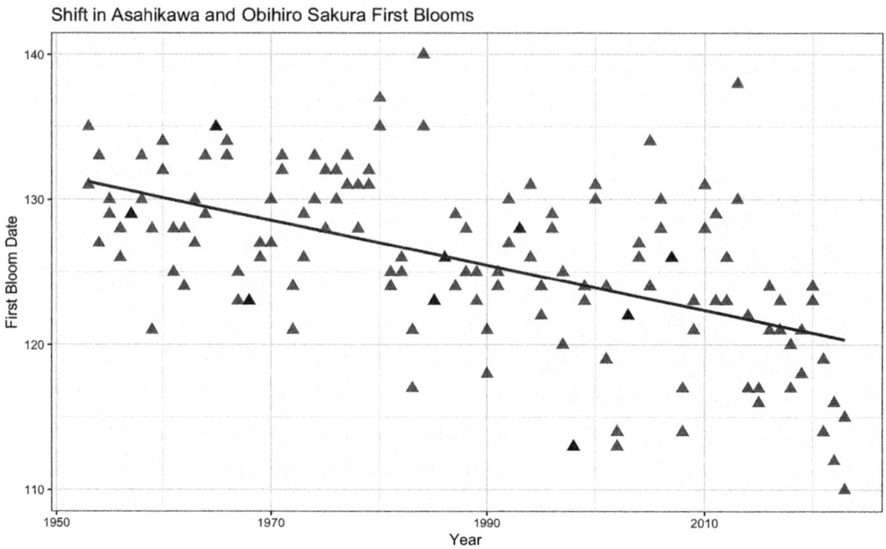

What does the code do?

- **Time series plot with ggplot2**:

  ggplot(data_cleaned, aes(x = year, y = doy)) + · · ·

  Uses ggplot2 to create a plot with year on the x-axis and doy on the y-axis, similar to the base R plot, but with more flexibility for customization and appearance.

- **Adding points**:

  geom_point(aes(size = 3), alpha = 0.5):

  Adds points to represent each first bloom date. The points are sized with a size of 3 and have transparency (alpha = 0.5).
  shape = 17 set shape into triangle, to check all available shape you can use this code:

```
# Code to display all available shapes in ggplot2
library(ggplot2)

shape_data < - data.frame(
 x = rep(1:5, each = 5)[1:25], # Adjust to match
length of shape
```

```
 y = rep(5:1, times = 5)[1:25], # Adjust to match
length of shape
 shape = 0:24
)

ggplot(shape_data, aes(x = x, y = y)) +
 geom_point(aes(shape = shape), size = 5) + # Plot
the shapes
 scale_shape_identity() + # Use shapes directly
 geom_text(aes(label = shape), vjust = -1.5) + #
Add labels for shape codes
 theme_void() + # Minimal theme
 labs(title = "Available Shapes in ggplot2")
```

Output:

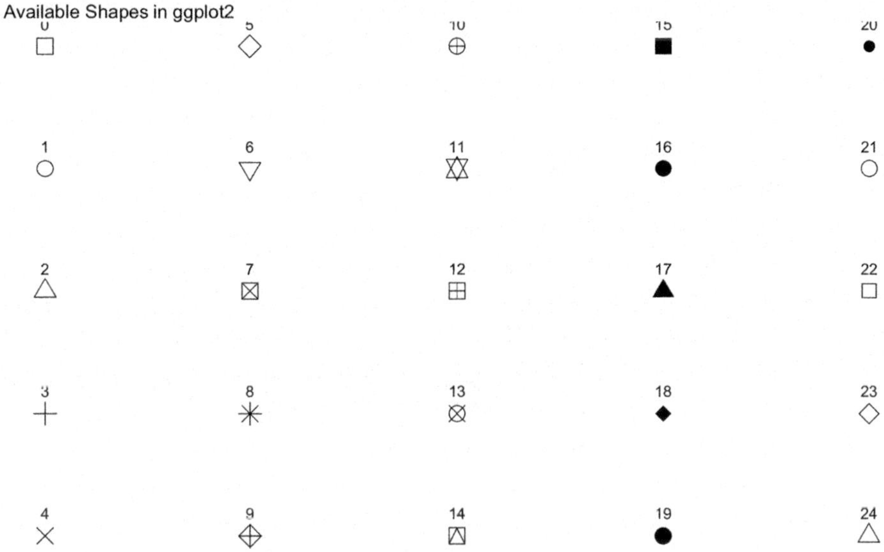

- **Adding linear regression line**:

 geom_smooth(method = "lm", se = FALSE):

 Adds a linear regression line (method = "lm") to show the trend of first bloom dates over time. The se = FALSE argument removes the shaded confidence area around the line.

- **Adding labels**:
  - labs(title = "Shift in Asahikawa and Obihiro Sakura First Blooms", x = "Year", y = "First Bloom Date"):

    Adds a title and axis labels.
- **Applying theme**:
  - theme_bw():

    Applies a clean black-and-white theme to the plot.

```
# Plot with confidence area (uncertainty)
ggplot(data_cleaned, aes(x = year, y = doy)) +
 geom_point() +
 geom_smooth(method = lm) +
 labs(title = "Shift in Sakura First Blooms Date",
  x = "Year",
  y = "First Bloom Date (DOY)")
```

Output:

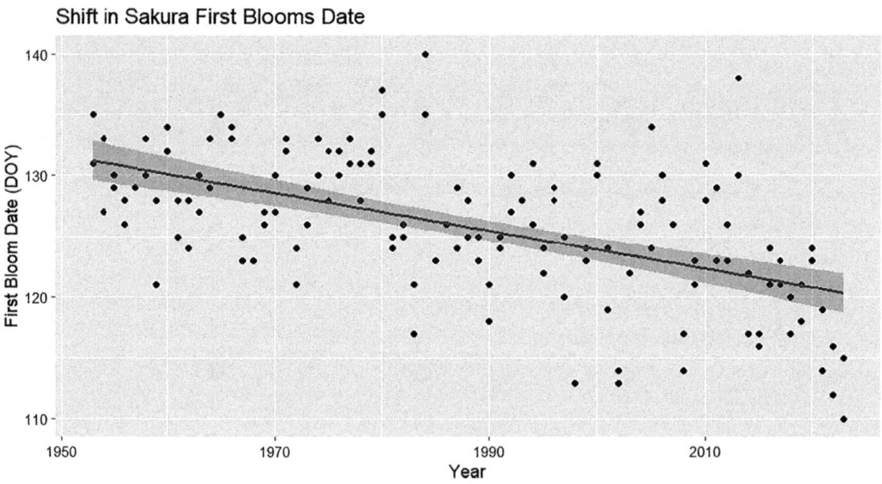

Storytelling of the sakura's shifting bloom:

Many years ago, in the 1950s, spring arrived in Japan with the first blooms of sakura (cherry blossom) trees appearing around May. These iconic trees are now blooming as early as late March, a shift of nearly two months. Historical records confirm this trend. For example, data from Kyoto, a city famous for its sakura, show that the average first bloom date has advanced by about 7 days since the 1950s (Aono & Kazui, 2008). As shown in the graph, the line slopes downward, clearly illustrating how the first blooms are occurring earlier and earlier with each passing decade.

The average temperature in Japan has been steadily increasing over the past few decades. According to the Japan Meteorological Agency (2020), the country's average temperature has risen by approximately 1.2°C since the early 20th century. Research indicates that for every 1°C increase in temperature, sakura blooming dates advance by about 2 to 3 days (Miller-Rushing et al., 2007). Another key factor is the length of daylight, a phenomenon known as photoperiodism. Sakura trees, like many plants, use day length as a cue to time their blooms. In spring, as days grow longer and nights shorten, the trees receive signals to start flowering. Climate change may amplify this effect by shifting seasonal patterns, causing daylight cues to occur earlier in the year (Körner & Basler, 2010).

What does the code do?

- **Confidence interval plot**:

- Similar to the previous ggplot2 plot, but this time the confidence interval around the linear regression line is displayed by removing the se = FALSE argument in geom_smooth.

Comparison:

- **Base R verus ggplot2**:

  Base R Plot: More manual customization is required, such as adding polygons for shading and placing text labels explicitly. It is less flexible for adding additional layers like regression lines or smooth plots.
  ggplot2 Plot: Provides an elegant and more compact way of adding features like points, regression lines, and confidence intervals. It also allows for a clean and customizable theme (theme_bw()), and layering is easier.

- **Shading for specific months:**

  In **Base R**, shading is manually done using the shade_month function, which requires more lines of code and attention to specific areas.
  In **ggplot2**, shading of months isn't done, but the plot offers more flexibility in plotting and enhancing the visual appeal with additional layers like confidence intervals.

From the figures, we can see a clear downward trend. This means that the first bloom dates have been happening earlier over time. For example, in the 1950s, Sakura typically bloomed around the 130th DOY (early May), but by the 2000s, the bloom dates shifted to around the 110th DOY (late April).

This change is likely related to rising global temperatures and changes in climate patterns, which influence the flowering times of plants. Earlier blooming may be a response to warmer spring temperatures, as plants react to seasonal cues like temperature and sunlight. Studies have shown that similar trends are observed in other regions, linking this shift to global climate change (Primack, R. B., et al. (2009)).

Forecasting with ARIMA

The data for a specific site ("Asahikawa") is isolated, and ARIMA is used for forecasting.

```
# Subset data for Asahikawa
Asahikawa < - subset(data_cleaned, Site = =
"Asahikawa")
Asahikawa[, c('Site', 'year', 'value', 'month',
'date')] < - list(NULL)

# Remove rows beyond 2018
pred_Asahikawa < - Asahikawa[-c(67:71),]

# Convert to time series
Asahikawa_ts_actual < - ts(Asahikawa, start =
c(1953, 1), frequency = 1)
Asahikawa_ts_pred < - ts(pred_Asahikawa, start =
c(1953, 1), frequency = 1)

# Fit ARIMA model
install.packages("forecast")
library(forecast)

model < - auto.arima(Asahikawa_ts_pred)

# Forecast next 5 values
forecast_data < - forecast(model, 5)
print(forecast_data)

# Plot the forecast
plot(forecast_data, main = "Forecasting for Sakura
First Bloom at Asahikawa")
lines(Asahikawa_ts_actual, type = "l", col =
"red")
```

Output:

```
> print(forecast_data)
     Point Forecast    Lo 80    Hi 80    Lo 95    Hi 95
2019       124.1097 117.2658 130.9537 113.6428 134.5766
2020       125.2081 118.1910 132.2251 114.4764 135.9397
2021       124.4961 117.4630 131.5293 113.7398 135.2525
2022       124.1874 117.1446 131.2303 113.4163 134.9586
2023       124.2968 117.1987 131.3949 113.4412 135.1524
```

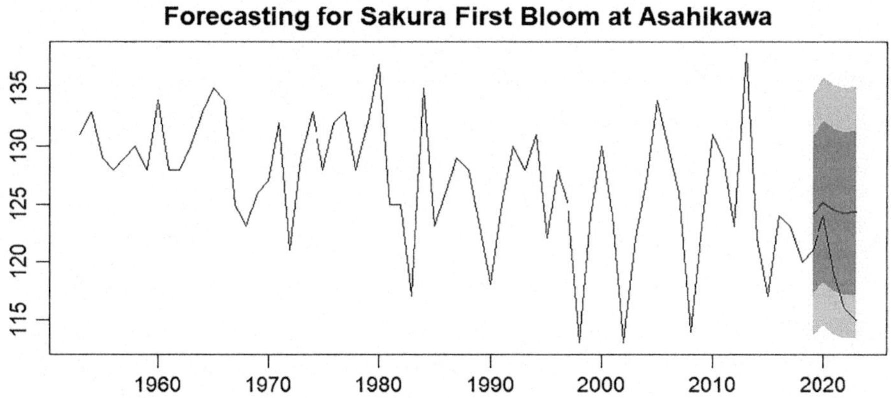

Challenges

Using data of "sakura_full_bloom_dates.csv" create multiple plots of:

- Line plot (X = Time, Y = DOY) of time series Sakura Full Bloom,
- Scatterplot (X = Time, Y = DOY) of Sakura Full Bloom,
- Scatterplot Shift of Sakura Full Bloom with Linear Line and Confidence Interval, and
- Forecasting of Sakura full bloom for year 2024–2030 and create a line plot

Expected results:

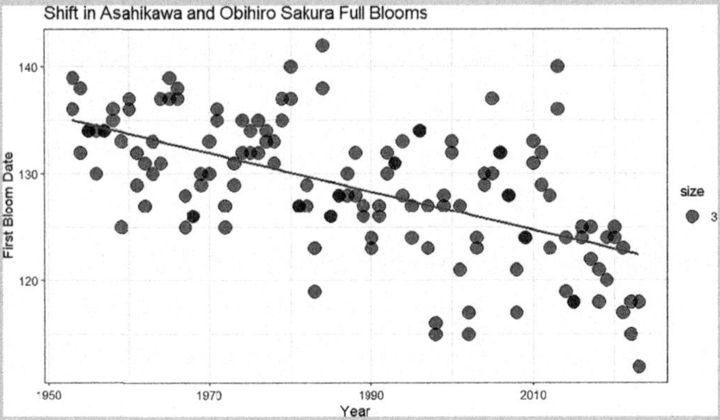

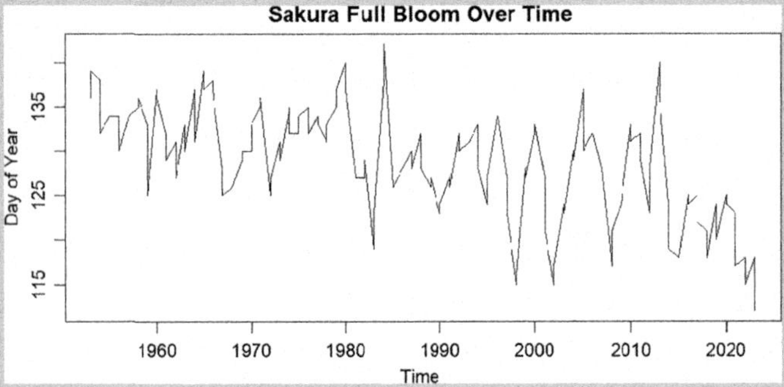

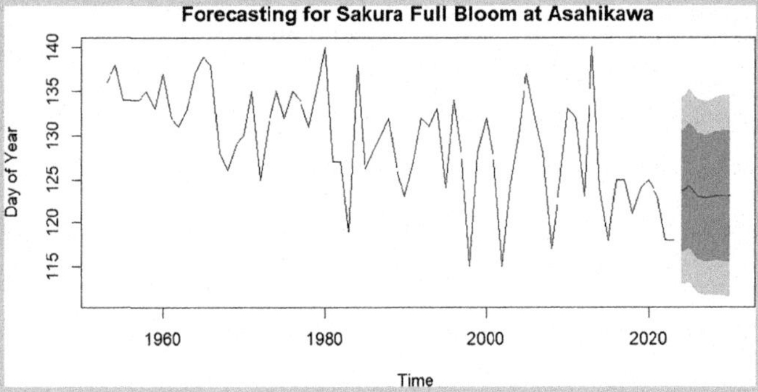

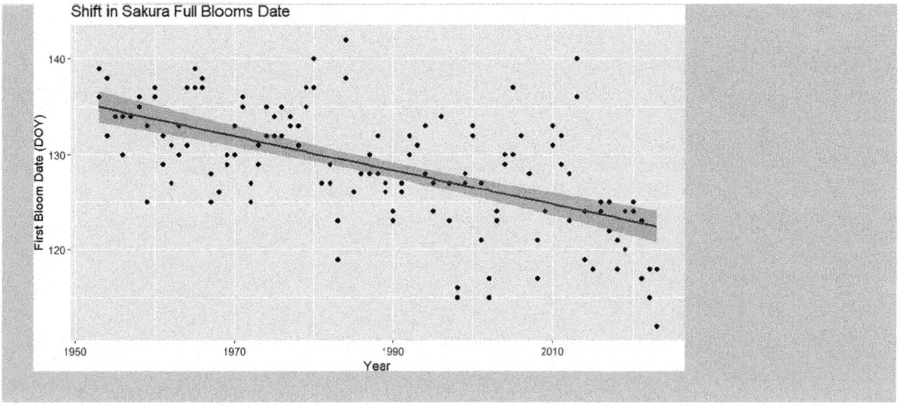

References

Aono, Y., & Kazui, K. (2008). Phenological data series of cherry tree flowering in Kyoto, Japan, and its application to reconstruction of springtime temperatures since the 9th century. *International Journal of Climatology, 28*(7), 905-914. https://doi.org/10.1002/joc.1594

Bishop, C. M. (2006). Pattern recognition and machine learning. Springer. ISBN: 978–0–387–31073–2. Available at https://link.springer.com/book/9780387310732

Dietterich, T. G. (2000). Ensemble methods in machine learning. In: Multiple classifier systems. MCS 2000. Lecture Notes in Computer Science, vol 1857. Springer, Berlin, Heidelberg. Available at https://doi.org/10.1007/3-540-45014-9_1

Japan Meteorological Agency. (2020). Climate change monitoring report 2020. Retrieved from https://www.jma.go.jp/jma/en/NMHS/ccmr/ccmr2020.pdf

Körner, C., & Basler, D. (2010). Phenology under global warming. *Science, 327*(5972), 1461-1462. https://doi.org/10.1126/science.1186473

Miller-Rushing, A. J., Katsuki, T., Primack, R. B., Ishii, Y., Lee, S. D., & Higuchi, H. (2007). Impact of global warming on a group of related species and their hybrids: cherry tree (Rosaceae) flowering at Mt. Takao, Japan. *American Journal of Botany, 94*(9), 1470-1478. https://doi.org/10.3732/ajb.94.9.1470

Primack, R. B., Higuchi, H., & Miller-Rushing, A. J. (2009). The impact of climate change on cherry trees and other species in Japan. *Biological Conservation, 142*(9). https://link.springer.com/chapter/10.1016/j.biocon.2009.03.016

Strubell, E., Ganesh, A., & McCallum, A. (2019). *Energy and Policy Considerations for Deep Learning in NLP*. Proceedings of the 57th Annual Meeting of the Association for Computational Linguistics, 3645–3650. Available at https://arxiv.org/abs/1906.02243

Taylor, S. J., & Letham, B. (2018). Forecasting at scale. PeerJ Computer Science. Available at https://peerj.com/preprints/3190/

Chapter 7
Working with Spatial Data

Abstract Spatial data is rapidly transforming data science, enabling nuanced insights across disciplines from environmental monitoring to urban planning. This chapter is one of the most unique in this book because it focuses on spatial data, a topic rarely covered in data science references. While many data science resources exist, few explore spatial data's unique aspects. Nowadays, most data includes location information, which can greatly enhance data science and decision-making. In this chapter, we'll explore how spatial data is represented and structured and how it's collected, stored, managed, analyzed, and visualized, as well as its various applications. We'll also discuss how to assess the uncertainty in spatial data, and we'll conclude with an explanation of common sources of error in spatial data, such as human, environmental, and instrument-related factors. In the next part of this chapter, we will practice working with the two main types of spatial data: vector and raster. Using Japan as our study case, we'll join population data (in CSV format) with Japan's prefecture-level administrative boundaries (in shapefile format). We'll then create population change data through simple calculations and visualize the results using static and dynamic maps. Furthermore, we'll work with earth observation satellite imageries to calculate the NDVI and create a land use land cover map using a machine learning algorithm and supervised method. We will also practice with the Nighttime Light (NTL) imagery of Black Marble datasets to visualize the changes in the NTL radiance image. We'll also practice extracting annual data from NTL and plotting it using bar plots in RStudio.

Relation to Other Chapters: Adds a spatial dimension to data science methods, essential for advanced techniques discussed in Chaps. 8 and 9.

F. Ramdani, *Data Science: Foundations and Hands-on Experience*,
https://doi.org/10.1007/978-981-96-4683-8_7

7.1 Introduction

Most data today includes location information, which is essential for many modern applications. However, only a few data science books cover spatial data or its practical uses. This chapter introduces the importance of spatial data and explores its real-world applications.

Historically, spatial data was mainly used in fields like geography, environmental science, agriculture, and climate studies. But now, social sciences also use spatial data. This is because spatial data does not just show "what" but also "where." Combined with geometric information, it helps decision-makers make more precise and accurate decisions. In spatial data science, the final output is often a map. These maps include points, lines, polygons, colors, and symbols that are sometimes self-explanatory.

Spatial data is also known as multidimensional data. Multidimensional data is a dataset with many different columns, or attributes, that can be organized and viewed in multiple dimensions. It is often used to understand complex systems and events through data analysis, machine learning, and data visualization.

Multidimensional data offers several benefits, making it a powerful tool in data analysis. One major advantage is its ability to discover hidden insights. When datasets contain multiple dimensions, or columns, analysts can explore relationships that may not be immediately obvious. For instance, combining financial, demographic, and behavioral data in retail can uncover hidden purchasing patterns among different customer groups. The more dimensions available, the greater the potential to extract valuable insights that might otherwise remain unnoticed.

Another advantage is the ability to group similar information. By organizing data into related dimensions, analysts can combine similar attributes, which simplifies the analysis process. For example, in a dataset of products, information about sales, profit, and cost can be grouped into a single dimension, making it easier to view and compare trends. This grouping approach enhances the clarity and usefulness of the data.

Multidimensional data also helps in visualizing complex datasets. Data analysis outcomes can be visually represented through graphs, charts, or 3D visualizations. For example, a 3D scatter plot can illustrate relationships across three variables, such as temperature, rainfall, and crop yield, allowing researchers to spot patterns more intuitively. Such visualizations are particularly valuable in presenting findings to stakeholders who may not have a technical background.

Furthermore, multidimensional data enables the detection of patterns, trends, outliers, and anomalies. With its "cubed" structure, every data point is visible, reducing the chances of missing critical insights. This capability is crucial for fields like finance, where outliers in transaction data may indicate fraudulent activities, or for environmental monitoring, where anomalies could signal potential natural disasters.

Examples of multidimensional data include spatial raster data, which is data collected over dimensions like space, time, depth, or height. This type of data is frequently used in remote sensing and climate studies. For example, satellite images capturing temperature changes over time can help scientists monitor global warming trends or assess the impact of natural disasters like hurricanes or wildfires.

"The ability to work with spatial data has become important for data scientists. If you want to set yourself apart from the crowd in the world of data science, then be good at spatial data processing and analysis."

7.2 Computer Representation

What was your first impression when you saw the Tokyo Skytree? Most likely, you were amazed by this tall structure. It stands 634 m high (including the antenna), with 32 floors above ground and three below. It was developed by Tobu Railway and designed by the architectural firm Nikken Sekkei. Construction began in 2008, and it was completed and opened in 2012.

All the descriptions above consist of string data containing text and some numbers. This data is quite simple, whereas the structure of the Tokyo Sky Tree is highly complex. Its design blends traditional Japanese aesthetics with cutting-edge technology, reflecting both cultural heritage and futuristic ambition. The structure features a tripod base, which gradually transitions into a cylindrical form as it rises, ensuring stability and elegance. This unique shape is engineered to withstand earthquakes and typhoons, utilizing a central column damping system inspired by traditional pagodas. The steel framework, reinforced with vibration-resistant materials, provides resilience against seismic activity, while the exterior lattice pattern, reminiscent of traditional Japanese motifs, adds a delicate beauty to its robust form. The Skytree's two observation decks, located at 350 and 450 m, are encased in glass, offering breathtaking 360 degree panoramic views of Tokyo while integrating seamlessly with the sleek, aerodynamic design. This complex structure is not only an engineering feat but also a symbol of Tokyo's harmony between innovation and tradition.

When you look at the Tokyo Sky Tree on a map, it is shown as a simple point with a surrounding area or polygon. A label, "Tokyo Sky Tree," is added to make it clear what the point represents. This is called modeling or simplification, where we create a simple version of real-world features to display in the digital or computer world. We use spatial data to represent features of the Earth in digital form.

Spatial data is information that includes a geographic location. It shows where things are and describes their characteristics on Earth's surface or in space. Spatial data usually comes with coordinates, like latitude and longitude (and sometimes altitude—*an elevation data* and time-stamped). These coordinates help locate data points within a reference system. When spatial data is combined with a specific projection and reference system, such as the World Geodetic System (WGS) 1984 or North UTM Zone 54, it becomes geospatial data.

How can a computer system store information about a complex structure like the Tokyo Sky Tree in a digital format? The process is similar to translation—real-world geographic features must be converted into a geographic information system (GIS) using computer representations. This translation involves simplifying each feature by representing it with geometric shapes and associated attributes.

A computer system can store geographic objects in two basic forms: **regular and irregular**. The regular form is known as raster, which consists of a set of regularly spaced and contiguous cells, each associated with specific field values. These values represent the attributes of the cells rather than individual points.

In contrast, the irregular form, referred to as vector data, represents georeferenced information using coordinate pairs within a geographic space. Vector data can be categorized into three basic forms: point, line, and area (or polygon), each representing distinct geometric features in the spatial domain.

Raster Representation

Geographic phenomena can be represented as shapes made up of pixels (Fig. 7.1), often derived from remotely sensed data such as satellite or drone imagery. This representation uses a model of the world as a continuous surface divided into a regular grid of cells, arranged systematically in rows and columns. Each cell within this grid must be uniform in size and is assigned a specific value, which could represent a variety of attributes, such as elevation, temperature, land cover type, or Nighttime Light. Additionally, every cell is georeferenced, meaning that it has coordinates that define its precise location on the Earth's surface.

This grid-based approach is particularly useful for representing areas or polygons, allowing for the analysis and visualization of spatial phenomena over a defined region. By maintaining consistency in cell size and value assignment, this method provides a structured and reliable way to model and interpret spatial data. Rasters data include various forms such as satellite images, aerial photos, elevation models, and scanned maps.

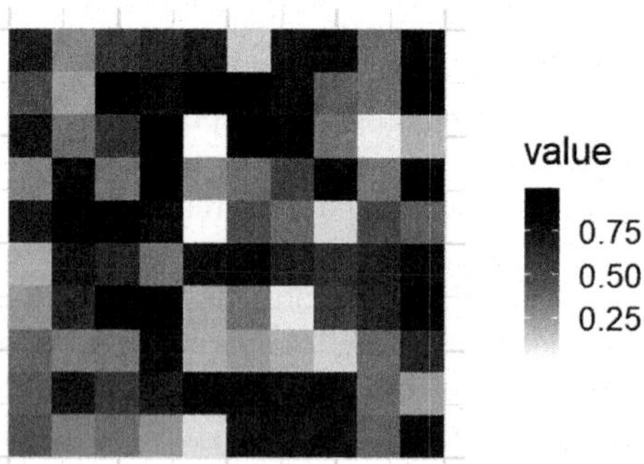

Fig. 7.1 Raster representation of pixels

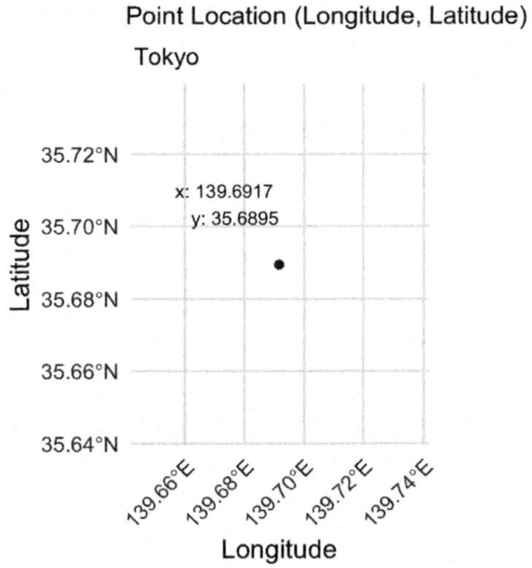

Fig. 7.2 Representation of point of spatial data

Vector Representation

Vector data is a fundamental representation in GIS that models geographic phenomena using three primary shapes: points, lines, and areas.

Points are used to represent discrete geographic phenomena that can be pinpointed at specific locations. Examples include cities, mountains, and towers, which are typically mapped as singular points on a map. Figure 7.2 illustrates the point of spatial data.

Lines are used to depict linear features that represent connections or pathways in geographic phenomena. These include road networks, rivers, and contours, which are essential for understanding transportation, hydrology, and elevation patterns. Figure 7.3 illustrates line in a spatial data.

Areas (polygons), on the other hand, represent phenomena that occupy a defined space. These are used to model features such as administrative boundaries, water bodies like lakes and seas, and various land uses such as buildings and football fields. Additionally, areas are critical for illustrating land cover types, such as forests, urban regions, agricultural lands, and other land classifications. Together, these vector shapes provide a versatile and precise way to model and analyze spatial data in GIS applications. Figure 7.4 illustrates a polygon of spatial data.

7.3 Spatial Data Architecture

Raster Data Architecture

As explained in the previous subchapter, raster data uses pixels or cells to represent features on the earth. A single raster data can have just one pixel or billions of

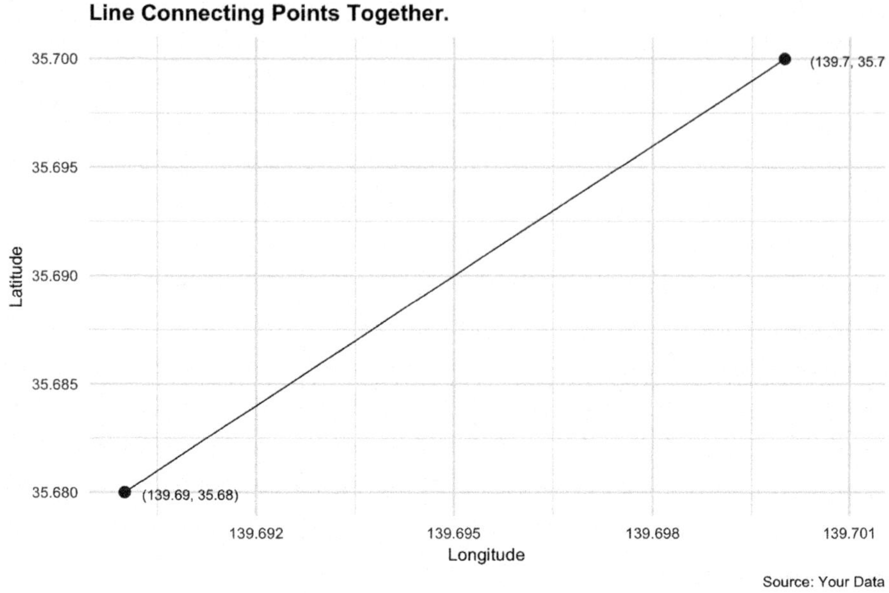

Fig. 7.3 Representation of line of spatial data

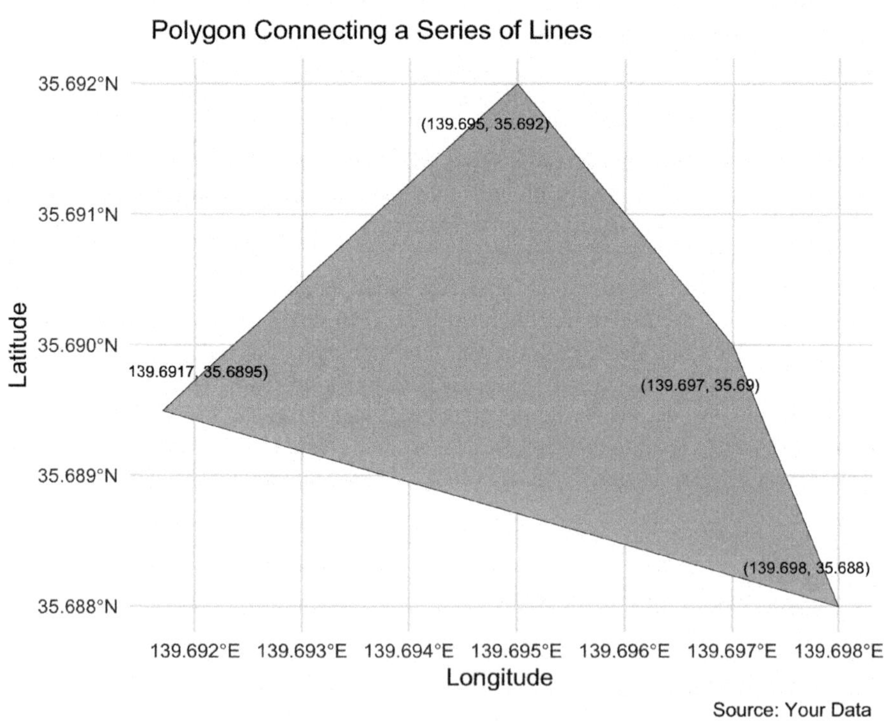

Fig. 7.4 Representation of polygon of spatial data

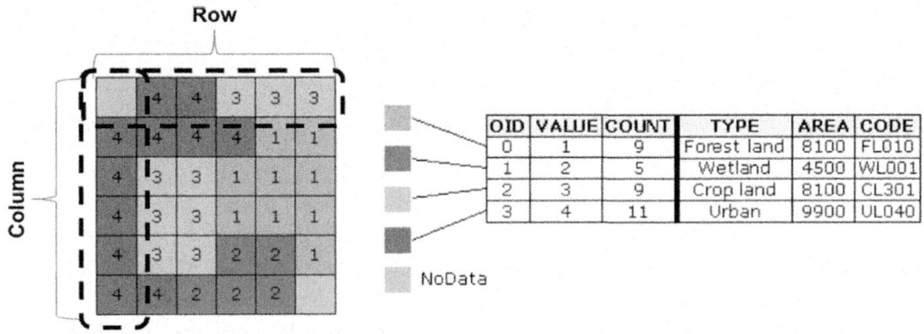

OID	VALUE	COUNT	TYPE	AREA	CODE
0	1	9	Forest land	8100	FL010
1	2	5	Wetland	4500	WL001
2	3	9	Crop land	8100	CL301
3	4	11	Urban	9900	UL040

Fig. 7.5 Illustration of raster data architecture

pixels. Raster data is made up of rows and columns, where each row and column contain values. These values can be shown in different colors. Each pixel has its own coordinates (longitude and latitude), and after some post-processing steps, raster data can store additional information such as ID, type, area, and code, as shown in Fig. 7.5.

Vector Data Architecture

Vector data is a fundamental structure in geospatial analysis, combining spatial and tabular components to represent real-world phenomena. The spatial aspect focuses on geometry, answering the question "where" by representing the real world using points, lines, or polygons. This approach simplifies reality by ignoring intricate details and emphasizing patterns.

Points are represented by coordinate pairs in two dimensions (x, y) or coordinate triplets in three dimensions (x, y, z). Points are often used to represent objects that don't have a clear size or shape but are important for defining locations, such as a Capital City or top of a mountain can be represented using a specific spot on a map. In addition to the geographical coordinates, each point can also have extra information attached to it, which is called attribute or thematic data. This extra data could include information such as the type of object at that location, its characteristics, or other related details. Following is an example of GeoJSON architecture of point vector data of Fig. 7.2:

```
• {
• "type": "FeatureCollection",
• "features":[
• {
• "type": "Feature",
• "geometry":{
• "type": "Point",
• "coordinates":[139.6917, 35.6895]
```

- },
- "properties":{}
- }
-]
- }

Lines are formed by connecting points together. These lines can be defined by two end nodes, or by additional internal nodes or vertices. Nodes and vertices are similar to points, but their main purpose is to help define the shape of the line and create a more accurate representation of a real-world feature. The straight sections of a line that connect consecutive nodes or vertices are called line segments. Lines, especially when connected together in a series, can represent networks, such as roads, transportation systems, or water systems, and are often used in applications like traffic monitoring or watershed management. Following is an example of GeoJSON architecture of line vector data of Fig. 7.3:

- {
- "type": "FeatureCollection",
- "features": [
- {
- "type": "Feature",
- "geometry": {
- "type": "LineString",
- "coordinates": [
- [139.6917, 35.6895],
- [139.7000, 35.7000]
-]
- },
- "properties": {}
- }
-]
- }

Polygons are created by connecting a series of lines, forming a boundary. In a polygon, the first and last node of the line must have the same coordinates to close the shape. This boundary model is sometimes referred to as the "topological data model" because it captures the relationships between different geographical features. For example, it can represent how one polygon might be adjacent or connected to another, providing important topological information about the layout of the area. Following is an example of GeoJSON architecture of polygon vector data of Fig. 7.4:

```
• {
• "type": "FeatureCollection",
• "features": [
• {
• "type": "Feature",
• "geometry": {
• "type": "Polygon",
• "coordinates": [
• [
• [139.6917, 35.6895],
• [139.6950, 35.6920],
• [139.6970, 35.6900],
• [139.6980, 35.6880],
• [139.6917, 35.6895]
• ]
• ]
• },
• "properties": {}
• }
• ]
• }
```

Vector data is linked to a backend database called the attribute table, which helps users analyze and query the data. This table makes it easy to visualize and map the data's details, which can include various types of information. These details, often referred to as the tabular component, answer questions like "what" by providing a database of specific information about a phenomenon. This information may include text, number, date, or measurements, such as area in hectares, length in millimeters, or size in square kilometers, giving an abstract overview of the phenomenon's details. Figure 7.6 Shows an example of this tabular component in vector data.

Tabular data can integrate seamlessly with spatial data through common attributes, such as prefecture names or unique IDs (to join or merge). Additionally, it can represent spatial features by mapping points using GPS coordinates (longitude and latitude) or associating address fields with a street network through geocoding. Other numeric or textual data, such as population, income, or GDP, can enrich the analysis by providing additional context and insights. Having understood the foundational architecture of spatial data, we now explore its acquisition methods.

	ID	POP10	POP19	POP2010	POP2019	POPULATION_CHANGE	geometry
1	Aichi	7411	7552	7411	7552	141	MULTIPOLYGON (((137.0016 34...
2	Akita	1086	966	1086	966	-120	MULTIPOLYGON (((139.8726 39...
3	Aomori	1373	1246	1373	1246	-127	MULTIPOLYGON (((141.5298 40...
4	Chiba	6216	6259	6216	6259	43	MULTIPOLYGON (((140.1086 35...
5	Ehime	1431	1339	1431	1339	-92	MULTIPOLYGON (((132.5617 32...
6	Fukui	806	768	806	768	-38	MULTIPOLYGON (((136.065 35....
7	Fukuoka	5072	5104	5072	5104	32	MULTIPOLYGON (((130.1284 33...
8	Fukushima	2029	1846	2029	1846	-183	MULTIPOLYGON (((140.9552 37...
9	Gifu	2081	1987	2081	1987	-94	MULTIPOLYGON (((137.2885 36...
10	Gumma	2008	1942	2008	1942	-66	MULTIPOLYGON (((139.1792 36...
11	Hiroshima	2861	2804	2861	2804	-57	MULTIPOLYGON (((132.494 34....
12	Hokkaido	5506	5250	5506	5250	-256	MULTIPOLYGON (((139.8 41.36...
13	Hyogo	5588	5466	5588	5466	-122	MULTIPOLYGON (((134.8239 34...
14	Ibaraki	2970	2860	2970	2860	-110	MULTIPOLYGON (((140.6799 35...
15	Ishikawa	1170	1138	1170	1138	-32	MULTIPOLYGON (((137.0446 37...
16	Iwate	1330	1227	1330	1227	-103	MULTIPOLYGON (((141.7068 40...
17	Kagawa	996	956	996	956	-40	MULTIPOLYGON (((133.5416 34...
18	Kagoshima	1706	1602	1706	1602	-104	MULTIPOLYGON (((128.4521 27...

Fig. 7.6 Attribute component of vector data

7.4 Spatial Data Acquisition

Spatial data acquisition (SDA) is the process of collecting data that represents the physical features and characteristics of the Earth's surface. This data helps us understand and map geographical areas, including landforms, structures, and other environmental aspects. There are different ways to gather spatial data, which can be broadly classified into two main types: primary data acquisition and secondary data acquisition.

Primary data acquisition involves gathering new data directly from the field. This is often done using specialized methods that are tailored to the specific needs of the project. Common techniques used for primary data collection include surveys, where information is gathered from people or places, and field measurements, where measurements are taken in person. Other methods include using Global Positioning System (GPS) devices to collect location data, aerial photography to capture images from the sky, Light Detection and Ranging (LiDAR) to measure distances and create detailed 3D models, and satellite imagery to capture large-scale images of the Earth's surface.

Secondary data acquisition refers to using existing data that other organizations or individuals have already collected. This data is typically obtained from government agencies, research institutions, or commercial providers. Secondary data include maps, environmental reports, and geospatial datasets available to the public or through specific databases.

However, due to technological development, today there is the third category of spatial data acquisition. Machine/sensor-generated data involves using modern technology, such as smartphones, CCTV cameras, social networking sites (SNS),

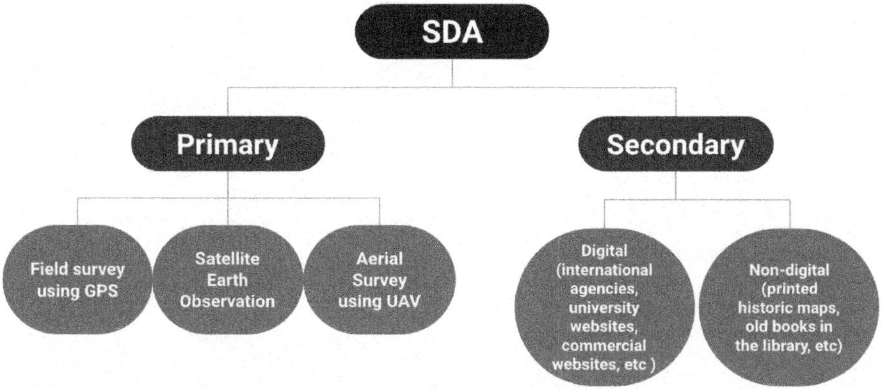

Fig. 7.7 Category of spatial data acquisition (SDA)

and other sensors, to collect data. These devices automatically gather information through built-in sensors, such as GPS, cameras, and motion detectors. This type of data collection is becoming increasingly popular due to the widespread use of smart devices and the ability to collect large amounts of data in real-time.

Each type of spatial data acquisition has its advantages, and the chosen method depends on the project's specific needs and the resources available. Figure 7.7 summarizes the categories of spatial data acquisitions.

Raster Data Acquisition

Earth observation satellites collect data from space using sensors that capture information about the Earth's surface. These sensors are powered by solar energy, which is reflected and emitted by objects on Earth. As this energy travels through the atmosphere, it interacts with atmospheric components, which can influence the quality and type of data collected by the satellite sensors.

The data collected by the satellite sensors is transmitted back to Earth through communication systems. This data is received by ground stations, where it is processed to remove noise or errors, ensuring that the information is accurate and useful. Once the data is processed, it is prepared for further analysis. Scientists interpret this data to study various aspects of the Earth's surface, such as land cover, vegetation, or temperature changes.

The data is stored in a geodatabase, a system that organizes and manages large amounts of spatial information. A geodatabase allows researchers to access, update, and analyze the data easily. The applications of this data are vast. It can be used for environmental monitoring, urban planning, disaster management, agriculture, and climate change studies. By understanding the data captured by earth observation satellites, researchers can make informed decisions to address global challenges and improve the sustainability of our planet. Figure 7.8 illustrates the process of earth observation satellite data.

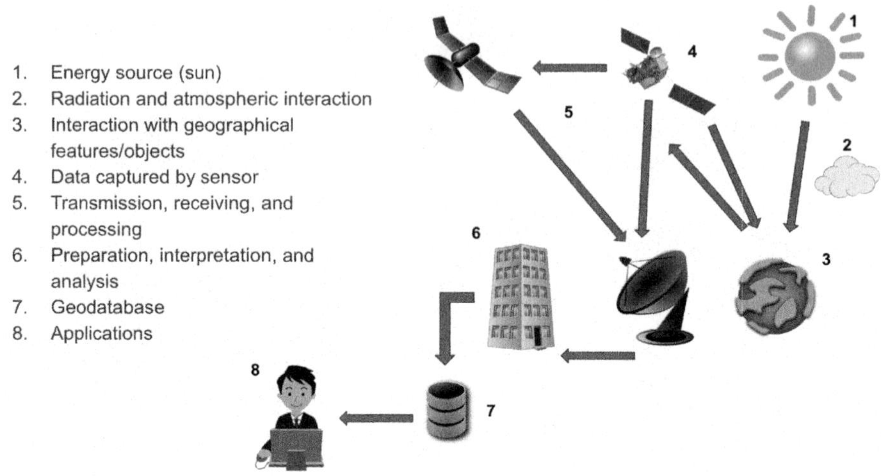

Fig. 7.8 Process of earth observation satellite data

Raw data of passive sensor of satellite images is visualized in black and white scale or single-band pseudocolor with the scale from 0 (black) to 255 (white) within the visible spectrum of electromagnetic (Fig. 7.9). It is very difficult for human eyes to distinguish the earth's features within this scale. Therefore, it is important to transform the visualization using a false color Red–Green–Blue (RGB) composite. Then we can easily distinguish the earth's features.

Vector Data Acquisition

Vector data is mostly acquired using the Global Position System (GPS). GPS can collect data in the form of points, lines, and polygons. Modern GPS can even store attribute data with huge storage, making field survey more convenient.

GPS is important because it helps you find out where you are and where you are going. Knowing your position is crucial when handling geographical data because

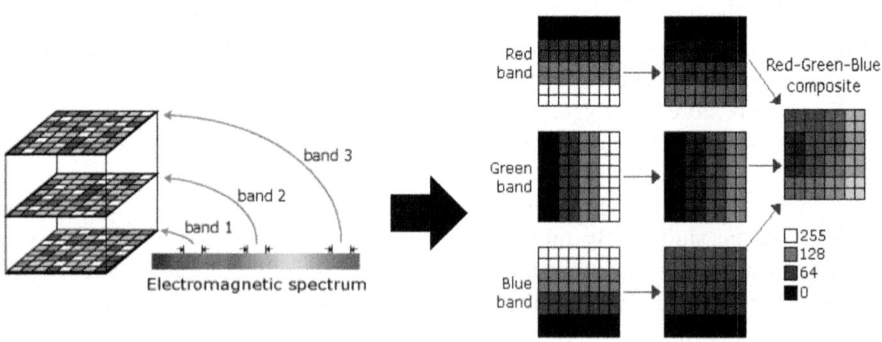

Fig. 7.9 Transforming the visualization using false color Red–Green–Blue (RGB) composite

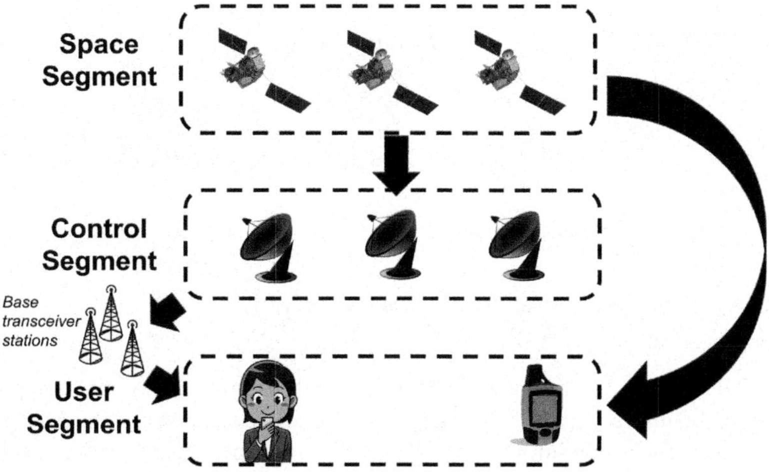

Fig. 7.10 Component of GPS

it allows you to map locations, track movements, and navigate accurately. GPS is a worldwide system that helps determine your exact location, no matter where you are on Earth.

GPS is a global radio-navigation system that uses satellites as reference points to calculate positions on Earth. The system works in three parts (Fig. 7.10):

1. **Space Segment**: The satellites orbiting the Earth.
2. **Control Segment**: The ground stations that monitor and control the satellites.
3. **User Segment**: The GPS receivers (GPSr) that receive the signals from the satellites.

GPS works by calculating the distances between the receiver on Earth and the satellites in space. These distances are determined by the time a radio signal travels from the satellite to the receiver. The GPS receiver uses the signals from the satellites to determine its position in terms of latitude and longitude on the Earth's surface.

The more satellites the GPS receiver can "see," the more accurate the position it can calculate. For best results, the receiver must have a clear sky view to communicate with the satellites. GPS doesn't work well in places like dense forests, caves, underwater, or inside buildings, where the signals may be blocked.

As of August 15, 2023, 83 GPS satellites have been built. Of these, 31 are operational and in use, 3 are in reserve or testing, 42 have been retired, 2 were lost during launch, and 1 prototype was never launched. For the system to work properly, at least 24 operational satellites are needed. The GPS can support up to 32 satellites, though typically 31 are operational at any given time. A GPS receiver needs at least four satellites to calculate its position in three dimensions—latitude, longitude, and altitude.

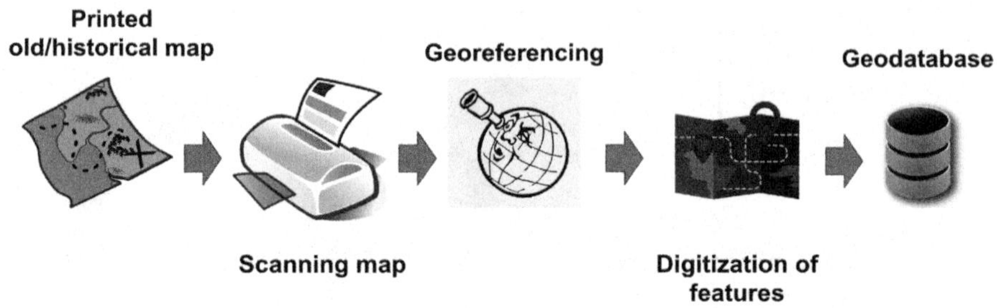

Fig. 7.11 Scanning old/historical map and creating geodatabase

The GPS in your smartphone works differently from conventional mapping and survey GPS. Smartphone GPS is designed for basic use and needs an internet connection to provide location information. It relies on multiple Base Transceiver Stations (BTS) to function. Without a connection to BTS, your smartphone cannot work properly or give accurate location data.

Collecting vector data with a smartphone GPS works well in cities or areas with a good internet connection. However, it is better to use conventional mapping or survey GPS devices for remote areas. Unlike smartphones, these devices have longer battery life, are more durable, and are designed for tough environments.

Another way to collect vector data is using various tools, such as a scanner to save an old map (Fig. 7.11). After scanning, we need to perform georeferencing, assigning coordinates to the scanned map. Then, we can create vector points, lines, or polygons from the scanned map using any GIS software. This process is called digitizing. The digitized data is stored in a geodatabase and can be used for further analysis.

A modern way to collect vector data is by using social networking services (SNSs). These online platforms allow users to create public profiles and connect with others. Users share their activities, and this data is stored in the cloud. We can request this data from the cloud with specific techniques, and the cloud sends back the information. Any location data can then be saved in a geodatabase for further analysis or applications (Fig. 7.12).

7.5 Spatial Data Storage

Raster Data Storage

Common formats for raster data storage include GeoTIFF, NetCDF, and GRID. GeoTIFF, or Georeferenced Tagged Image File Format, is a widely utilized raster data format designed for geospatial applications. It builds upon the Tagged Image File Format (TIFF) by embedding geospatial metadata, enabling precise geographic referencing.

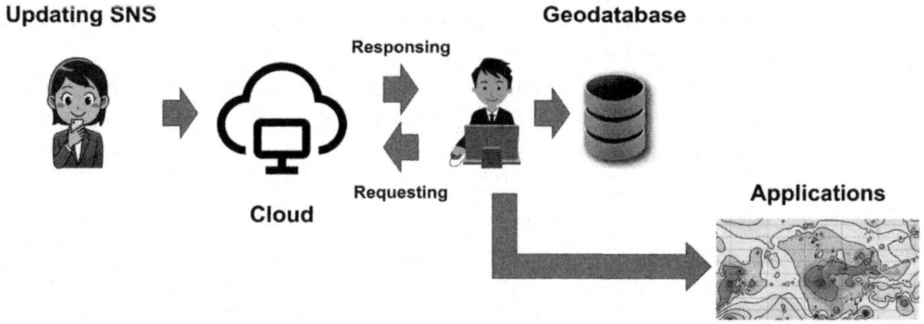

Fig. 7.12 Modern vector data acquisition

GeoTIFF supports single or multiple bands and accommodates a range of data types, such as integers and floating-point numbers. One of its standout features is georeferencing, which stores information about map projections, coordinate systems, and geotransformation parameters, such as corner coordinates and resolution. GeoTIFF also supports lossless compression methods, like LZW and DEFLATE, and lossy compression, such as JPEG, ensuring efficient storage without compromising essential data.

Its compatibility with various GIS software, including QGIS, ArcGIS, and GRASS GIS, enhances its interoperability, making it a preferred choice for data visualization. GeoTIFF files are easily rendered as maps or images thanks to its integration with the TIFF format.

GeoTIFF is extensively used in applications such as satellite imagery analysis, Digital Elevation Models (DEMs), and land cover or land use mapping, owing to its robust capabilities and versatility.

NetCDF is another raster data, short for Network Common Data Form, a versatile format specifically designed for storing multidimensional scientific data. Originating from atmospheric and oceanographic research needs, it has gained prominence in geospatial applications. NetCDF excels in managing variables across dimensions like time, latitude, longitude, and altitude, making it particularly suited for spatiotemporal datasets.

The format is self-describing, incorporating metadata for each variable and the entire dataset, ensuring clarity and usability. Its support for chunking and compression allows efficient storage of large datasets. NetCDF is widely adopted in scientific communities and is compatible with tools like QGIS, Python's xarray, and R's ncdf4 package, enhancing its interoperability across platforms.

NetCDF is commonly applied in climate modeling, weather predictions, oceanography, hydrology, and other spatiotemporal data analyses, such as tracking temperature changes over time. Its ability to handle complex datasets makes it a cornerstone in environmental and geospatial research.

While Esri develops GRID raster data, it is a proprietary raster format tailored for use with ArcGIS software. It is available in two variations: integer GRID for categorical data and floating-point GRID for continuous data. Unlike other formats,

GRID organizes data within a structured directory, consisting of multiple files that store spatial and attribute information.

A distinctive feature of Integer GRID is its support for attribute tables, which store additional information about each category in the data, enhancing analytical capabilities. However, the GRID format typically does not employ compression, which can result in larger file sizes. While primarily used within Esri's ecosystem, GRID data can be converted to other formats for broader compatibility.

Common applications of GRID include hydrological modeling tasks such as flow accumulation and watershed delineation, categorical land cover analysis, and suitability or cost surface evaluations. GRID remains a valuable tool for specialized GIS analyses within the ArcGIS environment despite its proprietary nature. Table 7.1 summarizes the difference between GeoTIFF, NetCDF, and GRID.

Vector Data Storage

The shapefile is a widely used vector data format developed by Environmental Systems Research Institute (ESRI), an American company specializing in GIS software (ArcGIS), mapping, and location intelligence. Shapefile consists of multiple components, with three mandatory files:.shp,.shx, and.dbf. The.shp file stores the geometry of features, the.shx file provides an index for these geometries, and the.dbf file holds attribute data in a tabular format. Shapefiles are broadly compatible with GIS software and are simple and lightweight, making them suitable for basic spatial data needs. However, they have limitations, such as a maximum file size of 2 GB, strict attribute formatting (e.g., column names are limited to 10 characters), and lack of support for advanced data types like complex geometries or topologies.

Another format of vector data is GeoJSON. GeoJSON is a JSON-based open format for encoding vector data that is human-readable and widely used for web applications. Its strengths lie in its lightweight nature and ease of use, making it ideal for web mapping and sharing spatial data over the internet. GeoJSON natively

Table 7.1 Differences between GeoTIFF, NetCDF, and GRID

Feature	GeoTIFF	NetCDF	GRID (Esri GRID)
Data type	Geospatial raster	Multidimensional scientific	Geospatial raster
Metadata	Embedded in file	Self-describing metadata	Directory structure
Compression	Supported	Supported (chunking)	Not supported
Software support	Broad (GIS and imaging)	Scientific and GIS tools	Primarily ArcGIS
Complexity	Moderate	Advanced (multidimensional)	Simple
Best for	Static maps, DEMs	Temporal datasets, modeling	Esri-centric workflows

supports the WGS 84 Coordinate Reference System (CRS). However, it is less efficient for large datasets, offers limited CRS support beyond WGS 84, and is unsuitable for handling complex geometries or attributes

Example of GeoJSON data structure

```
{
    "type": "Feature",
    "geometry": {"type": "Point", "coordinates":
[125.6, 10.1]},
    "properties": {"name": "Dinagat Islands"}.
  }
```

GeoPackage is an open format based on SQLite, designed to store both vector and raster data in a single file. It adheres to the Open Geospatial Consortium (OGC) standard. Its compact and efficient storage capabilities and support for advanced features such as spatial indexing and custom CRS make it a versatile choice. GeoPackage can handle large datasets better than shapefiles or GeoJSON and is cross-platform and open standard. However, it may not be supported by older GIS software and has a steeper learning curve compared to shapefiles.

The Geodatabase is a proprietary database format developed by Esri for storing, managing, and analyzing large spatial datasets. It is available in two main variants: the File Geodatabase (FGDB), which stores data in a folder structure on disk, and the Enterprise Geodatabase, which utilizes relational database systems like PostgreSQL or Oracle for advanced spatial data management. Geodatabases offer advanced capabilities such as versioning, topology rules, and complex data models, making them efficient for handling large datasets. They are tightly integrated with Esri's ArcGIS ecosystem. However, their proprietary nature limits compatibility outside the Esri ecosystem, and the Enterprise Geodatabase requires significant resources and expertise to implement.

Keyhole Markup Language (KML) is an XML-based format originally developed by Google for geographic data visualization, particularly in Google Earth. It excels in 3D visualization and interactive maps and is widely supported by web mapping platforms. KML files can include custom styles and multimedia elements. Despite its strengths, KML is not optimized for large datasets, and its XML structure can result in large file sizes compared to other formats. Additionally, it has limited capabilities for advanced geospatial analysis. The differences between Shapefile, GeoJSON, GeoPackage, Geodatabase, and KML is shown in Table 7.2.

Raster and vector data are different in format and structure; therefore, there are advantages and disadvantages of using these spatial data (Table 7.3).

Table 7.2 Differences between Shapefile, GeoJSON, GeoPackage, Geodatabase, and KML

Format	Best for	Strengths	Weaknesses
Shapefile	Basic GIS tasks	Simple and compatible	Size and attribute limitations
GeoJSON	Web applications	Lightweight and human-readable	Inefficient for large datasets
GeoPackage	Modern GIS needs	Compact, efficient, open standard	Limited support in older software
Geodatabase	Advanced spatial analysis	Powerful, large dataset handling	Proprietary, steep learning curve
KML	Visualization in Google Earth/Maps	Good for 3D and interactive maps	Large file size, limited analysis

Table 7.3 Differences between raster and vector data

Aspect	Raster data	Vector data
Advantages	• Simple to store and process • Handles continuous data (e.g., elevation) • Good for complex analyses (e.g., climate) • Easy to apply map algebra	• High precision and accuracy for shapes • Easy to update and edit features • Smaller file sizes for features • Powerful for overlay analysis
Disadvantages	• Large file sizes for high resolution • Requires large storage space • Can look blurry when zoomed in • Limited precision for boundaries	• Cannot handle continuous data well • More complex to analyze and process • Requires more effort for storage formats • Costly and time-consuming for updating

7.6 Spatial Data Management

Spatial data management involves collecting, storing, analyzing, and using location-based data to address real-world challenges by linking data to specific places. It comprises six key components: **data, software, hardware, methods, people, and networks** (Fig. 7.13). Each component plays an essential role in the overall process, enabling the use of spatial information effectively.

Data is the foundation of spatial data management. It includes information about where objects are located on Earth, typically represented in vector data (points, lines, and areas) and raster data (gridded data). Accurate and up-to-date data is crucial because the reliability of any analysis depends on the quality of the input data.

Software refers to the tools and programs used to handle spatial data. Popular examples include QGIS, GRASS GIS, RStudio, Python, and MANDARA (a free software) and ArcGIS (a commercial option). These programs allow users to store and manage

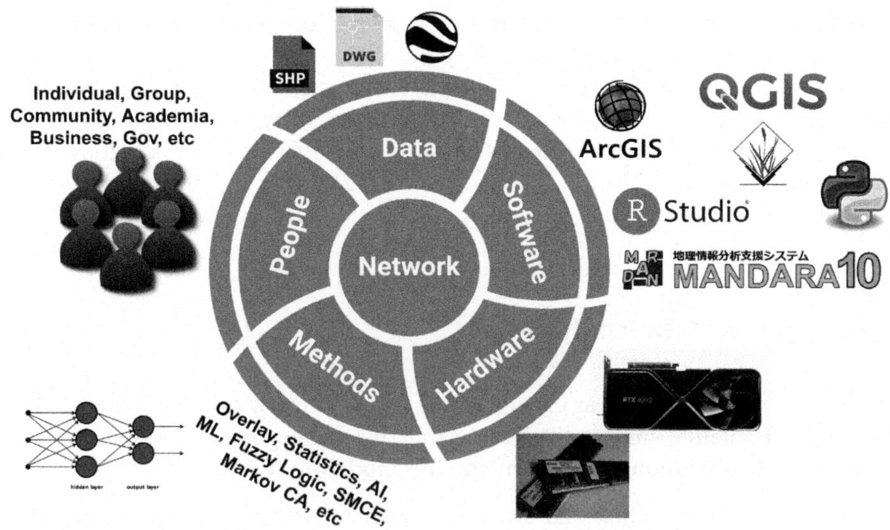

Fig. 7.13 Components of spatial data management

data in databases, visualize information on maps, and perform analyses, such as finding optimal routes or calculating environmental changes. Software simplifies complex tasks, making spatial data accessible and useful for decision-making.

Hardware encompasses the physical devices required for collecting, storing, processing, and analyzing spatial data. Examples include high-performance computers with advanced graphics cards and sufficient Random Access Memory (RAM) for data processing, GPS devices and drones for capturing location and imagery data and servers for storing, sharing, and accessing large datasets. Efficient and reliable hardware ensures that spatial data is collected and processed effectively, supporting accurate and timely analysis.

Methods (or sometimes also termed as **algorithms**) are the structured processes and techniques applied to manage spatial data. These include procedures for data collection, cleaning, combining different layers of information on a map, and analyzing. Following proper methods or algorithms ensures that spatial analysis results are both accurate and meaningful, which is essential for making informed decisions.

People are integral to the spatial data management system, serving as users and managers. These include researchers who analyze data, planners who design cities or conservation efforts using maps, and technicians who maintain the software and hardware. Skilled people are critical for formulating the right questions, effectively using tools, and interpreting results to address various challenges.

Networks connect all five components, enabling the sharing and access of spatial data. For example, the Internet is a global network allowing users to download satellite images or share maps online. Networks are essential for collaboration and accessing diverse datasets, especially in a globally connected world.

These components are interdependent, forming a cohesive GI system. Data provides the material for analysis, software processes and visualizes it, and skilled people interpret and apply it. Reliable hardware supports these activities, while networks facilitate collaboration and data sharing. These components ensure that spatial data management can effectively address complex real-world problems.

7.7 Spatial Data Analysis

Spatial data analysis involves understanding and working with geospatial data, such as maps or satellite images. There are four main categories of spatial analysis: **retrieval, classification, measurement, and modeling** (Fig. 7.14).

Retrieval involves finding and accessing specific information from spatial data, which can be done in several ways. **Interactive** retrieval allows users to click on a map or select an area to view detailed information about a location. **Attribute queries** enable searches based on specific criteria, such as "Cities with more than 1 million people within Japan." **Topological queries** analyze spatial relationships, such as identifying rivers within 1 km of a city or determining areas affected by tropical cyclones.

The other type of spatial data analysis is **classification**, which involves grouping spatial data into meaningful categories. For instance, a satellite image can be classified to distinguish forests, water bodies, or urban areas. This can be achieved through two approaches: **user-controlled** classification, where the user provides examples to guide the system, or **automatic** classification, where algorithms analyze patterns in the data to categorize it independently.

Measurement is another type of spatial data analysis focusing on calculating various spatial data aspects. This includes determining the **length of features** like roads or rivers, **measuring the area** of forests or lakes, **assessing the distance** between

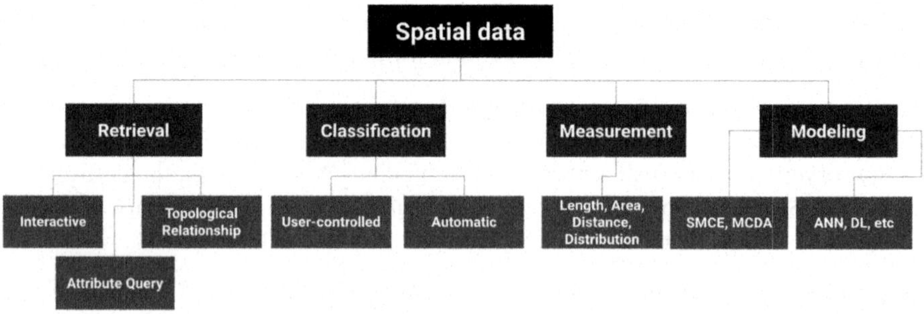

Fig. 7.14 Categories of spatial data analysis

places, or **analyzing the distribution** patterns of features such as health facilities in a city.

The advanced spatial data analysis is **modeling**, where we can use spatial data to simulate or predict outcomes, often leveraging advanced computational methods. Techniques like **Spatial Multicriteria Evaluation (SMCE)** or **Multicriteria Decision Analysis (MCDA)** can predict the flood susceptibility locations (Fig. 7.10) or **Artificial Neural Networks (ANN)** that can identify patterns to make predictions, such as forecasting crop yields based on satellite imagery. **Deep Learning (DL)**, a more advanced form of ANN, can handle highly detailed data, such as recognizing specific tree types in a forest. **Convolutional Neural Networks (CNNs)**, a kind of DL specialized for image analysis, can detect features like handicapped parking signs in a very high spatial resolution of satellite images.

Spatial data analysis provides the tools to answer questions and solve problems related to locations and their characteristics, ranging from simple mapping tasks to sophisticated computer-based modeling. In a simple sentence, spatial data analysis is a set of methods whose results change when the locations of the objects being analyzed change.

Spatial Data Analysis for Social Studies

Figure 7.15 illustrates how spatial data can be used in social studies by following steps. These steps include collecting different types of data, cleaning and preparing it, analyzing the information, and visually presenting the results using maps.

1. Data Collection

The first step involves gathering various types of data from different sources. This data includes:

- **Demographic Data**: Information about populations, such as age, gender, or the size of a population in a specific area.
- **Economic Data**: Details about income levels, employment rates, and the types of industries present in a region.
- **Crime Reports**: Records of criminal activities in different areas.
- **GIS Data**: Geospatial information, like maps, shows the locations and boundaries of physical areas.
- **Social Data**: Insights into people's behaviors, relationships, or trends within communities.

These diverse data types provide a foundation for understanding complex issues when combined.

2. Data Preprocessing

Before data analysis, proper preparation is essential. This process involves several key steps:

- **Data Cleaning:** Fixing errors, removing duplicate entries, and ensuring the data is complete and accurate.

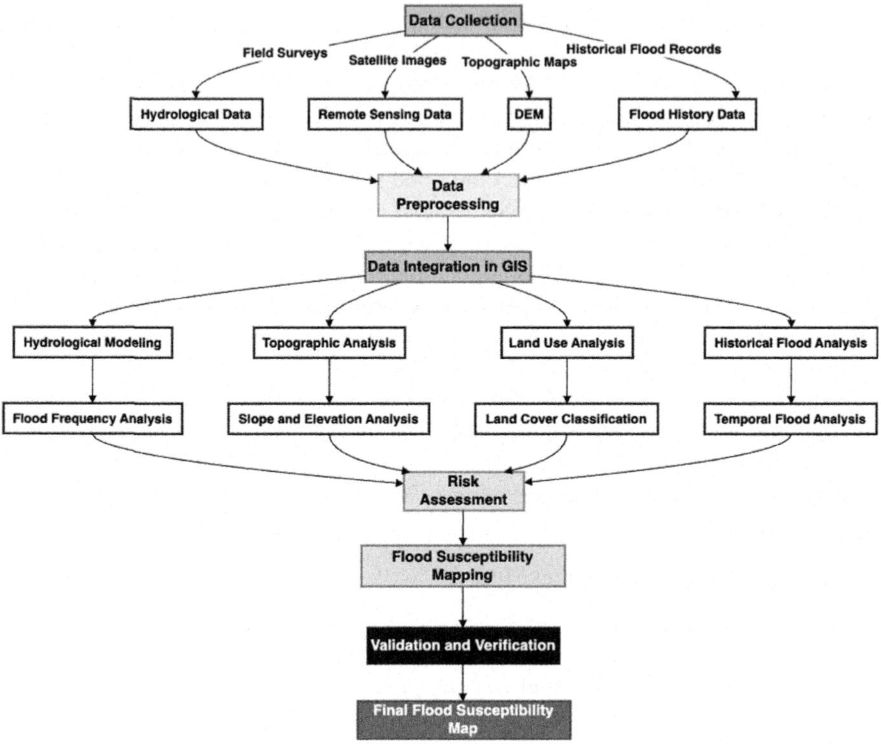

Fig. 7.15 Spatial multicriteria evaluation for flood susceptibility mapping

- **Data Normalization:** Standardizing the data so that all measurements and formats are comparable (e.g., converting all currency values to the same unit).
- **Data Integration:** Merging the cleaned and standardized data into a single, cohesive format, making it ready for analysis.

These steps guarantee the reliability and usability of the data.

3. Data Storage

Once preprocessing is complete, the data is stored in a central database. This storage system keeps all the information organized and accessible for the next steps. It acts as a hub for analysis and visualization.

4. Analysis and Modeling

The prepared data is then analyzed to answer specific questions and uncover patterns. Common methods include:

- **Correlation Analysis:** Studying relationships between variables, such as whether higher income levels are linked to lower crime rates.
- **Regression Analysis:** Using data to predict outcomes, like forecasting unemployment rates based on education levels.

- **Spatial Analysis:** Examining how information is distributed across physical locations, such as identifying urban and rural differences.
- **Machine Learning Models:** Using advanced algorithms to detect patterns, make predictions, or classify data.

These techniques help researchers understand the connections between various factors and provide insights into social or economic trends.

5. Model Evaluation

The analysis results need to be assessed using a confusion matrix for multiple classes or an ROC curve for single classes. Additionally, the model's uncertainty can be evaluated using accuracy, precision, or the F1-score, as discussed in Chap. 6.

6. GIS Visualization

Finally, the results are presented visually, making them easier to interpret. Visualization methods include:

- **Map Visualization:** Displaying data on maps to highlight geographic patterns, such as areas with high crime rates.
- **Heatmaps:** Showing areas with high or low values for specific variables, such as unemployment or population density.
- **Geostatistical Analysis:** Using advanced mapping techniques to explore trends or patterns over larger regions.

These visualizations make complex data accessible to policymakers, researchers, and the public. Figure 7.16 summarizes all of the steps of spatial data analysis for social studies.

Spatial data analysis bridges the gap between people and places. By combining social, economic, and geographic data, researchers can explore and address complex issues, such as the relationship between poverty and crime or how urban planning impacts communities. This approach is valuable in social studies, providing a solid foundation for making informed decisions and shaping effective policies.

7.8 Spatial Data Visualization

The final result of any spatial data analysis is a map. The map must follow the cartography principle to ensure the messages are well delivered to the stakeholders. Cartography is the study and practice of creating maps. The primary goal of cartography is to represent spatial information in a way that is visually clear, understandable, and useful for visualizing data patterns, making informed decisions, and communicating information effectively.

When we make a map, we use special elements to make it easy to understand. The map components that should appear are:

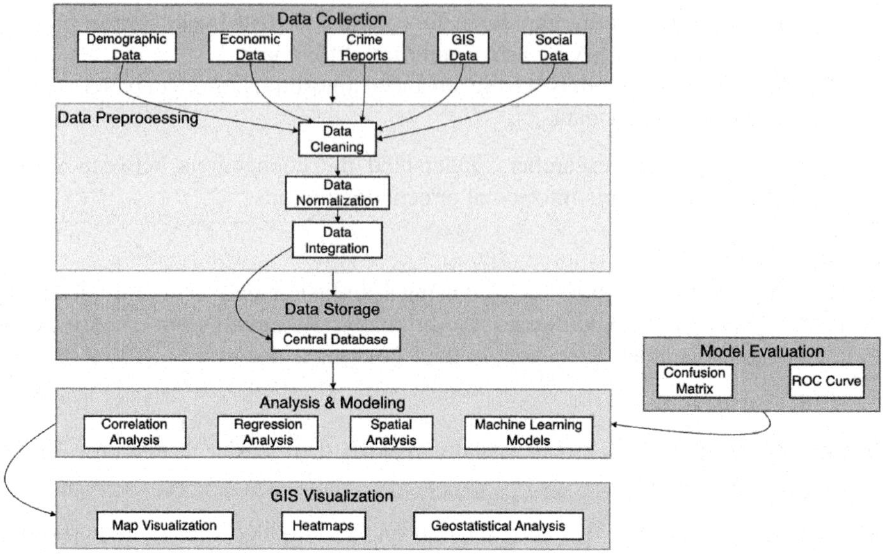

Fig. 7.16 Spatial data analysis for social studies

- **Main Title**: The title is like the headline of a newspaper. It tells you what the map is about. For example, "World's Annual Working Hours".
- **Main Map**: This is the map's focus—the area or region you want to show. For instance, if you're talking about rainfall in Japan, the map of Japan will be the center of attention.
- **Legend**: The legend is like a key. It explains what the map's colors, symbols, or lines mean. For example, blue might show rivers, and green might show forests. Remember to avoid overcrowded legends or poor color contrasts for accessibility.
- **Base Map**: The base map gives the background, like the shape of a country or city. It helps the viewer understand where everything is.
- **Scale**: The scale shows how big or small the features on the map are compared to real life. For example, it might say 1 cm on the map equals 1 km on the ground.
- **Orientation**: This typically involves displaying a compass or a north arrow, which indicates the direction of north to prevent confusion.
- **Information/Metadata**: Metadata is concise yet crucial information about a map, such as its creation date and data source. It enhances the credibility and reliability of the map.
- **Inset/Overview (Optional)**: A smaller map displayed within a larger map, providing context by showing a wider geographical area around the main focus of the larger map.
- **Grid (Optional)**: A grid is a system of lines, such as latitude and longitude, used to pinpoint locations on a map. It functions similarly to coordinates in a game.

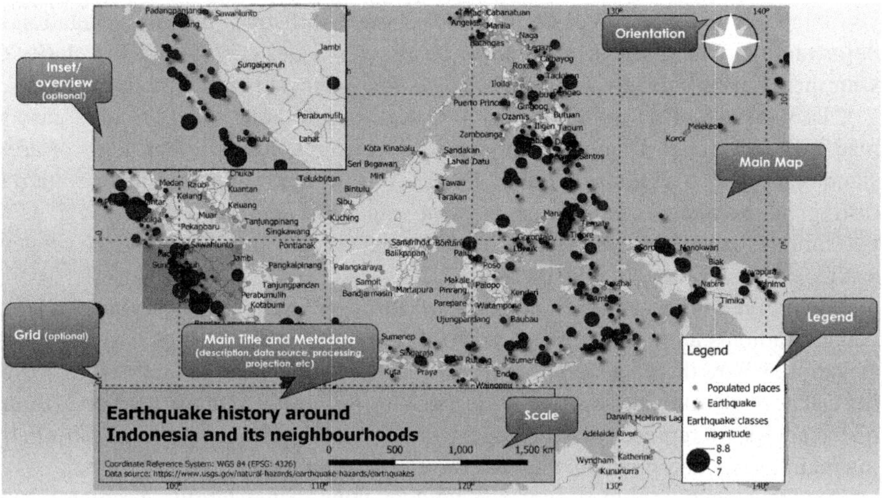

Fig. 7.17 Spatial data visualization of earthquake history around Indonesia and its neighborhood using cartography elements

When all these parts are included, the map becomes a powerful tool to share information visually (Fig. 7.17). It is clear, easy to read, and helps people understand spatial patterns, like where things are or how they are connected.

Principles of Using Color in Data Visualization

When creating visualizations, the colors you choose are important in helping users understand your data. It's essential to use natural colors that match what people typically associate with the concept or data you are presenting. This "intuitiveness" approach makes it easier for users to interpret and understand your visualization quickly.

For instance, certain colors are often linked to specific meanings. Red is commonly used for important or dangerous things, such as warnings or hazards. Blue is usually associated with water or anything wet, making it a natural choice when representing oceans, lakes, or rivers. Conversely, green is often connected to nature and vegetation, so it's a good choice when displaying forests, fields, or other natural areas. Selecting colors that align with these associations helps your audience quickly make sense of your data.

However, it is important not to overload your visualization with too many colors. Moderation is key in ensuring your visualization which remains clear and easy to interpret. Using just one main color can be effective for simple maps or charts, with additional colors used sparingly to highlight the most important parts of your data. Too many colors can confuse the viewer and distract from the main message.

Consistency is also crucial when using colors in your visualization. Stick to the same color scheme throughout to avoid confusion. If you need to change colors, do so intentionally to show a specific difference or change in the data. For example, you might switch from green to brown to show a shift from healthy vegetation to deforestation. Changing colors just for aesthetic reasons can disrupt the clarity of your message and make your audience question the meaning behind the colors.

Clarity should always be a priority. Colors should help make the data easy to read and understand. Using contrasting colors ensures that different items or areas stand out clearly. Avoid using colors that are too similar, as this can make it hard to distinguish between different categories or values in your data. For example, using two similar shades of green to show different vegetation types might confuse viewers, as they may not notice the distinction.

Be careful with how they are applied when using gradients or varying shades of color. Gradients are best used for showing continuous data, such as temperature or elevation, where the data smoothly transitions from one value to another. However, for categorical data, such as population groups or land use types, it's better to use distinct colors to represent each category rather than relying on gradients. This helps maintain clarity and prevents the data from becoming too complex.

Finally, always include a color legend in your visualization. A color legend explains what each color represents, helping users interpret the data correctly. Without a clear explanation of why certain color are used, your audience may misunderstand the meaning of your visualization, which can lead to confusion or misinterpretation of the data.

Color-Blind Map Design

Color-blind design in map cartography is essential for ensuring that maps are accessible and understandable to everyone, including individuals with color vision deficiencies. Approximately 8% of men and 0.5% of women worldwide have some form of color blindness, which affects their ability to distinguish certain colors, especially red and green. If a map relies heavily on these colors without considering color blindness, it can lead to misinterpretation of the data and exclude a significant portion of the audience.

Using color-blind-friendly palettes helps make maps more inclusive. For example, color schemes that rely on blues and oranges, or other contrasting hues that are distinguishable for people with color blindness, are often more effective. Additionally, adding patterns, textures, or labels as alternative ways to represent data can improve accessibility. This ensures that users can interpret the information accurately, regardless of their ability to perceive colors.

The importance of color-blind-friendly design is particularly significant in maps used for critical purposes, such as disaster management, public health, or urban planning. In these contexts, clear communication of spatial information can directly impact decision-making and public safety. Inclusive design not only promotes equity but also improves the overall usability of the map for all users.

Cartographers can test their designs using tools like the Coblis (Color Blindness Simulator) or software features that simulate how maps will appear to users with different types of color blindness. By doing so, they can identify and address potential issues before finalizing their maps.

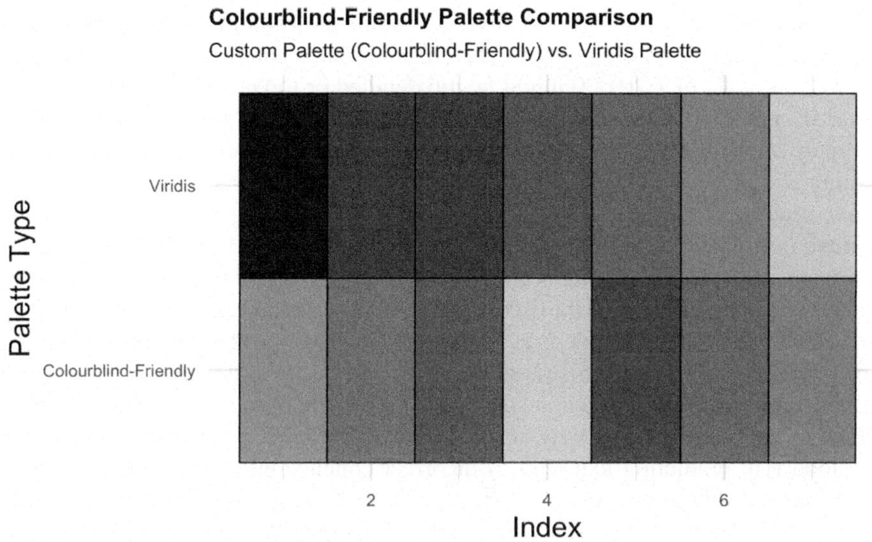

Fig. 7.18 Color-blind-friendly palette

Brewer (1994) emphasizes the importance of selecting perceptually effective color schemes in thematic mapping. These studies highlight that incorporating color-blind design is not merely a technical detail but a vital part of creating functional and inclusive maps. Figure 7.18 illustrates the custom palette that color-blind-friendly.

7.9 Uncertainty of Spatial Data

Having learned about spatial data, its analysis, and various applications, it is important to understand that spatial data is not flawless. Like any other data type, it has errors and limitations, especially concerning uncertainty. Uncertainty in spatial data can arise from several sources, and it is crucial to recognize these to make more accurate interpretations and decisions. Generally, there are three main types of uncertainty in spatial data: spatial scale, measurement scale, and temporal scale.

The first type of uncertainty is related to **spatial scale**. Spatial scale refers to how data is represented across different geographic areas. Errors may arise when the data does not cover the entire study area, leading to incomplete or inaccurate analysis. For example, a dataset may be collected for a specific region, but it might not cover the full area needed for a particular study. Additionally, the spatial resolution or scale at which the data is collected may not match the scale required for the analysis. This mismatch can lead to errors in interpretation, as different spatial scales can highlight different patterns and relationships.

The second type of uncertainty involves the **measurement scale**. Measurement scale refers to the level of detail or generalization in the data. For instance, a dataset created at a scale of 1:20,000 might be too detailed or too generalized compared to a map designed at a scale of 1:100,000. The level of detail affects the precision and accuracy of the data. Additionally, measurement errors can occur due to issues with positional accuracy, which is influenced by the projection, coordinate system, and datum used when collecting or processing the data. These technical aspects can lead to small discrepancies in the positioning of features, causing potential inaccuracies.

Finally, the **temporal scale** is another important source of uncertainty. Temporal scale refers to the periods data is collected and used for analysis. Errors can occur when data from different periods is combined, which can lead to misleading conclusions. For example, using census data from 2010 to analyze current economic problems might not provide an accurate picture of the present situation, as the data may not reflect recent changes. Similarly, using outdated Digital Elevation Models (DEMs) for flood risk prediction can lead to incorrect conclusions, as the landscape may have changed due to new developments or natural events. Temporal errors can be especially significant when studying rapidly changing phenomena, such as climate or urbanization.

Understanding spatial, measurement, and temporal uncertainties is essential when working with spatial data. Acknowledging these limitations helps ensure that the analysis is as accurate as possible and that the results are appropriately interpreted.

Sources of Error in Spatial Data

When working with spatial data, errors can occur for many reasons. These errors can come from different sources and are usually divided into three main types: human, environmental, and instrument. Each type of error has its causes and effects on data accuracy. Understanding these errors is important for improving our ability to work with spatial data and ensure more reliable results. Let's look at each of these errors in simple terms.

1. Human Errors

Human errors are mistakes that happen when people make incorrect decisions or actions. These errors can happen in various ways, often because of misinterpretation, judgment issues, or fatigue. Here are two common examples:

- **Misreading an Instrument**: Sometimes, people may misinterpret the reading of an instrument. For example, if someone reads a measuring scale from the wrong angle, they might record the wrong number. This can happen with simple tools like rulers or more complex instruments used for spatial measurements.
- **Judgment Errors**: People often must make estimates, especially when measuring things that are not easy to see or clearly defined. For example, measuring an aquifer (underground water source) is tricky because the water is hidden and cannot be directly observed. Similarly, the boundaries of a soil unit may be difficult to determine because they are not always clear. In both cases, judgments must be made, and those judgments can lead to errors.

2. Environmental Errors

Environmental factors are things in the surroundings that can affect the accuracy of measurements. These factors are not always under our control, but they can influence the data in important ways. Here are a few examples:

- **Temperature Changes**: Temperature can cause instruments to expand or contract slightly, leading to inaccurate readings. For instance, instrument metal parts might expand in hot weather and shrink in cold weather, affecting measurements that rely on precise dimensions.
- **Gravity Variations**: Gravity is not the same everywhere on Earth. It can vary slightly from place to place. This variation can affect very sensitive measurements, such as those used in geodesy or for measuring the shape of the Earth. These small differences can sometimes cause errors in spatial data.
- **Magnetic Declination**: Earth's magnetic field is not the same everywhere when using a compass. In some places, the magnetic north is different from the true north. This variation, called magnetic declination, can lead to errors in direction measurements, especially when precise directions are needed for spatial analysis.

3. Instrument Errors

The instruments themselves are not perfect. Every tool used to measure spatial data has its limitations. These limitations can lead to errors related to the instrument's precision and resolution. Here are two common types of instrument errors:

- **Limited Precision**: Instruments can only measure to a certain level of detail. For example, a ruler marked in millimeters cannot measure anything smaller than a millimeter. Similarly, GPS systems used for mapping may have limited precision, with some systems providing accuracy within 3–5 m, while more advanced systems can be accurate to millimeters. If the instrument's precision is not fine enough for the task, the results can be inaccurate.
- **Resolution**: Resolution refers to the smallest change that an instrument can detect. If an instrument's resolution is too low, it may not be able to capture the details necessary for accurate measurements. For example, a low-resolution camera might not capture fine details of the landscape, which could affect spatial analysis in fields like land use mapping.

Understanding the different types of errors—**human, environmental, and instrument errors**—helps us make better decisions when working with spatial data. Scientists, engineers, and researchers often take steps to minimize these errors, such as double-checking measurements, using higher-quality instruments, and accounting for environmental factors. By recognizing and correcting errors, we can ensure that the data we collect is as reliable and accurate as possible, essential for making informed decisions in fields like environmental science, urban planning, and many other areas.

7.10 Spatial Inference and Reasoning

Statistical inference was covered in Chap. 4 of this book. Meanwhile, spatial inference and reasoning involve drawing conclusions based on the arrangement and relationships of objects in space. In simple terms, spatial inference and reasoning refer to thinking spatially.

Spatial inference is when we use existing data or patterns to make educated guesses or predictions about areas we do not have direct information about. For example, if we know how a disease spreads in one part of a city, we might infer how it could spread in other parts of the city based on the patterns we've observed.

Spatial reasoning is the ability to understand and think about how objects and places are arranged in space and how they relate to one another. It helps us figure out things like distances, directions, and how objects might interact based on their location. For example, figuring out how far a store is from a house or how different roads connect.

These skills are important in spatial data analysis because they help us make sense of complex information about locations, like environmental data, traffic patterns, or population distribution. By using spatial inference and reasoning, we can make better decisions, predict future trends, and find solutions to problems related to geography and space.

Easy to Digest Box

Spatial data is information about where things are located in the world. It's like a map that shows where different places, objects, or events are. In data science, spatial data helps us understand patterns, relationships, and changes in the world by showing how things are connected to each other and their surroundings.

For example:

- *If we want to know where to plant trees in a city to make the air cleaner, we use spatial data to find the best spots based on where there is less pollution or where more people live.*
- *If we want to know how far apart different schools are, we use spatial data to measure the distance between them on a map.*
- *If we want to see how much we lost the forests, we can use spatial data to see the different areas where they were and track changes over time.*

Spatial data helps us answer not only "where" questions but also "how," which are very important for making good decisions about the world around us!

7.11 Summary of Key Points

- Spatial data refers to information that has a geographic or locational component. When it is assigned with coordinates, such as latitude and longitude, it is called geospatial data.
- A computer system might store geographic objects in two basic forms: regular (raster) and irregular (vector).
- Vector has three basic types: point (0D), line (1D), polygon (2D).
- Spatial data always have geometry (where) and tabular (what).
- Spatial data acquisition refers to the process of collecting and gathering data: primary, secondary, machine/sensor-generated.
- Raster representation is simple and easy for map algebra but difficult to represent the real world in detail and requires large space for storage. While vector is complex topology, easy to represent the real world in detail but in-efficient for map algebra analysis and more update-intensive.
- Five components in spatial data management: data, software, hardware, method/algorithms, and people.
- Basic spatial analysis: retrieval, classification, measurement, and modeling.
- Principle of colors: intuitive, moderation, consistency, clarity, classification, and explainable.
- Uncertainty of spatial data: spatial, measurement, and temporal scales.
- Source of errors: human, environmental, and instrument.

7.12 Hands-on Experience

Working with RStudio

In this part, you will learn how to import vector data into RStudio, join the attribute table with population data by Prefecture, calculate the population changes over time, and visualize the final map with clear thematic layers. For raster data, you will learn how to import satellite imagery, visualize it in a false color composite to enhance specific features, and calculate the Normalized Difference Vegetation Index (NDVI) to analyze vegetation health and land cover. Additionally, you will explore how to perform supervised classification for land use and land cover, allowing you to categorize the land based on specific features or types. You will also learn how to visualize Digital Elevation Models (DEM) to understand terrain variations and landscape features. Finally, you will be introduced to working with Nighttime Lights (NTL) data, which is one of the most commonly used spatial datasets in economic studies, enabling you to explore patterns of economic activity, urbanization, and infrastructure development. Through these steps, you will gain valuable skills in spatial data analysis and visualization that are applicable to a wide range of environmental and socio-economic studies.

Practice 7

Working with Vector Data

Learning Objectives

Install and Load Required Packages:

- Install necessary R packages (sf, tmap, leaflet, dplyr, ggplot2, readxl) for spatial data manipulation and visualization.
- Demonstrate how to load the libraries after installation to enable their use in analysis.

Data Preparation:

- Import Excel files into R using the readxl package.
- Select and clean relevant data columns to prepare for further analysis.
- Handle missing values by removing or imputing data where necessary.
- Rename columns for clarity and convert relevant columns to numeric data types.
- Calculate new variables (e.g., population change between 2010 and 2019) and save the processed data as a CSV file.

Working with Vector Data and Shapefile Processing:

- Load and read shapefile data using the sf package for spatial data manipulation.
- Validate the geometries of the shapefile data and address any invalid geometries if necessary.
- Select and rename columns for consistency between the shapefile and population data.
- Merge population data with shapefile data using the dplyr package for data wrangling.

Data Visualization with Maps:

- Create quick maps using the tmap package to visualize population data for 2010, 2019, and population change.
- Switch between interactive and static map views to explore data.
- Customize the layout and design of maps, including adding titles, legends, and borders.
- Use different styles and palettes (e.g., RdBu) to enhance map clarity and visual appeal.
- Add additional elements to maps, such as a scale bar, compass, and histograms in legends.

Interactive and Customized Maps:

- Switch to interactive mode using tmap_mode("view") to allow dynamic zooming and panning.
- Add more advanced features to maps, such as compass styles, scale bars, and customized legends for better data presentation.

Using OpenStreetMap and Esri Imagery as Base Maps:

- Integrate OpenStreetMap as a base map layer to provide contextual geographic information.
- Use Esri World Imagery as a base map and combine it with population change data visualizations.
- Add customized map features, such as bubbles representing population change, and style them for better clarity.

Data Exploration and Mapping Techniques:

- Use the tm_bubbles function to represent population changes with varying bubble sizes and color.
- Customize legend text and titles, adjusting color for visual accessibility and clarity.

Implement different map visualizations with varied base maps, such as osm and esri-imagery.

Download Required Data

To begin, you need to download the following data files:

1. Administrative boundary shapefile data for Japan (level 1):
   - File name: "jpn_adm_2019_SHP.zip" you must unzip the file and put into the same working folder as the Excel file.
   - Size: 6.2 MB.
   - Download link: (https://data.humdata.org/dataset/cod-xa-jpn_
2. Population data by prefecture in Excel format:
   - File name: "Population by Prefecture".
   - Size: 31.1 KB.
   - Download link: (https://www.stat.go.jp/english/data/nenkan/70nenkan/1431-02.html_

Create a new working folder and ensure that all necessary files are placed in the same directory. Then check the current working directory, set working directory where you save the files if needed:

```
# Check the current working directory
getwd()

# Set working directory
setwd("/path/to/your/folder") # Replace with your
directory
```

Install and load required packages

```
install.packages(c("sf", "tmap", "leaflet")) #
Install if not already installed
library(sf)
library(dplyr)
library(ggplot2)
library(tmap)
library(leaflet)
```

Data Preparation

1. Import the Excel file and extract relevant columns.
2. Remove missing values and rename the columns.
3. Calculate the population change between 2010 and 2019 and save as CSV file.

```
# Import Excel file
library(readxl)
japan_pop < - read_excel("y700203000.xlsx")

# Create a new dataframe with selected columns
japan_pop < - japan_pop[,c(3, 28, 34)]

# Remove missing values
japan_data < - na.omit(japan_pop)

# Rename columns
colnames(japan_data)[c(1, 2, 3)] < - c("ID",
"POP10", "POP19")

# Convert population columns to numeric
japan_data$POP2010 < - as.numeric(japan_data$POP10)
japan_data$POP2019 < - as.numeric(japan_data$POP19)
```

```
# Calculate population change
japan_data$POPULATION_CHANGE < - japan_data$POP19 -
japan_data$POP10

# Remove the row for "Japan" in the ID column
japan_data < - subset(japan_data, ID ! = "Japan")
View(japan_data)

# Save the cleaned data to a CSV file
write.csv(japan_data, "japandata.csv", row.names =
FALSE)
```

Shapefile Processing

1. Load the shapefile data and validate geometries.
2. Remove unnecessary columns and rename the relevant ones.
3. Join the shapefile data with the population data.

```
# Read the shapefile data
japan_admin < - st_read("jpn_admbnda_adm1_
2019.shp")

# Check for invalid geometries
is_valid < - st_is_valid(japan_admin)

# Fix invalid geometries if necessary
if (!all(is_valid)) {
 japan_admin < - st_make_valid(japan_admin)
}

# Select only the prefecture name column
japan < - japan_admin % > % select(ADM1_EN)

# Rename column header
colnames(japan)[1] < - "ID"

# Replace prefecture name discrepancies
library(stringr)
rep_str < - c('Gunma' = 'Gumma', 'Hyōgo' = 'Hyogo',
'Kōchi' = 'Kochi', 'Ōita' = 'Oita')
japan$ID < - str_replace_all(japan$ID, rep_str)
```

```
# Remove all spaces from the "ID" column
japan$ID < - str_trim(japan$ID) # It is an
important step! If you missed this, the result will
be NA.

# Merge population data with shapefile data
merge_data < - left_join(japan, japan_data, by =
"ID")
```

Data Visualization

Use the "tmap" package to create maps showing population data and changes. I wrote the script in this chapter using tmap v3, but future updates in tmap v4 will introduce slight changes to the map-making code.

```
# Quick map of 2010 population
tm_shape(merge_data) +
 tm_polygons("POP2010") +
 tm_layout(title.size = 1.5, legend.text.size =
1.2, legend.title.size = 1.3) +
tmap_options(check.and.fix = TRUE, max.categories
= 47)
```

Output:

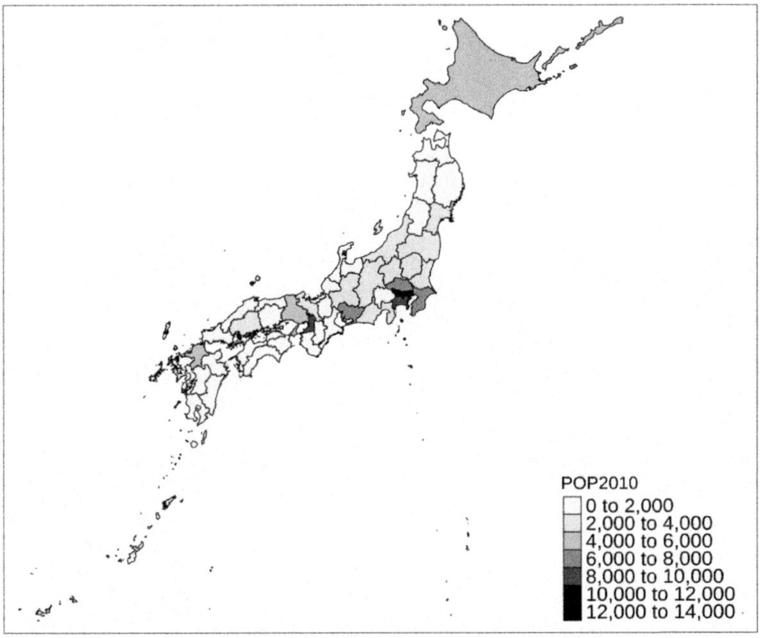


```
# Quick map of 2019 population
tm_shape(merge_data) +
 tm_polygons("POP2019") +
 tm_layout(title.size = 1.5, legend.text.size =
1.2, legend.title.size = 1.3) +
 tmap_options(check.and.fix = TRUE, max.categories
= 47)
```

Output:

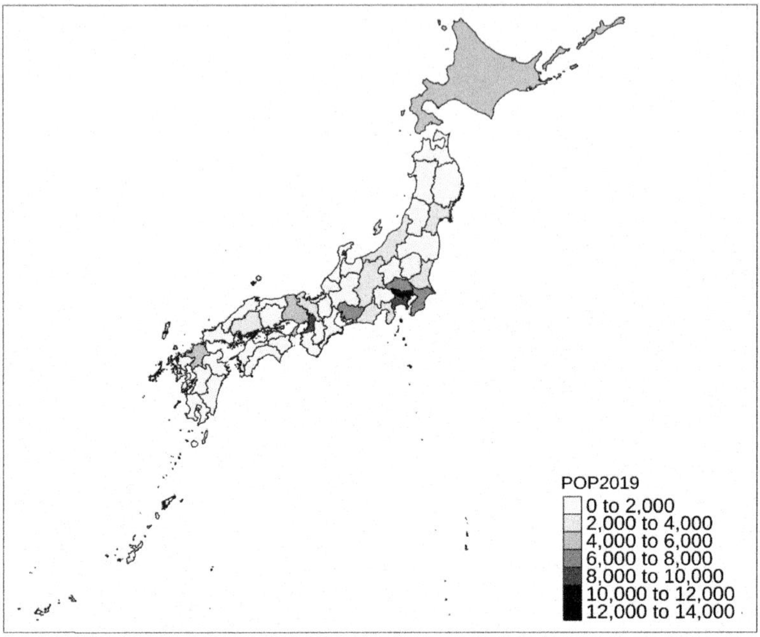


```
# Quick map of population change
tm_shape(merge_data) +
 tm_polygons("POPULATION_CHANGE") +
 tm_layout(title.size = 1.5, legend.text.size =
1.2, legend.title.size = 1.3) +
 tmap_options(check.and.fix = TRUE, max.categories
= 47)
```

Output:

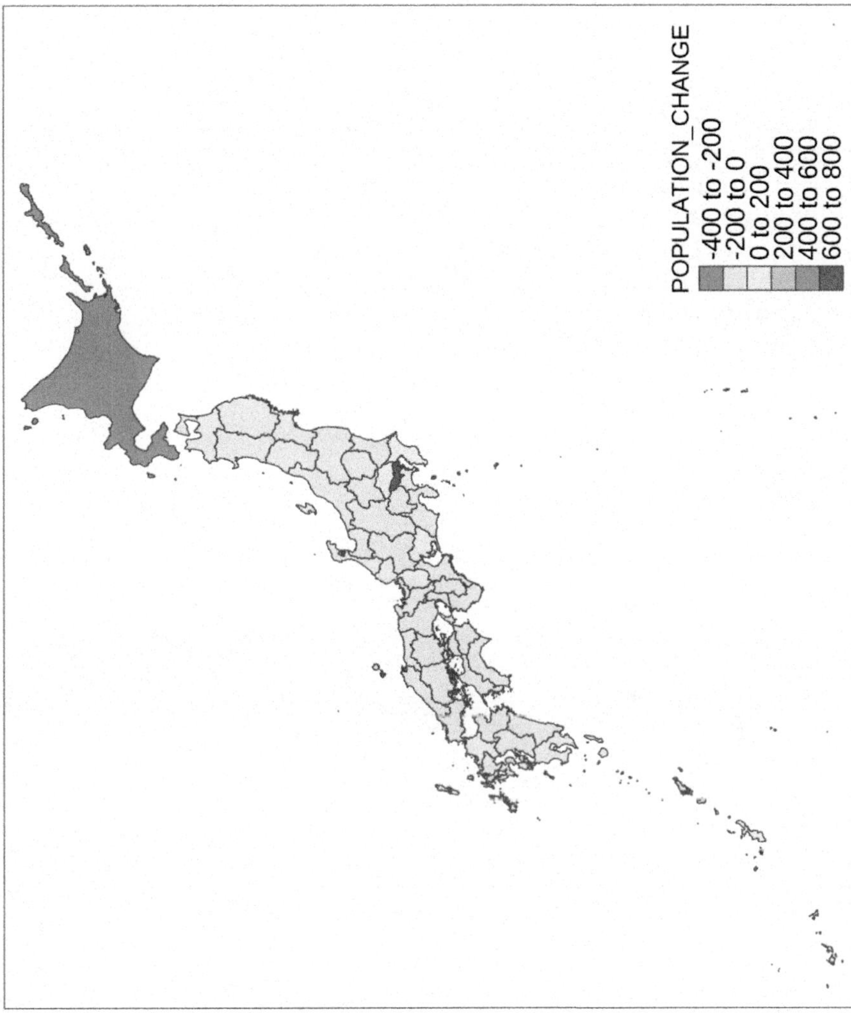
POPULATION_CHANGE
-400 to -200
-200 to 0
0 to 200
200 to 400
400 to 600
600 to 800

```
# Switch to interactive map view
tmap_mode("view")

# Customized map with layout
tm_shape(merge_data) +
  tm_fill("POPULATION_CHANGE", palette = "RdBu",
   style = "pretty", title = "Population Changes")
+
 tm_borders(alpha = 0.4) +
 tm_compass(type = "arrow", position = c("right",
"top")) +
 tm_layout(main.title = "Japan Population Changes
(2010 to 2019)",
   main.title.position = "center",
   main.title.color = "blue",
   legend.text.size = 0.7,
   legend.title.size = 1,
   legend.position = c("right", "bottom"),
   frame = FALSE)
```

Output:

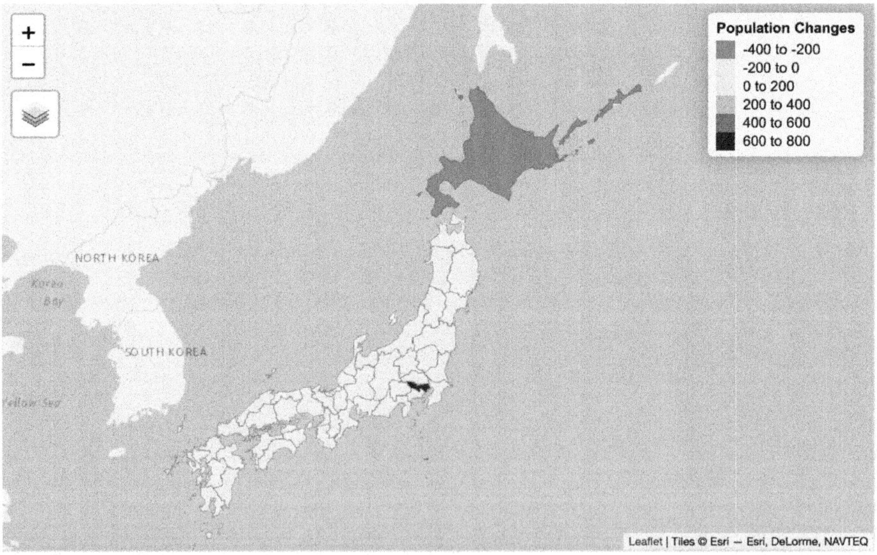

This interactive view will allow us to dynamically zoom-in and zoom-out the map.

```
# Switch back to plot view
tmap_mode("plot") #or you can use ttm()

# Map with histogram in legend
tm_shape(merge_data) +
 tm_fill("POPULATION_CHANGE", style = "pretty", n
= 5,
   palette = "RdBu", title = "Population Changes",
legend.hist = TRUE) +
 tm_layout(
  main.title = "Japan Population Changes (2010 to
2019)",
  main.title.position = "center",
  main.title.color = "blue",
  main.title.size = 2 # Increase main title font
size
 ) +
 tm_borders(alpha = 0.4) +
 tm_compass(type = "rose", position = c("right",
"top"), size = 2)
```

Output:

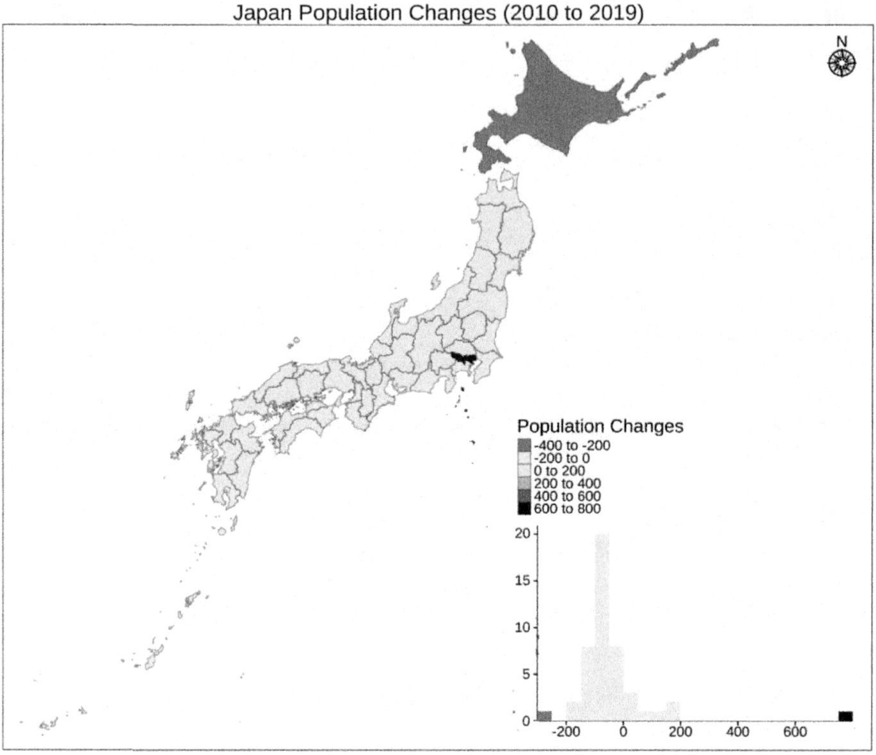


```
# Add scale bar and change compass style
tm_shape(merge_data) +
 tm_fill("POPULATION_CHANGE", style = "pretty", n
= 5,
   palette = "RdBu", title = "Population Changes")
+
 tm_layout(
 main.title = "Japan Population Changes (2010 to
2019)",
 main.title.position = "center",
  main.title.color = "blue",
  main.title.size = 2 # Increase main title font
size
 ) +
 tm_borders(alpha = 0.4) +
```

```
 tm_compass(type = "4star", position = c("right",
"top"), size = 2) +
 tm_scale_bar(
  text.size = 0.8, # Increase font size of scale
bar text
  color.dark = "black",
 color.light = "white",
 lwd = 1
 )
```

Output:

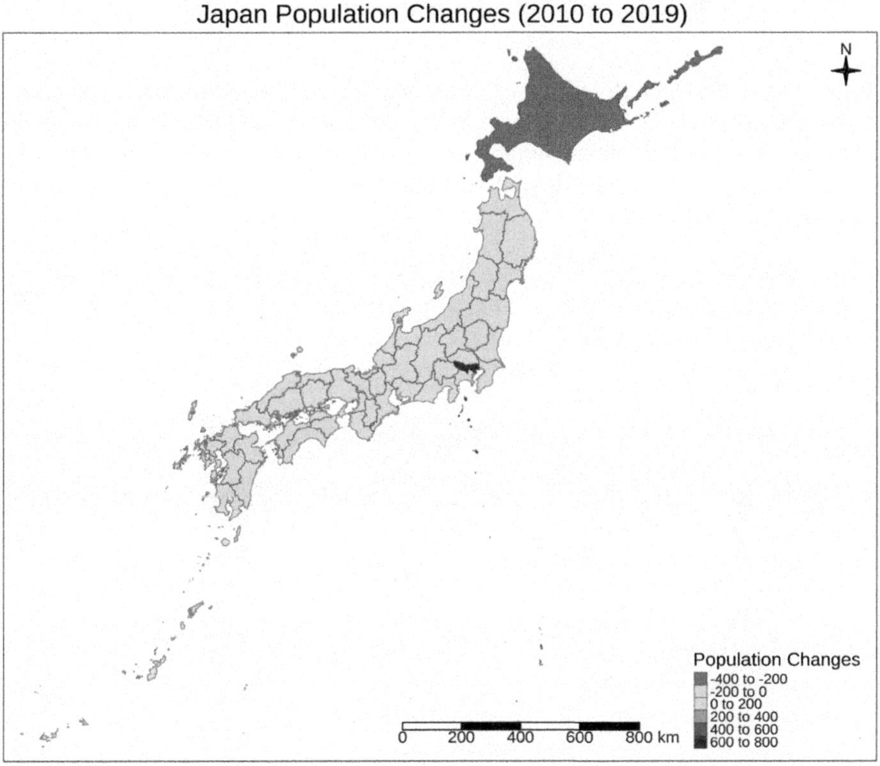

To change the color palette, you can use library(RColorBrewer) and use simple code:

```
library(RColorBrewer)
display.brewer.all()
```

Output:

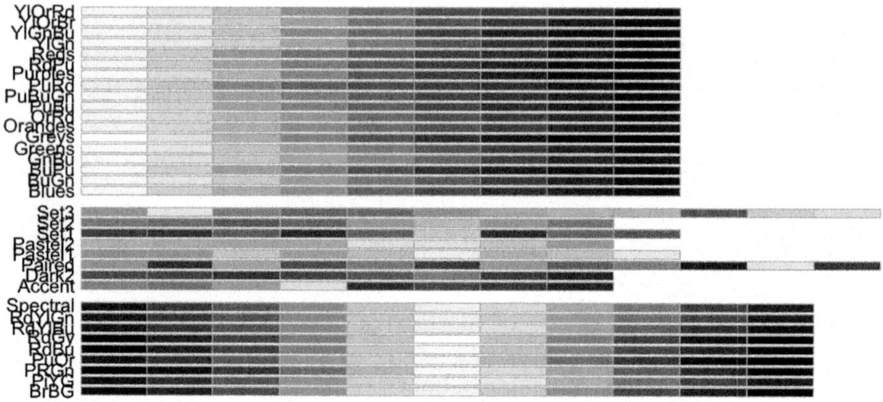

You can also use OpenStreetMap as a basemap for your map; however, you have to make sure Java is available in your system. You can download Java from http://www.java.com and check the most suitable installer for your system. For macOS users, make sure to download the ARM64 version of the JRE if you are running on an M series system (ARM64).

```
# Adds OpenStreetMap as base map
library(tmaptools)
library(OpenStreetMap)

osm_world < - read_osm(merge_data)

japan_pop_changes <- tm_shape(osm_world) + tm_rgb()
+
 tm_shape(merge_data) +
 tm_fill("POPULATION_CHANGE", palette = "RdBu",
   style = "pretty", title = "Population Changed
(1,000)") +
 tm_borders(alpha = 0.4) +
 tm_compass(type = "8star", position = c("right",
"top"), size = 2) +
 tm_layout(main.title = "Japan Population Changes
(2010 to 2019)",
   main.title.position = "center",
   main.title.color = "black",
   legend.text.size = 0.7,
   legend.title.size = 1,
```

```
    legend.position = c("right", "bottom"),
    frame = F) +
  tm_scale_bar(position = c("left", "bottom")) #to
save the map as high-resolution PNG you can write:
tmap_save(japan_pop_changes, filename = "japan_
population_changes.png", width = 4000, height =
3000, dpi = 300)
```

Output:

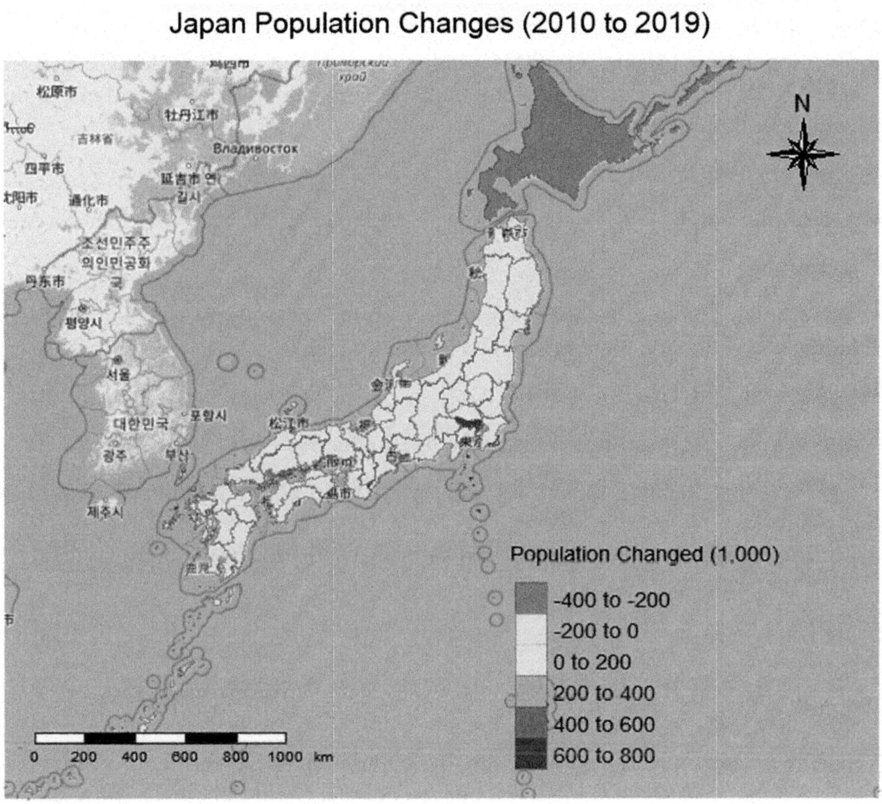

What Does the Code Do?

Load Required Libraries:

- library(tmaptools) loads tools for working with spatial data.
- library(OpenStreetMap) loads functions for accessing and visualizing OpenStreetMap data.

Load OpenStreetMap Data:

- osm_world < - read_osm(merge_data) reads the OpenStreetMap data for the region specified in merge_data and stores it in the osm_world object.

Base Map and Layers:

- tm_shape(osm_world) + tm_rgb() adds the OpenStreetMap base layer to the map, displaying it in RGB (colored) format.

Overlay Population Data:

- tm_shape(merge_data) adds the spatial data from merge_data (which likely contains population information) to the map.
- tm_fill("POPULATION_CHANGE", palette = "RdBu", style = "pretty", title = "Population Changed (1,000)") color areas based on the "POPULATION_CHANGE" attribute, with a color palette ranging from red to blue and displaying values in thousands.

Borders and Transparency:

- tm_borders(alpha = 0.4) adds borders around the regions with 40% transparency.

Compass:

- tm_compass(type = "8star", position = c("right", "top"), size = 2) adds an 8-star compass rose to the map, positioned at the top-right.

Map Layout and Title:

- tm_layout(...) customizes the map layout, including:

  The title ("Japan Population Changes (2010 to 2019)"), centered with black color.
  The legend settings (e.g., text and title sizes, position at the bottom-right).
  Frame removed (frame = F).

Scale Bar:

- tm_scale_bar(position = c("left", "bottom")) adds a scale bar at the bottom-left of the map.

The red areas indicate regions where the population decreased significantly, with changes ranging from -400 to -200 thousand people. Light pink areas show smaller population declines, from -200 to 0. Blue shades represent population increases. The darker the blue, the higher the population growth, with the darkest blue areas showing increases of 600 to 800 thousand people.

From the map, we can see that most regions in Japan experienced a decline in population during this period, especially in rural areas. Conversely, the Tokyo metropolitan area stands out with a large population increase, highlighted in dark blue. This reflects the trend of urbanization, where people move from rural areas to cities for better job opportunities, education, and services.

The data likely reflects the impact of Japan's aging population and low birth rate, which have led to overall population decline in many areas. However, urban centers, such as Tokyo, continue to grow due to internal migration.

Additionally, you can use imagery as your base map. Since we are now using imagery, it's important to adjust the color of the legend, scale bar, and north arrow to white. Then you can change the visualization of the population change using bubbles. Refer to the code below for guidance:

```
# Option: Esri World Imagery
esri_imagery < - read_osm(merge_data, type =
"esri-imagery")

tm_shape(esri_imagery) +
 tm_rgb() +
 tm_shape(merge_data) +
 tm_bubbles(size = "POPULATION_CHANGE",
   col = "red", # Set the color of circles
   border.col = "white", # Add a white border for
visibility
   scale = 1.5, # Adjust the size scale of bubbles
   title.size = "Population Change (1,000)") +
 tm_borders(alpha = 0.4) +
 tm_compass(type = "8star", position = c("right",
"top"), size = 2,
   color.light = "white", # Set "N" and compass
face to white
   color.dark = "white") + # Set border lines of
the compass to white
  tm_layout(main.title = "Japan Population Changes
(2010 to 2019)",
   main.title.position = "center",
   main.title.color = "black",
   legend.text.size = 0.7,
   legend.title.size = 1,
   legend.text.color = "white", # Set legend text
to white
   legend.title.color = "white", # Set legend title
to white
   legend.position = c("right", "bottom"),
   frame = FALSE) +
tm_scale_bar(position = c("left", "top"),
   text.color = "white") # Scale bar text to white
```

Output:

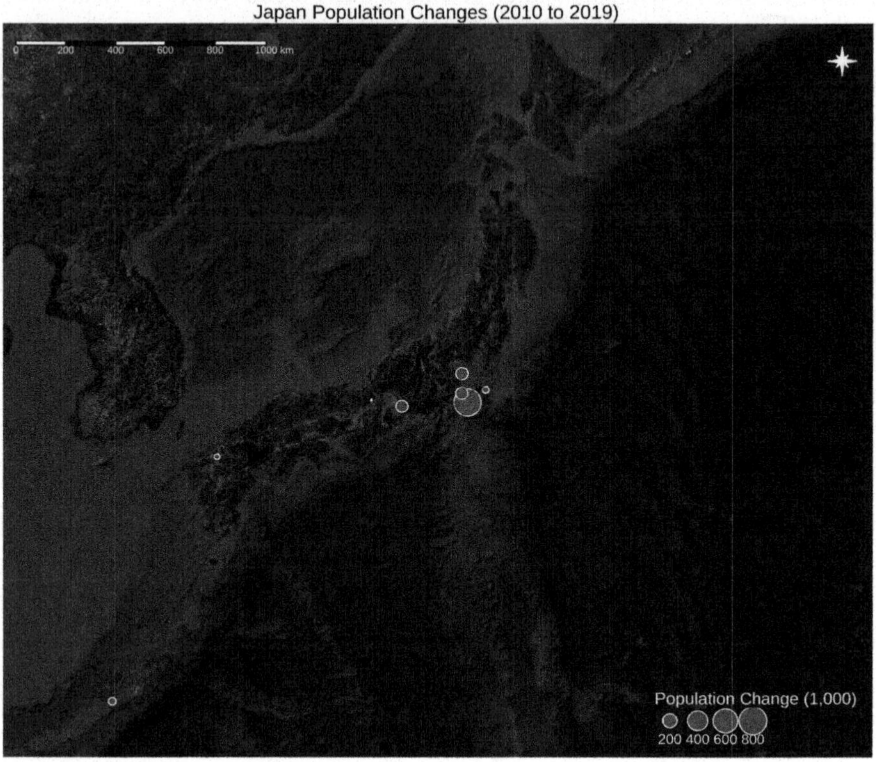

What Does the Code Do?

Changed tm_fill to tm_bubbles

- Replaced the filled choropleth visualization with circle markers proportional to population change.

Added Size Parameter

- The size parameter in tm_bubbles determines the size of the circles based on the POPULATION_CHANGE variable.

Bubble Styling

- col = "blue" sets the circle color.
- border.col = "white" ensures the circles are outlined in white for better visibility.

Size Scaling

- scale = 1.5 adjusts the bubble size scaling factor; you can tweak this value for better visualization.

Scale Bar

- tm_scale_bar(position = c("left", "top")) adds a scale bar at the top-left of the map.

What is the difference between the colored areas and the bubbles based on the "POPULATION_CHANGE" attribute? Which map is better and easier to understand?

Working with Raster Data

Learning Objectives

Understanding the Setup and Environment:

- Demonstrate the importance of setting and checking the working directory in R.
- Explain how to install and load required packages in R for geospatial analysis.

Loading and Combining Raster Data:

- Learn how to load Sentinel-2 bands as SpatRaster objects using the terra package.
- Combine multiple raster bands into a single multilayer SpatRaster object.
- Understand how to visualize raster data through RGB composites.

Calculating and Visualizing NDVI:

- Learn how to calculate the Normalized Difference Vegetation Index (NDVI) using the Red and NIR bands of Sentinel-2 imagery.
- Understand how to classify NDVI values into different categories based on defined thresholds.
- Visualize NDVI and its classification using color palettes.

Performing Raster Classifications:

- Understand how to classify NDVI raster into different classes and calculate the area in hectares for each class.
- Learn how to use randomForest or decision tree models (e.g., rpart) for land use/land cover (LULC) classification.
- Learn how to refine classification results using sieve analysis to remove small noise patches.

Working with Land Use Land Cover (LULC) Data:

- Learn how to load and manipulate shapefiles using the sf package in R.
- Generate random sampling points for LULC classification based on polygon features.

- Train a decision tree model to classify satellite imagery into different LULC classes.

Creating and Saving Classified Maps:

- Learn how to visualize and interpret classified raster maps using custom colorschemes.
- Save the classified raster maps as GeoTIFF files for further analysis.

Working with Digital Elevation Model (DEM) Data:

- Understand how to load and visualize DEM data using the raster and rasterVis packages in R.
- Learn how to create 3D visualizations of DEM data using the rayshader package.

Analyzing Nighttime Light (NTL) Data:

- Learn how to fetch and process Nighttime Light data from NASA using the blackmarbler package.
- Mask raster data to focus on specific regions of interest and apply log transformations to improve data interpretability.
- Calculate and visualize the difference in NTL data between two time periods to identify changes in radiance.

Using R for Geospatial Data Analysis and Visualization:

- Demonstrate the ability to perform geospatial analysis tasks such as calculating NDVI, classifying land cover, and visualizing environmental changes.
- Develop proficiency in using R packages like terra, rpart, ggplot2, and rayshader to handle, analyze, and visualize raster and vector geospatial data.

In this section, you will learn how to visualize raster data, calculate NDVI, and perform land use and land cover classification using the Classification and Regression Tree (CART) classifier. Before starting, you need to search for and download satellite image raster data. Visit https://browser.dataspace.copernicus.eu/, register for an account, log in, and then search for and download the required data. For this practice, we will use Sentinel-2 MSI L1C data for Inashiki City, Ibaraki Prefecture, Japan.

Setting Up the Environment

Before starting any project in R, it's important to check the current working directory. This tells us where files will be saved or read from by default. To check it, we use:

```
# Check the current working directory
getwd()
```

If the working directory is not set to the folder you are working in, you can set it using setwd():

```
# Set working directory
setwd("/path/to/your/folder") # Replace with your
directory
```

Installing and Loading Required Packages

Next, you need some packages for analysis. Use install.packages() to install the necessary tools, and library() to load them for use.

```
# Install required packages
install.packages('randomForest')
install.packages(c("randomForest", "terra"))

# Load the packages
library(randomForest)
library(terra)
```

Reading and Combining Sentinel-2 Satellite Data

Satellite data is often provided in layers, or bands, each representing different parts of the light spectrum, which can be used for various analyses. For Sentinel-2 data is typically delivered as a zip file, so you will need to unzip it before use. A tutorial on how to download and process this data is available at https://sites.google.com/view/ramdani-lab/videos. Look for the video titled *Supervised Classification Using the Dzetsaka Plugin.*

```
# Load Sentinel-2 bands as SpatRaster objects
b3 < - rast('2024-05-11-00:00_2024-05-11-23:59_
Sentinel-2_L1C_B03.tiff') # Band Green
b4 < - rast('2024-05-11-00:00_2024-05-11-23:59_
Sentinel-2_L1C_B04.tiff') # Band Red
```

```
b6 < - rast('2024-05-11-00:00_2024-05-11-23:59_
Sentinel-2_L1C_B06.tiff') # Band Vegetation Red
Edge
b8 < - rast('2024-05-11-00:00_2024-05-11-23:59_
Sentinel-2_L1C_B08.tiff') # Band NIR
```

We then combine these bands into a multilayer SpatRaster object, which allows us to work with them together.

```
sentinel < - c(b3, b4, b6, b8)
names(sentinel) < - c('Green', 'Red', 'Red.Edge',
'NIR')
names(sentinel) # to check the names
print(sentinel) # to check the complete metadata
```

Output:

```
> print(sentinel)
class       : SpatRaster
dimensions  : 1658, 2500, 4  (nrow, ncol, nlyr)
resolution  : 9.535367, 9.39556  (x, y)
extent      : 432045.2, 455883.7, 3971065, 3986643  (xmin, xmax, ymin, ymax)
coord. ref. : WGS 84 / UTM zone 54N (EPSG:32654)
sources     : 2024-05-11-00:00_2024-05-11-23:59_Sentinel-2_L1C_B03.tiff
              2024-05-11-00:00_2024-05-11-23:59_Sentinel-2_L1C_B04.tiff
              2024-05-11-00:00_2024-05-11-23:59_Sentinel-2_L1C_B06.tiff
              2024-05-11-00:00_2024-05-11-23:59_Sentinel-2_L1C_B08.tiff
names       : Green, Red, Red.Edge, NIR
```

To visualize the data, you can create a false color composite (FCC):

```
# Plot the RGB false color composite (FCC) - false
color of vegetation (NIR-Red-Green)
plotRGB(sentinel, r = 4, g = 2, b = 1, stretch =
"lin")
plotRGB(sentinel, r = 4, g = 2, b = 1, stretch =
"his")
```

Output:

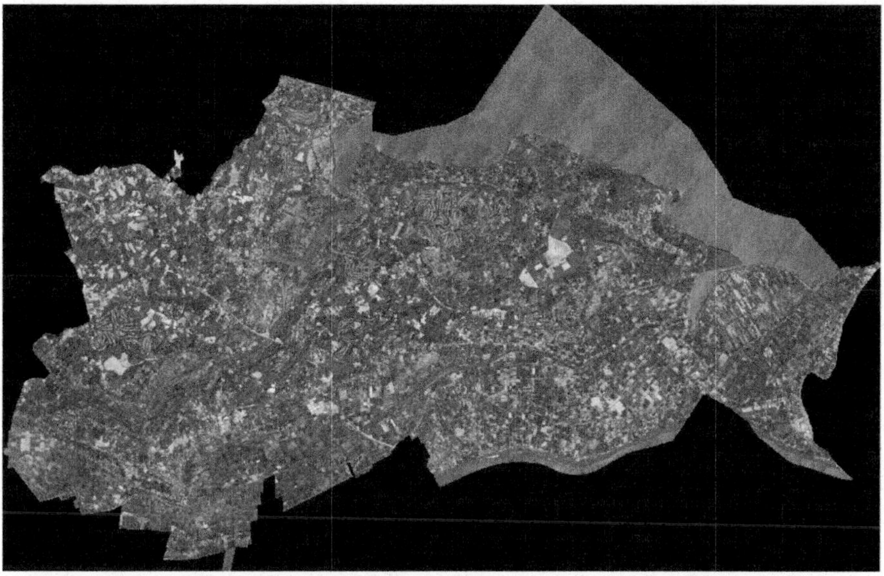

Calculating NDVI

The Normalized Difference Vegetation Index (NDVI) is a commonly used metric to assess vegetation health. It is calculated using the red and near-infrared bands:

```
# Calculate NDVI
NDVI < - (b8 - b4) / (b8 + b4)

# Plot NDVI with a terrain colorpalette
plot(NDVI, col = rev(terrain.color(10)))
```

Output:

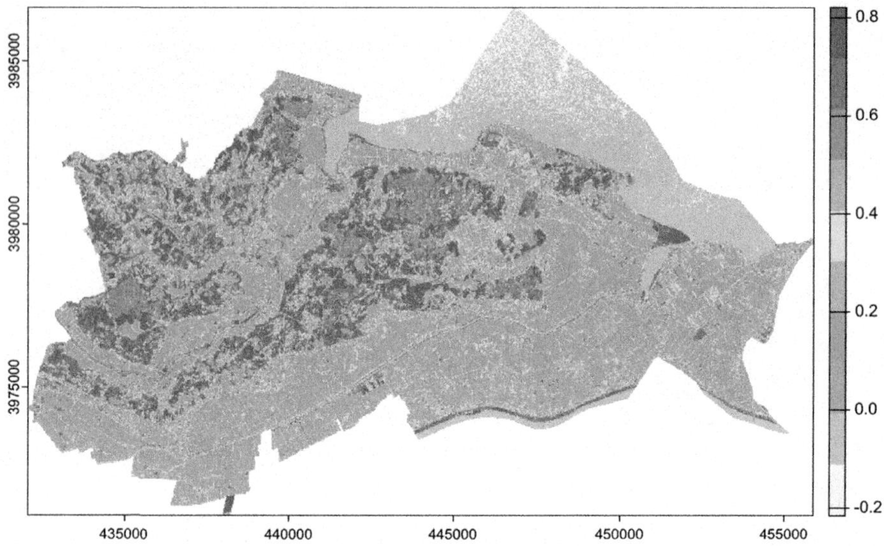

Then we can calculate the area (ha) and percentage of NDVI classes. But first we need to get the summary for the threshold adjustment.

```
# Check NDVI statistics
print(summary(NDVI))
```

Output:

```
> print(summary(NDVI))
 X2024.05.11.00.00_2024.05.11.23.59_Sentinel.2_L1C_B08
 Min.   :-0.16
 1st Qu.: 0.10
 Median : 0.22
 Mean   : 0.28
 3rd Qu.: 0.49
 Max.   : 0.82
 NA's   :44666
```

```
# Check for NA pixels
NDVI_NA_count < - sum(is.na(NDVI[]))
print(paste("Number of NA pixels in NDVI:", NDVI_
NA_count))

# Define thresholds and classify NDVI
thresholds < - c(-0.2, 0, 0.2, 0.4, 0.5, 0.78) #
Adjust thresholds as needed. We get these numbers
from the previous code

NDVI_classes < - classify(NDVI, thresholds,
include.lowest = TRUE)

# Check classified raster
plot(NDVI_classes, main = "NDVI Classes")
```

Output:

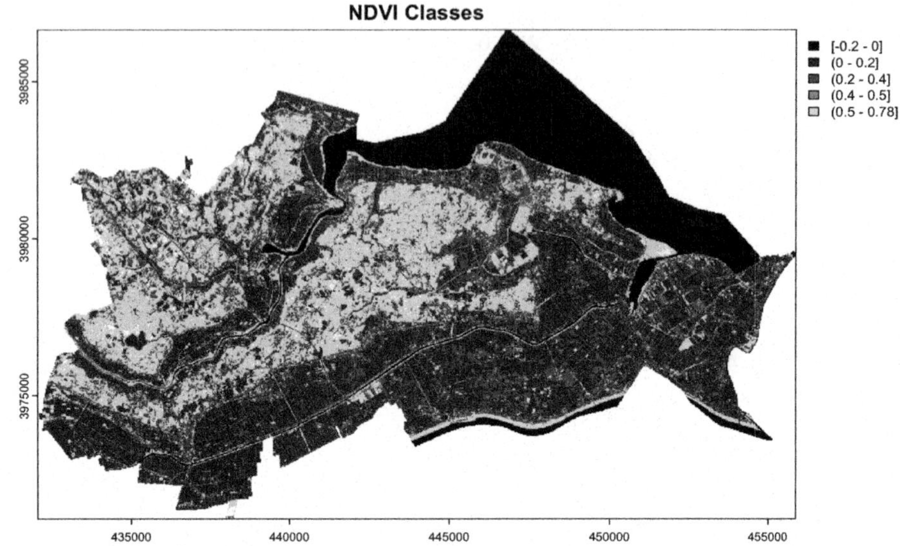

Calculate NDVI class areas in hectares

Furthermore, we can define the class and calculate the area in ha for each class of NDVI using the following code:

```
# Frequency table of classes
NDVI_table < - freq(NDVI_classes)
print(NDVI_table)

# Define class labels
class_labels < - c("Very high", "High", "Medium",
"Low", "Very low")

# Calculate class areas in hectares
class_area_ha < - table(values(NDVI_classes)) *
prod(res(NDVI_classes)) / 10,000

# Assign class labels
names(class_area_ha) < - class_labels

# Convert to a data frame
total_area < - sum(class_area_ha)
NDVI_class_area_df < - data.frame(
```

```
 Class = names(class_area_ha),
 Area_Ha = as.numeric(class_area_ha),
 Percentage = as.numeric(class_area_ha) / total_
area * 100
)

# Print the result
print(NDVI_class_area_df)

# Save as CSV
write_csv(NDVI_class_area_df, “NDVI_Classes_Area_
Percentage.csv”)
```

Output:

```
> print(NDVI_class_area_df)
      Class  Area_Ha Percentage
1 Very high 3119.205  15.231784
2      High 6551.635  31.993116
3    Medium 4712.807  23.013703
4       Low 1309.960   6.396829
5  Very low 4784.658  23.364569
```

Land Use Land Cover (LULC) Classification

For LULC analysis using earth observation satellite data, it is essential to create training data first. You can use QGIS software to generate this training data. Typically, training data containing land use information is stored in shapefiles. To load and view these files, you can use the sf package in R.

```
# Install and load the sf package
install.packages(“sf”)
library(sf)

# Load a shapefile
shapefile < - st_read(“ROI.shp”)
print(shapefile)

# Plot the shapefile
plot(shapefile[“geometry”])
```

```
text(shapefile, shapefile$Class)
```

Output:

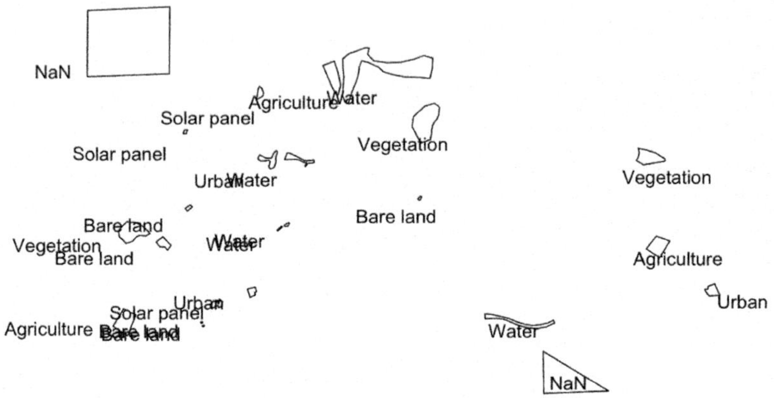

Then we need to create sample random points within the shapefile's polygons:

```
# Generate random points within each polygons.
set.seed(123)

# Convert shapefile to SpatVector and sample points
shapefile_vect < - vect(shapefile)
ptsamp < - spatSample(shapefile_vect, 300, method =
"random")
plot(ptsamp, "Class")
```

Output:

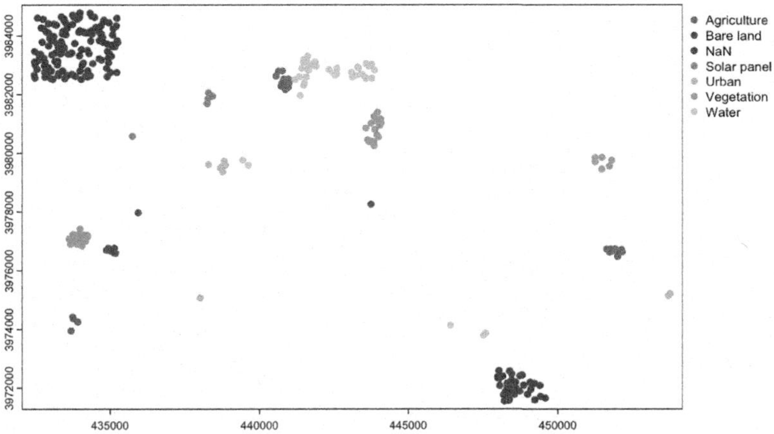

Training a Classification Model

After extracting the reflectance values for the sampled points, combine this data with land use information for classification.

```
# Extract reflectance values
df < - extract(sentinel, ptsamp, ID = FALSE)

# Combine land-use class with reflectance values
sampdata < - data.frame(class = ptsamp$Class, df)
```

Use the rpart package to train a decision tree model for classification:

```
# Train a decision tree model
install.packages("rpart")
library(rpart)

cartmodel < - rpart(as.factor(class) ~., data =
sampdata, method = 'class', minsplit = 5)

# Visualize the model
plot(cartmodel, uniform = TRUE, main =
"Classification Tree")
text(cartmodel, cex = 1)
```

Output:

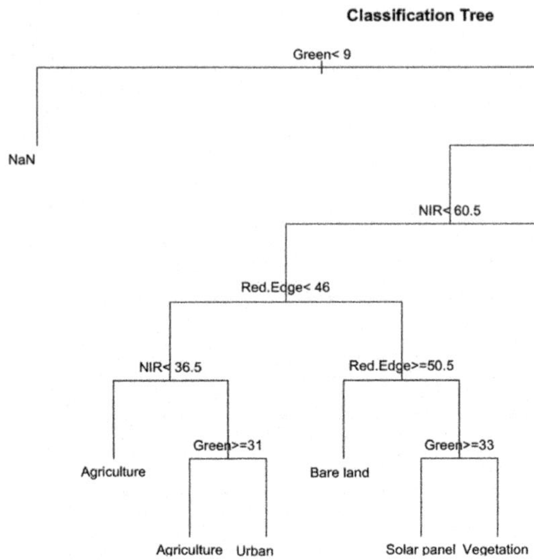

Classifying the Raster Data

Use the trained model to classify the satellite imagery into different land use and land cover (LULC) classes:

```
# Predict LULC classes
classified < - predict(sentinel, cartmodel, na.rm =
TRUE)

# Plot classified raster
plot(classified)
```

Output:

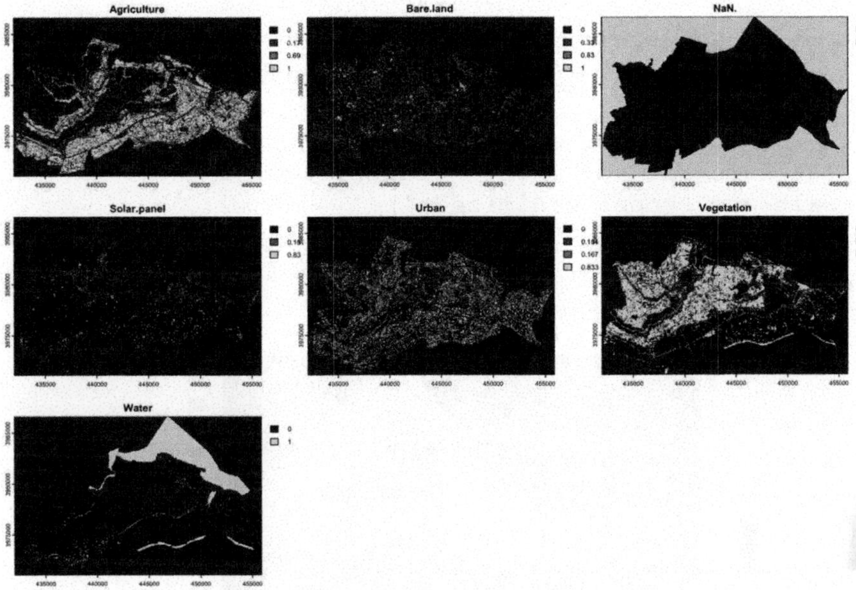

To determine the most likely LULC class for each cell:

```
# Identify the class with the highest probability
lulc < - which.max(classified)
```

Refining the Classified Data

Then we can do sieve analysis to minimize the salt-and-pepper issue in the classified image. The salt-and-pepper issue in satellite image classification refers to a common problem where classified images show a scattered, noisy appearance, with individual pixels being assigned to different classes inconsistently, creating a speckled effect. This problem typically arises in pixel-based classification methods, where each pixel is classified independently without considering its spatial context or neighboring pixels.

```
# Perform sieve analysis to remove small patches
(salt-and-pepper noise)
# Define a minimum patch size (e.g., 5 pixels)
lulc_sieved < - sieve(lulc, threshold = 5)

# Set up a top-down layout
```

```
par(mfrow = c(2, 1)) # 2 rows, 1 column

# Plot the raw classified map
plot(lulc, main = "Classified Map(Raw)")

# Plot the processed classified map
plot(lulc_sieved, main = "Classified Map
(Salt-and-Pepper Minimized)")
```

Output:

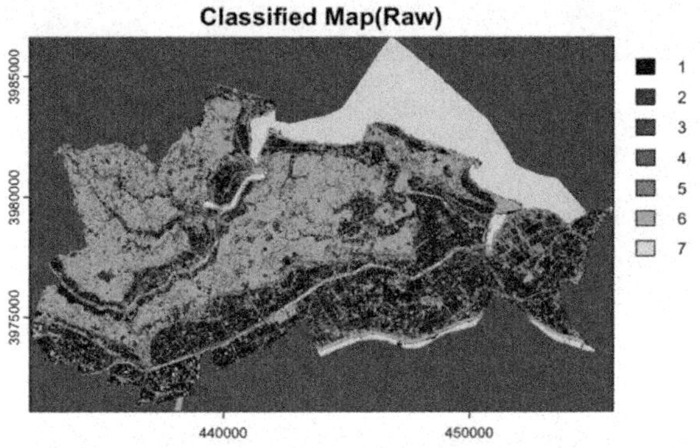

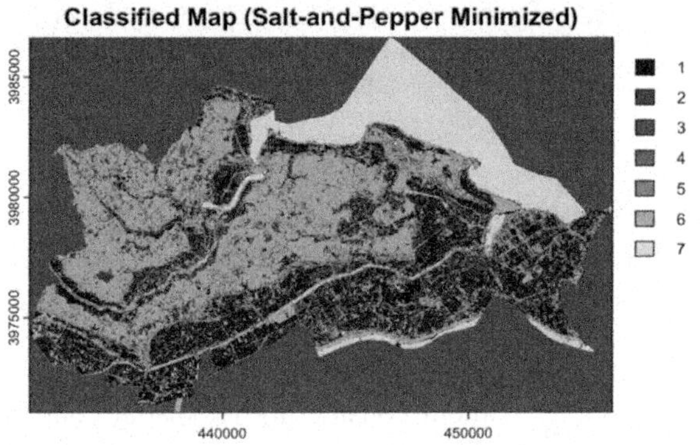

Creating a Final Map

Assign names and color to the LULC classes to create an easily interpretable map. Then you can save the classified map as a GeoTIFF file into the working folder, and open it using QGIS for further analysis or advance map layout using Layout Manager of QGIS.

```
# Load necessary library
library(tmap)

# Assign class names and color using a two-column
data frame
cls < - c("Agriculture", "Urban", "NaN",
"Solar.Panel", "Bareland", "Vegetation", "Water")
df < - data.frame(id = 1:7, class = cls)
levels(lulc_sieved) < - df

# Define custom color
mycolor < - c("purple", "red", "white", "grey",
"orange", "green", "blue")

# Create the map using tmap
map < - tm_shape(lulc_sieved) +
tm_raster(palette = mycolor, title = "Legend") +
tm_layout(
main.title = "Land Use Land Cover Map",
main.title.size = 2, # Increase main title size
legend.title.size = 1.5, # Increase legend title
size
legend.text.size = 1.2, # Increase legend text size
legend.outside = FALSE,
legend.position = c("right", "top"),
frame = FALSE # Optionally remove the frame
) +
tm_scale_bar(
text.size = 1 # Increase scale bar text size
) +
tm_compass(
position = c("left", "top"),
text.size = 1 # Increase compass text size
)

# Plot the map
map

# Save the classified map as a GeoTIFF file into
the working folder
writeRaster(lulc_sieved, "classified_map_
sieved.tif", overwrite = TRUE)
```

Output:

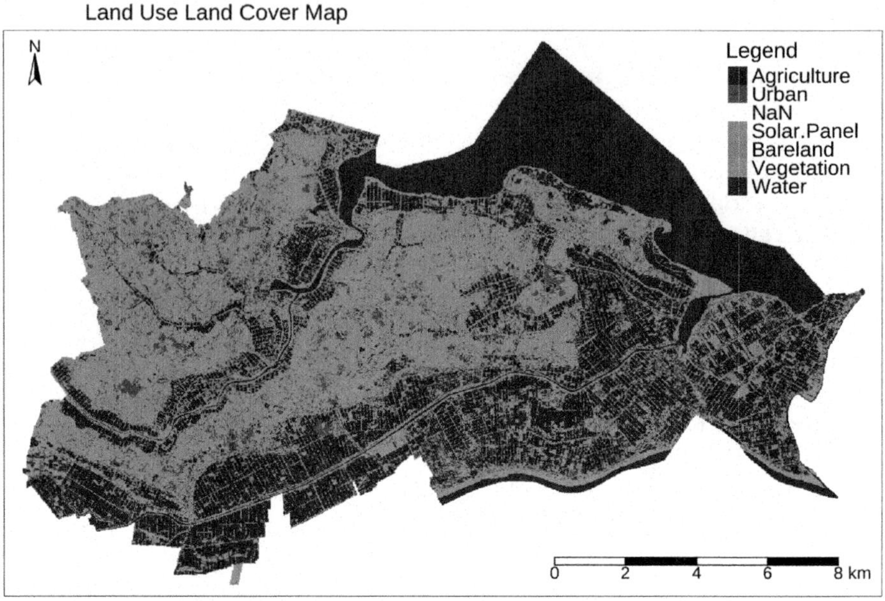

Calculating the Area (ha)

Finally, we then calculate the area of each class in ha as well as the percentage using the code:

```
# Calculate the area of each class in the sieved
classified map (lulc)

# Define class labels
class_labels < - c("Agriculture", "Urban", "NaN",
"Solar.Panel", "Bareland", "Vegetation", "Water")

# Calculate class areas in hectares
class_area_ha < - table(values(lulc_sieved)) *
prod(res(lulc_sieved)) / 10,000

# Assign class labels
names(class_area_ha) < - class_labels

# Remove the "NaN" class from calculations
class_area_ha < - class_area_ha[names(class_area_
ha) ! = "NaN"]
```

```
# Convert to a data frame
total_area < - sum(class_area_ha)
class_area_df < - data.frame(
 Class = names(class_area_ha),
 Area_Ha = as.numeric(class_area_ha),
 Percentage = as.numeric(class_area_ha) / total_
area * 100
)

# Save as CSV
write.csv(class_area_df, "class_area_results.csv",
row.names = FALSE)

# Print the result
print(class_area_df)
```

Output:

```
> # Print the result
> print(class_area_df)
        Class   Area_Ha Percentage
1 Agriculture 6000.6113  29.122125
2       Urban 1038.6809   5.040919
3 Solar.Panel  244.8498   1.188303
4    Bareland 2801.1961  13.594746
5  Vegetation 7337.0897  35.608313
6       Water 3182.5633  15.445594
```

As of 2024, we now have a clearer understanding of the land use in Inashiki City, Ibaraki Prefecture. The city is predominantly covered by vegetation and agricultural lands, which together shape most of the landscape, accounting for 36% and 29% of the total area, respectively. Water bodies and bare land also play a notable role, covering over 15% and 13%, respectively. In contrast, urban or built-up areas are relatively limited, occupying just 5% of the city's land. Additionally, solar panel installations, while still a small fraction, make up more than 1% of the total land use, reflecting the city's efforts to incorporate renewable energy infrastructure.

Working with DEM Data

In this part, you will learn how to visualize Digital Elevation Model (DEM) data step by step. We will use the ALOS Global Digital Surface Model provided by JAXA, which can be accessed at: https://www.eorc.jaxa.jp/ALOS/en/dataset/aw3d30/aw3d30_e.htm. Scroll down to Sect. 4 on the webpage, where you will find detailed instructions to register and download the DEM data. Please note that you must create an account, register, and log in before you can access and download the files.

The downloaded data will be in a.zip file, so you need to unzip it first and place the contents into your working directory. Inside the unzipped folder, you will find several files. The Digital Elevation Model (DEM) data can be identified as the file with the largest size or the one that has a suffix ending in "_DSM".

ALPSMLC30_N035E138_DSM.tif	Mar 10, 2020 at 17:44	25.9 MB	TIFF image
ALPSMLC30_N035E138_HDR.txt	Mar 10, 2020 at 17:44	1 KB	Plain Text
ALPSMLC30_N035E138_LST.txt	Mar 10, 2020 at 17:44	15 KB	Plain Text
ALPSMLC30_N035E138_MSK.tif	Mar 10, 2020 at 17:44	13 MB	TIFF image
ALPSMLC30_N035E138_QAI.txt	Mar 10, 2020 at 17:44	7 KB	Plain Text
ALPSMLC30_N035E138_STK.tif	Mar 10, 2020 at 17:44	13 MB	TIFF image

For this exercise, we will focus on visualizing the DEM of Mount Fuji, one of Japan's most iconic landmarks. This will give you practical experience in handling and analyzing DEM data.

Checking the Working Directory and Loading Required Packages

Always check and set your working directory to ensure that files are available and R can access the required files.

```
# Check the current working directory
getwd()

# Set working directory
setwd("/path/to/your/folder") # Replace with your
directory
```

Then, we need to load some R packages that will help us process and visualize the DEM. The raster packages are used to handle spatial data, while rasterVis helps with advanced plotting. The rayshader package allows us to create 3D visualizations with shading effects.

```
# Load required packages
library(raster)
library(rasterVis)
```

```
library(rayshader)
```

Load the DEM Data

We use the raster function from the raster package to load the DEM file. This function reads the elevation data and creates a raster object, which we can manipulate in R. After loading, we plot the DEM using a color palette that represents elevation levels.

```
# Load the DEM data
dem < - raster("ALPSMLC30_N035E138_DSM.tif")

# Plot the DEM
plot(dem, col = topo.color(20))
```

Output:

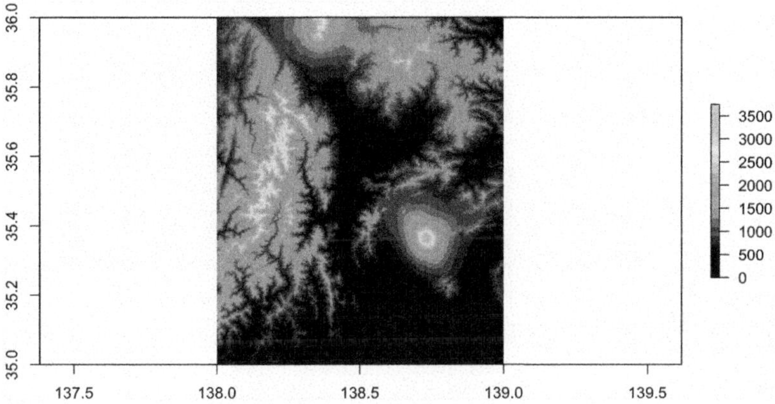

The plot() function displays the DEM using the topo.color() palette, where different colors represent different elevations. For example, green might represent lowlands, while brown or white could represent higher elevations.

Visualize DEM with rasterVis

The levelplot() function from the rasterVis package provides another way to visualize the DEM. This method produces a more polished plot and uses the terrain.color palette for a smooth gradient of color.

```
# Visualize the DEM
```

```
levelplot(dem, margin = FALSE, col.regions =
terrain.color(255))
```

Output:

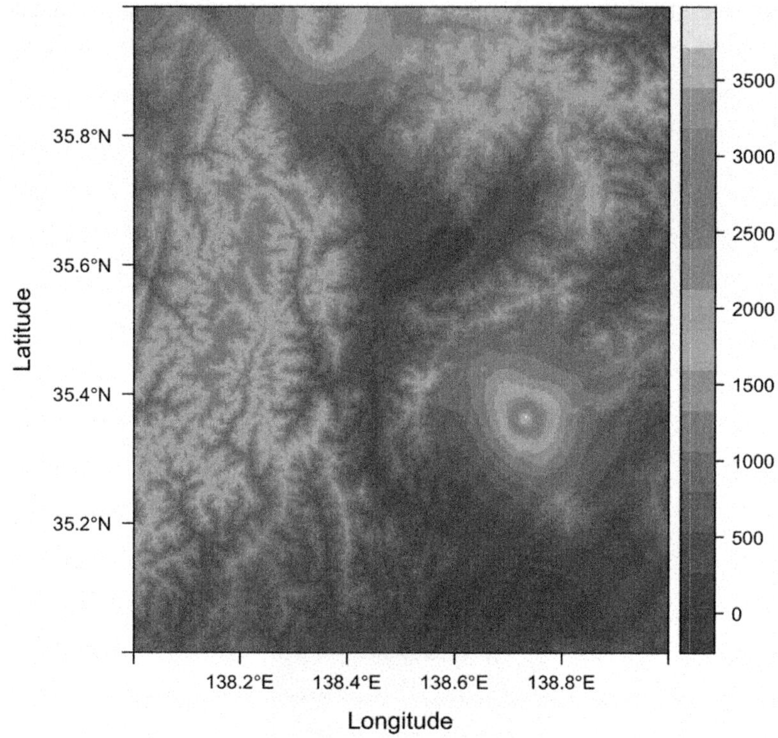

This visualization helps us better understand the terrain by giving a clear and continuous representation of elevation.

Convert Raster to Matrix

To create a 3D visualization, we need to convert the raster data into a matrix. The raster_to_matrix() function from the rayshader package transforms the raster data into a format that can be used for 3D plotting.

```
# Convert raster to matrix
fuji.new < - raster_to_matrix(dem)
```

Create a 3D Visualization with Rayshader

Finally, we use the rayshader package to create a 3D visualization of the DEM. The sphere_shade() function adds shading based on the sun angle, and the plot_map() function renders the 3D view.

```
# Visualize the DEM using hillshade technique
fuji.new % > % sphere_shade(sunangle = 45, texture
= "desert") % > %
 plot_map()
```

Output:

In this example, the sphere_shade() function uses a sun angle of 45 degrees and applies a "desert" texture, which makes the DEM look realistic. The result is an interactive and visually appealing 3D map of Mount Fuji.

Working with Nighttime Light Data

Nighttime Lights (NTL) data is an important resource for understanding human activities, urbanization, economic development, and even the impact of war. By analyzing changes in NTL data over time, we can identify patterns of growth or decline in specific regions. In this example, we will process and analyze NTL data for Palestine for the years 2014 and 2024, using R programming. Below is a step-by-step breakdown of the process:

Setup: Load Required Packages

To start, we load the necessary R packages. These packages allow us to work with geospatial data, manipulate raster data, and create visualizations.

```
# Setup: Load packages
library(blackmarbler)
library(geodata)
library(sf)
library(terra)
library(ggplot2)
library(tidyterra)
library(lubridate)
```

NASA Bearer Token Authentication

To access the Nighttime Lights data from NASA, you need an authentication token. The token is used to authenticate requests to NASA's servers. Make sure to replace the token below with your valid token. To get your own token, follow the guide from https://worldbank.github.io/blackmarbler/

```
# NASA bearer token
bearer < - "your_NASA_bearer_token_here"
```

Define Region of Interest (ROI)

Here, we define the region of interest as Palestine. First, we check the country codes and filter for Palestine using its country code ("PSE"). The **gadm** function retrieves the region's administrative boundaries.

```
# Define Region of Interest (ROI)
# Check country codes
cc < - country_codes()
head(cc)

# Query for Palestine
p < - country_codes(query = "Palestin")
p

# Define ROI
```

```
roi_sf < - gadm(country = "PSE", level = 1, path =
tempdir())

# If you have this message: "The geodata server
appears to be down. Hopefully it will be back
soon." Just wait a couple of minutes or hours.
```

Output:

```
> p <- country_codes(query="Palestin")
> p
         NAME ISO3 ISO2                             NAME_ISO  NAME_FAO NAME_LOCAL SOVEREIGN
173 Palestine  PSE   PS PALESTINIAN TERRITORY, OCCUPIED Palestine   Filastin Palestina
      UNREGION1 UNREGION2 continent
173 Western Asia      Asia      Asia
```

If your study area is different, you can replace “Palestine” in the code above with your area of interest, such as “North Korea,” and then verify the country code again.

Fetch Nighttime Lights Data

Using the **bm_raster** function from the blackmarbler package, we fetch NTL data for Palestine for the years 2014 and 2024. The product ID “VNP46A3” refers to the monthly NTL data product, while “VNP46A2” is for daily, and “VNP46A4” is for the yearly NTL data product.

```
# Fetch Nighttime Lights Data for 2014 and 2024
r2014 < - bm_raster(roi_sf = roi_sf, product_id =
"VNP46A3", date = "2014-06-01", bearer = bearer)
r2024 < - bm_raster(roi_sf = roi_sf, product_id =
"VNP46A3", date = "2024-06-01", bearer = bearer)

#if you have the following message, just continue:
Warning message:
Failed to open 'https://ladsweb.modaps.eosdis.nasa.gov/archive/allData/5000/
VNP46A3/2014/153.csv': The requested URL returned error: 404
```

Mask and Log-Transform Data

To focus on the area within the region of interest, we mask the raster data using the administrative boundaries. Then, we apply a log transformation to the data to reduce skewness and enhance interpretability.

```
# Mask and Log-transform Data
r2014 < - terra::mask(r2014, roi_sf)
r2024 < - terra::mask(r2024, roi_sf)

# Log-transform data
r2014[] < - log(r2014[] + 1)
r2024[] < - log(r2024[] + 1)
```

Compute Difference Between Years

Next, we calculate the difference in NTL radiance between 2024 and 2014. This difference highlights areas with increased or decreased radiance over the decade.

```
# Compute Difference
r_diff < - r2024 - r2014
```

Visualize the Changes

Finally, we create a map to visualize the changes in NTL radiance. The map uses a gradient colorscheme to represent areas of increase (red), decrease (black), and no change (white).

```
# Plot Change Map
change_map < - ggplot() +
 geom_spatraster(data = r_diff) +
 scale_fill_gradient2(low = "black", mid =
"white", high = "red", midpoint = 0, na.value =
"transparent",
   name = "Change in NTL") +
 labs(title = "Change in Nighttime Lights Radiance
(2014-2024)") +
 coord_sf() +
 theme_minimal() +
 theme(plot.title = element_text(face = "bold",
hjust = 0.5))

print(change_map)
```

Output:

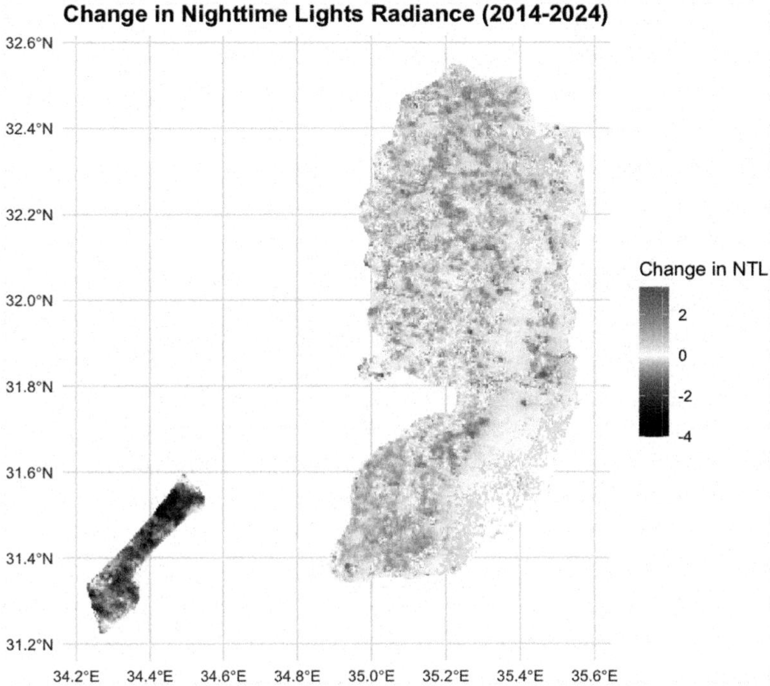

The map illustrates the change in Nighttime Light brightness in Palestine (West Bank and Gaza) between 2014 and 2024. The color on the map indicates the extent of this change, with red areas representing an increase in brightness, while white areas show minimal change. In the West Bank, there are more red areas than black, suggesting a growth in economic activity and development during this period. In contrast, Gaza has predominantly black areas, reflecting a decline in brightness due to the intense and repeated attacks from the occupying army.

Extracting the NTL Trends and Plot Using Barplot

Furthermore, you can extract and plot the monthly trends of Nighttime Light (NTL) data, you can start by using the ggplot2 package to visualize the data. The process usually takes a while.

```
# Extract Monthly Trends for NTL
ntl_df_monthly < - bm_extract(roi_sf = roi_sf,
product_id = "VNP46A3",
date = seq.Date(from = as.Date("2023-01-01"),
to = as.Date("2024-06-01"),
```

```
by = "month"), bearer = bearer, check_all_tiles_
exist = FALSE)

# Plot monthly trends
ntl_df_monthly |>
 ggplot() +
 geom_col(aes(x = date, y = ntl_mean), fill =
"darkorange") +
 facet_wrap(~NAME_1) +
 labs(x = NULL,
 y = "NTL Luminosity",
 title = "Palestine Admin Level 1: Monthly Average
Nighttime Lights") +
 scale_x_date(labels = scales::date_format("%b
%Y"),
 breaks = scales::date_breaks("2 month")) +
 theme_minimal() +
 theme(strip.text = element_text(face = "bold"),
 axis.text.x = element_text(angle = 45, hjust =
1)) # Diagonal x-axis labels
```

Output:

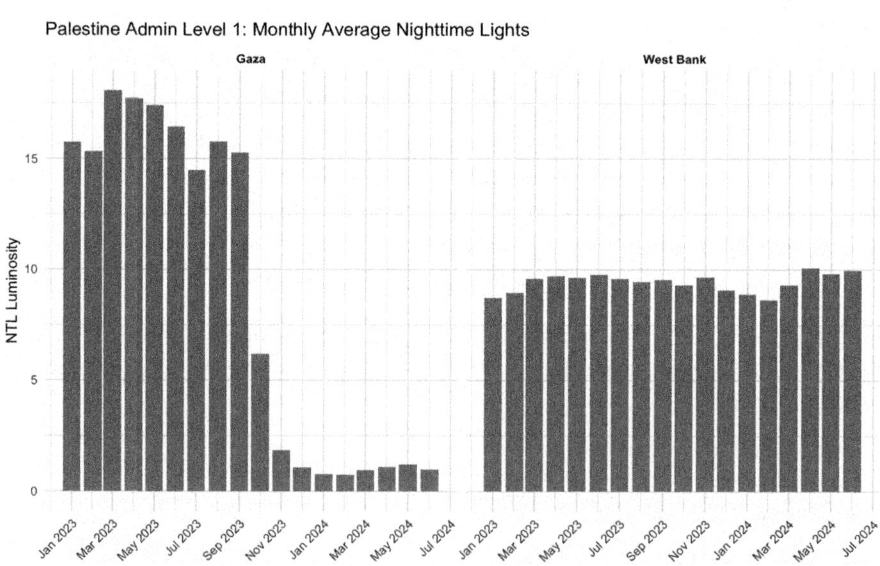

Once the plot is created, you may want to save the data and any raster files for further analysis.

```
# Save Data and Rasters
write.csv(ntl_df_monthly, "NTL_Trends_2014_
2024.csv", row.names = FALSE)
writeRaster(r_diff, "NTL_Change_2014_2024.tif",
filetype = "GTiff", overwrite = TRUE)
```

What Does the Code Do?

- We start by extracting the monthly trends from the dataset. We use the bm_extract function, specifying the region of interest (roi_sf) and the product ID ("VNP46A3"). The time range is from January 2023 to June 2024, with the data divided into monthly intervals. The bearer token is provided for authentication, and we set check_all_tiles_exist to FALSE to allow for missing data tiles.
- We are plotting a bar chart (geom_col) with the ntl_df_monthly dataset. The x-axis represents the date, and the y-axis shows the average NTL values (ntl_mean). Each facet (or subplot) represents a different administrative region (defined by NAME_1), which is helpful for comparing trends across different areas.
- The labs function is used to set the axis labels and title. The x-axis labels are formatted to show the month and year, with a break every two months (scales::date_breaks("2 month")). The theme_minimal() function is applied for a clean, simple plot background. Additionally, the x-axis labels are tilted by 45 degrees using element_text(angle = 45, hjust = 1) to improve readability, especially if there are many dates.
- The write.csv function is used to save the ntl_df_monthly data as a CSV file, which can be useful for further analysis or sharing. Additionally, the writeRaster function saves the raster data (r_diff) into a GeoTIFF file, which stores the changes in NTL from 2014 to 2024.

Challenges

Using data of "y700223000.xlsx" create two maps of "Japan's Net Migration By Prefectures 2019" complete with map's components (Title, Legend, Scale, and Compass)

Data source: https://www.stat.go.jp/english/data/nenkan/70nenkan/1431-02.html

Scroll down and find data **Migration 2–23 "Migrants by Prefecture(Excel:15.7 KB)"**

Expected results:

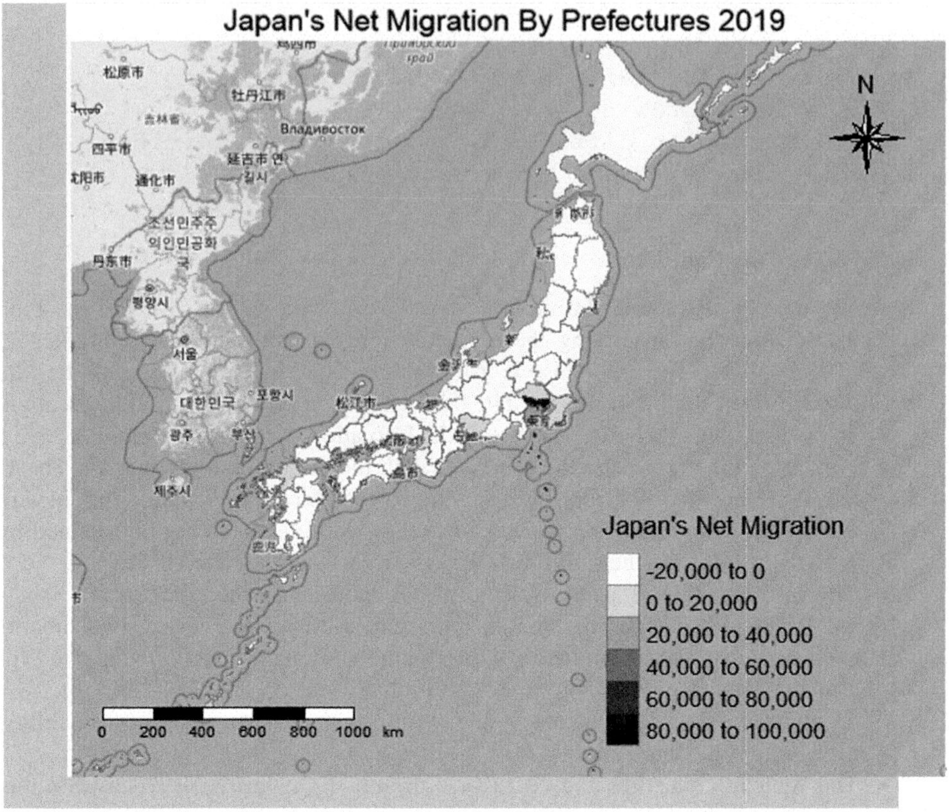

Challenges

Using monthly NTL data of Blackmarble, analysis the NTL changed of North Korea from 2014 to 2024 and visualize as a map

Expected results:

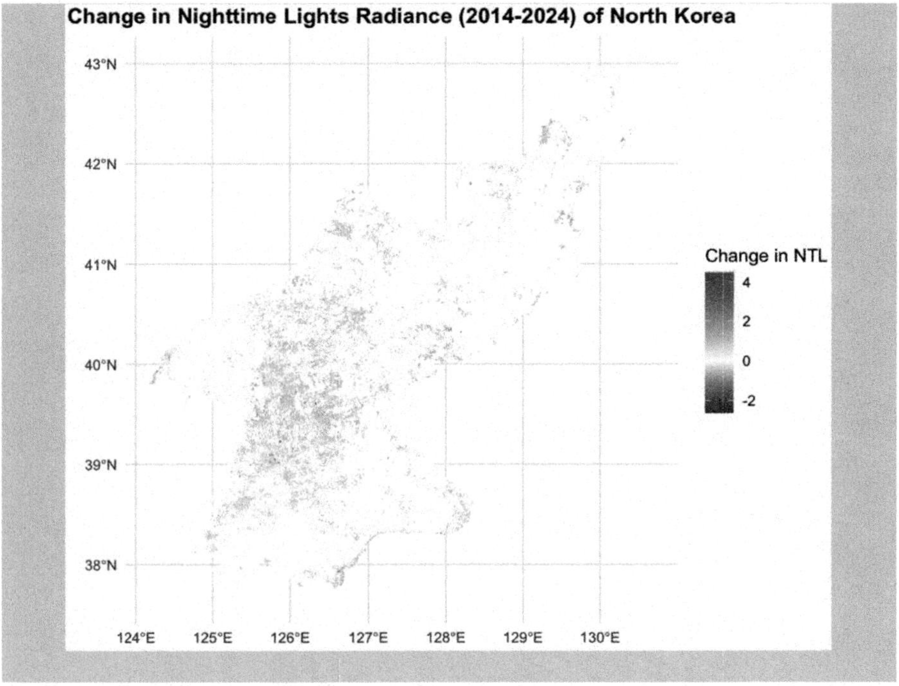

Reference

Brewer, C. A. (1994). Guidelines for use of the perceptual dimensions of color for mapping and visualization. In *Visualization in Modern Cartography* (pp. 123–147). Elsevier.

Chapter 8
Web Scraping and Data Mining

Abstract This chapter explores modern data science approaches, with a focus on web scraping and data mining. It covers fundamental topics, including the definitions and brief history of web scraping and data mining, their working principles, applications, types, and the tools and architectures involved. The advantages and limitations of these techniques, their integration, and future challenges in the field are also discussed. The second part of the chapter provides hands-on practice using COVID-19 pandemic data from Japan, involving data preprocessing tasks such as renaming headers, deleting rows, updating values, converting data to numeric format, and creating bar plots. Furthermore, spatial data on Japan's administrative boundaries is integrated with the cleaned COVID-19 data to produce visualizations.

Relation to Other Chapters: Provides hands-on techniques for data extraction, supporting later NLP tasks (Chap. 9) and ethical considerations (Chap. 10).

8.1 Introduction

In the world of data science, web scraping and data mining are powerful techniques for collecting and analyzing data. Today, the Internet is a vast resource of information, offering data from various fields, such as business, health, education, and the environment. This data is crucial for research, decision-making, and developing solutions to real-world problems.

However, the data we find online is often unorganized and may contain errors, missing values, or irrelevant information. To make the data useful for analysis, it must be cleaned, structured, and sometimes enriched with additional details. This process ensures that the insights we gain are accurate and reliable.

F. Ramdani, *Data Science: Foundations and Hands-on Experience*,
https://doi.org/10.1007/978-981-96-4683-8_8

8.2 Definition

Web scraping

Web scraping refers to the process of extracting data from websites automatically. It involves using software or programming techniques to access and gather information from web pages. Web scraping allows you to retrieve data that may not be readily available in a structured format, such as data displayed on websites without an Application Programming Interface (API).

The process typically involves sending Hypertext Transfer Protocol (HTTP) requests to a website's server, retrieving the Hypertext Markup Language (HTML) content of the web pages, and then parsing and extracting the desired data from the HTML using techniques like regular expressions, XPath, or HTML parsing libraries. The extracted data can be saved to a local file or database for further analysis or use.

Keep in mind that web scraping can sometimes have legal consequences, as every country has its own set of rules and regulations. In some cases, individuals may be prohibited from web scraping, but it may be legally allowed if conducted for research purposes or by accredited journalistic organizations. Always ensure you understand and comply with the specific laws in the jurisdiction where the scraping is being conducted.

Data mining

Data mining is the process of discovering patterns, relationships, and insights from large sets of data. It involves extracting valuable information from vast amounts of structured or unstructured data, often stored in databases, data warehouses, or other data repositories. Data mining utilizes various techniques and algorithms to analyze the data and uncover hidden patterns or knowledge that can be used for decision-making, prediction, and optimization.

The primary goal of data mining is to transform raw data into actionable knowledge, enabling organizations and individuals to make informed and data-driven decisions. It involves several steps, including data collection, data preprocessing, data transformation, data modeling, pattern discovery, and result interpretation.

***Data mining** is like being a detective who looks through lots of information (or data) to find hidden patterns, trends, or useful facts. Imagine you have a huge box of LEGO bricks. Data mining is when you look at all the pieces and try to find the most common colors or shapes, or maybe see if certain pieces are often used together.*

- ***What is data mining?***
- *Finding out what kinds of toys are most popular in a store by looking at lots of sales data.*
- *Figuring out what time of day students do their homework the most by looking at school surveys.*
- *Discovering which books kids like to read by looking at a library's checkout history.*

- ***What is not data mining?***
- *Just looking at a single toy or book without comparing it to anything else.*
- *Asking one person what time they do their homework, without looking at information from other students.*
- *Making guesses without checking the patterns in all the data.*

In simple terms, data mining is about looking at lots of information and using that to find something interesting or useful, instead of just guessing.

8.3 Brief History

Web scraping

Web scraping originated alongside the growth of the World Wide Web (www) in the 1990s. Initially, it was primarily used for extracting data from websites for indexing purposes by search engines like AltaVista and Yahoo.

In the early days (1990), web scraping involved writing custom scripts or programs to parse and extract information from HTML web pages. As the Internet evolved in the early 2000s, web scraping became more sophisticated, with the emergence of tools and frameworks that facilitated automated data extraction.

In the mid-2000s, the rise of social media and e-commerce platforms created a need for web scraping to gather data for market research, sentiment analysis, price comparison, and other purposes.

However, in the late 2000s, web scraping also raised ethical and legal concerns, leading to debates around data ownership, copyright infringement, and website terms of service.

Data mining

The concept of data mining began to take shape in the 1960s to 1970s as researchers started exploring techniques to analyze large volumes of data. The advent of powerful computers in the 1980s and 1990s allowed for more sophisticated data analysis methods, including statistical modeling and machine learning algorithms.

In the late 1990s, data mining gained significant attention with the growing availability of vast amounts of digital data and the need to extract meaningful insights from it. In the 2000s, the field of data mining expanded rapidly, with various industries adopting its techniques to identify patterns, make predictions, and gain valuable knowledge from their data.

8.4 How Does It Work

Web scraping

Web scraping involves the process of extracting data from websites and transforming it into a structured format for analysis or further use. The following section is a step-by-step explanation of the web scraping process, along with commonly used tools and methodologies.

1. Identify the target website

The first step in web scraping involves determining the website from which you want to extract data. This could be any publicly accessible website containing the desired information, such as e-commerce platforms, news sites, or government portals. At this stage, it's crucial to review the website's terms of service to ensure your scraping activities comply with its policies and legal requirements.

2. Inspect the website

Once you have identified the target website, you need to analyze its structure. This involves examining the website's HTML code to understand how the data is organized. Most modern web browsers offer built-in developer tools (such as Chrome's DevTools or Firefox's Inspector) that allow you to view and interact with the HTML elements of a webpage. By inspecting the page, you can identify the specific tags, classes, or IDs associated with the data you want to extract.

3. Choose a scraping tool

Selecting the appropriate tool or programming language for web scraping depends on your familiarity and the complexity of the task. Popular choices include:

- R: Provides packages like rvest for scraping and parsing HTML.
- Python: Known for its robust libraries like BeautifulSoup for parsing HTML, Scrapy for large-scale scraping, and Selenium for interacting with dynamic web pages.
- Other tools: Browser extensions, such as Web Scraper for Chrome, can be useful for beginners or quick tasks.
- Send an HTTP request

The next step involves sending an HTTP request to the target website's server. This request fetches the HTML content of the page you want to scrape. R's httr package can handle this task efficiently. The request specifies the webpage's URL, and the server responds with the required data unless restricted by measures such as CAPTCHA or anti-scraping mechanisms.

5. Retrieve the HTML content

Upon receiving the server's response, your program captures the raw HTML content of the webpage. This HTML document contains the structure and data of the page, which will be parsed and processed in the subsequent steps.

6. Parse the HTML

Parsing the HTML involves converting the raw HTML content into a format your program can navigate. Libraries like R's rvest allow you to traverse the HTML tree and locate specific elements based on their tags, classes, or IDs. This step is crucial for isolating the relevant data from other elements of the webpage.

7. Extract the desired data

Once the required elements are identified, you can extract the relevant data. This could include text from paragraphs, values from tables, links from anchor tags, or images from img tags. Advanced scraping tasks may involve handling JavaScript-rendered content using tools like Selenium.

8. Store or process the data

After extraction, the data needs to be saved or processed for further use. Common formats for storing the data include CSV files, JSON, or databases like MySQL or MongoDB. For instance, In R, you can use the dplyr and tidyr packages to transform the extracted data into a structured data frame for analysis.

What is web scraping used for?

Data extraction

Web scraping plays a crucial role in extracting vast amounts of data from websites, encompassing various types of information such as product details, pricing, customer reviews, news articles, and social media activity. This process enables businesses and organizations to acquire data that would otherwise be difficult to collect manually. The extracted data can be utilized for diverse purposes, including market research, competitor analysis, and sentiment analysis. For example, companies can track competitor pricing trends or analyze customer reviews to understand consumer preferences. Such applications highlight the value of web scraping in supporting data-driven decision-making processes.

Research and analysis

In academic and scientific domains, researchers rely on web scraping to collect datasets for their studies. The ability to extract data from multiple sources efficiently allows researchers to analyze trends, test hypotheses, and generate insights. For instance, a social scientist might scrape social media posts to study public opinions on climate change, while an economist could gather financial data for market trend analysis. Web scraping, therefore, enhances the scope and accuracy of research by providing access to a broad range of information in a time-efficient manner.

Lead generation

Businesses use web scraping to gather contact information, such as email addresses, phone numbers, or social media profiles, from online sources. This data is essential for lead generation, enabling companies to identify potential customers or clients. By building robust marketing databases, businesses can create targeted campaigns and improve their sales prospecting efforts. For instance, a startup might use web scraping to compile a list of prospective clients in a specific industry, streamlining their outreach process and enhancing the effectiveness of their marketing strategies.

Data mining

Data mining involves the process of uncovering meaningful patterns, trends, and insights from large datasets using a combination of statistical methods, machine learning, and database systems. Following are the key steps in how data mining works, explained in more detail.

1. Data preparation

The first step in data mining is data preparation, which involves gathering and cleaning data to ensure it is suitable for analysis. Data can come from various sources, such as databases, web servers, sensors, or surveys. The collected data often contains errors, inconsistencies, or missing values that need to be addressed. Cleaning involves removing duplicates, handling missing values, and correcting errors. Once cleaned, the data is transformed into a consistent format that aligns with the objectives of the analysis. This step ensures that the data is reliable and ready for the next stages of data mining. Data preparation is crucial because the quality of insights derived from data mining heavily depends on the quality of the input data.

2. Data exploration

After data preparation, exploratory data analysis (EDA) is performed to understand the dataset's characteristics and structure. EDA involves summarizing the data using descriptive statistics, such as mean, median, and standard deviation, and visualizing patterns through charts and graphs. Common techniques include histograms for understanding distributions, scatter plots for identifying relationships, and box plots for spotting outliers. Through EDA, researchers can identify initial patterns, trends, or anomalies in the data, which helps in selecting the most appropriate data mining techniques later. It also provides insights into potential issues, such as skewed data or imbalances between classes in classification problems. Figure 8.1 provides a comprehensive visual summary of key insights derived from the Groceries dataset, which consists of transactional data from a supermarket.

3. Feature Selection

Feature selection is the process of identifying the most relevant attributes or variables in the dataset for analysis. Not all features in a dataset are useful; some may be redundant, irrelevant, or even misleading. By selecting only the most relevant features, analysts can simplify the model, improve computational efficiency, and

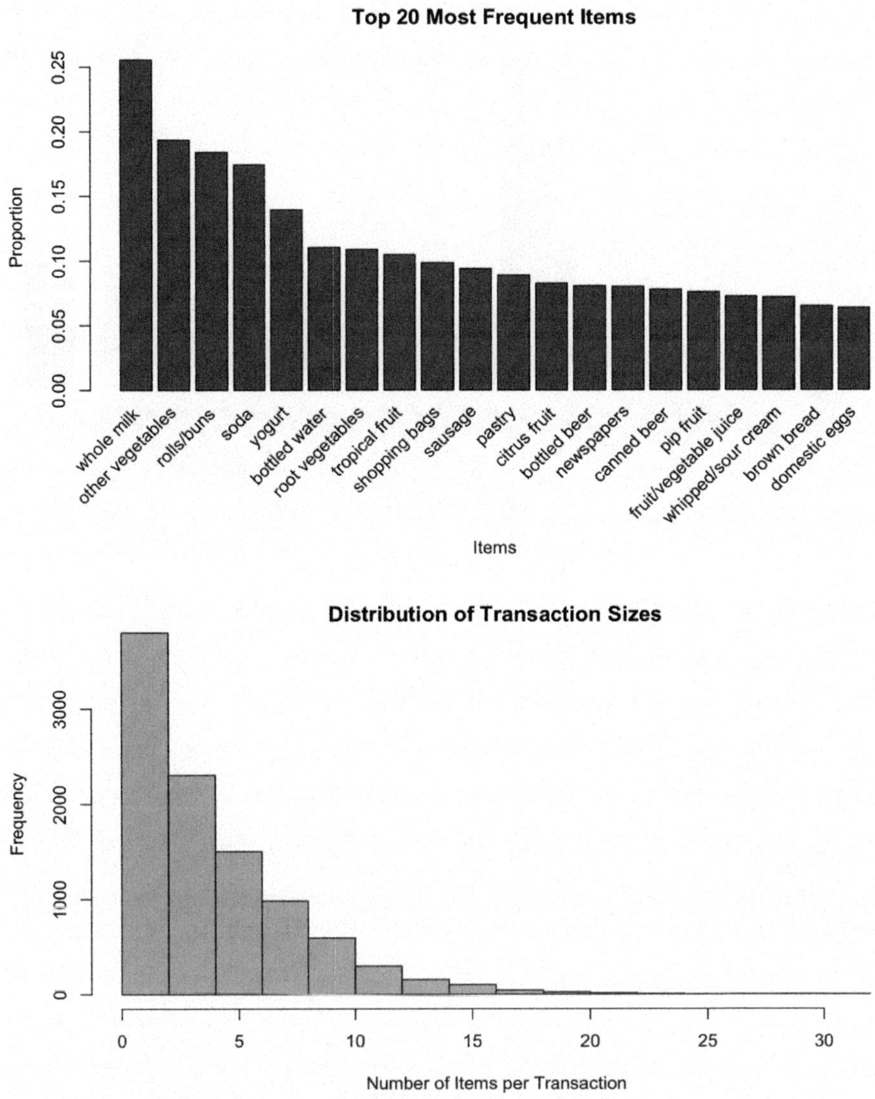

Fig. 8.1 Illustration of the top 20 most frequent items, distribution of transaction sizes, item frequency (support > 5%), and matrix of the first 100 transactions using the Groceries dataset that is preloaded with the arules package. It contains transactional data for a supermarket

enhance accuracy. Methods for feature selection include statistical techniques like correlation analysis, dimensionality reduction methods such as Principal Component Analysis (PCA), or algorithm-specific techniques like feature importance scores in random forests. For example, in predicting house prices, features such as location, size, and age of the house might be more relevant than the paint color.

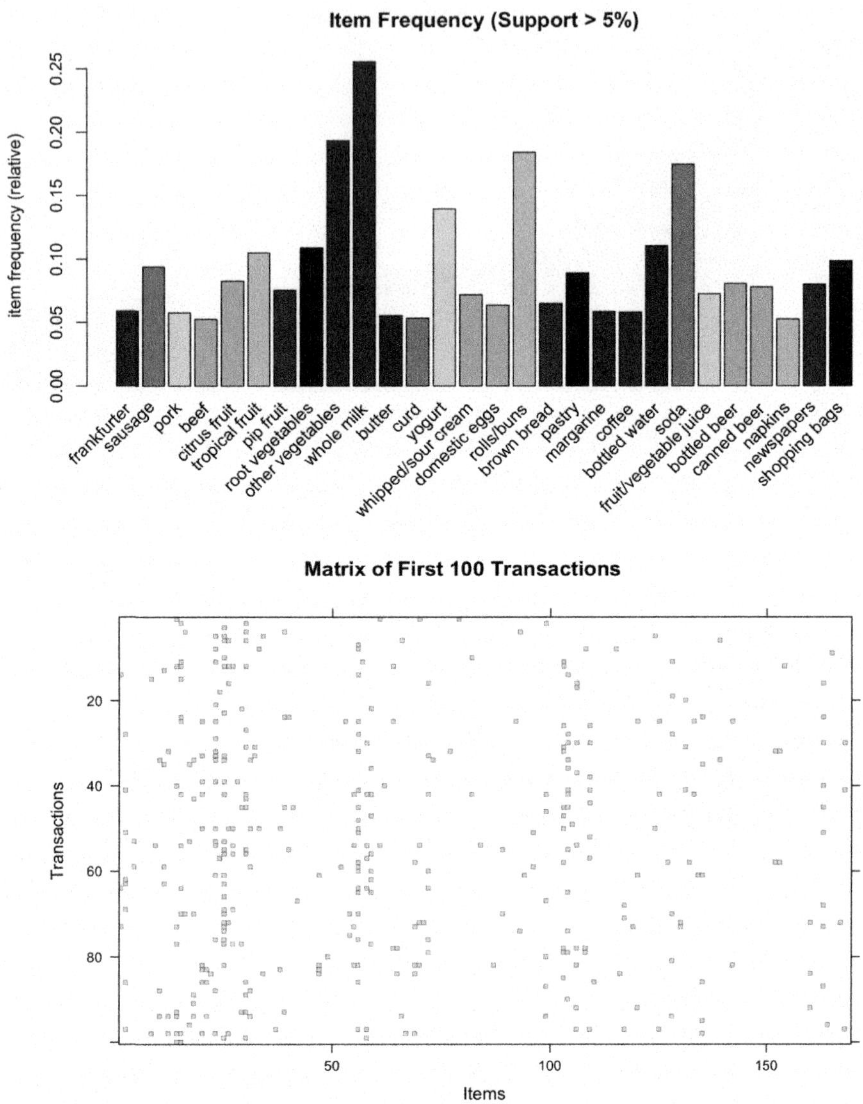

Fig. 8.1 (continued)

4. Data Mining Techniques

Once the data is prepared and relevant features are selected, data mining techniques are applied to uncover patterns or make predictions. Different techniques address different types of problems:

- **Classification**: Classification assigns data points to predefined categories or groups based on their attributes. It is widely used in applications like spam email detection or medical diagnosis. Popular algorithms include decision trees, which create tree-like structures for decision-making; support vector machines (SVM), which find optimal boundaries between classes; and Naive Bayes, which uses probabilities for classification tasks. Figure 8.2 presents a decision tree model applied to the Groceries dataset for classification purposes.

- **Regression**: Regression predicts a continuous numerical value based on input variables. For instance, predicting a house's price based on its features involves regression. Common algorithms include linear regression, which fits a straight line, and polynomial regression, which models nonlinear relationships. Figure 8.3 shows the prediction frequency based on Item (numeric representation) using Groceries data

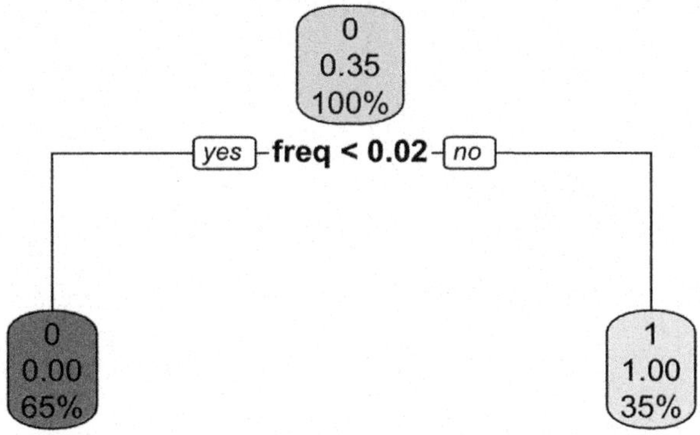

Fig. 8.2 Decision tree of Groceries dataset for classification tasks. A binary target variable is created where items with a frequency greater than a specified threshold (e.g., 2%) are labeled as frequent (1), and less frequent items are labeled as 0

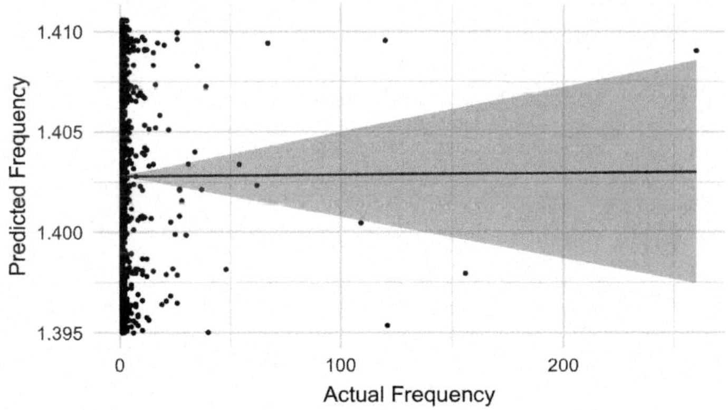

Fig. 8.3 Scatterplot of Groceries data, regression: actual versus predicted frequencies

- **Clustering**: Clustering groups similar data points based on patterns or similarities, often used in customer segmentation or image compression. Algorithms like K-means divide data into clusters, hierarchical clustering creates tree-like structures, and DBSCAN identifies dense regions in the data. Figure 8.4 presents the results of clustering analysis on the Groceries dataset using K-means and hierarchical clustering techniques. To enhance visualization, PCA was applied to reduce the dimensionality of the data.
- **Association rule mining**: This technique uncovers interesting associations between items in a dataset, commonly used in market basket analysis. The Apriori algorithm is one such method, identifying frequent item sets and generating rules like, "If a customer buys bread, they are likely to buy butter." Figure 8.5 shows the scatterplots, graph visualizations for better interpretation, and rules where the item "whole milk" is on the right-hand side using the Groceries dataset.

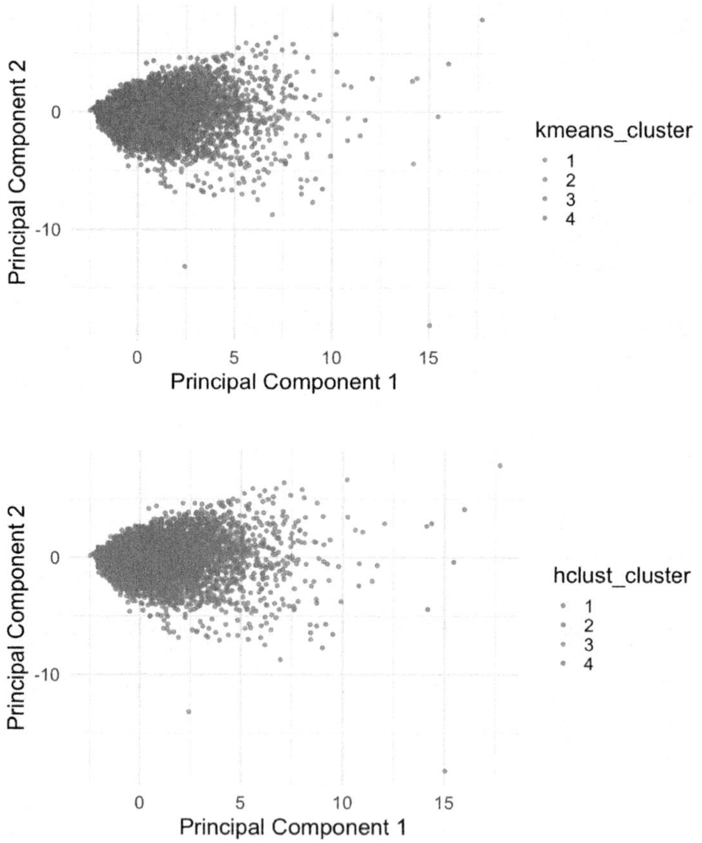

Fig. 8.4 Clustering using K-means and hierarchical clustering of Groceries dataset (PCA was used to reduce dimensions for better visualization)

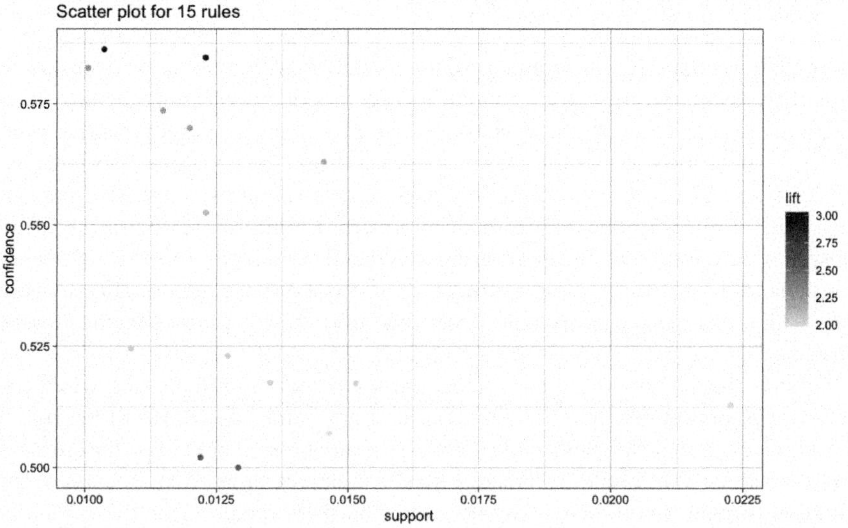

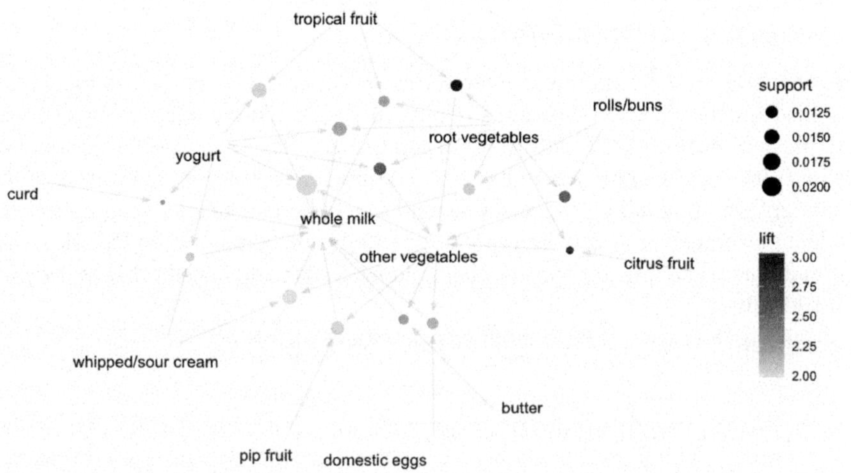


```
> milk_rules <- subset(rules, rhs %in% "whole milk")
> inspect(head(sort(milk_rules, by = "lift"), 10))
     lhs                                rhs          support    confidence coverage   lift     count
[1]  {curd, yogurt}                  => {whole milk} 0.01006609 0.5823529  0.01728521 2.279125  99
[2]  {other vegetables, butter}      => {whole milk} 0.01148958 0.5736041  0.02003050 2.244885 113
[3]  {tropical fruit, root vegetables} => {whole milk} 0.01199797 0.5700483  0.02104728 2.230969 118
[4]  {root vegetables, yogurt}       => {whole milk} 0.01453991 0.5629921  0.02582613 2.203354 143
[5]  {other vegetables, domestic eggs} => {whole milk} 0.01230300 0.5525114  0.02226741 2.162336 121
[6]  {yogurt, whipped/sour cream}    => {whole milk} 0.01087951 0.5245098  0.02074225 2.052747 107
[7]  {root vegetables, rolls/buns}   => {whole milk} 0.01270971 0.5230126  0.02430097 2.046888 125
[8]  {pip fruit, other vegetables}   => {whole milk} 0.01352313 0.5175097  0.02613116 2.025351 133
[9]  {tropical fruit, yogurt}        => {whole milk} 0.01514997 0.5173611  0.02928317 2.024770 149
[10] {other vegetables, yogurt}      => {whole milk} 0.02226741 0.5128806  0.04341637 2.007235 219
```

Fig. 8.5 The scatterplots, graph visualizations, and rules where the item “whole milk” is on the right-hand side

5. Model Evaluation and Validation

After applying data mining techniques, the models must be evaluated to ensure their reliability. Evaluation involves comparing the model's predictions against known outcomes to measure accuracy. Metrics such as precision (correct positive predictions), recall (ability to identify all positive cases), and the F1 score (harmonic mean of precision and recall) are commonly used. Cross-validation methods, like k-fold cross-validation, help ensure the model's generalizability by testing it on different subsets of the data. Proper evaluation ensures that the model performs well on unseen data and is not overfitting or underfitting. Figure 8.6 shows the rules quality metric and rules with the highest support, confidence, and lift for evaluation using the Groceries dataset.

Support means how often the rule's item sets appear in the dataset, while confidence is the probability that the items on the right-hand side (RHS) of the rule will appear, given that the left-hand side (LHS) items are present, and lift is the strength of the rule compared to random chance; a lift > 1 indicates a positive association. Rules with high support, confidence, and lift can be used for recommendations, bundling, or store layouts (e.g., placing frequently bought items together).

6. Interpretation and Knowledge Discovery

The final step in data mining is interpreting the results and extracting meaningful insights from the discovered patterns. This involves explaining relationships between variables, identifying key factors influencing outcomes, and translating technical findings into actionable decisions. For example, a retailer might discover that customers who buy baby products also tend to buy certain snacks, leading to better product placement strategies. Interpretation bridges the gap between technical analysis and practical applications, enabling organizations to make data-driven decisions that add value.

From Fig. 8.6, we can have three interpretations as follow:

- `{other vegetables, yoghurt}` → `{whole milk}` has high support, which means many transactions in the dataset include other vegetables, yoghurt and whole milk,
- `{citrus fruit, root vegetables}` → `{other vegetables}` with a confidence of 0.58 means 58% of transactions containing citrus fruit and root vegetables also include other vegetables.
- `{citrus fruit, root vegetables}` → `{other vegetables}` with a lift of 3.029 means citrus fruit, root vegetables, and other vegetables are 3.1 times more likely to be bought together than by chance.

	support	confidence	coverage	lift	count
1	0.01006609	0.5823529	0.01728521	2.279125	99
2	0.01148958	0.5736041	0.02003050	2.244885	113
3	0.01230300	0.5525114	0.02226741	2.162336	121
4	0.01087951	0.5245098	0.02074225	2.052747	107
5	0.01464159	0.5070423	0.02887646	1.984385	144
6	0.01352313	0.5175097	0.02613116	2.025351	133
7	0.01037112	0.5862069	0.01769192	3.029608	102
8	0.01230300	0.5845411	0.02104728	3.020999	121
9	0.01199797	0.5700483	0.02104728	2.230969	118
10	0.01514997	0.5173611	0.02928317	2.024770	149
11	0.01291307	0.5000000	0.02582613	2.584078	127
12	0.01453991	0.5629921	0.02582613	2.203354	143
13	0.01220132	0.5020921	0.02430097	2.594890	120
14	0.01270971	0.5230126	0.02430097	2.046888	125
15	0.02226741	0.5128806	0.04341637	2.007235	219

```
Rules with highest support:
> inspect(head(sort(rules, by = "support"), 5))
    lhs                                      rhs          support    confidence coverage   lift     count
[1] {other vegetables, yogurt}            => {whole milk} 0.02226741 0.5128806  0.04341637 2.007235 219
[2] {tropical fruit, yogurt}              => {whole milk} 0.01514997 0.5173611  0.02928317 2.024770 149
[3] {other vegetables, whipped/sour cream} => {whole milk} 0.01464159 0.5070423  0.02887646 1.984385 144
[4] {root vegetables, yogurt}             => {whole milk} 0.01453991 0.5629921  0.02582613 2.203354 143
[5] {pip fruit, other vegetables}         => {whole milk} 0.01352313 0.5175097  0.02613116 2.025351 133
> cat("\nRules with highest confidence:\n")

Rules with highest confidence:
> inspect(head(sort(rules, by = "confidence"), 5))
    lhs                                 rhs                 support    confidence coverage   lift     count
[1] {citrus fruit, root vegetables}  => {other vegetables} 0.01037112 0.5862069  0.01769192 3.029608 102
[2] {tropical fruit, root vegetables} => {other vegetables} 0.01230300 0.5845411  0.02104728 3.020999 121
[3] {curd, yogurt}                   => {whole milk}       0.01006609 0.5823529  0.01728521 2.279125  99
[4] {other vegetables, butter}       => {whole milk}       0.01148958 0.5736041  0.02003050 2.244885 113
[5] {tropical fruit, root vegetables} => {whole milk}       0.01199797 0.5700483  0.02104728 2.230969 118
> cat("\nRules with highest lift:\n")

Rules with highest lift:
> inspect(head(sort(rules, by = "lift"), 5))
    lhs                                 rhs                 support    confidence coverage   lift     count
[1] {citrus fruit, root vegetables}  => {other vegetables} 0.01037112 0.5862069  0.01769192 3.029608 102
[2] {tropical fruit, root vegetables} => {other vegetables} 0.01230300 0.5845411  0.02104728 3.020999 121
[3] {root vegetables, rolls/buns}    => {other vegetables} 0.01220132 0.5020921  0.02430097 2.594890 120
[4] {root vegetables, yogurt}        => {other vegetables} 0.01291307 0.5000000  0.02582613 2.584078 127
[5] {curd, yogurt}                   => {whole milk}       0.01006609 0.5823529  0.01728521 2.279125  99
```

Fig. 8.6 Rules quality metric and rules with the highest support, confidence, and lift for evaluation using the Groceries dataset

What is data mining used f or?

Data mining is a powerful tool that allows organizations to analyze vast amounts of data to uncover valuable insights and make informed decisions. It is widely used across various domains to address specific challenges and opportunities such as:

Business intelligence

Data mining enhances business intelligence by helping organizations analyze their operational data to identify trends, patterns, and relationships. These insights are crucial for improving business performance. For example, companies use data mining to perform customer segmentation, analyze markets, forecast demand, and identify opportunities for cross-selling or upselling. By leveraging these techniques, businesses can gain a competitive advantage and optimize their operations.

Fraud detection

In industries like finance, insurance, and telecommunications, data mining is employed to detect fraudulent activities. By analyzing patterns and anomalies in data, organizations can identify suspicious transactions, fraudulent claims, or abnormal behaviors. For example, financial institutions use data mining to monitor transactions for unusual activity, enabling early detection of potential fraud and minimizing losses.

Customer relationship management (CRM)

Data mining is an integral part of CRM systems, helping organizations analyze customer data to derive insights for targeted marketing campaigns, customer segmentation, and personalized recommendations. It enables businesses to understand customer preferences, behaviors, and loyalty patterns. For instance, e-commerce platforms analyze purchase histories to suggest products tailored to individual customer needs.

Risk analysis

Risk assessment and management benefit greatly from data mining techniques. By analyzing historical data, organizations can identify factors contributing to risks in areas like finance, insurance, healthcare, and security. This enables them to make informed decisions to mitigate risks and optimize strategies. For example, insurers use data mining to assess risk profiles of clients, aiding in policy pricing and fraud prevention.

Healthcare and medicine

In healthcare, data mining is used to analyze patient records, medical data, and clinical trials. It assists in disease diagnosis, predicting treatment outcomes, and identifying patterns in patient care. For instance, machine learning algorithms can analyze data to predict the likelihood of diseases or discover adverse drug interactions, contributing to better patient care and medical research.

Market research

Data mining supports market researchers in analyzing large volumes of data to understand consumer preferences, market trends, and competitive landscapes. This helps identify target audiences, optimize pricing strategies, and guide product launches.

For example, retailers analyze customer purchase data to determine seasonal demand and adjust inventory accordingly.

Recommender systems

Online platforms such as e-commerce websites, streaming services, and social media platforms utilize data mining algorithms for personalized recommendations. By analyzing user behavior, preferences, and historical data, these systems suggest relevant products, movies, or content, enhancing the user experience. For instance, Netflix recommends shows based on users' viewing histories and preferences.

8.5 Coupling Web Scraping and Data Mining

Coupling web scraping and data mining is a powerful approach for gathering and analyzing information from online sources. **In the data collection stage**, web scraping allows users to extract information from a wide range of sources, such as websites, social media platforms, and online marketplaces. This process involves using automated tools or scripts to systematically collect the desired data, which could include text, images, or structured content like tables or lists.

After collection, the next step is data preprocessing, where the raw data is cleaned, transformed, and formatted into a structured format suitable for analysis. This involves removing duplicates, handling missing values, and standardizing data formats to ensure consistency and usability. Once the data is ready, various **data mining techniques** can be applied to extract meaningful patterns and insights. For example, clustering, classification, and association rule mining are commonly used to identify trends, group similar items, or discover relationships in the data.

Exploratory data analysis (EDA) is another crucial step, where the data is visualized and analyzed to uncover its characteristics and any hidden patterns. This step provides a deeper understanding of the dataset, allowing researchers or decision-makers to refine their focus or hypotheses.

The ultimate goal of integrating web scraping and data mining is **knowledge discovery and decision-making**. By leveraging insights gained from these techniques, organizations can understand market trends, customer preferences, and emerging opportunities. This process empowers businesses and researchers to make informed, data-driven decisions that can lead to strategic advantages in their respective fields.

Figure 8.7 summarizes how web scraping and data mining are connected. It is divided into three sections: **Website**, **database**, and **applications**.

1. **Website**: The process begins with a website that contains information in the form of HTML content. A user sends an HTTP request to the website to access the information. The website responds by sending back the HTML content.

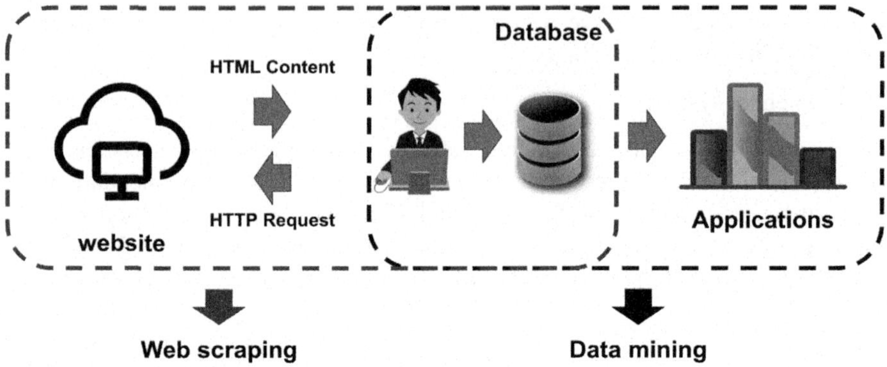

Fig. 8.7 Integration of web scraping and data mining

2. **Database**: After the data is collected from the website, it is stored in a database. This step involves organizing the raw data so it can be easily analyzed and processed.
3. **Applications**: The stored data is then used in various applications. These applications process and analyze the data to create visualizations or insights, such as charts and graphs.

Web scraping is the process of collecting data from websites, while data mining refers to analyzing and extracting useful patterns or information from the collected data. Together, these processes are useful for gaining insights from large amounts of online information.

What is (and is not) data mining?

Data mining is the process of discovering patterns, trends, or relationships within large datasets. For example, it could involve identifying groups of similar articles in a journal database, such as clustering research papers based on their topics or keywords. Another example of data mining is analyzing prefectural-level data to identify patterns related to COVID-19, such as infection rates, recovery trends, or demographic impacts. These tasks involve advanced techniques, such as statistical analysis, machine learning, artificial intelligence, or spatial analysis to extract and map meaningful insights from raw data.

On the other hand, not every activity related to data or searching qualifies as data mining. For instance, looking for books about "data science" in a library catalog or querying a web search engine for general information does not constitute data mining. These activities involve retrieving or searching for specific information but do not analyze or extract patterns from large datasets. Unlike data mining, these tasks rely on existing indexing systems and do not require complex analytical methods.

8.6 Type of Web Scraping and Data Mining

Type of web scraping

HTML parsing

HTML parsing is one of the simplest methods of web scraping. In this approach, the scraper fetches the HTML content of a web page and extracts the desired information directly from the source code. This method works best for straightforward tasks where the data is neatly organized and easy to identify within the HTML structure.

API scraping

Application Programming Interface (API) scraping is a more advanced and reliable method compared to HTML parsing. It involves sending HTTP requests to web APIs and extracting the required data from the structured responses, typically in JSON or XML format. This approach ensures clean and well-structured data, eliminating the need for parsing messy HTML. Many websites provide APIs for developers to access their data, making this technique more efficient and less prone to errors.

DOM parsing

DOM parsing leverages the Document Object Model (DOM) of an HTML document to extract information using advanced navigation and manipulation techniques. By treating the webpage as a hierarchical structure of elements, DOM parsing allows scrapers to traverse and interact with different nodes efficiently. This method is particularly helpful for complex scraping tasks, such as extracting deeply nested data or interacting with dynamic elements on a page.

Dynamic scraping

Dynamic scraping addresses the challenges posed by websites that generate content dynamically using JavaScript. Traditional scraping methods may fail to capture such content as it does not appear in the initial HTML. Instead, dynamic scraping uses headless browsers or browser automation tools to load the webpage and execute JavaScript to render the content.

Image scraping

Image scraping focuses on extracting images from websites. This technique is widely used for tasks such as building image datasets, analyzing metadata, or gathering visual content for machine learning projects. The process often involves downloading images and, in some cases, extracting associated metadata such as captions or tags.

Text scraping

Text scraping is the process of extracting textual content from web pages, such as articles, blog posts, or product descriptions. The extracted text can be used for various applications, including sentiment analysis, natural language processing (NLP), or creating large-scale text datasets. This method is particularly valuable for tasks like monitoring trends, analyzing customer reviews, or training machine learning models on text data.

Types of data mining techniques

Data mining involves various techniques that are designed to address specific business problems and provide valuable insights. Each technique has its unique approach to analyzing data, and understanding the nature of the business problem is crucial in selecting the right method. Choosing an appropriate technique ensures that the analysis yields the best possible results. Broadly, data mining techniques can be categorized into two main types: **Predictive data mining** and **descriptive data mining**.

1. Predictive data mining

Predictive data mining focuses on using historical data to forecast future outcomes. As the name suggests, this type of analysis helps predict potential scenarios, aiding businesses in strategic decision-making. Predictive data mining techniques are particularly useful in industries like finance, marketing, and healthcare, where understanding future trends is critical. It can be further divided into four subtypes:

- **Classification analysis**: Used to classify data into predefined categories, such as determining whether a customer is likely to churn or not.
- **Regression analysis**: Helps in identifying relationships between variables to predict continuous outcomes, such as sales figures.
- **Time series analysis**: Analyzes data points collected over time to detect trends and patterns, often used in stock market predictions. Figure 8.8 illustrates a time series plot using synthetic data, where the first plot shows basic time series data with red points and blue lines. The second plot includes a smoothed trend line (green color) to help visualize potential trends.

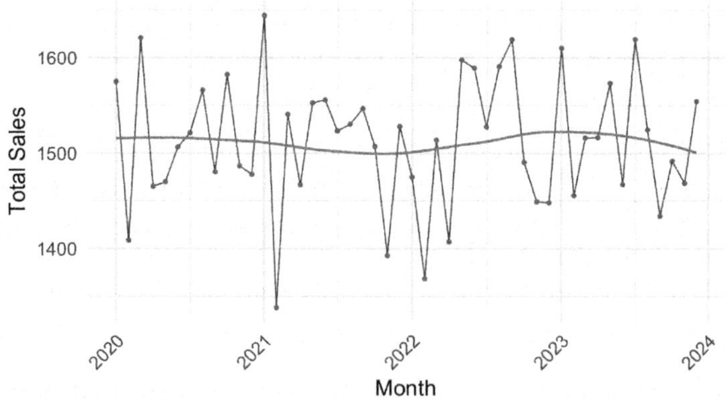

Fig. 8.8 Time series visualization with trend analysis using synthetic data

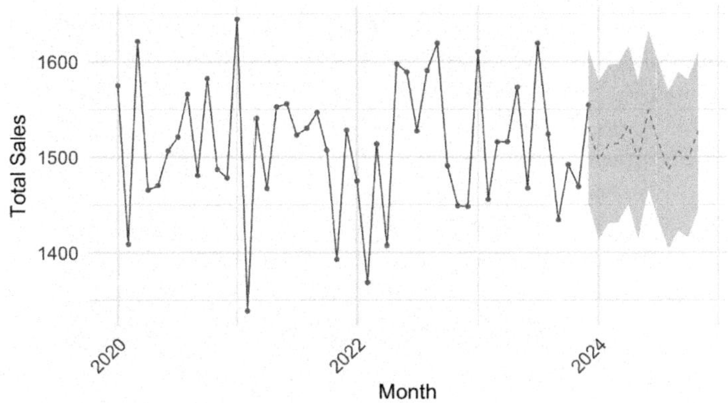

Fig. 8.9 Forecasting groceries sales (next 12 months) using synthetic data

- **Prediction analysis**: Focuses on forecasting future events based on historical data trends. Figure 8.9 shows the forecasting groceries sales (next 12 months) using synthetic data.

2. Descriptive data mining

Descriptive data mining aims to understand and summarize the underlying patterns in existing data. Unlike predictive techniques, descriptive analysis focuses on explaining past events and generating insights from the data at hand. This approach is essential for exploring data structures and identifying correlations. It can also be divided into four subtypes:

- **Clustering analysis**: Groups similar data points together, useful for market segmentation and customer profiling.
- **Summarization analysis**: Generates compact representations of the dataset, such as creating a summary of customer demographics.
- **Association rules analysis**: Identifies relationships between variables, often used in market basket analysis to find products frequently bought together.
- **Sequence discovery analysis**: Detects patterns in sequential data, such as analyzing customer purchase behavior over time. Figure 8.10 shows a bar plot of top ten frequent sequential patterns to detect patterns in sequential data, in this case identifying which products are often bought together or in a specific order, and provides insights into customer purchase behavior over time.

These data mining techniques enable businesses to extract actionable knowledge from vast datasets, driving better decision-making and strategic planning. For example, predictive approaches have been instrumental in fraud detection and personalized marketing, while descriptive techniques support inventory management and customer segmentation.

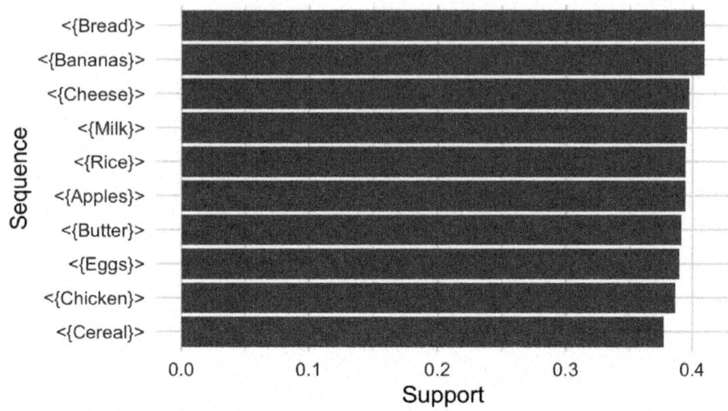

Fig. 8.10 Bar plot of top 10 frequent sequential patterns for analyzing customer purchase behavior

8.7 Data Mining Architecture

Data sources play a crucial role in the success of data mining processes. The primary sources include databases (DB), data warehouses (DW), the World Wide Web (WWW), text files, and various other documents. For data mining to yield meaningful results, it requires a vast amount of historical data to identify trends and patterns effectively. However, data from these sources is often incomplete, inconsistent, or stored in diverse formats, making preprocessing a vital step. Before feeding the data into the database or data warehouse server, it must go through cleaning, integration, and selection processes. This ensures the data is accurate, complete, and formatted uniformly. Additionally, since excessive information is often collected, only relevant data is selected and passed to the server, optimizing the subsequent analysis.

The **database or data warehouse** server stores the processed data and serves as the primary repository for data mining activities. It allows for the retrieval of relevant data based on user requests, forming the foundation for further exploration and analysis. The **data mining engine**, a core component of any data mining system, performs key analytical tasks such as association, classification, clustering, prediction, and time-series analysis. These tasks utilize specialized tools and software to uncover hidden insights and valuable knowledge from the data stored in the warehouse.

Another critical component is the **pattern evaluation module**, which assesses the quality and relevance of discovered patterns. Using threshold values, it filters out uninteresting patterns and focuses on those deemed significant. This module often works closely with the data mining engine to refine results and may use a coordinated approach to enhance efficiency depending on the data mining technique employed.

To bridge the gap between complex algorithms and users, the **graphical user interface (GUI)** provides an intuitive way to interact with the data mining system. It simplifies operations, allowing users to navigate and extract insights without understanding the underlying complexities. Finally, the **knowledge base** enhances the

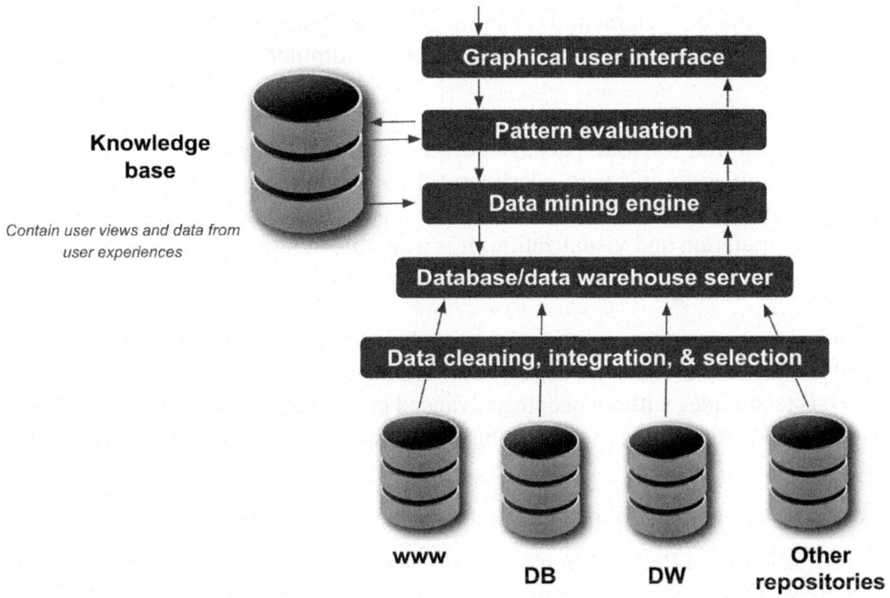

Fig. 8.11 Architecture of data mining

entire process by storing user preferences, expert knowledge, and system-generated insights. It acts as a dynamic repository that feeds into the data mining engine and pattern evaluation module, ensuring outputs are both accurate and contextually relevant. Together, these components form a robust data mining architecture capable of transforming raw data into actionable knowledge. Figure 8.11 provides a detailed visualization of the data mining architecture, outlining its key components and processes.

8.8 Data Mining Tools

Web scraping and data mining tools are essential for extracting and analyzing large amounts of data from various sources. These tools are divided into free and commercial categories, each serving different needs and user levels. Below is a list of popular tools that fall into these two categories.

Free tools

RapidMiner (community edition)

RapidMiner is a robust data mining tool that provides powerful capabilities for data analysis and machine learning. The Community Edition is free to use, offering a wide range of features that help users explore data and build models. It is commonly used in research and development to perform advanced analytics and machine learning tasks. It is available at https://altair.com/altair-rapidminer.

DataMelt

DataMelt is a free software package designed for data analysis, scientific computation, and simulation. It is particularly useful for handling large datasets and building complex models. Researchers and data scientists often use it for tasks that require heavy computation and visualization. It is available at https://datamelt.org/.

Orange data mining

Orange is an open-source data mining tool with a simple, visual interface that is ideal for beginners. It allows users to explore machine learning algorithms and data analysis techniques without needing advanced programming skills. Orange is widely used in academic settings for teaching data science. It is available at https://orangedatamining.com/.

BeautifulSoup (Python library)

BeautifulSoup is a Python library used for web scraping, particularly for extracting data from HTML and XML documents. It is easy to use and is commonly employed for tasks such as scraping website content for research or business purposes. It is available at https://beautiful-soup-4.readthedocs.io/en/latest/.

Scrapy

Scrapy is an open-source framework for building web scraping applications. It is designed to handle large amounts of data and allows users to efficiently scrape websites. This tool is popular among developers for its flexibility and ability to handle complex scraping tasks. It is available at https://scrapy.org/.

Commercial tools

Tableau

Tableau is a commercial data mining and visualization tool that helps users understand their data through interactive dashboards. It is widely used in business environments to analyze and visualize data, making it easier to communicate insights and trends. Tableau is available at https://www.tableau.com/.

Knime

KNIME is a comprehensive data mining platform that offers machine learning, analytics, and data mining tools. Known for its user-friendly interface, KNIME is a powerful tool for professionals who need to analyze large datasets and build predictive models. KNIME is available at https://www.knime.com/.

Alteryx

Alteryx is a data mining platform that provides tools for data transformation, cleaning, and analysis. Its intuitive drag-and-drop interface makes it easy for users to perform complex tasks without deep programming knowledge. It is commonly used by business analysts for data preparation and analysis. Alteryx is available at https://www.alteryx.com/.

DataRobot

DataRobot is a commercial machine learning platform that automates the process of building and deploying machine learning models. It is designed for users who may not have extensive programming experience, allowing them to develop models quickly and easily. DataRobot is available at https://www.datarobot.com/.

WebHarvy

WebHarvy is a commercial web scraping software that offers a point-and-click interface for extracting data from websites. Users can scrape data without any coding knowledge, making it accessible for non-technical users who need to collect information from the web. WebHarvy is available at https://www.webharvy.com/.

8.9 Advantages and Disadvantages

Advantages and disadvantages of web scraping

One of the major benefits of web scraping is **automated data collection**. This process eliminates the need for manual data entry, saving significant time and effort. By using web scraping tools, users can gather large amounts of data quickly and efficiently. Another advantage is its **cost-effectiveness**. Unlike hiring personnel for data entry or purchasing data from third-party providers, web scraping provides a more affordable option for businesses and researchers. Web scraping also gives users **access to publicly available data** on websites. This can include information such as product prices, customer reviews, or social media trends, which are valuable for market research and decision-making. Additionally, web scraping helps businesses make **data-driven** decisions by providing up-to-date and comprehensive datasets. For example, e-commerce platforms can use web scraping to monitor competitors' pricing strategies and adjust their prices accordingly. Moreover, web scraping is **highly scalable**, meaning that modern tools can extract data from numerous websites at once. This scalability makes it ideal for big data applications, where large volumes of data need to be processed quickly.

However, web scraping also has its challenges. One of the primary concerns is **legal and ethical** issues. Many websites prohibit scraping in their terms of service, and scraping these sites without permission can result in legal action or account bans. Additionally, websites often implement anti-scraping measures such as CAPTCHAs or IP **blocking** to prevent automated scraping, which can disrupt the scraping process and increase the resources needed to bypass these barriers. Another disadvantage is the issue of **inconsistent data**. Websites frequently update their structure or content, which can cause scraping scripts to break and require constant maintenance to keep them working. The initial setup for web scraping can also be **costly**. While web scraping may be affordable in the long run, setting up a robust scraping system and ensuring legal compliance can involve significant initial expenses.

Furthermore, there is the potential for **misuse**. Web scraping can be used for harmful purposes, such as spamming, stealing intellectual property, or invading user privacy, which raises important ethical concerns. Lastly, scraped data can sometimes be **poor quality**, containing errors, duplicates, or outdated information. This data requires thorough cleaning and validation before being used for analysis or decision-making.

Most privacy laws do not explicitly require websites to implement measures to protect against data scraping. Instead, the responsibility typically falls on organizations to define the rules in their terms of service and enforce them accordingly. However, this approach leaves significant gaps in safeguarding user privacy. Privacy laws should take a more proactive stance by mandating robust protections against data scraping, as unauthorized scraping can expose personal data to misuse (Solove, 2024).

For example, if a company were to directly transfer large volumes of personal information to third parties without user consent, such an act would clearly violate numerous privacy regulations, including the General Data Protection Regulation (GDPR) in the EU or the California Consumer Privacy Act (CCPA) in the USA. More detail about GDPR and CCPA will be explained in Chap. 10.

Similarly, failing to prevent third parties from extracting this data through scraping is effectively equivalent to sharing or selling it without consent, as it results in the same erosion of user privacy. Addressing this loophole through stricter legal requirements would strengthen data protection frameworks and ensure organizations prioritize user rights over convenience or profit.

Advantages and disadvantages of data mining

Data mining is a powerful technique that helps organizations uncover valuable patterns and insights from large datasets. The advantages of data mining include its ability to provide **knowledge-based** data, enabling organizations to make data-driven decisions and implement profitable changes in their operations and production processes. Compared to other statistical data analysis tools, data mining is **cost-efficient**, making it accessible for many organizations. It supports the decision-making process by identifying hidden patterns and predicting future trends and behaviors. Additionally, data mining techniques can be **seamlessly** integrated into existing systems or incorporated into new platforms. This quick and efficient process allows users, even those new to the field, to analyze vast amounts of data in a short time, contributing to better strategic planning and business performance.

However, the disadvantages of data mining include **ethical and technical challenges**. For instance, organizations may misuse customer data by selling it to third parties for financial gain, raising privacy concerns. Reports indicate that companies like American Express have sold customer credit card purchase data, while platforms like Meta have been criticized for selling user data, such as locations and browsing behavior, for targeted advertising. Moreover, many data mining tools **require advanced training** to operate, making them less accessible for non-experts. The diversity in data mining algorithms also complicates the selection of appropriate tools, as different algorithms yield varying results. Furthermore, data mining techniques are **not always accurate**, which can lead to significant errors or undesirable consequences in critical applications, such as healthcare or financial forecasting.

8.10 Future Challenges

The future of web scraping and data mining faces several challenges, which need to be addressed to ensure the accuracy and effectiveness of these techniques. One of the main challenges is **data quality**. Data often contains errors, missing values, outliers, or inconsistencies, which can lead to incorrect or misleading results. To handle these issues, data preprocessing and cleaning techniques are essential. However, these steps can be time-consuming and require significant resources, especially when dealing with large datasets.

Another challenge is the **volume and dimensionality** of data. With the rapid growth of digital data, data mining techniques often need to manage massive datasets. The sheer size of the data makes storage, processing, and analysis complex tasks. As a result, advanced methods and tools are needed to handle and extract valuable insights from such large volumes of data.

The **complexity of real-world** data is also a significant issue. Much of the data available today is unstructured, heterogeneous, and complex. This diversity makes it difficult to develop algorithms that can effectively mine all types of data. Researchers and data scientists are continuously working to create more advanced techniques that can manage and process these complex datasets.

Domain-specific challenges add another layer of complexity to data mining. Different fields or industries have unique characteristics, and understanding the specific context and constraints of each domain is vital. For example, data mining techniques that work well in one area, such as healthcare, may not be effective in another, like finance. Therefore, domain knowledge plays a crucial role in applying data mining techniques successfully.

Lastly, **privacy and security** concerns are significant when it comes to data mining. Many data mining processes involve extracting insights from sensitive and personal information, raising concerns about how this data is used and protected. Striking a balance between effective data mining and ensuring privacy and security is a delicate issue that requires careful consideration of ethical standards and legal regulations.

Easy to Digest Box

Web scraping and data mining are important in data science because they ***help gather and understand information*** *from the internet and other places. With web scraping and data mining, we can do:*

1. ***Finding patterns***: *Just like finding the most popular ice cream flavor, data mining helps us see patterns in huge amounts of data.*
2. ***Saving time***: *Web scraping can quickly gather data from many websites, saving a lot of time that would be spent doing it manually.*
3. ***Helping make decisions***: *If scientists are studying how weather changes affect crops, they can use web scraping to gather all the weather information they need and use data mining to see how it affects crop growth.*

8.11 Summary of Key Points

- Web scraping refers to collecting and structuring the data from web sources in a more convenient format. It involves no processing or review of the data.
- Data mining refers to analyzing large datasets to reveal useful information and patterns. It does not require data processing or extraction.
- The data mining types can be divided into two basic parts: (1) Predictive data mining analysis and (2) descriptive data mining analysis.
- Domain-specific challenges and privacy and security are still the main future challenges.

8.12 Hands-on Experience

Working with RStudio

Web scraping and mapping COVID-19 Data in Japan

This part demonstrates how to use **RStudio** to scrape data from the web, clean and process it, and create visualizations, including maps. We use various R libraries, including rvest for web scraping, tidyverse for data manipulation, ggplot2 for plotting, and tmap for creating maps. Let's begin step by step.

Practice 8

Learning Objectives

Understand the Basics of Setting up an R Environment:

- Learn how to check and set the working directory in R.

- Install and load necessary libraries for web scraping and data manipulation (e.g., rvest, tidyverse).

Acquire skills in web scraping:

- Learn how to scrape data from a webpage (e.g., COVID-19 statistics from Wikipedia).
- Explore and inspect the scraped HTML content.
- Extract relevant tables from HTML documents and convert them into data frames.

Data cleaning and transformation:

- Clean the extracted data by renaming columns, removing unnecessary rows, and correcting specific data points.
- Convert data types (e.g., from text to numeric) for analysis and visualization.

Data visualization using bar plots:

- Create bar plots to visualize the distribution of COVID-19 cases by prefecture using ggplot2.
- Explore different ways to visualize data, such as cumulative cases by region.

Save data for future use:

- Learn how to export data to a CSV file for storage or further analysis.

Mapping COVID-19 data:

- Load shapefiles representing Japan's administrative boundaries.
- Prepare and clean spatial data for visualization (e.g., removing unnecessary columns, renaming columns).
- Merge COVID-19 data with spatial data (shapefiles) for mapping purposes.

Creating maps with spatial data:

- Visualize COVID-19 data on a map using the tmap package.
- Add base maps, thematic fills, and other map elements (e.g., borders, compass, legends, and titles).
- Customize map aesthetics and layout to improve readability and presentation.

Advanced map customization:

- Classify regions based on the number of COVID-19 cases (e.g., high, medium, low).
- Use color schemes to visualize classified data on the map.
- Add advanced map features such as scale bars, logos, and credits.

Apply mapping skills for effective data communication:

- Use maps to communicate complex data insights clearly and visually.
- Incorporate additional map elements (e.g., logos, credits, compass) to enhance the map's informative value.

Setting up the environment

We start by checking the working directory, setting it, and installing and loading the required libraries. The working directory is set to the folder where we store the data files.

```
# Check the current working directory
getwd()
# Set working directory
setwd("/path/to/your/folder") # Replace with your
directory
# Install and load necessary libraries
# install.packages(c("rvest", "tidyverse") #
Install if not already installed
library(rvest).
library(tidyverse)
```

Web scraping COVID-19 data

The COVID-19 statistics are scraped from a Wikipedia page. After loading the webpage into an R object, we extract and inspect its content.

```
# Web Scraping
covid < - read_html("https://en.wikipedia.org/wiki/Statistics_of_
the_COVID-19_pandemic_in_Japan")
# Checking the data
class(covid)
covid
# Viewing raw text data
html_text(covid)
```

We extract the relevant table from the HTML document and clean the data.

```
# Extracting table elements
tab< - covid %>% html_nodes("table")
```

```
# Select and convert Table 1
tab < - tab[[1]] % > % html_table(header = TRUE, fill =
TRUE)
# Rename column headers and remove unnecessary rows
tab < - tab % > % setNames(c("Island", "Region",
"Prefecture", "Cases", "Deaths"))
tab < - tab[-c(1, 49, 50, 51, 52),]
# Correct specific data points
tab$Prefecture[43] < - "Nagasaki Prefecture"
tab$Cases[43] < - 1246
```

Visualizing COVID-19 data
To visualize the data, we create a bar plot showing cases by prefecture.

```
# Convert data types
tab$Cases < - as.numeric(tab$Cases)
tab$Deaths < - as.numeric(tab$Deaths)
# Create a bar plot.
ggplot(tab) + geom_col(aes(x = Prefecture, y = Cases,
fill = factor(Region))) + theme(axis.text.x = element_
text(size = 5, angle = 45, vjust = 0.5)) + labs(title =
"COVID-19 Cases by Prefecture", x = "Prefectures", y
= "Cases", fill = "Prefecture")
```

Output:

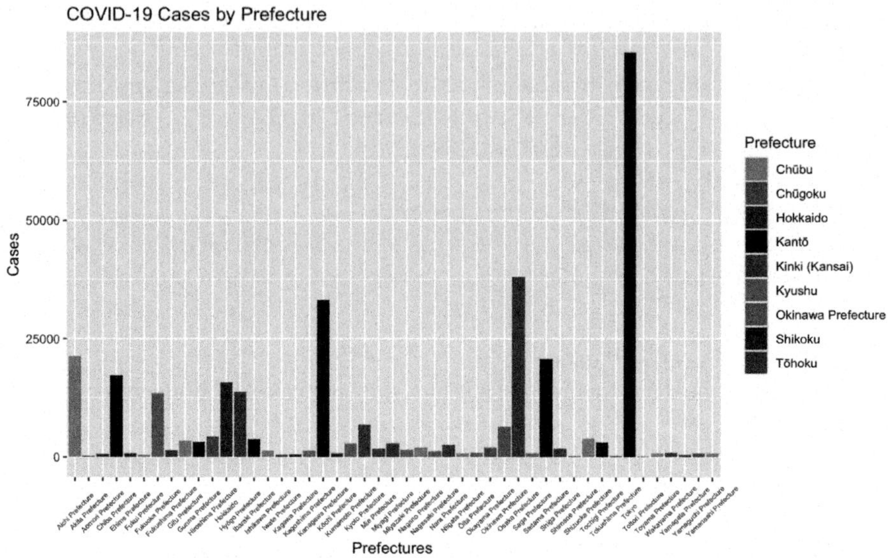

We can also visualize in a simpler way using the following code; it will plot the COVID-19 cases by Region.

```
# Create a new dataframe with cumulative cases by
Region
tab_new < - tab % > %
group_by(Region) % > %
mutate(Total_Cases = cumsum(Cases))
# Plot in cumulative
ggplot(tab_new, aes(x = Island, y = Cases, fill =
factor(Region))) +
geom_col() +
theme(axis.text.x = element_text(size = 9, angle = 45,
vjust = 0.5)) +
labs(title = "COVID-19 Cases by Region", x = "Region",
y = "Cases", fill = "Region")
```

Output:

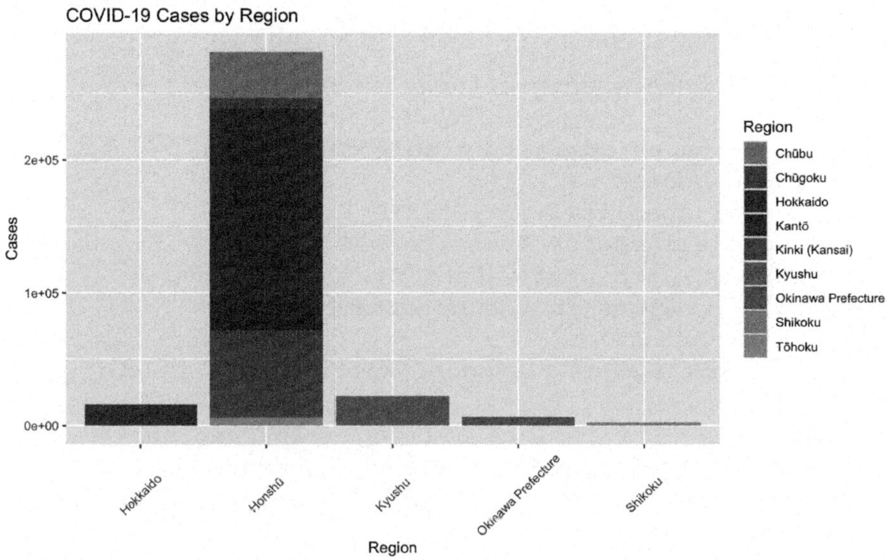

Finally, if needed you can save the data in CSV format using the code:

```
# Save in CSV format
write.csv(tab,"your/path/jpn_covid19.csv",
row.names = FALSE) # change with your path
```

Mapping COVID-19 Data in Japan

To create a map, we load Japan's administrative boundaries from a shapefile and merge it with the COVID-19 data.

```
# Load shapefile and libraries
library(sf)
library(dplyr)
library(tmap)
japan_admin < - st_read("jpn_admbnda_adm1_2019.shp")
#make sure the shapefile is stored in the working
directory
# Check if the shapefile has any invalid geometries
is_valid< - st_is_valid(japan_admin)
# If the shapefile has invalid geometries, fix them
using st make_valid()
```

```
if (!all(is_valid)) {
japan_admin <- st_make_valid(japan_admin)
}
# Delete unnecessary columns except Prefecture's
name
japan <- japan_admin %>% select(ADM1_EN)
# Rename header
colnames(japan)[c(1)] <- c("ID")
# Remove all spaces from the "ID" column
japan$ID <- str_trim(japan$ID)
# replace values in the dataframe
library(stringr)
rep_str = c('Hyōgo' = 'Hyogo','Kōchi' = 'Kochi','Ōita' =
'Oita')
japan$ID <- str_replace_all(japan$ID, rep_str)
# Remove "Prefecture" from each element
tab_new$Prefecture < - gsub("Prefecture", "", tab_
new$Prefecture)
tab_new$Prefecture < - str_replace_all(tab_
new$Prefecture, rep_str)
# Delete unnecessary columns except "Prefecture",
"Cases"
tab_new <- tab_new[, c("Prefecture", "Cases")]
# Rename header
colnames(tab_new)[c(1)] <- c("ID")
# Remove all spaces from the "ID" column
tab_new$ID <- str_trim(tab_new$ID)
# Merge data to shapefile
merge_data <- left_join(japan, tab_new, by = "ID")
japan_covid <- merge_data
```

We then use the tmaptools and OpenStreetMap package to visualize the data on a map. But before that, make sure you have Java installed in your system. If it is not, visit the following website to download:

For Windows: https://www.oracle.com/java/technologies/downloads/#jdk23-windows

For MacOS: https://www.oracle.com/java/technologies/downloads/#jdk23-mac

```
# Install and load required the libraries
install.packages(c("OpenStreetMap", "tmaptools",
"rJava"))
```

```
library(rJava)
library(OpenStreetMap) # make sure you have Java in
your system
library(tmaptools)
# Create a bounding box for base map
osm_world <- read_osm(japan_covid)
# Plot map with tmap
tm_shape(osm_world) + tm_rgb() +
tm_shape(japan_covid) +
tm_fill("Cases", palette = "YlOrRd", # you can add
(-YlOrRd) to create opposite color
style = "pretty", title = "Number of Cases") +
tm_borders(alpha = 0.4) +
tm_compass(type = "arrow", position = c("right",
"top")) +
tm_layout(main.title = "COVID-19 Pandemic in Japan",
main.title.position = "center",
main.title.color = "red",
legend.text.size = 0.7,
legend.title.size = 1,
legend.position = c("right", "bottom"),
frame = T)
```

Output:

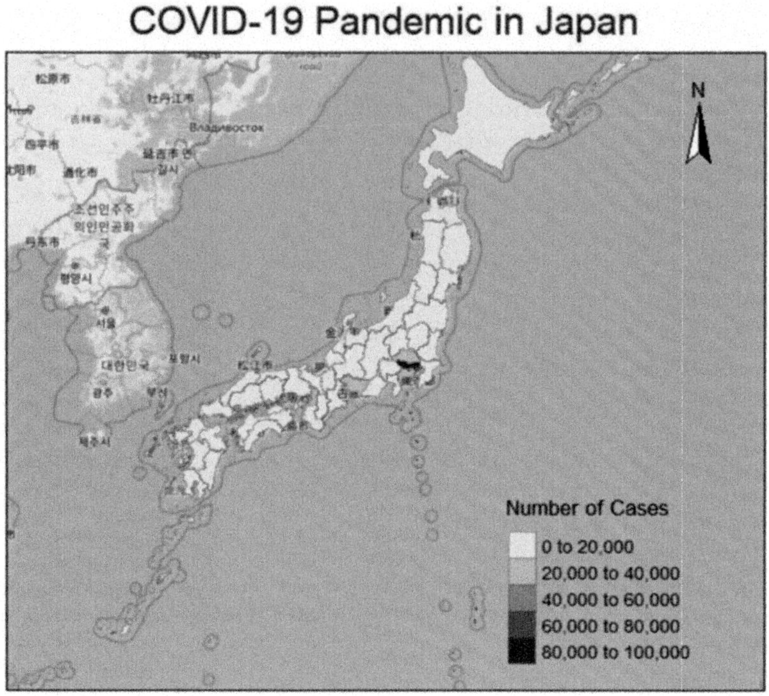

Advanced mapping

For advanced mapping, we classify prefectures by the number of cases into **high**, **medium**, and **low** and visualize the classified data.

```
# Reclassify cases
japan_covid$Classification < - "Low"
japan_covid$Classification[japan_covid$Cases > 12000]
< - "High"
japan_covid$Classification[japan_covid$Cases > =
2000 & japan_covid$Cases < = 12000] < - "Medium"
#Noted: When reclassifying, always check the data
first. For example, 12,000 is classified as "high"
here, but in your dataset, it might be considered
"low."
# Create classification map
# Plot reclass map using tmap
tm_shape(osm_world) + tm_rgb() +
 tm_shape(japan_covid) +
```

```
 tm_fill("Classification", palette = "Spectral",
 style = "pretty", title = "Classification Cases") +
 tm_borders(alpha = 0.4) +
 tm_compass(type = "4star", position = c("right",
"top")) +
 tm_layout(main.title = "COVID-19 Pandemic in Japan",
 main.title.position = "center",
 main.title.color = "red",
 panel.labels = c("as of 2021/01/17"),
 panel.label.color = "black",
 legend.text.size = 0.7,
 legend.title.size = 1,
 legend.position = c("right", "bottom"),
 frame = T) +
 tm_scale_bar(position = c("left", "bottom")) +
 tm_logo ("https://web.dpipe.tsukuba.ac.jp/wp-content/uploads/sites/19/
2018/05/UTLogo2.png",
 height = 1.5) +
 tm_credits("Data source: multiple sources",
fontface = "italic", align = "right") +
 tm_credits("Author: Data Science Class", fontface =
"bold", align = "right") +
 tm_legend(position = c("left", "top"), bg.color =
"grey80") +
 tm_style("natural", frame.lwd = 5)
```

Output:

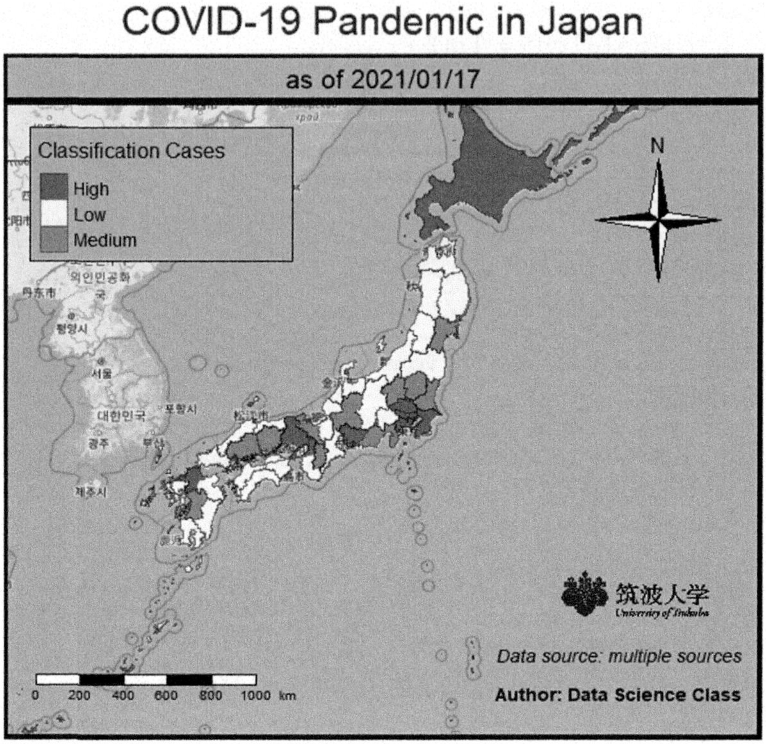

What does the code do?

Reclassify COVID-19 cases:

- Assigns the value "low" to all rows in the classification column of the japan_covid dataset.
- Updates the classification to "high" for rows where the cases exceed 12,000.
- Updates the classification to "medium" for rows where the cases are between 2000 and 12,000 (inclusive). If you want the legend shows in order, you need to modify the script. Convert to ordered factor to control legend order japan_covid$Classification <- factor(japan_covid$Classification, levels = c("Low", "Medium", "High"))

Prepare a classification map:

- Uses the tmap package to create a map displaying the classifications of COVID-19 cases.
- The base map (osm_world) is rendered with RGB imagery using tm_rgb().

Map visualization for COVID-19 classifications:

- The classification column in japan_covid is visualized using colored fills (tm_fill) with a "spectral" palette and a "pretty" style.
- Adds borders around regions using tm_borders.

Enhancements for map readability:

- Adds a **compass** with a 4-star design in the top-right corner (tm_compass).
- Includes a **title** "COVID-19 Pandemic in Japan" centered at the top in red.
- Displays a **panel label** with the date ("as of 2021/01/17").

Map legend and layout configuration:

- Adjusts **legend text and title size**, positions the legend at the bottom-right, and applies a frame around the map.
- Adds a **scale bar** at the bottom-left of the map (tm_scale_bar).

Branding and credits:

- Includes a **university logo** at the top of the map (tm_logo).
- Adds credits for the data source and authorship, styled with different font weights and alignments (tm_credits).

Styling and framing:

- Applies a "natural" style theme and sets a thick border around the map using frame.lwd = 5.

Reference

Solove, D. J. (2024). Artificial intelligence and privacy. 77 Florida Law Review (forthcoming Jan 2025), GWU Legal Studies Research Paper No. 2024-36, GWU Law School Public Law Research Paper No. 2024-36, Available at https://doi.org/10.2139/ssrn.4713111

Chapter 9
Natural Language Processing and Sentiment Analysis

Abstract In this chapter, natural language processing (NLP) and sentiment analysis are introduced by defining their key concepts, exploring their historical evolution, and explaining how they complement each other. Various types, architectures, and tools used in these fields are examined, with a focus on their advantages, limitations, and practical applications. Future challenges and emerging trends in NLP and sentiment analysis are also discussed. The second part of the chapter provides hands-on experience using R for text and sentiment analysis, covering data preparation, cleaning, and visualization of the most frequently occurring words, along with the creation of a word cloud to effectively represent the processed data.

Relation to Other Chapters: Extends web scraping data sources (Chap. 8) to textual analysis, Building a bridge to ethical concerns in Chap. 10.

9.1 Introduction

Natural language processing (NLP) is a vital area within artificial intelligence (AI) that empowers computers to process, understand, and respond to human language in meaningful ways. This rapidly evolving technology forms the backbone of numerous everyday applications, such as virtual assistants like Siri and Alexa, automated customer service chatbots, and real-time translation tools like Google Translate. At its essence, NLP focuses on developing algorithms and computational methods that enable machines to interpret, analyze, and even generate human language, bridging the gap between human communication and machine understanding. Sentiment analysis is a key area of NLP that helps extract insights into human emotions and opinions expressed in written text, playing a crucial role in fields like marketing, social media monitoring, and public opinion analysis (Bird et al., 2009; Jurafsky & Martin, 2023). This chapter explores the fundamental aspects of NLP, including its history, core techniques, and diverse applications, with special attention to sentiment analysis.

F. Ramdani, *Data Science: Foundations and Hands-on Experience*,
https://doi.org/10.1007/978-981-96-4683-8_9

9.2 Definition

Natural language processing

Natural language processing is an interdisciplinary field that combines linguistics, computer science, and AI to analyze and interpret human language. Unlike structured data, human language is complex, ambiguous, and context-dependent, making NLP an essential tool for extracting meaningful insights. Its fundamental tasks include:

1. Tokenization

Tokenization breaks text into smaller units like words or sentences. For instance, the sentence "*I love data science*" would be tokenized into individual words: *I*, *love*, *data*, *science*. Tokenization underpins most NLP pipelines by preparing text for computational analysis.

2. Part-of-speech (POS) tagging

POS tagging assigns grammatical labels—such as nouns, verbs, or adjectives—to words. For instance, in the sentence "*She plays soccer,*" *she* would be tagged as a pronoun and *play* as a verb. This helps machines grasp the syntactic roles of words in sentences.

3. Named entity recognition (NER)

NER identifies entities such as names, locations, or dates within the text. For example, in the sentence "*Ultraman visited Paris in 2024,*" *Ultraman* would be tagged as a person, and *Paris* as a location.

4. Stemming and lemmatization

These techniques reduce words to their base forms, aiding in uniform text representation. For instance, *runs*, *running*, and *ran* are reduced to their root form, *run*. Lemmatization ensures the reduced form is a valid dictionary word, enhancing semantic interpretation. Figure 9.1 illustrates all of these tasks using a sentence of ***"Sato and Ito went to the University of Tsukuba to study data science techniques in 2025."***

Sentiment analysis

Sentiment analysis, often referred to as opinion mining, is a specialized application of natural language processing (NLP) that aims to determine the emotional tone or subjective information conveyed in a piece of text. This process involves examining text to uncover underlying sentiments such as emotions, opinions, attitudes, and the polarity of the sentiment, which could be positive, negative, or neutral. Sentiment analysis can be performed on various sources of text data, including social media posts, customer reviews, survey responses, news articles, and more (Liu, 2012; Pang & Lee, 2008).

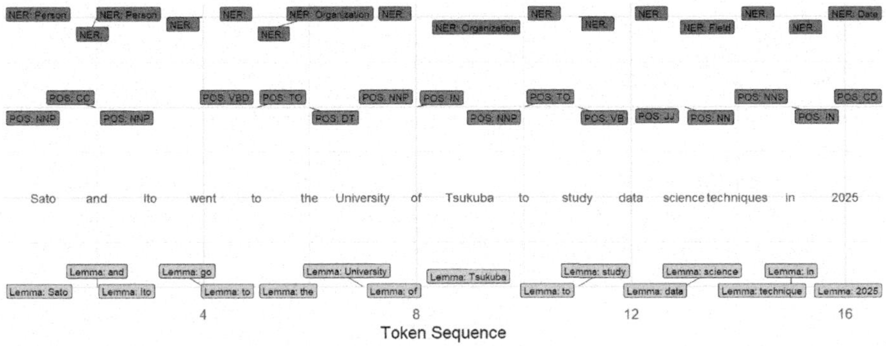

Fig. 9.1 Illustration of the tokenization, where the token is shown in blue, POS tagging in green, NER in red, and lemma in yellow

The primary objective of sentiment analysis is to automatically classify the sentiment expressed in a text into categories (e.g., positive, negative, or neutral) or to conduct a more detailed analysis by assigning numerical sentiment scores or estimating the intensity of emotions (Medhat et al., 2014). This technology has a wide range of practical applications, such as gauging public opinion on products and services, monitoring social media trends, predicting fluctuations in financial markets, enhancing customer support strategies, and refining product development based on user feedback.

Key methods in sentiment analysis include:

- **Rule-based approaches**: These rely on predefined lexicons of positive and negative words.
- **Machine learning models**: Algorithms like Naive Bayes and support vector machines classify sentiment based on labeled training data.
- **Deep learning models**: Advanced architectures like recurrent neural networks (RNNs) and transformers analyze complex linguistic patterns.

Natural language processing (NLP) is a way for computers to understand and work with human language, like how we talk or write. It helps computers read, listen, and even respond to us in a way that makes sense. For example, when you ask Siri or Alexa a question, NLP helps them understand what you're saying and give an answer.
Sentiment analysis is a special part of NLP. It helps the computer figure out if a piece of text (like a sentence or tweet) is happy, sad, angry, or any other feeling. Imagine you read a message like "I love playing video games!"—the computer can say that it's a happy sentence. But if the message says "I hate doing homework," the computer can tell that it's a sad or angry sentence.

Example

1. ***NLP:*** *If you talk to a robot and say, "What's the weather like today?" the robot will use NLP to understand your words and answer, "It's sunny today!":*
2. ***Sentiment analysis:*** *If you read a comment like "I love this course!" the computer can say it's a positive or happy feeling. But if the comment says, "This course is boring," it can tell it's a negative or sad feeling.*

9.3 Brief History

1940s–1950s: Early beginnings

The roots of natural language processing (NLP) can be traced back to foundational advancements in computing and artificial intelligence in the mid-twentieth century. In 1943, Warren McCulloch and Walter Pitts introduced the "McCulloch-Pitts Neuron," a computational model of neural networks that provided theoretical insights into how machines could process information similarly to the human brain. This work was pivotal for early computational approaches to language processing. The 1950s marked the emergence of machine translation as a focal area of NLP research. Notable among these efforts was the Georgetown Experiment in 1954, which showcased a system capable of translating Russian sentences into English. This demonstration was primarily rule-based, relying on extensive human-crafted grammar and syntax rules. Such rule-based methods set the tone for the initial decades of NLP research, despite their inherent limitations in scalability and flexibility.

1960s: Challenges and setbacks

The 1960s saw a surge of interest in creating machines that could interact naturally with humans, exemplified by projects like ELIZA (1964), a program designed to simulate conversation. However, ELIZA's reliance on pattern-matching algorithms without true comprehension highlighted the limitations of early NLP systems. The enthusiasm of the 1950s waned by 1966 when the Automatic Language Processing Advisory Committee (ALPAC) report revealed that machine translation research had failed to deliver practical results, leading to funding cuts. This setback contributed to the first "AI Winter," where progress in NLP stagnated due to a lack of resources and optimism.

1970s–1980s: Rule-based and statistical models

During the 1970s and 1980s, rule-based systems continued to dominate NLP. These systems relied on meticulously crafted linguistic rules, requiring significant manual effort to encode syntactic and semantic structures. The landscape began to shift in the 1980s with the introduction of statistical models, driven by the increasing availability of computational power and data. IBM's work on statistical methods, such as Hidden Markov Models (HMMs), replaced manually encoded grammar rules with probabilistic approaches. These methods demonstrated greater adaptability and scalability, signaling a paradigm shift in NLP research.

1990s: Statistical NLP

The 1990s were a transformative period for NLP, marked by the adoption of statistical techniques and machine learning models. Researchers leveraged a large corpora of text to train models for tasks such as part-of-speech tagging, parsing, and machine translation. Techniques like n-grams became foundational tools for analyzing text, enabling systems to predict word sequences based on statistical probabilities. This era saw the rise of data-driven methods, which consistently outperformed rule-based systems in accuracy and efficiency. The availability of annotated datasets and computational resources further accelerated progress.

2000s: Rise of sentiment analysis

The early 2000s marked the emergence of sentiment analysis as a distinct application within NLP. Researchers developed algorithms to identify and classify opinions, emotions, and attitudes expressed in text, a capability that quickly found applications in domains like marketing, customer feedback analysis, and political discourse. Concurrently, the first neural network-based language models were proposed in 2001, heralding a new era of AI-driven NLP. These models began to leverage distributed word representations, setting the stage for significant advancements in language understanding.

2010s–present: Deep learning and self-supervised models

The 2010s marked a groundbreaking era in natural language processing (NLP), largely fueled by advancements in deep learning and self-supervised learning methods. A significant milestone came in 2013 with the development of models like `word2vec`, which introduced word embeddings capable of capturing semantic relationships between words. This innovation transformed key NLP applications such as machine translation and sentiment analysis by making them more accurate and context-aware (Mikolov et al., 2013).

By 2018, the emergence of transformer-based architectures revolutionized the field even further. Models like Bidirectional Encoder Representations from Transformers (BERT) and Generative Pretrained Transformer (GPT) achieved unprecedented levels of performance across a wide range of NLP tasks, from text classification to question answering (Vaswani et al., 2017). These self-supervised models, trained on vast amounts of textual data, demonstrated a remarkable ability to understand and generate human-like language. Their versatility has led to widespread adoption in diverse industries, including digital marketing, customer service, healthcare, and social media analytics.

Today, applications like sentiment analysis continue to be pivotal, benefiting from the steady progress in deep learning and the expanding role of artificial intelligence in everyday life. These tools not only enhance decision-making for businesses but also improve user experiences in domains such as content recommendation and brand monitoring, reflecting the transformative impact of NLP advancements over the past decade.

9.4 How It Works

Text preprocessing

Text preprocessing is a crucial initial step in sentiment analysis, designed to clean and prepare textual data for analysis. This process involves several tasks to standardize the input data and remove irrelevant or noisy information that may interfere with model performance. Common steps include the removal of punctuation, which eliminates unnecessary symbols that do not contribute to the sentiment; removal of stopwords, such as "the," "and," or "is," which are high-frequency words with little semantic meaning; and removal of special characters or numbers that do not hold relevance to the context of the text. Another key component is tokenization, a process that breaks the text into individual words or tokens, enabling further analysis at a granular level. Advanced preprocessing may also include lemmatization (reducing words to their base forms) or stemming (trimming words to their root forms). These techniques help ensure that variations of words like "running" and "ran" are treated as equivalent. Preprocessing is essential for reducing dimensionality and ensuring the text is in a form that machine learning models can interpret effectively.

Feature extraction

After preprocessing the text, the next crucial step is feature extraction, where meaningful features or attributes are identified to serve as inputs for machine learning models. This process bridges the gap between unstructured text data and structured formats that models can analyze effectively. One widely used method is calculating word frequency counts, which measure how often specific words occur in the text. Another common approach involves using n-grams, which are sequences of consecutive words or tokens—such as bigrams like "very good" or trigrams like "not very good"—to capture contextual relationships between words. Techniques like part-of-speech (POS) tagging identify grammatical categories (e.g., nouns, verbs, and adjectives), while syntactic dependency parsing maps the grammatical relationships between words in a sentence, providing deeper insights into sentence structure.

Advanced feature extraction techniques go further in capturing semantic meaning and context. For instance, term frequency–inverse document frequency (TF-IDF) highlights important words by balancing their frequency in a document against their occurrence across a collection of documents. Word embeddings, such as Word2Vec, GloVe, or fastText, represent words as dense vectors in a high-dimensional space, capturing their semantic relationships and contextual usage. These methods allow machine learning models to better understand patterns, relationships, and meanings within text data.

Feature extraction is an essential step in text processing, transforming raw, unstructured text into a structured representation suitable for computational analysis. Without it, machine learning models would struggle to extract meaningful insights from textual data (Mikolov et al., 2013).

Sentiment classification

Sentiment classification involves identifying and assigning a specific sentiment label—such as positive, negative, or neutral—to a piece of text. This process plays a key role in sentiment analysis and relies on machine learning or statistical techniques trained using labeled datasets. These datasets include text samples that have been annotated with corresponding sentiment labels, helping the model recognize patterns and relationships within the data. Commonly used models range from simple algorithms like logistic regression, which is easy to implement, to more advanced techniques such as Support Vector Machines (SVM), known for their ability to handle high-dimensional data effectively.

Statistical methods like Naive Bayes classifiers are also widely used because they offer a good balance between simplicity and performance, especially in text classification tasks. Sentiment classification forms the foundation of sentiment analysis, enabling businesses and researchers to extract valuable insights from text data, such as customer feedback or social media posts. For more detailed information on this topic, see Pang and Lee's seminal paper on sentiment analysis (Pang & Lee, 2008) or explore modern advancements discussed in surveys like Liu's "Sentiment Analysis and Opinion Mining" (Liu, 2012).

Model training

Model training involves selecting and applying algorithms to build a predictive model that can classify sentiment accurately. Traditional models such as Naive Bayes and SVM are computationally efficient and work well for smaller datasets. However, for more complex or large-scale sentiment analysis tasks, deep learning models like recurrent neural networks (RNNs) and transformers have proven to be highly effective. RNNs, including variants like long short-term memory (LSTM) networks, excel at capturing sequential patterns in text, making them ideal for sentiment analysis. Transformers, such as BERT and GPT, leverage attention mechanisms to capture contextual relationships across sentences and documents. The choice of algorithm depends on factors like dataset size, computational resources, and the complexity of the sentiment analysis task.

Sentiment prediction, post-processing, and analysis

Once the model is trained, it can be used to predict the sentiment of new, unseen text data. The preprocessed text is input into the trained model, which assigns a sentiment label based on learned patterns. Post-processing may involve aggregating sentiment scores across multiple text samples, normalizing outputs, or combining results with metadata for a more holistic analysis. These results can be applied in diverse domains, such as understanding customer feedback, monitoring brand sentiment on social media, or identifying trends in public opinion. Sentiment analysis outcomes often

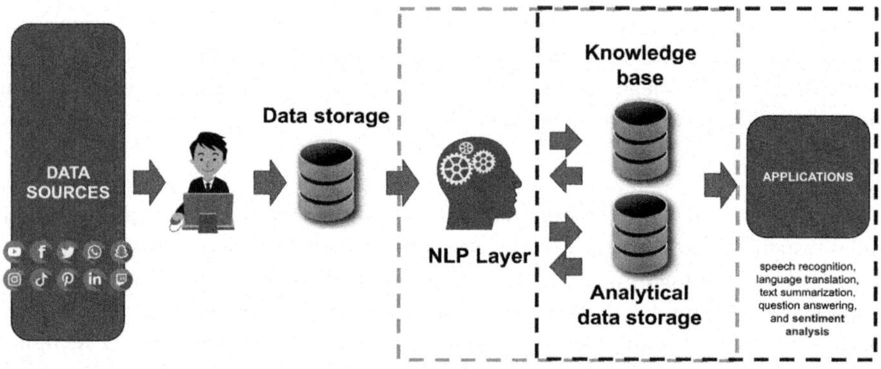

Fig. 9.2 Illustration of how NLP and sentiment analysis work

inform decision-making processes, guiding marketing strategies, public relations efforts, or policy decisions.

Figure 9.2 shows how data flows through a system designed for natural language processing (NLP) applications. The process starts with **data sources**, such as social media platforms (e.g., YouTube, Facebook, Twitter, TikTok, and others). A researcher or system collects this data and stores it in a **data storage system**, which organizes and keeps the data safe for further processing.

The **NLP layer** then analyzes the data using artificial intelligence. This layer is the advanced processing of language, such as understanding text or speech. The processed information is then divided into two parts: a **knowledge base**, which stores important facts and information, and an **analytical data storage**, where deeper analysis is conducted.

The results are used in **applications** such as speech recognition, language translation, text summarization, question answering, and sentiment analysis. These applications make the data useful for real-world purposes.

9.5 What Is NLP and Sentiment Analysis for?

As discussed in the earlier section, natural language processing (NLP) serves as the backbone of sentiment analysis, a method used to identify the emotional tone embedded within a piece of text. Sentiment analysis goes a step further by categorizing these emotions into three main categories: positive, negative, and neutral. This technique is extensively applied to extract meaningful insights from textual data, offering a deeper understanding of user opinions, customer feedback, or public sentiment. This combination of NLP and sentiment analysis has transformative applications across industries such as follows:

Customer feedback analysis

Businesses frequently collect customer feedback through surveys, reviews, and social media interactions. Sentiment analysis automates the process of analyzing this feedback by extracting meaningful insights from text data. For instance, analyzing reviews on e-commerce platforms helps businesses identify common customer concerns, preferences, or praise for specific features. This understanding allows companies to improve their products and services, enhance customer experience, and build stronger customer relationships. Studies have shown that companies effectively utilizing sentiment analysis can improve customer satisfaction and loyalty.

Social media monitoring

Social media platforms are a treasure trove of public opinion, making them an ideal target for sentiment analysis. Organizations monitor conversations around topics, events, or their brand to gauge public perception. For example, analyzing tweets during a product launch or a marketing campaign helps track the campaign's reception in real-time. Additionally, sentiment analysis identifies potential issues or crises by flagging negative trends. For example, detecting a surge in negative mentions of a product can prompt immediate intervention. This proactive approach to managing public perception can significantly protect and enhance a brand's reputation.

Market research

In market research, sentiment analysis helps companies analyze vast amounts of unstructured text, such as customer surveys, product reviews, or online forums. By understanding how consumers feel about products, trends, and competitors, businesses can make data-driven decisions. For instance, analyzing sentiment from online discussions about emerging products can reveal untapped market needs or preferences. This method is also widely applied to assess how a competitor's product resonates with consumers, offering insights that drive strategic planning.

Brand reputation management

Brand reputation is critical in today's competitive landscape, and sentiment analysis offers a way to measure and manage it effectively. By continuously analyzing mentions of their brand across digital platforms, companies can detect changes in sentiment and identify potential PR crises. For example, detecting a spike in negative feedback about a new advertising campaign allows a company to respond swiftly to prevent lasting damage to its reputation. This capability provides businesses with the tools to not only react to crises but also to strengthen their relationship with customers.

Financial analysis

Sentiment analysis is increasingly utilized in the financial sector to gauge market sentiment and predict trends. By analyzing news articles, earnings call transcripts, and social media posts, financial institutions can extract valuable insights into market moods and public perception of specific stocks or sectors. For instance, a surge in negative sentiment about a company due to a controversial decision can be an indicator of falling stock prices, guiding investment decisions. This application highlights how sentiment analysis can complement traditional financial models to provide a more holistic understanding of market dynamics.

9.6 Methods, Architectures, and Tools

Sentiment analysis methods

Rule-based methods

Rule-based methods in sentiment analysis rely on predefined rules, patterns, and linguistic structures to identify and classify sentiments in text. These rules are often constructed based on domain-specific knowledge or general sentiment patterns, such as identifying positive or negative words (e.g., "good," "bad") or detecting modifiers that change sentiment intensity (e.g., "very happy," "not satisfied"). Rule-based systems are interpretable and require no training data, making them suitable for applications where labeled datasets are unavailable. However, their limitations include poor generalization to new domains and difficulty in capturing nuanced sentiments, such as sarcasm or complex context.

Machine learning (ML) approaches

Machine learning (ML) techniques use algorithms that are trained on datasets with labeled examples to recognize patterns and connections between the features of text and sentiment categories (e.g., positive, negative, neutral). Common ML methods like Naive Bayes, support vector machines (SVM), and random forests are often employed to make these predictions. These models rely on feature engineering, which involves identifying important aspects of the text—such as word counts, combinations of adjacent words (n-grams), or values like term frequency–inverse document frequency (TF-IDF)—to extract meaningful information. One of the strengths of ML-based methods is their flexibility, allowing them to be adapted to different domains, compared to rule-based systems, which are often more rigid. However, ML approaches need large volumes of labeled data to work effectively, which can be a limitation. Over time, advancements in extracting relevant features and fine-tuning models have led to significant improvements in the performance and accuracy of sentiment analysis across a wide range of tasks. This progress has made machine learning a powerful tool for analyzing emotions in text, from customer reviews to social media posts (Cambria & White, 2014).

Lexicon-based methods

Lexicon-based methods depend on predefined sentiment lexicons or dictionaries containing words and phrases annotated with their sentiment scores. Examples include SentiWordNet and AFINN. These methods calculate the overall sentiment of a text by aggregating the sentiment scores of the words or phrases it contains. They are straightforward and interpretable, making them useful for initial analyses and applications with limited computational resources. However, these methods struggle with contextual understanding, such as when sentiment shifts due to negation or domain-specific language.

Deep learning approaches

Deep learning approaches have revolutionized sentiment analysis by leveraging models capable of learning hierarchical and contextual representations of text. Recurrent neural networks (RNNs), including LSTM and Gated Recurrent Units (GRU), are effective in capturing temporal dependencies in sequential data. Convolutional neural networks (CNNs), although primarily designed for image processing, excel in capturing local patterns in text, such as phrase-level sentiment. The advent of transformers, including BERT and GPT models, has further improved sentiment analysis by enabling models to capture global dependencies and nuanced contextual information. Deep learning approaches often outperform traditional methods in tasks requiring a deep understanding of language.

Text representation architectures

Bag-of-Words (BoW) model

The Bag-of-Words (BoW) model is a technique for representing text by treating it as a collection of individual words, without considering the order or grammar of those words. In this model, a document-term matrix is created, where each row represents a document and each column corresponds to a unique word found across all documents. The values in this matrix indicate the frequency of each word's occurrence in the document. Although BoW is straightforward and computationally efficient, it has limitations. Since it ignores word order and grammatical structure, it cannot capture the context or meaning behind word usage, making it less suitable for tasks that require understanding the deeper relationships between words or the nuances of sentence structure (Manning et al., 2008). As a result, it is often less effective for more complex language tasks, such as sentiment analysis or machine translation, where context plays a crucial role (Jurafsky & Martin, 2023).

Recurrent neural networks (RNNs)

Recurrent neural networks (RNNs) are a type of machine learning model specifically created to handle data that comes in sequences, such as time series or text. They work by maintaining internal states, also called "hidden states," that help capture the relationships between data points over time. This ability to understand the sequence of data makes RNNs especially useful for tasks like classifying text, analyzing sentiment, and identifying named entities (like people or places). However, RNNs are not perfect and have limitations, particularly when dealing with long sequences. To address these issues, more advanced versions like LSTM networks and Gated Recurrent Units (GRU) were developed. These variants help prevent a common problem in RNNs known as the "vanishing gradient" problem, allowing the model to learn long-term dependencies in data more effectively. However, despite their advantages, RNNs can still be computationally intensive and challenging to use in parallel, which makes them slower for large-scale tasks (Chung et al., 2014; Hochreiter & Schmidhuber, 1997).

Convolutional neural networks (CNNs)

Convolutional neural networks (CNNs), initially designed for image processing tasks, have been successfully adapted for natural language processing (NLP). These networks work by using convolutional layers that can identify local patterns within data, such as n-grams, which are sequences of n words that frequently appear together. This makes CNNs particularly useful for tasks like sentiment analysis, where understanding short sequences of text is key. One of the main advantages of CNNs is their computational efficiency—they can process text data in parallel, which speeds up processing and makes them suitable for real-time applications, such as chatbots or live feedback systems. However, CNNs have limitations when it comes to modeling long-range dependencies in text, meaning they may struggle to understand context from earlier parts of a sentence or document that influence later parts. This can affect their performance on more complex NLP tasks, especially when compared to other models like transformers, which are better at capturing long-term relationships in text (Vaswani et al., 2017).

Transformer models

Transformer-based models have significantly changed the field of NLP by utilizing self-attention mechanisms to better understand the relationships between different parts of a text. This allows them to capture global dependencies and context across long distances within the text. Popular models such as BERT and GPT are trained on large datasets, which allows them to learn language patterns and structures. They are then fine-tuned for specific tasks, such as sentiment analysis, text summarization, and question answering, and have set new performance standards in these areas.

These transformer models are particularly powerful because they can consider the context of words in both directions (from left to right and right to left), unlike previous models that processed text in one direction. This ability to understand the full context of a sentence or paragraph has made them highly effective for complex NLP tasks, including sentiment analysis, machine translation, and even creative text generation. However, despite their impressive capabilities, transformers require a lot of computational power to train and run, which can make them difficult to deploy on systems with limited resources (Vaswani et al., 2017; Radford et al., 2019).

Free tools and libraries for NLP and sentiment analysis

Natural language toolkit (NLTK)

The natural language toolkit (NLTK) is a crucial Python library that plays a significant role in the field of NLP. It is widely used for both research and the development of practical applications. NLTK provides a wide range of tools that assist in performing fundamental NLP tasks. These include tokenization, which breaks text into individual words or sentences; stemming, which simplifies words to their root forms; lemmatization, which transforms words into their dictionary or base forms; part-of-speech (POS) tagging, which identifies the grammatical categories of words in sentences; and sentiment analysis, which helps determine the emotional tone of text.

In addition to these functionalities, NLTK offers access to various linguistic resources such as WordNet, a large lexical database of English. Its modular design, which allows users to select only the tools they need, and its extensive documentation make NLTK accessible to both beginners and experienced researchers. While it remains one of the most popular libraries for NLP tasks, it's worth noting that NLTK's performance can be slower when compared to more modern libraries, like SpaCy or Hugging Face's Transformers, which are often optimized for speed and efficiency in larger-scale applications.

NLTK has been praised for its educational value, making it an ideal choice for those new to NLP. However, for large-scale, production-level NLP tasks, researchers may turn to alternatives that offer faster processing speeds. These considerations highlight the importance of choosing the right tool based on the specific needs of a project (Bird et al., 2009).

spaCy

spaCy is a powerful and efficient Python library designed for natural language processing (NLP). It's built for both speed and ease of use, allowing users to perform tasks such as tokenization (breaking text into individual words or phrases), named entity recognition (NER, identifying people, organizations, and other entities in text), part-of-speech (POS) tagging (labeling words with their grammatical role), and dependency parsing (understanding the grammatical structure of sentences). One of the key features that sets spaCy apart is its use of pretrained models, which makes it easier to handle complex tasks like sentiment analysis (determining the mood or emotion behind text) and recognizing entities. Moreover, spaCy can easily work with popular deep learning frameworks like PyTorch and TensorFlow, which makes it ideal for deploying machine learning models in real-world applications.

TextBlob

TextBlob is an intuitive and user-friendly Python library built on top of NLTK and pattern. It simplifies common NLP tasks, such as sentiment analysis, text translation, noun phrase extraction, and spell correction, through an easy-to-use API. TextBlob's sentiment analysis capabilities use a combination of rule-based algorithms and lexicon-based approaches, making it suitable for straightforward tasks. While it lacks the advanced capabilities and speed of spaCy, its simplicity and readability make it a popular choice for beginners or projects with limited computational demands.

Valence Aware Dictionary and sEntiment Reasoner (VADER)

VADER is a specialized sentiment analysis tool designed for short, informal text, such as social media posts and customer reviews. It employs a lexicon and rule-based approach to determine the polarity (positive, negative, neutral) and intensity of sentiments. Its primary advantage lies in its ability to handle slang, emoticons, and punctuation-based emphasis (e.g., exclamation marks). VADER is lightweight, language-agnostic (to some extent), and integrates easily into Python workflows, making it a popular choice for social media analytics and customer feedback analysis.

Stanford CoreNLP

Stanford CoreNLP is a comprehensive Java-based library developed by Stanford University. It provides tools for tokenization, POS tagging, NER, sentiment analysis, dependency parsing, and more. Its robust architecture and high accuracy make it ideal for complex NLP tasks and research projects. While CoreNLP primarily runs on Java, wrappers are available for Python, R, and other languages, broadening its accessibility. CoreNLP also supports multilingual processing, making it a valuable resource for global projects. However, its Java foundation may present a learning curve for those unfamiliar with the language.

Considerations for usage

These tools and libraries are widely adopted in academia and industry due to their efficiency, versatility, and accessibility. However, it is essential to review their licenses and terms of use to ensure they align with your project requirements. For example, spaCy offers an open-source license but requires attribution, while Stanford CoreNLP has more restrictive licensing terms. Understanding these details is critical to ensuring ethical and legal compliance in your projects.

9.7 NLP Using R: Architecture and Tools

Bag-of-Words (BoW) model

The **Bag-of-Words (BoW)** model is a popular and straightforward method in natural language processing (NLP). It works by representing text as a set of individual words, ignoring grammar and the order in which the words appear, but keeping track of how often each word is used. Figure 9.3 shows Bag-of-Words matrix of three sentences: "I love data science and machine learning!", "Data science is fascinating and exciting.", and "Learning R is a great way to explore data science.". In this model, each document is turned into a vector, which is essentially a list of numbers. Each number represents how frequently a specific word from the overall vocabulary appears in the document. The BoW model is commonly used in various text analysis tasks, such as identifying spam emails, categorizing topics, and grouping similar documents together. By focusing on word frequency, BoW allows for simple and effective analysis of large amounts of text (Manning et al., 2008). However, while

```
Bag-of-Words Matrix:
> print(bow_matrix)
    Terms
Docs data learn love machin scienc excit fascin explor great way
   1    1     1    1      1      1     0      0      0     0   0
   2    1     0    0      0      1     1      1      0     0   0
   3    1     1    0      0      1     0      0      1     1   1
```

Fig. 9.3 Bag-of-Words matrix representation of sample sentences in data science context

it is easy to use, it does not capture the meaning or context of words, which is a limitation in more advanced NLP applications.

Tools:

- **tm package**: The **tm (text mining)** package in R provides several tools to preprocess text data, such as removing stopwords, punctuation, and other noise. It also includes functions to create a document-term matrix (DTM), which is essential for implementing the BoW model. This package allows users to clean and tokenize text data before applying machine learning algorithms to process it further. Functions like `tm_map()` enable users to manipulate and preprocess text data efficiently.

Documents with similar word frequencies might have similar content and words with high frequencies across documents are likely key topics in the corpus. The row index (`[1,]`, `[2,]`, etc.) represents a document:

- `[1,]` is the first document.
- `[2,]` is the second document, and
- `[3,]` is the third document.

The column names (e.g., `data`, `learn`, `love`, etc.) are the unique words extracted from the corpus. The cell values (e.g., `1`, `0`, `1`) show how many times each word appears in that document.

Term Frequency–Inverse Document Frequency (TF-IDF)

The **term frequency–inverse document frequency (TF-IDF)** model offers an improvement over the Bag-of-Words (BoW) approach by enhancing how the importance of words is determined. While BoW treats every word in the same way, TF-IDF assigns greater significance to words that appear frequently within a specific document but are rare across the entire collection of documents (the corpus). This feature makes TF-IDF especially useful for identifying distinctive terms that can help differentiate one document from another. The TF-IDF value is calculated by multiplying two components: term frequency (TF), which indicates how often a word appears in a document, and inverse document frequency (IDF), which gauges the rarity of a word across the corpus. By emphasizing the significance of less common terms and downplaying the influence of frequent but less meaningful words (such as "the," "is," or "and"), TF-IDF helps to focus on terms that are more relevant to the

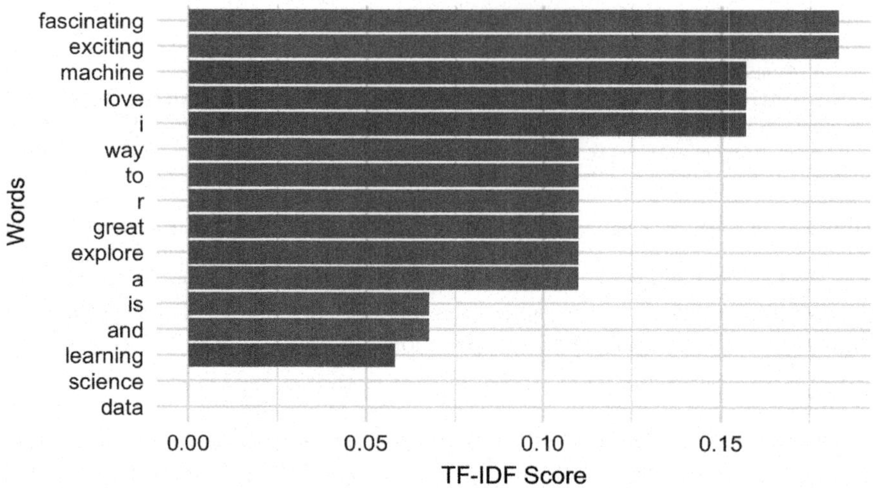

Fig. 9.4 TF-IDF scores for word relevance and document summarization

document's unique content. This approach is widely used in text mining, information retrieval, and natural language processing (NLP) tasks (Manning et al., 2008; Salton & Buckley, 1988). Figure 9.4 illustrates a bar chart plotted to show the TF-IDF scores of the words using three sentences: "I love data science and machine learning!", "Data science is fascinating and exciting.". Words with higher TF-IDF scores are highly relevant and unique to a specific document, making them valuable as keywords for summarization. In contrast, words with lower TF-IDF scores are either commonly found throughout the corpus (e.g., "data," "science") or frequently appear across multiple documents, making them less useful for distinguishing one document from another.

Tools:

- **tm package**: The **tm package** provides the function `weightTfIdf()` to compute TF-IDF values from a document-term matrix. This function adjusts the document-term matrix by incorporating the IDF score, allowing users to generate weighted document-term matrices for more accurate text classification or clustering tasks. The package also provides functions like `DocumentTermMatrix()` to create the initial DTM from raw text data.

Word embeddings

Word embeddings are a way to represent words as numerical values in a high-dimensional space, where words with similar meanings are placed close to each other. Unlike traditional methods such as BoW or TF-IDF, which focus on how often words appear in a text, word embeddings go a step further by considering the relationships between words. They do this by analyzing the context in which words appear in large amounts of text. Models like `Word2Vec` and `GloVe` are

```
> print("Similar words to 'data' (Word2Vec):")
[1] "Similar words to 'data' (Word2Vec):"
> print(similar_words("data", word_vectors_word2vec))
   science          r       love    explore        and
0.45971705 0.17163667 0.16433887 0.13611797 0.09510757
> # Find similar words for "data" using GloVe embeddings
> print("Similar words to 'data' (GloVe):")
[1] "Similar words to 'data' (GloVe):"
> print(similar_words("data", word_vectors_glove))
   science       love        and    explore         to
0.25371027 0.12870631 0.08833348 0.05950131 0.04723402
```

Fig. 9.5 Word-level relationships using Word2Vec and GloVe with cosine similarity analysis

used to create these embeddings, learning word relationships based on their usage patterns in a large corpus of text. This approach helps capture both the meaning (semantics) and the structure (syntax) of language. As a result, word embeddings have improved the performance of many natural language processing (NLP) tasks, including machine translation, sentiment analysis, and question answering (Mikolov et al., 2013; Pennington et al., 2014). Figure 9.5 illustrates the word-level relationships that were created using Word2Vec and GloVe packages using three sentences: "I love data science and machine learning!", "Data science is fascinating and exciting.". Cosine similarity is calculated to find words similar to a given word (e.g., "data"). The word "data" is most similar to "science," indicating they are often used in related contexts and words like "love" and "explore" are less similar but still contextually related to "data."

Tools:

- **wordVectors package**: The **wordVectors** package in R provides functions to work with pretrained word embeddings, such as `Word2Vec` and `GloVe`. It allows users to compute word similarities, find analogies (e.g., "king" − "man" + "woman" = "queen"), and perform vector arithmetic. The package also supports the training of custom word embeddings from a corpus, enabling users to tailor embeddings for specific domains or applications.

Sentiment analysis

Sentiment analysis is a popular task in natural language processing (NLP) that focuses on identifying the emotional tone or sentiment in a piece of text. The sentiment is generally categorized as positive, negative, or neutral, and this technique is widely applied in various fields, including social media monitoring, analyzing customer feedback, and conducting market research. The goal of sentiment analysis is to understand how people feel about certain topics, products, or services based on the text they produce. To perform sentiment analysis, text is typically classified by examining words or phrases that signal specific emotions or opinions. There are two main approaches for carrying out sentiment analysis: lexicon-based methods and machine learning models. Lexicon-based approaches rely on predefined lists of words with assigned sentiments, while machine learning models use statistical techniques to learn patterns in data. These models often depend on prelabeled datasets to train algorithms, enabling them to predict sentiment in new, unseen text (Cambria et al., 2013; Pang & Lee, 2008).

Tools:

- **tm package**: The **tm package** provides various text classification algorithms, such as **Naive Bayes**, **support vector machines (SVM)**, and **random forest**, which are widely used for sentiment analysis tasks. These algorithms can be applied to the preprocessed text data (such as tokenized and stemmed words) to classify the sentiment of text documents.
- **sentimentr package**: The **sentimentr** package provides a rule-based sentiment analysis approach. It assigns sentiment scores to individual words based on predefined sentiment dictionaries and then combines these scores to calculate the overall sentiment of a sentence or document. This method is particularly useful for analyzing short texts, such as tweets or product reviews. Figure 9.6 provides a visualization of the sentiment scores in a bar plot using three sentences: "I love data science and machine learning!", "Data science is fascinating and exciting.". In such plot, positive scores indicate positive sentiment (e.g., happiness, excitement, love) while negative scores indicate negative sentiment (e.g., sadness, anger, frustration), and scores close to zero indicate neutral sentiment.

Neural Networks

Neural networks have become an essential tool in NLP, playing a critical role in tasks such as understanding emotions in text (sentiment analysis), translating languages, and identifying specific information like names or places (named entity recognition).

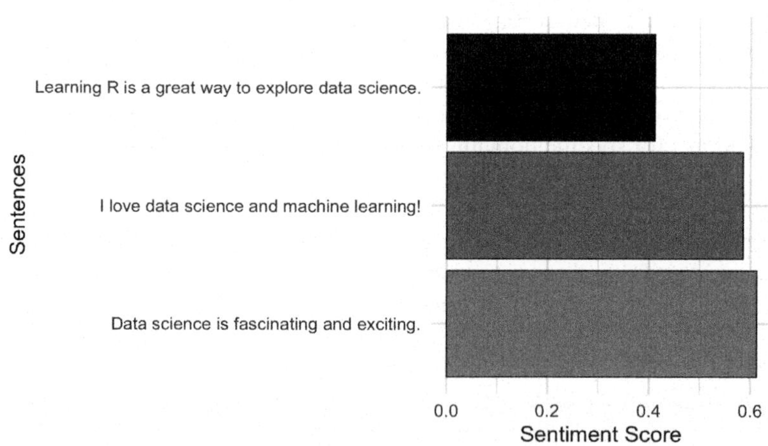

Fig. 9.6 Visualization of the sentiment scores in a bar plot

In particular, deep learning models—such as RNNs, LSTM networks, and transformers—have significantly advanced NLP. These models improve the accuracy of predictions and allow for a deeper understanding of the text. They are able to identify connections between words that are far apart in a sentence, which is crucial for tasks that involve sequences, like processing language. This is because language is often composed of patterns and relationships that span over long stretches of text, and these models are well-suited to capture such complexities. Tools like R offer frameworks that allow researchers and developers to apply neural network-based models to various NLP tasks, helping them tackle challenges more effectively (Goodfellow et al., 2016; Vaswani et al., 2017).

Tools:

- **keras package**: The **keras** package in R provides an interface to the popular deep learning framework Keras, which runs on top of TensorFlow or Theano. Keras allows users to build and train neural networks with a high-level API, making it accessible even for beginners. It provides modules for creating sequential models, adding layers (such as LSTM, dense, or Conv1D), and compiling models for training. This package is often used for advanced NLP tasks, including sentiment analysis, text classification, and named entity recognition.
- **text package**: The **text** package in R provides tools for text preprocessing, including tokenization and embedding generation, and is specifically designed for NLP tasks. It also allows the creation of deep learning models, particularly for tasks like sentiment analysis and topic modeling. This package integrates seamlessly with Keras and TensorFlow, enabling users to train complex neural networks for text data efficiently.

9.8 Advantages and Disadvantages

Advantages of natural language processing

Text summarization

One of the significant advantages of NLP is its ability to automatically generate summaries from large documents or articles. Text summarization is vital for users who need quick access to key information without sifting through lengthy content. Automated summarization techniques can provide concise, relevant insights by identifying the most important sections of a text, thus improving user experience and decision-making. This capability is particularly useful in industries such as journalism, research, and business, where time is of the essence.

Efficiency

NLP significantly enhances efficiency by automating the processing of vast volumes of text data. Human efforts that would otherwise be spent on manual data processing and analysis can be reduced, allowing businesses and organizations to focus on strategic tasks. For instance, NLP techniques such as named entity recognition and part-of-speech tagging can quickly sift through data to extract relevant information, enabling rapid insights. This automation saves time and effort, making it a powerful tool for applications in areas such as customer service, market research, and data management.

Language understanding

NLP enables computers to understand and interpret human language, allowing for more natural interactions with users. By processing syntactic structures and semantic meanings, NLP technologies can enable systems like chatbots, virtual assistants, and search engines to understand user queries and provide contextually appropriate responses. This advancement is crucial for improving communication between humans and machines, fostering more accurate and efficient interactions across various applications, such as customer support and virtual healthcare.

Data extraction

One of the key advantages of NLP is its ability to extract valuable information from unstructured text. This includes identifying entities, relationships, and concepts that are vital for data mining and knowledge extraction. For example, NLP can identify names of people, places, or organizations in a news article, providing structured data that can be further analyzed or integrated into other systems. This capability is particularly useful in industries such as healthcare, finance, and legal fields, where accurate and timely information is critical.

Machine translation

Machine translation is another important advantage of NLP, as it allows for the translation of text between languages, thus breaking down language barriers. With advancements in NLP, automated translation tools, such as Google Translate, have become more accurate, facilitating communication between people who speak different languages. This has vast applications in international business, travel, and education, as it enables individuals and organizations to connect across linguistic divides.

Disadvantages of natural language processing

Ambiguity

Natural language is inherently ambiguous, and NLP models can struggle to accurately interpret context or determine the intended meaning of words or phrases. For instance, the word "bank" could refer to a financial institution or the side of a river, and NLP systems may misinterpret the meaning without understanding the context in which the word is used. This challenge is compounded in languages with multiple meanings for words or phrases.

Cultural and contextual bias

NLP models can inadvertently reflect biases embedded in the training data, leading to unfair or inaccurate results, especially in sensitive areas such as gender, race, and religion. These biases are often a result of the data being sourced from historical texts or specific demographic groups. If not carefully managed, this bias can perpetuate discrimination or skewed interpretations of language.

Language complexity

Different languages present unique challenges in NLP due to their varying grammatical structures, syntax, and cultural contexts. For example, languages like Japanese, Chinese or Arabic have different sentence constructions and vocabulary compared to English, which can make it difficult for NLP models trained in one language to perform equally well in others. This linguistic diversity creates challenges for developing universal NLP systems that are robust across all languages.

Domain specificity

NLP models trained on general language data may not perform well in specialized domains such as medicine, law, or technology, where specialized terminology and nuanced meanings are common. For instance, medical texts contain complex jargon that may require domain-specific models to ensure accurate interpretation. Without proper adaptation or retraining, NLP systems may fail to understand domain-specific language, leading to errors in analysis.

Data requirements

To function optimally, NLP models often require large amounts of high-quality, annotated training data. This data must be representative of the target language and domain, and acquiring and annotating this data can be both time-consuming and costly. In many cases, the lack of sufficient or diverse data can hinder the performance of NLP models, particularly in less commonly spoken languages or specialized fields.

Advantages of sentiment analysis

Customer support

Sentiment analysis plays a pivotal role in customer support by automatically categorizing and prioritizing customer feedback. It can identify negative sentiments or unresolved issues, ensuring that they are quickly addressed by support teams. This automation enhances customer service efficiency, enabling companies to respond faster and more effectively to customer concerns.

Customer insight

Sentiment analysis provides valuable insights into customer opinions, preferences, and emotions, helping businesses understand their target audience better. This understanding can drive product development, marketing strategies, and customer experience improvements. By analyzing sentiment from various sources, such as reviews and social media, companies can adapt their offerings to meet customer expectations.

Brand monitoring

Sentiment analysis enables organizations to monitor their brand's reputation in real-time by analyzing online discussions. Positive or negative sentiments expressed on social media platforms, forums, and review sites can be tracked, helping businesses proactively manage their public image. This ability to gauge public opinion provides companies with the insights needed to adjust marketing tactics or address emerging issues.

Market research

Sentiment analysis can be a powerful tool for market research by analyzing public sentiment toward products, services, or trends. By identifying consumer attitudes and opinions, businesses can make more informed decisions about product launches, promotions, or market positioning. This enables companies to stay ahead of trends and better align their strategies with consumer preferences.

Social media analysis

Sentiment analysis is widely used for social media analysis, where large volumes of text data are generated daily. By analyzing sentiments in social media posts, companies can gain a better understanding of public opinion, monitor trending topics, and identify emerging issues. This analysis is especially valuable in crisis management, allowing businesses to quickly respond to negative sentiment before it escalates.

Disadvantages of sentiment analysis

Contextual challenges

One of the main drawbacks of sentiment analysis is its difficulty in understanding the context of certain statements. Sentiment analysis tools may struggle to detect sarcasm, irony, or subtle nuances in text. For instance, a statement like "Great, another delay" may be classified as positive, even though it is likely expressing frustration. Without contextual awareness, sentiment analysis models may misinterpret the true sentiment of a statement.

Subjectivity

Sentiment analysis is inherently subjective, as different people may interpret the same text differently. One individual may view a product review as positive, while another may see it as negative due to personal preferences or cultural differences. This subjectivity makes it difficult to achieve 100% accuracy, especially in cases where the sentiment is not clearly expressed.

Accuracy

Achieving high accuracy in sentiment analysis can be challenging due to the complexities of human emotion and expression. Sentiment can be influenced by various factors such as tone, context, and individual biases, making it difficult for automated systems to consistently interpret sentiment correctly. Furthermore, sentiment analysis models may struggle to deal with mixed or neutral sentiments, which are often prevalent in real-world data.

Data limitations

The accuracy of sentiment analysis heavily depends on the quality and diversity of the training data. Biased or unrepresentative data can lead to inaccurate sentiment classifications. For instance, a sentiment analysis model trained primarily on positive reviews may struggle to classify negative sentiments accurately. As a result, ensuring the availability of high-quality, diverse datasets is essential for building robust sentiment analysis models.

Multilingual challenges

Sentiment analysis in multilingual environments presents its own set of challenges. Language-specific nuances, such as idioms, slang, and cultural context, can significantly affect the accuracy of sentiment analysis in different languages. Moreover, the availability of high-quality training data for each language is not always guaranteed, which can lead to less reliable results in multilingual applications.

9.9 Future Challenges

Privacy and security

One of the most significant challenges in the development and deployment of natural language processing (NLP) models is ensuring the privacy and security of the data used to train these models. Many NLP systems rely on large datasets, which often contain personal or sensitive information, such as communication logs, health data, and financial records. The need to gather and process this data for model training poses a considerable risk to individual privacy, especially with the growing use of personal data in various applications like healthcare, customer service, and marketing. Thus, researchers must strike a delicate balance between leveraging rich datasets for model improvement and safeguarding privacy. Techniques such as differential privacy, federated learning, and secure multi-party computation are emerging as potential solutions, allowing models to learn from data without exposing sensitive information. Ensuring that these privacy-preserving techniques are both effective and scalable remains a critical challenge for the future.

Handling noisy and informal text

Another key challenge in NLP is dealing with noisy and informal text, which is increasingly prevalent on social media, messaging platforms, and user-generated content. Text in these domains often contains misspellings, abbreviations, slang, and non-standard grammar, which makes it difficult for traditional NLP models to accurately process and understand the content. For example, sentiment analysis models that typically rely on well-formed sentences may struggle with informal or unconventional expressions, leading to misinterpretations of sentiment. To improve the robustness of NLP systems, researchers must develop techniques that can better handle noise and variance in language, such as spelling correction algorithms, context-aware models, and advanced preprocessing methods. Moreover, handling mixed-language text, such as code-switching or multilingual content, remains a crucial area of research to enhance NLP performance in real-world applications.

Emotion detection

While sentiment analysis focuses primarily on classifying text as positive, negative, or neutral, understanding the full spectrum of emotions expressed in text is much more complex. Human emotions are nuanced, and their expression can vary significantly across different cultures, contexts, and individual personalities. Developing NLP models capable of detecting and understanding emotions like joy, anger, surprise, and fear, as well as more subtle emotional states such as frustration or empathy, requires more than just analyzing sentence-level sentiment. Fine-grained annotation of emotional content and the development of emotion-specific models are essential to address this challenge. Moreover, the ambiguity inherent in textual data (e.g., sarcasm, irony, or mixed emotions) further complicates emotion detection tasks. Researchers are focusing on multimodal emotion recognition, which combines text with other data sources, such as facial expressions or voice tone, to improve the accuracy of emotion detection. However, more work is needed to refine models capable of understanding emotions in varied and diverse textual contexts.

Explainability and interpretability

Modern NLP models, especially those based on deep learning, face significant criticism for being "black boxes." This term refers to the models' lack of transparency regarding how they make decisions. This opacity is particularly concerning in fields like healthcare, finance, and law, where understanding why a model reaches a certain conclusion is critical. In these high-stakes areas, being unable to explain the reasoning behind a model's decision can erode trust and accountability, which can limit the widespread use and effectiveness of these technologies. As a result, improving the explainability and interpretability of NLP models has become an important area of research.

Researchers are exploring various techniques to enhance the transparency of these models, including attention mechanisms, saliency maps, and model-agnostic interpretability methods (Chen et al., 2018; Ribeiro et al., 2016). These approaches aim to reveal how models weigh different pieces of input data when making decisions. However, the challenge lies in making these explanations accurate and easy to understand, particularly for individuals who are not experts in machine learning. This means that, while progress is being made, there is still much work to be done to ensure that the explanations provided by NLP models are both useful and accessible. Ultimately, developing models that are interpretable and trustworthy is essential to encourage their adoption in sensitive and impactful areas, ensuring they are used ethically and responsibly.

Easy to Digest Box

Natural language processing, or NLP, is like teaching computers how to read, write, and understand human language. Imagine you're talking to a friend, and you use words to share your thoughts and feelings. Computers don't naturally understand words like we do—they mostly understand numbers and codes. NLP helps computers learn how to make sense of the words we say or type so they can talk to us or help us solve problems.

Sentiment means feelings—like being happy, sad, angry, or excited. Sentiment Analysis is when a computer tries to figure out how someone feels by looking at the words they use. For example, if someone writes, "This movie is amazing! I loved it," the computer might decide that the person feels happy or excited about the movie. If someone says, "This was the worst day ever," the computer might guess that the person feels upset.

In data science, we use NLP and sentiment analysis to understand people better. Imagine you're a toy store owner, and you want to know if kids like your toys. You could collect reviews where people say things like, "This toy is so much fun!" or "This toy broke too quickly." By using sentiment analysis, a computer could read all the reviews and tell you how many people feel happy about your toys and how many feel disappointed. This way, you can make better toys that kids will love.

9.10 Summary of Key Points

- Natural language processing (NLP) is a subfield of artificial intelligence (AI). It is used to understand, interpret, and generate human language in a way that is meaningful and useful.
- Sentiment analysis is a specific application of NLP that focuses on determining the sentiment or subjective information expressed in a piece of text. To identify emotions, opinions, attitudes, and polarity (positive, negative, or neutral).
- Types of NLP: Rule-based methods, machine learning (ML) approaches, lexicon-based methods, deep learning approaches.
- Multilingual and language complexity is one of many disadvantages of NLP.
- NLP models often work as black boxes, making it challenging to understand the reasoning behind their predictions.

9.11 Hands-on Experience

Working with RStudio

Practicing with natural language processing (NLP)

In this practice, we will work through an example that involves text preprocessing, exploring word frequencies, and performing sentiment analysis using R. Below is a detailed guide to help you understand and apply the concepts.

Practice 9

Learning Objectives

Preprocess Text Data:

- Gain proficiency in using the `tm` package for text preprocessing tasks.
- Learn how to clean text data by converting to lowercase, removing punctuation, numbers, and common stopwords.
- Understand how to handle text encoding issues and create a text corpus.
- Learn how to apply stemming and whitespace removal in text data.

Create and manipulate a Term-Document Matrix (TDM):

- Learn how to create a Term-Document Matrix (TDM) using the `TermDocumentMatrix()` function.
- Understand how to sort words by frequency and display the top frequent words in a dataset.

Visualize Word Frequencies:

- Understand how to create a bar plot to visualize word frequencies.
- Learn how to use the `wordcloud` package to visualize frequent words in a more engaging format.
- Explore the use of `wordcloud2` for creating customized word clouds with different shapes and designs.

Perform Sentiment Analysis:

- Learn how to perform sentiment analysis on text data using the `syuzhet` library.
- Understand how to visualize sentiment scores with bar plots to assess the overall sentiment of the text.

Visualize and Analyze Advanced Sentiment Data:

- Learn how to combine word frequencies with sentiment analysis results to create a comparison cloud.

- Understand the use of sentiment lexicons (e.g., "bing" sentiment lexicon) and how to visualize positive and negative sentiments in a word cloud.

Enhance Text Analysis with Advanced R Packages:

- Learn how to use `reshape2` and `tidytext` packages to manipulate and analyze text data in more complex ways.
- Understand how to join sentiment data with word frequencies and use functions like `acast()` for reshaping the data for advanced visualizations.

Downloading and loading data

Always check the current working directory, set working directory where you save the files if needed:

```
# Check the current working directory
getwd()
# Set working directory
setwd("/path/to/your/folder") # Replace with your
directory
```

First, we need to download the dataset from the provided link and set up the working directory. The data we used in this practice is from https://github.com/finnstats/finnstats/blob/main/Data1.csv

```
# Load the dataset
Apple <- read.csv("Data1.csv", header = T)
# View the structure of the dataset
str(apple)
```

Text preprocessing

Text preprocessing is a crucial step in NLP to clean and prepare text for analysis. We use the **tm** package to remove unnecessary characters, punctuation, numbers, and common stopwords. Additional steps like stemming and whitespace removal are also applied.

```
# Load the tm library
library(tm)
# Convert text encoding and create a corpus
Corpus         <         - iconv(apple$text) #If error:
iconv(apple$text, 'UTF-8', 'ASCII')
Corpus <- Corpus(VectorSource(corpus))
# Text cleaning: lowercasing, removing punctuation,
numbers, and stopwords
# ONLY FOR MAC USER put it before "tolower" function
#corpus <- tm_map(corpus, PlainTextDocument)
Corpus <- tm_map(corpus, tolower)
```

```
Corpus <- tm_map(corpus, removePunctuation)
Corpus <- tm_map(corpus, removeNumbers)
Cleanset <- tm_map(corpus, removeWords, stopwords('english'))
#No worries if you see a "Warning message:…". Just continue.
# Remove URLs and specific words
removeURL <- function(x) gsub('http[[:alnum:]]*', '', x)
cleanset <- tm_map(cleanset, content_transformer(removeURL))
cleanset <- tm_map(cleanset, removeWords, c('aapl', 'apple'))
# Replace specific words and apply stemming
Cleanset <- tm_map(cleanset, gsub, pattern = 'stocks', replacement = 'stock')
Cleanset <- tm_map(cleanset, stemDocument)
# Remove extra whitespaces
Cleanset <- tm_map(cleanset, stripWhitespace)
#No worries if you see a "Warning message:…". Just continue.
# Inspect the first five documents in the cleaned corpus
inspect(cleanset[1:5])
```

Output:

```
> inspect(cleanset[1:5])
<<SimpleCorpus>>
Metadata:  corpus specific: 1, document level (indexed): 0
Content:  documents: 5

[1] rt optionsnipp beat ep revenu see q rev bb est b
[2] rt optionsnipp beat ep revenu see q rev bb est b
[3] let see break timer
[4] NA
[5] wow suppos throwaway quarter beat million revenu trillion dollar compani
```

Analyzing word frequencies

After cleaning the text, we create a Term-Document Matrix (TDM) to analyze word frequencies. Words are sorted by their frequency, and the top words are visualized.

```
# Create a Term-Document Matrix
Tdm < - TermDocumentMatrix(cleanset)
Tdm < - as.matrix(tdm)
# Sort words by frequency
tdm_v < - sort(rowSums(tdm), decreasing = TRUE)
tdm_d < - data.frame(word = names(tdm_v), freq = tdm_v)
# Display the top 10 most frequent words
head(tdm_d, 10)
# Visualize the top 20 frequent words
barplot(tdm_d[1:20,]$freq,
 las = 2,
 names.arg = tdm_d[1:20,]$word,
 col = "lightgreen",
 main = "Top 10 Most Frequent Words",
 ylab = "Word Frequencies").
```

Output:

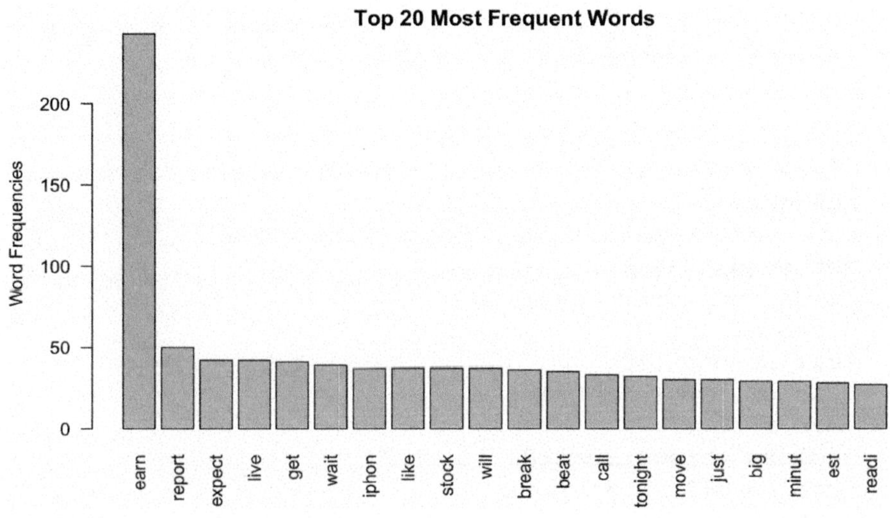

Visualizing word frequencies

To explore the word frequencies further, we use bar plots and word clouds. Word clouds provide an engaging way to visualize the importance of words in the dataset.

```
# Bar plot for words with frequency >= 25.
w < - rowSums(tdm).
w < - subset(w, w >= 25).
barplot(w,
```

```
  las = 2,
  col = rainbow(50),
  ylab = 'Count',
  main = 'Words Frequency').
```

Output:

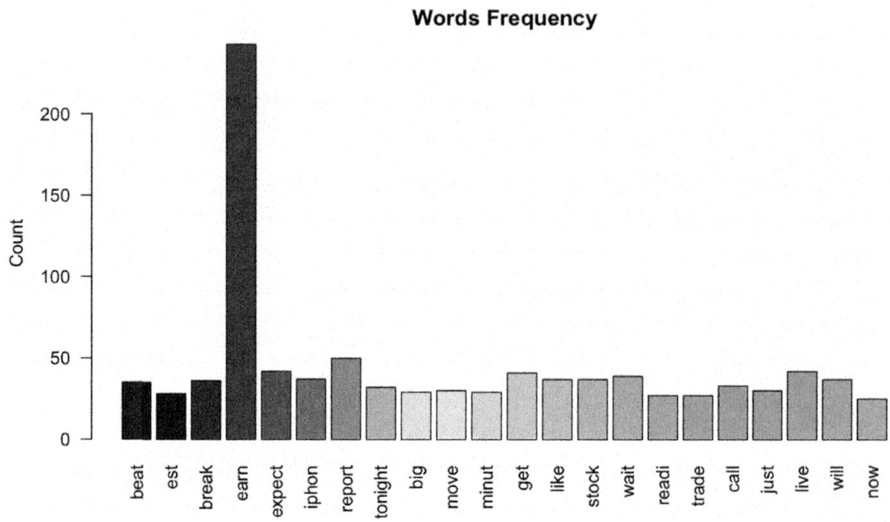


```
# Word cloud visualization
library(wordcloud) #install the package first if
needed.
w <- sort(rowSums(tdm), decreasing = TRUE)
set.seed(123)
wordcloud(words = names(w),
  freq = w,
  max.words = 150,
  random.order = FALSE,
  min.freq = 5,
  colors = brewer.pal(8, 'Dark2'),
  scale = c(5, 0.3),
  rot.per = 0.7).
```

Output:

```
# Wordcloud2 for a customized design
install.packages("wordcloud2")
library(wordcloud2)
w<- data.frame(names(w), w)
colnames(w)<- c('word', 'freq')
set.seed(123)
wordcloud2(w,
 size=0.7,
 shape='diamond',
 rotateRatio=0.5,
 minSize=1).
```

Output:

Sentiment analysis

Sentiment analysis helps us understand the emotions conveyed in the text. Using the **syuzhet** library, we extract sentiment scores and visualize them.

```
# Load sentiment analysis libraries
library(syuzhet)
library(ggplot2)
# Extract sentiments from text
tweets < - iconv(apple$text)
s < - get_nrc_sentiment(tweets)
#FOR MAC USER IF ERROR!
S < - get_nrc_sentiment(tweets, cl = NULL, language
= "english", lowercase = F) #it will takes time, be
patient.
# Plot sentiment scores.
barplot(colSums(s),
 las = 2,
 col = rainbow(10),
 ylab = 'Count',
 main = 'Sentiment Scores of Tweets').
```

Output:

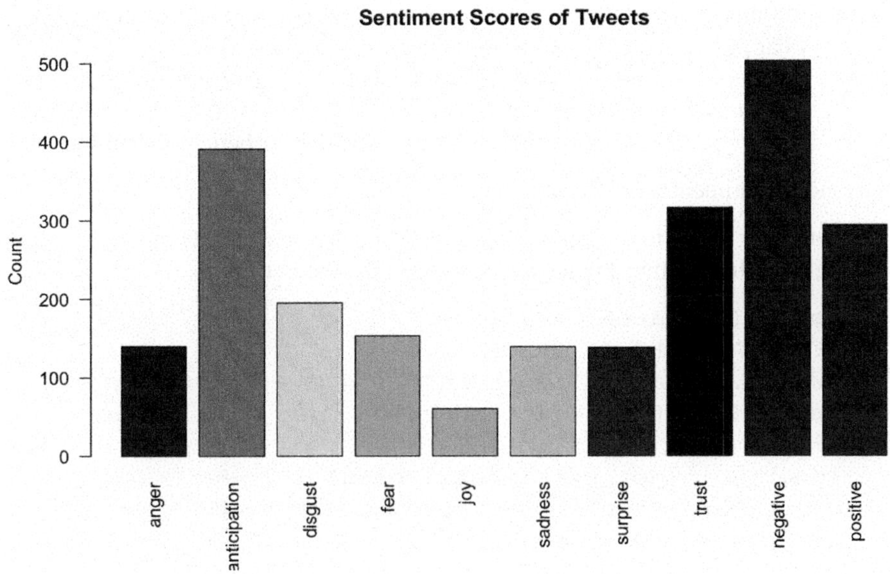

What does the code do?

This code performs sentiment analysis on a dataset of tweets related to "Apple stock performance in the Wall Street" and visualizes the sentiment scores. Following is a breakdown of what it does:

1. **Load required libraries**:
   - syuzhet: Used for text sentiment analysis.
   - ggplot2: Used for plotting, though it is not used directly in this snippet.
2. **Prepare the text data**:
   - The apple$text object presumably contains the text of tweets.
   - The iconv function converts the text into a readable encoding to avoid character encoding issues.
3. **Sentiment analysis**:
   - get_nrc_sentiment(tweets) computes sentiment scores for each tweet based on the NRC sentiment lexicon. This lexicon categorizes words into emotions (e.g., joy, anger, sadness) and sentiment (positive or negative).
   - The commented line with cl = NULL and language = "english" provides an alternative method for Mac users if an error occurs, with parameters allowing custom settings for case sensitivity and language.

4. **Visualize sentiment scores**:

   - colSums(s) calculates the total count of each sentiment across all tweets.
   - A bar plot is created with these summed sentiment scores.
   - The plot uses rainbow colors for bars, labels the y-axis as "count," and titles the plot as "sentiment scores of tweets."
   - las = 2 ensures the axis labels are perpendicular for better readability.

Advanced sentiment word visualization

We combine word frequencies and sentiments to create a comparison cloud, highlighting the positive and negative words in the dataset.

```
library(reshape2)
# FOR MAC USER IF ERROR!
Install.packages("tidytext")
library(tidytext) #for function 'get_sentiments'
w %>%
 inner_join(get_sentiments("bing")) %>%
 count(word, sentiment, sort = TRUE) %>%
 acast(word ~ sentiment, value.var = "n", fill = 0) %>%
 comparison.cloud(colors = c("red", "green"),
 max.words = 100).
```

Output:

What does the code do?

This R code analyzes the sentiment of words in a dataset and visualizes the results as a comparison word cloud. Following is a step-by-step explanation:

1. **Library loading**:

   - `reshape2`: Provides functions for reshaping data, such as acast.
   - `tidytext`: Offers tools for text mining, including sentiment analysis with predefined sentiment lexicons like "bing."

2. **Pipeline explanation**: The code uses a series of operations (% > % pipes) to process the data:

- **`inner_join(get_sentiments("bing"))`**:

  Joins the dataset w with the "bing" sentiment lexicon.
  The "bing" lexicon categorizes words into two sentiment categories: "positive" and "negative."
  Only words in both w and the "bing" lexicon are retained.

- **`count(word, sentiment, sort = TRUE)`**:

  Counts the occurrences of each word and its associated sentiment (positive or negative).
  The sort = TRUE argument ensures the results are sorted by count.

- **`acast(word ~ sentiment, value.var = "n", fill = 0)`**:

  Reshapes the data into a matrix where rows are words, columns are sentiment categories ("positive" and "negative"), and values are the word counts.
  fill = 0 ensures missing values are replaced with 0.

- **`comparison.cloud(colors = c("red", "green"), max.words = 100)`**:

  Creates a comparison word cloud, with "red" representing negative words and "green" representing positive words.
  Displays up to 100 words based on their frequency.

References

Bird, S., Klein, E., & Loper, E. (2009). *Natural language processing with Python.* O'Reilly Media.

Cambria, E., Schuller, B., Xia, Y., & Havasi, C. (2013). New Avenues in Opinion Mining and Sentiment Analysis. *IEEE Intelligent Systems, 8 (2), 15–21, https://doi.org/10.1109/MIS.2013.30

Cambria, E., & White, B. (2014). Jumping NLP curves: A review of natural language processing research. *IEEE Computational Intelligence Magazine, 9*(2), 48–57. https://doi.org/10.1109/MCI.2014.2307227

Chen, J., Song, L., & Ustun, B. (2018). Learning to explain: An information-theoretic perspective on model interpretation. *Proceedings of the 35th International Conference on Machine Learning*, 883–892. Available at https://arxiv.org/abs/1802.07814

Chung, J., Gulcehre, C., Cho, K., & Bengio, Y. (2014). Empirical evaluation of gated recurrent neural networks on sequence modeling. arXiv preprint arXiv:1412.3555. https://doi.org/10.48550/arXiv.1412.3555

Devlin, J., Chang, M. W., Lee, K., & Toutanova, K. (2019). BERT: Pre-training of Deep Bidirectional Transformers for Language Understanding. *Proceedings of NAACL-HLT*. Available at https://aclanthology.org/N19-1423/

Goodfellow, I., Bengio, Y., & Courville, A. (2016). *Deep Learning.* MIT Press.

Hochreiter, S., & Schmidhuber, J. (1997). Long short-term memory. *Neural Computation, 9*(8), 1735–1780. https://doi.org/10.1162/neco.1997.9.8.1735

Jurafsky, D., & Martin, J. H. (2023). *Speech and Language Processing* (3rd ed.). Pearson.

Liu, B. (2012). *Sentiment Analysis and Opinion Mining*. Morgan & Claypool Publishers.
Manning, C. D., Raghavan, P., & Schütze, H. (2008). *Introduction to Information Retrieval*. Cambridge University Press.
Medhat, W., Hassan, A., & Korashy, H. (2014). Sentiment analysis algorithms and applications: A survey. *Ain Shams Engineering Journal, 5*(4), 1093–1113. https://doi.org/10.1016/j.asej.2014.04.011
Mikolov, T., Chen, K., Corrado, G., & Dean, J. (2013). Efficient estimation of word representations in vector space. *arXiv preprint* arXiv:1301.3781. Available at https://arxiv.org/abs/1301.3781
Pang, B., & Lee, L. (2008). *Opinion Mining and Sentiment Analysis*. Foundations and Trends in Information Retrieval. Available at https://www.cs.cornell.edu/home/llee/omsa/omsa.pdf
Pennington, J., Socher, R., & Manning, C. D. (2014). Glove: Global Vectors for Word Representation. *Empirical Methods in Natural Language Processing (EMNLP)*. https://doi.org/10.3115/v1/D14-1162
Radford, A., Narasimhan, K., Salimans, T., & Sutskever, I. (2019). Language models are unsupervised multitask learners. *OpenAI Blog*. Available at https://cdn.openai.com/better-language-models/language_models_are_unsupervised_multitask_learners.pdf
Ribeiro, M. T., Singh, S., & Guestrin, C. (2016). "Why should I trust you?" Explaining the predictions of any classifier. *Proceedings of the 22nd ACM SIGKDD International Conference on Knowledge Discovery and Data Mining*, 1135–1144. Available at https://arxiv.org/abs/1602.04938
Salton, G., & Buckley, C. (1988). Term-weighting approaches in automatic text retrieval. *Information Processing & Management, 24*(5), 513–523. https://doi.org/10.1016/0306-4573(88)90021-0
Vaswani, A., Shazeer, N., Parmar, N., Uszkoreit, J., Jones, L., Gomez, A. A., Kaiser, Ł., & Polosukhin, I. (2017). Attention Is All You Need. *Advances in Neural Information Processing Systems (NeurIPS)*. Available at https://arxiv.org/abs/1706.03762

Chapter 10
Ethics and Reproducibility

Abstract The final chapter focuses on two fundamental topics in data science: ethics and reproducibility. Ethics and reproducibility are defined, emphasizing their importance in data handling. The principles of information ethics are examined, along with their connections to law, morality, and common sense. Examples of how different countries regulate personal information are provided to offer a global perspective. Key elements and best practices for ensuring reproducibility in research are outlined to reinforce the importance of transparent and repeatable methodologies. The second part introduces practical implementation using RStudio to create a project with Git. The process begins with setting up a GitHub account, creating a new repository, and installing Git on Windows or Mac. Subsequently, practical exercises include using "commit" and "push" commands to update the project on GitHub.

Relation to Other Chapters: This chapter synthesizes previous chapters' methods, focusing on ethical, reproducible practices, ensuring readers are equipped for responsible data science applications.

10.1 Introduction

The rapid growth of the information society has brought significant advancements but also new ethical challenges. Ethics, which refers to principles that govern behavior to avoid harm or discomfort to others, plays a crucial role in managing these challenges. In data science, ethical practices ensure responsible data handling, fostering trust and protecting individuals' rights. This chapter explores the principles of information ethics, legal frameworks, and reproducibility as fundamental aspects of ethical data science practices.

F. Ramdani, *Data Science: Foundations and Hands-on Experience*,
https://doi.org/10.1007/978-981-96-4683-8_10

10.2 Ethics in Data Science

Definition and Principles

Ethics, as defined by Merriam-Webster Dictionary, is the principles of conduct governing an individual or a group. Another definition is a set of moral issues or aspects. As an individual, ethics means a moral principle.

In information society, information ethics refers to what must be observed in order not to cause harm or inconvenience to others. The law stipulates **"what not to do,"** however, the ethics can be thought of as **"actions to be taken."** When working in an information society, the simple principle is **"do not cause trouble to others"** or **"do not make others uncomfortable."**

Ethical Challenges in Data Handling

Collecting and processing data bring immense benefits, such as enhanced decision-making and business insights. However, unethical practices, such as invasive profiling or excessive tracking, can lead to discomfort or privacy concerns among users. For instance, algorithms predicting customer behavior based on browsing history may overstep boundaries, leaving users uneasy about their personal information.

Severson's Four Principles of Information Ethics

Severson's Four Principles of Information Ethics, introduced in 1997, provide a framework for ethical decision-making in the use and management of information. These principles include four key statements: **respect for intellectual property**, which emphasizes acknowledging and protecting the rights of creators; **respect for privacy**, which ensures individuals' personal information is safeguarded and not misused; **fair representation**, which involves presenting information honestly and accurately without bias; and **non-maleficence or "doing no harm,"** which stresses avoiding actions that could cause harm to others. Along with these principles, Severson outlined a four-step method to guide individuals in addressing complex ethical situations. This approach serves as a practical tool for ensuring ethical conduct in information practices, particularly in today's digital age, where issues such as copyright, data privacy, and misinformation are increasingly significant.

The first step, "**Get the facts straight,"** emphasizes the importance of fully understanding the situation by gathering accurate and comprehensive information. Without a clear grasp of the facts, it becomes challenging to make informed ethical decisions. The second step is to "**Identify the moral dilemma,"** which involves recognizing and defining the ethical conflict, such as competing interests or values, that requires resolution. The third step, "**Evaluate using ethical principles,"** encourages applying established ethical concepts, such as respecting privacy, ensuring fairness, and promoting justice, to assess potential courses of action. Finally, the fourth step, "**Test the solution,"** calls for critically evaluating the proposed solution to ensure it is not only effective but also defensible under public scrutiny. This systematic framework helps individuals and organizations navigate complex ethical challenges responsibly, ensuring that decisions align with moral and societal standards.

10.3 Relationship Between Ethics, Law, Morality, and Common Sense

In the book "Data Science: How It Works" by Toshikatsu Masui (2022, in Japanese), there is an interesting figure showing the relationship between ethics, law, morality, and common sense. It shows how these concepts interact and influence each other, highlighting the distinctions between autonomous and heteronomous approaches, as well as individual (human) and societal (social) aspects (Fig. 10.1).

Ethics reflects its autonomous nature. Ethics involves self-governed principles and rational thinking to determine right and wrong. It often guides professional and personal decision-making processes independently of external rules. **Law**, on the other hand, represents a heteronomous and social framework. Laws are established by governments or authorities to regulate behavior and ensure order in society. Unlike ethics, laws are enforceable and are created based on societal agreements or norms.

Morals emphasize their connection to individual (human) values. Morality is shaped by cultural, religious, and personal beliefs about what is right or wrong. It is more subjective than law and ethics. **Common sense** highlights its reliance on intuitive and shared human understanding. It bridges practical reasoning and everyday social interactions, providing guidance based on collective experiences.

Ethics and morals align more with autonomous decision-making. In other words, you can control yourself using your own judgment or reason. In this case, ethics and moral control our sense of right and wrong instead of law. While ethics and law align more with social influences. Law is not just imposed from above (by authority), and ethics is not just personal—instead, they grow out of social life, and are developed together with people. Law and common sense lean towards heteronomy (being controlled by something outside of yourself, from "hetero" = other, and "nomos" = law). While common sense and morality lean towards humans as individuals. Our moral

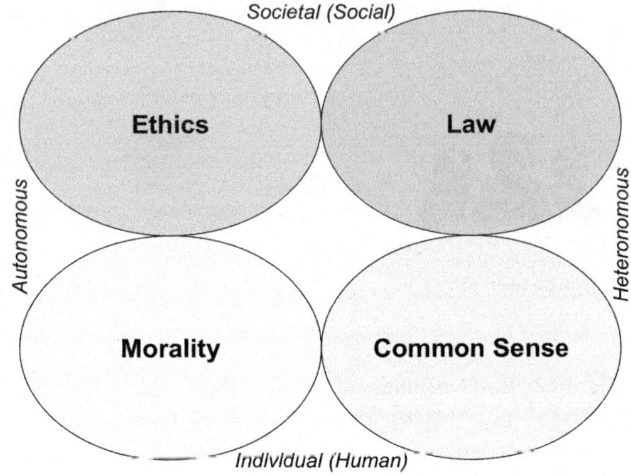

Fig. 10.1 Relationship between ethics, law, morality, and common sense. Inspired by "Data Science: How It Works" by Toshikatsu Masui (2022, in Japanese)

principles and our common-sense judgment work together in a way that values real people's feelings, needs, and situations. These elements form a dynamic framework for guiding human behaviour and societal norms.

10.4 Responsibilities and Balancing

Responsibilities of Users and Those Who Handle the Data

The concept of data ethics emphasizes the responsibilities of both users and those who handle the data, as presented in Fig. 10.2. It highlights the importance of transparency and ethical practices in data usage.

At the bottom left, there are users. These users are the data providers. They express the condition that their data should only be used when necessary and are informed of its purpose. This reflects the principle of user awareness and consent, which is critical in ethical data collection.

On the right side, individuals or entities handling data are depicted. These include analysts who process data and businesses that use the data to improve their operations, such as marketing or product distribution. A red dashed circle surrounds them, signifying the need for ethical conduct among those who manage, analyze, and use data. This includes respecting user privacy, avoiding misuse, and ensuring data security.

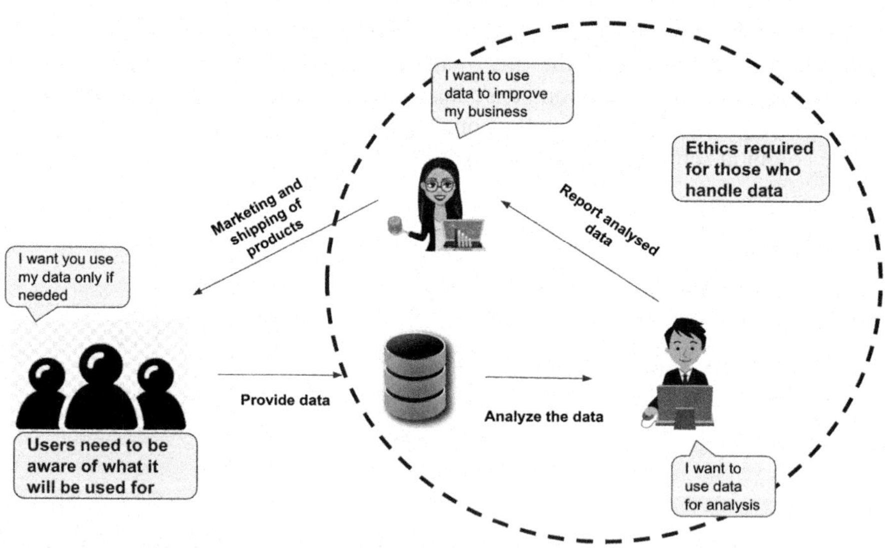

Fig. 10.2 Responsibilities of users and those who handle the data. Inspired by "Data Science: How It Works" by Toshikatsu Masui (2022, in Japanese)

The figure connects the users to the businesses and analysts through arrows. These arrows indicate data flow: users provide their data, which is then analyzed by professionals. Businesses use the analyzed data to make decisions, such as improving services or marketing strategies. This emphasizes the role of transparency in ensuring that all stakeholders understand how data is being used.

Figure 10.2 emphasizes the shared responsibility in maintaining data ethics—users need to be aware of their rights, while data handlers must adhere to ethical principles to maintain trust and accountability in data practices.

Balancing Between Public Interest and Company Profit

Achieving a balance between public interest and company profit is a critical challenge in today's data-driven world, requiring organizations to align ethical responsibilities with business objectives while ensuring transparency, fairness, and societal well-being. Figure 10.3 shows a balance between two aspects, public interest and company profit, presenting a conflict of priorities. The left side, representing the public interest, includes three key responsibilities: **duty of care, ensuring safety,** and **care for the environment.** These elements highlight the ethical and moral obligations to protect people and the planet. In the case of conflict between public interest and company profit, as data science researchers we must always have a basic principle to "Protect public safety in the event of conflict!"

On the right side, representing company profit, the priorities include **confidentiality, retention of credit,** and **business continuity.** These focus on maintaining the company's financial stability and operations, which are essential for long-term profitability. The scale visually symbolizes the need for a balance between these two aspects. Companies must navigate these conflicts carefully to uphold their social responsibilities while ensuring their survival and growth.

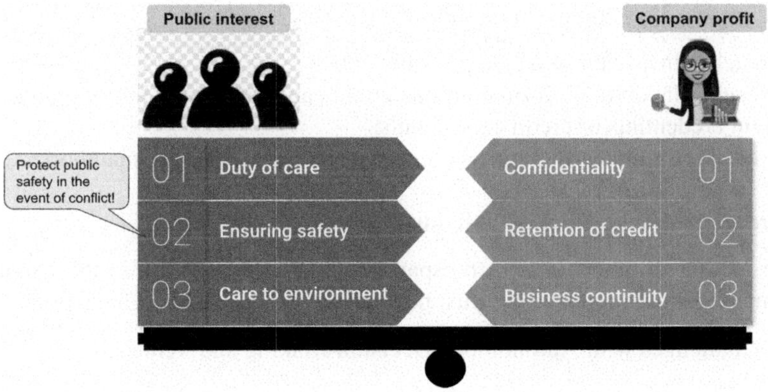

Fig. 10.3 Balancing between public interest and company profit. Inspired by "Data Science: How It Works" by Toshikatsu Masui (2022, in Japanese)

This balance is vital in industries where safety, environmental sustainability, and ethics intersect with economic objectives. Effective corporate governance and ethical frameworks can help organizations address these dilemmas responsibly.

10.5 Japan and Global Perspectives on Data Privacy

Data Privacy in Japan

The ethical handling of data often intersects with legal regulations. Examples include Japan's Personal Information Protection Law (個人情報保護法). The Personal Information Protection Law (PIPL) in Japan establishes legal guidelines for the handling of personal information. The law ensures individuals' personal information is managed responsibly and with their consent. According to the law, "personal information" is defined as data containing identifiable details about an individual, including a personal identification code. This framework was strengthened by a revision in June 2020, which came into effect in April 2022. The revision introduced the concept of "Personal Related Information," requiring explicit consent when sharing personal data with third parties. A summary of the law can be found at https://www.moj.go.jp/content/001345599.pdf.

Reporting Duties and Expanded Rights

Under the revised law, individuals' rights to manage their personal data have been expanded. Individuals can now request the suspension of the use of their personal data if they believe it has been misused. Additionally, businesses handling personal information have new responsibilities, including the obligation to notify the Personal Information Protection Commission and inform affected individuals in the event of a data breach. This applies in the following cases:

1. Breaches involving sensitive personal data.
2. Breaches involving information that could cause economic harm, such as stolen login credentials or credit card details.
3. Breaches for unlawful purposes, such as data stolen through unauthorized access or ransomware attacks.
4. Breaches affect over 1000 individuals.

These measures aim to ensure transparency and accountability in the handling of personal information, fostering trust between individuals and organizations.

Legal Challenges with Autonomous Decision-Making and Vehicles

The rise of autonomous decision-making systems, particularly in autonomous vehicles, has introduced new ethical and legal challenges. Discussions in Japan have focused on the need to disclose the logic and decision-making processes of these systems, as well as determining liability in accidents involving autonomous vehicles. To address these issues, the Road Traffic Act was amended in April 2020, allowing autonomous vehicles to operate under certain conditions. These amendments aim to balance innovation with public safety and accountability.

Privacy Regulations for Facial Recognition

Facial recognition data is categorized as personal information and is subject to strict privacy regulations under Japan's general information protection framework. For example, facial recognition systems implemented for crime prevention cannot be repurposed for marketing without obtaining consent. This ensures that sensitive biometric data is not misused and that its collection and usage remain ethical.

Geolocation Privacy Concerns

Geolocation data, such as GPS information, is also treated as personal information under Japanese law. The collection of precise location data often requires the explicit consent of the individual due to privacy concerns. If geolocation data is collected via mobile communication services provided by telecommunications companies, it is further protected under Japan's secrecy of communication provisions. These regulations emphasize the importance of safeguarding location data from unauthorized access or use.

Drone Usage and Privacy

The increasing use of drones for various purposes has raised privacy concerns. Drone operations in Japan are regulated by laws such as the Aviation Act, which imposes restrictions on the flight of unmanned aerial vehicles, and local government ordinances. To address privacy risks, particularly when drones capture images or videos, the Ministry of Internal Affairs and Communications (MIC) has issued guidelines on the responsible use of such data, especially when shared online. These measures aim to ensure drone technology is utilized responsibly while protecting individuals' privacy.

In Japan, starting June 20, 2022, all unmanned aerial vehicles (UAVs) weighing 100 g or more (including drones and radio-controlled aircraft) must be registered. Without registration, you cannot fly your UAV outdoors. For more information, visit https://www.mlit.go.jp/koku/koku_ua_registration.html.

Japan's PIPL and related regulations provide a robust framework for safeguarding personal data in an era of rapid technological advancement. From autonomous vehicles to drones, geolocation tracking, and facial recognition systems, these laws aim to balance innovation with individual rights. By requiring consent, imposing reporting obligations, and addressing emerging technologies, the legal system seeks to create a safer and more transparent digital landscape.

Global Perspectives on Data Privacy

General Data Protection Regulation (GDPR)

The General Data Protection Regulation (GDPR) is a comprehensive data protection law enacted by the European Union (EU) to safeguard personal information. It was designed to give EU citizens greater control and protection over their personal data, ensuring transparency and accountability in how businesses and organizations handle such information. One of the key features of GDPR is the right for individuals to request the deletion of their personal data, especially if it has been compromised or is no longer necessary for the purpose it was collected. This regulation reflects the EU's commitment to prioritizing data privacy as a fundamental human right.

GDPR imposes strict penalties on businesses and organizations that fail to comply with its requirements. Even minor violations can result in fines of up to 2% of the company's annual global turnover or €10 million, whichever is higher. For more severe infringements, the penalties double, reaching up to 4% of annual turnover or €20 million. These fines highlight the seriousness of GDPR and its role in encouraging businesses to adopt robust data protection practices. According to the European Commission, GDPR has significantly influenced global data protection laws and practices since its enforcement in May 2018.

California Consumer Privacy Act (CCPA)

The California Consumer Privacy Act (CCPA) is a groundbreaking privacy law in the United States that aims to protect the personal data of California residents. If a California resident signs up for a service or interacts with a company, the organization must carefully handle their personal information following the CCPA. For example, data such as cookies and IP addresses, which can potentially identify individuals, are treated as personal data under this regulation. This ensures companies handle such data responsibly, promoting transparency and respecting the privacy of consumers.

In January 2023, the CCPA was amended and renamed the California Privacy Rights Act (CPRA), introducing additional protections for consumers. Before the amendment, the CCPA granted California residents several important rights, including:

- The right to know about the personal information a business collects about them and how it is used or shared.
- The right to request the deletion of personal information collected from them (with specific exceptions).
- The right to opt out of the sale or sharing of their personal information.
- The right to non-discrimination for exercising their privacy rights under the CCPA.

The CPRA amendment further expanded these rights, emphasizing stronger protections for sensitive data. New rights introduced in 2023 include:

- The right to correct inaccurate personal information that a business holds about them.
- The right to limit the use and disclosure of sensitive personal information, such as health data or financial details.

These changes reflect a growing awareness of the need for stronger privacy protections in a digital age where data misuse can have significant consequences. Together, GDPR and CCPA/CPRA set global benchmarks for data privacy, influencing legislation worldwide and empowering individuals to take control of their personal information.

Table 10.1 Data protection regulations around the globe

Country(s)	Regulations	Summary
Singapore Thailand	Personal Data Protection Act (PDPA) https://www.pdpc.gov.sg/overview-of-pdpa/the-legislation/personal-data-protection-act https://thainetizen.org/wp-content/uploads/2019/11/thailand-personal-data-protection-act-2019-en.pdf	• Regulates the collection, use, and disclosure of personal data • Provides individuals with rights over their data • Requires organizations to obtain consent for data processing
Brazil	Lei Geral de Proteção de Dados (LGPD) https://www.planalto.gov.br/ccivil_03/_ato2015-2018/2018/lei/l13709.htm	• Establishes principles for personal data processing • Introduces requirements for data protection • Grants individuals rights over their data
South Africa	Protection of Personal Information Act (POPIA) https://popia.co.za/	• Regulates the processing of personal information • Sets conditions for lawful processing of data • Establishes rights for data subjects
China	Cybersecurity Law (CL) Data Security Law (DSL) Personal Information Protection Law (PIPL) https://personalinformationprotectionlaw.com/	• Requires network operators to comply with certain security obligations, conduct data localization, and restrict the transfer of personal information outside of China • Focuses on data security and the protection of personal information. It establishes requirements for data processing, and cross-border data transfers and introduces penalties for non-compliance
Canada	Personal Information Protection and Electronic Documents Act (PIPEDA) https://laws-lois.justice.gc.ca/eng/acts/p-8.6/	• Governs the collection, use, and disclosure of personal information by private sector organizations • Establishes principles for privacy protection and individuals' rights regarding their personal data

For further details, you may consult the European Commission's GDPR portal and California's official privacy laws website at https://gdpr-info.eu/ and https://oag.ca.gov/privacy/ccpa, respectively. However, for the data protection regulations around the world are summarized in Table 10.1.

10.6 Reproducibility

Definition

Reproducibility in data science refers to the ability to recreate or reproduce the results of a data analysis or experiment using the same data, code, and methods. It is a fundamental principle in scientific research and an essential aspect of data science practice. The goal is to ensure that the findings and conclusions drawn from a study can be independently verified and validated by others.

Another definition is the ability to obtain the same result even if an operation is performed multiple times. When publishing the result of an experiment in a paper, it would be a problem if the same results were not obtained when other people conducted the experiment under the same conditions.

A word similar to reproducibility is **idempotency**. It is a mathematical term that means that after performing an operation, you can repeat the same operation over and over again to get the same result.

Key Practices and Considerations

Reproducibility is a cornerstone of scientific research, ensuring that results can be independently verified and trusted by others. To achieve reproducibility, researchers must adhere to key elements and best practices across different stages of their work. This involves careful documentation, transparency in processes, and the sharing of resources. Below, we explore these practices in detail.

Parameter Settings

One of the fundamental aspects of reproducibility is documenting all parameter settings and hyperparameters used in an analysis. These parameters include model configurations, data preprocessing steps, and any tuning performed to optimize results. When these settings are recorded, other researchers can replicate the experiment under the same conditions, providing a foundation for validating the original findings. For instance, in machine learning research, specifying parameters like learning rates, batch sizes, and number of iterations can significantly impact the reproducibility of the results.

Randomness Control

Many analyses rely on random processes, such as random number generation or stochastic algorithms. To ensure reproducibility, researchers must control randomness by fixing a random seed or using a mechanism to replicate the same random behavior. This prevents unintentional variations in results due to the randomness inherent in the process. For example, in Monte Carlo simulations or data splitting during model training, fixing the random seed ensures consistent results across multiple runs.

Documentation and Reporting

Detailed documentation and thorough reporting are crucial for reproducibility. Researchers should clearly describe the methodology, assumptions, limitations, and potential biases involved in their analysis. This includes outlining every step of the data processing and analysis pipeline. Comprehensive documentation not only aids reproducibility but also enhances transparency, allowing others to critically evaluate the work. Clear reporting practices strengthen the credibility of scientific research and facilitate its extension by future researchers.

Open Data and Open Source

Sharing data and code openly is another essential practice to promote reproducibility. Making datasets publicly available and using open-source tools and libraries empower other researchers to verify results and build on previous work. For example, platforms like GitHub or Zenodo enable researchers to share their code, while repositories like Kaggle or the Open Science Framework facilitate open data sharing. These practices not only enhance reproducibility but also foster collaboration and innovation in the scientific community.

Data Documentation

To ensure reproducibility, it is vital to document all aspects of the data used in a study. This includes its source, collection methods, preprocessing steps, and any transformations applied. Proper data documentation enables others to understand the dataset fully and replicate the analysis accurately. For instance, metadata standards, such as those outlined in the FAIR principles (Findable, Accessible, Interoperable, Reusable), provide a framework for comprehensive data documentation.

Code Reproducibility

Providing access to the code used for data processing, analysis, and modeling is critical for reproducibility. This includes sharing scripts written in programming languages such as R, along with details about dependencies and libraries used. Tools like Git and GitHub offer effective version control and facilitate collaboration, ensuring that changes to the codebase are tracked and reproducible workflows are maintained.

Environment Reproducibility

Lastly, documenting the computational environment is crucial for ensuring reproducibility. This includes recording details about software versions, operating systems, hardware configurations, and any other relevant dependencies. Tools like Docker and Conda can help researchers replicate computational environments precisely, minimizing discrepancies due to system differences.

Reproducibility is a vital aspect of trustworthy and credible scientific research. Researchers can foster a culture of transparency and collaboration by following these key practices—such as documenting parameter settings, controlling randomness, sharing data and code, and ensuring environment reproducibility. These efforts not only validate scientific findings but also pave the way for further innovation and discovery.

10.7 Git and GitHub as Tools for Collaboration

Git

Git is a version control system that helps track file changes, especially in software development. It is designed to be fast, reliable, and able to manage changes across multiple users working on the same project. Git allows for distributed workflows, meaning that each person working on a project has their copy of the entire codebase, and they can work on it independently. This system is especially useful for developers because it ensures that the code is consistently updated and that changes are kept secure, even in a complex and fast-paced development environment. Git also supports nonlinear workflows, which means developers can work on different parts of the code at the same time without overwriting each others' work. This makes collaboration easier and more efficient. Key concepts and features of these tools include:

Repository

A repository, often shortened to "repo," is a core concept in version control. It is essentially a collection of files, along with a complete history of changes made to those files over time. This history allows developers to revert to previous versions, compare changes, and collaborate effectively. Repositories can exist either on a local machine or a remote server. A local repository resides on an individual developer's computer, enabling offline work. A remote repository, on the other hand, is stored on a server accessible via the Internet, allowing multiple developers to share and synchronize their work.

Commit

A commit represents a snapshot of the repository at a specific moment. It captures the changes made to files and stores them along with a unique identifier, often called a hash. This identifier allows developers to track and reference specific commits in the project's history. Each commit typically includes a message summarizing the changes, making it easier to understand the progression of the project. Committing changes ensures that every modification is recorded, providing a reliable audit trail.

Branch

A branch is a fundamental feature that facilitates parallel development. It acts as a separate line of work within the repository, enabling multiple developers to work on different tasks simultaneously without interfering with one another. For example, one branch might focus on adding a new feature, while another addresses a bug fix. Branches can be created as needed and merged back into the main branch once the work is complete. This approach enhances team productivity and helps maintain a clean and organized codebase.

Merge

Merging is the process of combining changes from different branches into a single branch. This step integrates the work done in various branches, ensuring that updates and improvements are consolidated. For example, when a feature branch is complete, its changes can be merged into the main branch to make them available to all developers. Version control systems often provide tools to resolve conflicts that arise when two branches modify the same part of a file. Proper merging practices are crucial for maintaining the project's stability and preventing errors.

Push and Pull Requests

Push and pull requests are features provided by Git hosting platforms like GitHub. A push refers to sending local commits to a remote repository, making the changes accessible to the team. A pull request, on the other hand, allows developers to propose changes to a project by submitting their branch for review. Team members can then examine the proposed changes, leave comments, suggest modifications, and approve or reject the request. This process promotes collaboration, ensures code quality, and facilitates knowledge sharing within the team. Pull requests are particularly valuable in open-source projects, where contributors from around the world can participate.

GitHub

GitHub is a web-based hosting service for Git repositories. It provides a platform for collaboration and allows developers to share, contribute to, and manage their Git repositories.

GitHub has become a popular platform for open-source projects, enabling collaboration between developers worldwide. It also offers additional features and integrations, such as actions, project management tools, continuous integration, and deployment services, to enhance the development workflow. GitHub extends Git's functionality, offering features like:

Remote Repository Hosting

GitHub is a platform that hosts code repositories in the cloud, providing a centralized location where developers can store and access their projects. This cloud hosting allows developers to keep their code in a secure place, ensuring that it's available from anywhere with an Internet connection. By using GitHub, developers can work remotely without needing to be in the same physical location, making collaboration more flexible and efficient.

Collaboration

One of the key features of GitHub is its ability to support collaboration among developers. The platform enables developers to clone repositories, which means they can make a copy of the code on their computers. Once they make changes or improvements to the code in their local environment, they can push these changes back to the central repository. Other developers who are working on the same project can then fetch these updates, allowing everyone to contribute and collaborate on the code. This process ensures that the project continues to grow and improve, with multiple developers adding their expertise.

Issue Tracking

GitHub also offers a built-in issue-tracking system, which is an essential tool for managing tasks and problems within a project. Team members can create issues to report bugs, suggest new features, or track progress on different parts of the project. Issues can be assigned to specific developers, allowing for clear responsibility and efficient task management. This feature enhances communication between team members, making it easier to keep everyone on the same page about what needs to be done and what has already been addressed.

Pull Requests and Code Review

Pull requests are another important feature of GitHub, enabling developers to propose changes to a project. When a developer has made changes to the code, they can submit a pull request to the team. This request invites other team members to review the changes and provide feedback before those changes are merged into the main project. Pull requests facilitate discussions about the code, allowing the team to ensure the changes are beneficial and do not introduce new issues. It's an essential part of the code review process, ensuring that the final product meets the project's standards.

GitHub Pages

Additionally, GitHub provides a service called GitHub Pages, which allows developers to host static websites directly from their repositories. This feature is particularly useful for showcasing projects, writing documentation, or creating personal websites. Developers can easily publish their work online without needing to set up external hosting services, making it a convenient way to display their portfolios or project-related content.

How GitHub Works

The process involves three key components: **the working directory, the local repository, and the online or remote repository**. Figure 10.4 illustrates the interactions between users and their collaborators when working on the same project.

Working Directory: This is where users create, edit, and manage their files locally on their computer. Once changes are made and ready to be saved, they can be committed to the local repository.

Local Repository: The local repository stores all committed changes made in the working directory. Users can make multiple commits to save different versions of their files. If they want to update their local repository with changes made by others, they can pull updates from the remote repository. Merging happens when combining changes from the local repository or other sources.

Remote Repository: This is an online server where files and code are shared and stored. Users can clone the repository to download its contents to their local machine. After making changes locally, users push updates to the remote repository so collaborators can access them. Similarly, they can fetch updates from the remote repository to see new changes but need to pull them into their working directory to start using them.

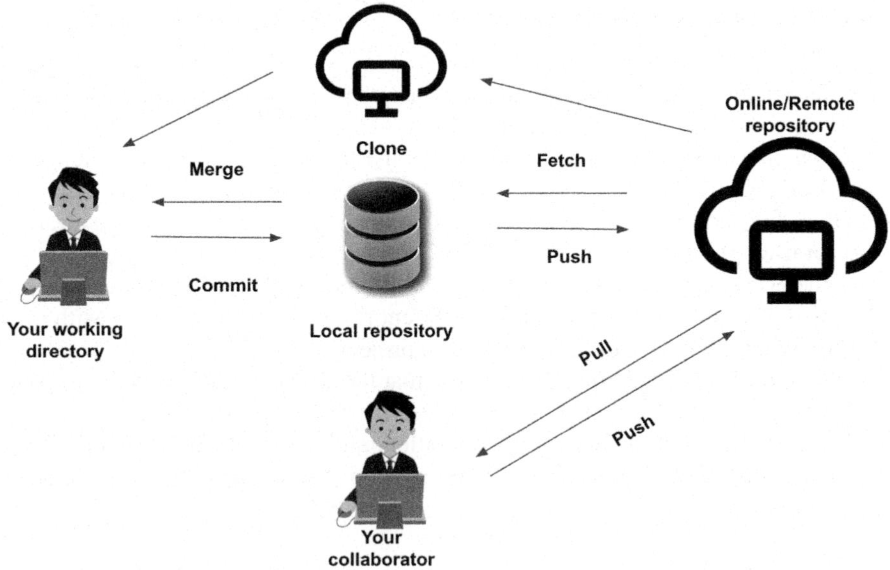

Fig. 10.4 Illustration of how GitHub work

Figure 10.4 also highlights the interaction between a user and a collaborator. Both individuals can push their changes to the remote repository and pull updates to synchronize their local versions, ensuring seamless collaboration.

Git is widely used in software development and other fields for tracking changes, enabling teamwork, and maintaining organized version histories. GitHub, GitLab, and Bitbucket host remote repositories for teams and individuals.

Easy to Digest Box

When scientists or people use data to solve problems or answer questions, they need to be honest and fair. This is called "ethics." It's like when you're playing a game, and you follow the rules so everyone has a fair chance to win. In data science, ethics means using the data the right way, not tricking people, and respecting others' privacy. For example, if you use someone's information, you need to ask for permission first and keep it safe.

Then, what is reproducibility? Imagine you build a LEGO castle, and your friend wants to build the exact same one. If you tell them exactly how to do it, step by step, they should be able to build the same castle. In data science, "reproducibility" means sharing your steps, tools, and the data you used so others can repeat your work and get the same results. It's important because it helps people trust that your results are true and not made up.

10.8 Summary of Key Points

- In the information society, the simple principle is "do not cause trouble to others" or "do not make others uncomfortable."
- Severson's Four Principles of Information Ethics: (1) respect for intellectual property, (2) respect for privacy, (3) fair representation, (4) doing no harm.
- Ethics are required for those who handle data while users need to be aware of what it will be used for.
- In the event of a conflict, always prioritize protecting the public interest.
- Different countries or regions have different rules, always complying with these rules when dealing with the data science project.
- The goal of reproducibility is to ensure that the findings and conclusions drawn from a study can be independently verified and validated by others.
- There are many platforms for collaboration, and one of them is GitHub. It will allow us to collaborate and allow developers to share, contribute to, and manage their repositories.

10.9 Hands-on Experience

Working with RStudio

Practice 10

1. Learning Objectives

Understand GitHub Account Creation

- Learn how to create a GitHub account by signing up on the GitHub platform with their username, email, and password.

Create a New GitHub Repository

- Learn how to set up a new repository on GitHub, providing a name, and optional description, and selecting the visibility settings.

Install Git on Computer

- Learn how to download and install Git for Windows or macOS, following the correct installation procedures.

Configure Git Credentials in RStudio

- Learners how to set up their GitHub credentials (username and email) in RStudio using the usethis package.

Enable Git for Version Control in RStudio

- Learn how to enable Git in RStudio by configuring version control settings and generating an SSH key.

Commit and Push Changes to GitHub

- Learn how to commit changes in RStudio, write meaningful commit messages and push code to a GitHub repository.

Verify Successful Code Upload

- Learn how to confirm the successful upload of their code by verifying the presence of their script in their GitHub repository.

Setting Up GitHub and R for Version Control

Step 1: Create a GitHub Account

To get started, you need a GitHub account. Follow these steps:

1. Open your web browser and go to GitHub Sign Up Page: https://github.com/signup
2. Fill in the required information (username, email, password) and follow the instructions to create your GitHub account.

Step 2: Create a New Repository

After setting up your GitHub account:

1. Log in to your GitHub account.
2. Click on the "+" icon in the top-right corner and select **New Repository**.
3. Provide a name for your repository, add an optional description, and choose whether it should be public or private.
4. Click **Create Repository**.

Step 3: Install Git for Windows

If you don't already have Git installed on your computer:

1. Go to the Git for Windows website: https://gitforwindows.org/ or https://git-scm.com/downloads/mac for macOS users. I suggest you download the "Binary installer"
2. Download the installer and follow the installation instructions.

Step 4: Configure Git in RStudio

Now that Git is installed, you need to configure it in RStudio. Open RStudio and run the following codes in the R console to set up your Git credentials:

```
# Install and load required packages
install.packages("usethis")
library(usethis)

use_git_config(user.name = "your-user-name",
user.email = "your-email@mail.com")
```

Replace your-user-name and your-email@mail.com with your actual GitHub username and email address.

Step 5: Enable Git in RStudio

1. In RStudio, click on **File** > **New Project** > **Version Control** > **Git**.
2. Then, go to **Tools** > **Global Options**. In the Global Options window, navigate to the **Git/SVN** section.
3. Click on **Create RSA Key** to generate an SSH key. Save it and copy it to your clipboard.
4. Add the SSH key to your GitHub account by navigating to **Settings** > **SSH and GPG keys** on the GitHub website.

Step 6: Commit and Push Your Code

1. Create a new R script in RStudio.
2. Go to the **Git** tab in RStudio and check the box next to your script file.
3. Type a commit message in the commit message window (e.g., "Initial commit") and click the **Commit** button.
4. Click on the **Push** icon in the Git tab.
5. When the "Authorize Git Credential Manager" window appears, click on **Authorize git-ecosystem**.

Step 7: Verify Your Repository

Finally, go to your GitHub repository page and check if the script has been successfully uploaded. You should see your file listed there.

All R scripts written in this book are available here:

You can also access it through this URL: https://github.com/fatwaramdani/Data-Science-Foundations-and-Hands-on-Experience.

Reference

Masui, T. (2022). *Data science: How it works*. Shoesha, Japan (in Japanese).

Bibliography

Agresti, A., & Finlay, B. (2009). *Statistical methods for the social sciences*. Pearson. Available at https://www.pearson.com/en-us/subject-catalog/p/statistical-methods-for-the-social-sciences/P200000006062/9780137546060

Babbie, E. R. (2016). *The practice of social research*. Cengage Learning. Available at https://faculty.cengage.com/works/9780357360767

Bishop, C. M. (2006). *Pattern recognition and machine learning*. Springer. Available at https://link.springer.com/book/9780387310732

Bouchekioua, Y., Blaisdell, A. P., Kosaki, Y., Tsutsui-Kimura, I., Craddock, P., Mimura, M., & Watanabe, S. (2021). Spatial inference without a cognitive map: The role of higher-order path integration. *Biological Reviews of the Cambridge Philosophical Society, 96*(1), 52–65. https://doi.org/10.1111/brv.12645

Box, G. E. P., Jenkins, G. M., & Reinsel, G. C. (2015). *Time series analysis: Forecasting and control*. Wiley. ISBN: 978-1-118-61919-3.

Breiman, L. (2001). Random forests. *Machine Learning, 45*(1), 5–32. https://doi.org/10.1023/A:1010933404324

Breiman, L., Friedman, J. H., Olshen, R. A., & Stone, C. J. (1986). *Classification and regression trees*. Wadsworth & Brooks/Cole. ISBN: 9781315139470.

Brewer, C. A. (2005). *Designing better maps: A guide for GIS users*. ESRI. ISBN: 9781589484405.

Cairo, A. (2012). *The functional art: An introduction to information graphics and visualization*. New Riders. Available at https://ptgmedia.pearsoncmg.com/images/9780321834737/samplepages/0321834739.pdf

Chang, K. (2019). *Introduction to geographic information systems*. McGraw-Hill Education.

Cohen, J. (1988). *Statistical power analysis for the behavioral sciences*. Routledge. Available at https://www.routledge.com/Statistical-Power-Analysis-for-the-Behavioral-Sciences/Cohen/p/book/9780805802832?gad_source=1&gclid=Cj0KCQiAlsy5BhDeARIsABRc6ZuwRlD2Mkgl_yrqmitOPVuRpv17Xk_Fle2wy7-PyOnIJlbLGuSAfegaAl8fEALw_wcB

Cortes, C., & Vapnik, V. (1995). Support-vector networks. *Machine Learning, 20*(3), 273–297. https://doi.org/10.1007/BF00994018

Cumming, G., & Finch, S. (2005). Inference by eye: Confidence intervals and how to read pictures of data. *American Psychologist, 60*(2), 170–180. https://doi.org/10.1037/0003-066X.60.2.170

Doebelin, E. O. (2004). *Measurement systems: Application and design*. McGraw-Hill.

Esri GRID Documentation: https://desktop.arcgis.com/en/arcmap/10.3/manage-data/raster-and-images/esri-grid-format.htm

Few, S. (2009). *Now you see it: Simple visualization techniques for quantitative analysis*. Analytics Press. https://archive.org/details/nowyouseeitsimpl0000fews

F. Ramdani, *Data Science: Foundations and Hands-on Experience*,
https://doi.org/10.1007/978-981-96-4683-8

Field, A. (2013). *Discovering statistics using IBM SPSS statistics*. SAGE. Available at https://uk.sagepub.com/en-gb/eur/discovering-statistics-using-ibm-spss-statistics/book285130

Fischer, M., & Getis, A. (2010). *Handbook of applied spatial analysis: Software tools, methods and applications*. Springer. https://doi.org/10.1007/978-3-642-03647-7

Forum, W. E. (2025). The future of jobs report 2025. Available at https://reports.weforum.org/docs/WEF_Future_of_Jobs_Report_2025.pdf

Freedman, D., Pisani, R., & Purves, R. (2007). *Statistics* (4th Ed.). W.W. Norton & Company. Available at https://homepages.dcc.ufmg.br/~assuncao/EstatCC/Slides/Extra/FPPExpObs.pdf

Friedman, J. H. (2001). Greedy function approximation: A gradient boosting machine. *Annals of Statistics, 29*(5), 1189–1232. Available at https://projecteuclid.org/journals/annals-of-statistics/volume-29/issue-5/Greedy-function-approximation-A-gradient-boosting-machine/10.1214/aos/1013203451.full

Gandomi, A., & Haider, M. (2015). Beyond the hype: Big data concepts, methods, and analytics. *International Journal of Information Management, 35*(2), 137–144. Available at https://www.sciencedirect.com/science/article/pii/S0268401214001066

Gawlikowski, J., Tassi, C. R. N., Ali, M., Lee, J., Humt, M., Feng, J., Kruspe, A., Triebel, R., Jung, P., Roscher, R. & Shahzad, M. (2023). A survey of uncertainty in deep neural networks. *Artificial Intelligence Review, 56*, 1513–1589. Available at https://doi.org/10.1007/s10462-023-10562-9

GDAL Documentation on GeoTIFF: https://gdal.org/drivers/raster/gtiff.html

Gelfand, A. E., Diggle, P. J., Fuentes, M., & Guttorp, P. (2010). *Handbook of spatial statistics*. Taylor and Francis. https://doi.org/10.1201/9781420072884

Gelman, A., Carlin, J., & Rubin, D. (2014). *Bayesian data analysis*. CRC Press. Available at http://www.stat.columbia.edu/~gelman/book/BDA3.pdf

GeoJSON. *The GeoJSON format specification*. https://geojson.org/

Goodchild, M. F., & Longley, P. A. (2015). Geographic information systems and science (4th Ed.). Wiley. ISBN: 978-1-119-12845-8.

Goodfellow, I., Bengio, Y., & Courville, A. (2016). *Deep learning*. MIT Press. Available at https://mitpress.mit.edu/9780262035613/deep-learning/

Hair, J. F., Black, W. C., Babin, B. J., & Anderson, R. E. (2019). *Multivariate data analysis*. Cengage Learning. Available at https://www.amazon.co.jp/-/en/Joseph-Hair/dp/1473756545

Heuvelink, G. B. M., Burrough, P. A., & Stein, A. (1989). Propagation of errors in spatial modelling with GIS. *International Journal of Geographical Information Systems, 3*(4), 303–322. https://doi.org/10.1080/02693798908941518

Hosmer, D. W., Lemeshow, S., & Sturdivant, R. X. (2013). *Applied logistic regression* (3rd Ed.). Wiley. ISBN: 978-0-470-58247-3.

Hyndman, R. J., & Athanasopoulos, G. (2018). *Forecasting: Principles and practice*. OTexts. Available at https://otexts.com/fpp3/

INSEE—EUROSTAT. (2018). *Handbook of spatial analysis*. Available at https://ec.europa.eu/eurostat/web/products-manuals-and-guidelines/-/insee-estat-spatial-ana

Introduction to NetCDF: https://climatedataguide.ucar.edu/climate-data-tools-and-analysis/netcdf

James, G., Witten, D., Hastie, T., & Tibshirani, R. (2013). *An introduction to statistical learning*. Springer. Available at https://doi.org/10.1007/978-1-0716-1418-1

James, G., Witten, D., Hastie, T., & Tibshirani, R. (2013). *An introduction to statistical learning: With Applications in R* (Vol. 112). Springer. https://doi.org/10.1007/978-1-0716-1418-1

Jean, N., Burke, M., Xie, M., Davis, W., Lobell, D. B., & Ermon, S. (2016). Combining satellite imagery and machine learning to predict poverty. *Science, 353*(6301), 790–794. Available at https://doi.org/10.1126/science.aaf7894

Krejcie, R. V., & Morgan, D. W. (1970). Determining sample size for research activities. *Educational and Psychological Measurement, 30*(3), 607–610.

Krizhevsky, A., Sutskever, I., & Hinton, G. E. (2012). ImageNet classification with deep convolutional neural networks. In *Advances in neural information processing systems* (pp. 1097–1105). Available at https://proceedings.neurips.cc/paper_files/paper/2012/file/c399862d3b9d6b76c8436e924a68c45b-Paper.pdf

Kuhn, M., & Johnson, K. (2013). *Applied predictive modeling*. Springer; Gelman, A., & Hill, J. (2006). *Data analysis using regression and multilevel/hierarchical models*. Cambridge University Press. Available at https://doi.org/10.1007/978-1-4614-6849-3

Lakshminarayanan, B., Pritzel, A., & Blundell, C. (2017). Simple and scalable predictive uncertainty estimation using deep ensembles. Available at https://arxiv.org/abs/1612.01474

LeCun, Y., Bengio, Y., & Hinton, G. (2015b). Deep learning. *Nature, 521*(7553), 436–444. https://doi.org/10.1038/nature14539

LeCun, Y., Bengio, Y., & Hinton, G. (2015). Deep learning. *Nature*. Available at https://www.nature.com/articles/nature14539

Levontin, P., & Walton, J. L. (2020). *Visualising uncertainty: A short introduction*. AU4DM. Available at https://spiral.imperial.ac.uk/bitstream/10044/1/80424/2/VUI_221219.pdf

McClave, J. T., Benson, P. G., & Sincich, T. (2017). *Statistics for business and economics*. Pearson. Available at https://www.pearson.com/en-gb/subject-catalog/p/statistics-for-business-and-economics-global-edition/P200000007231?view=educator&tab=table-of-contents

Moore, D. S., McCabe, G. P., & Craig, B. A. (2021). *Introduction to the practice of statistics* (6th Ed.). W. H. Freeman. The Excel manual is available at https://bcs.whfreeman.com/webpub/statistics/ips6e/manuals/student_excel_manual/ips6e.ex.st.pdf

NetCDF Documentation: https://www.unidata.ucar.edu/software/netcdf/

OGC. GeoPackage Standards. https://www.geopackage.org/

QGIS Documentation: https://qgis.org/

Ramdani, F. (2024). *Exploring the Earth with QGIS: A guide to using satellite imagery at its full potential*. Springer. https://doi.org/10.1007/978-3-031-46042-5

Rumelhart, D. E., Hinton, G. E., & Williams, R. J. (1986). Learning representations by back-propagating errors. *Nature*. Available at https://www.nature.com/articles/323533a0

Spiegelhalter, D. (2019). *The art of statistics: How to learn from data*. Penguin Random House.

Sullivan, L. M. (2018). *Essentials of biostatistics in public health* (3rd Ed.). Jones & Bartlett Learning. ISBN: 9781284288735.

Sutton, R. S., & Barto, A. G. (2018). *Reinforcement learning: An introduction*. MIT Press. Available at https://mitpress.mit.edu/9780262039246/reinforcement-learning/

Tabachnick, B. G., & Fidell, L. S. (2013). *Using multivariate statistics*. Pearson. Available at https://www.pearson.com/en-us/subject-catalog/p/using-multivariate-statistics/P200000003097/9780137526543?tab=table-of-contents

Taylor, S. J., & Letham, B. (2018). Forecasting at scale. *PeerJ Computer Science*. Available at https://peerj.com/preprints/3190/

Thapa, K., & Bossler, J. (1992). Accuracy of spatial data used in geographic information systems. Available at https://www.asprs.org/wp-content/uploads/pers/1992journal/jun/1992_jun_835-841.pdf

Tukey, J. W. (1977). *Exploratory data analysis*. Addison-Wesley; Friendly, M. (2008). A brief history of data visualization. In *Handbook of data visualization*. Springer. Available at https://doi.org/10.1007/978-0-387-32833-1_136

Unwin, A. (2015). *Graphical data analysis with R*. CRC Press. Available at https://doi.org/10.1201/9781315370088/graphical-data-analysis-antony-unwin

Wickham, H., & Grolemund, G. (2016). *R for data science: Import, tidy, transform, visualize, and model data*. O'Reilly Media. Available at https://r4ds.hadley.nz/

Wickham, H., & Grolemund, G. (2017). *R for data science*. O'Reilly Media. Available at https://www.oreilly.com/library/view/r-for-data/9781492097396/

The manufacturer's authorised representative in the EU is Springer Nature Customer Service Centre GmbH, Europaplatz 3, 69115 Heidelberg, Germany. If you have any concerns regarding our products, please contact ProductSafety@springernature.com

Printed and bound by CPI Group (UK) Ltd, Croydon, CR0 4YY
01/10/2026
02225853-0013